Che Guevara

Che Guevara

The Romantic Revolutionary

Allan Todd

PEN & SWORD
HISTORY

First published in Great Britain in 2024 by
Pen & Sword History
An imprint of Pen & Sword Books Limited
Yorkshire – Philadelphia

ISBN 978 1 39904 273 4

A CIP catalogue record for this book is
available from the British Library

Typeset by Mac Style
Printed in the UK by CPI Group (UK) Ltd, Croydon, CR0 4YY.

MIX
Paper | Supporting responsible forestry
FSC® C013604

Pen & Sword Books Limited incorporates the imprints of After the Battle, Atlas, Archaeology, Aviation, Discovery, Family History, Fiction, History, Maritime, Military, Military Classics, Politics, Select, Transport, True Crime, Air World, Frontline Publishing, Leo Cooper, Remember When, Seaforth Publishing, The Praetorian Press, Wharncliffe Local History, Wharncliffe Transport, Wharncliffe True Crime and White Owl.

For a complete list of Pen & Sword titles please contact

PEN & SWORD BOOKS LIMITED
47 Church Street, Barnsley, South Yorkshire, S70 2AS, England
E-mail: enquiries@pen-and-sword.co.uk
Website: www.pen-and-sword.co.uk
or
PEN AND SWORD BOOKS
1950 Lawrence Rd, Havertown, PA 19083, USA
E-mail: uspen-and-sword@casematepublishers.com
Website: www.penandswordbooks.com

Dedication

For Franz Fanon's 'Wretched of The Earth' – and all those modern-day Don and Doña Quixotes struggling to right the world's wrongs and to oppose its injustices, wherever they exist.

Contents

Acknowledgements

When I started writing this biography, I expected just to find more detailed specifics about what I understood to be the main areas of Che's brief life. One of the unexpected delights, soon after work had begun, was to discover aspects of his life and work which I hadn't known: aspects that led Jean-Paul Sartre to describe him as 'an intellectual [and] the most complete human being of our age'. I hope that at least some readers will be similarly surprised and delighted.

I would like to thank the following friends and *compañeros* for kindly reading, and offering constructive criticism on, early drafts of various chapters: Jacqui Petrie, Ken and Di Barrell, Chrissie Parfitt, Ian Rycroft, Charlotte Christensen, Paul Wilmott, Chris Jones, Simon Hannah, Ian Parker, and Michael Tucker. I was also fortunate to receive, once again, useful feedback from two of my ex-History students, Nicky Barrell and Patrick Fitzgerald; while Penelope Read (Robinson), a 1960s' classmate, offered many insightful suggestions. An unexpected bonus was being able to chat with Celia Watson, who is distantly related to Che via the Irish side of his family – and lives in Keswick!

Thanks are also due to Sarah-Beth Watkins and Laura Hirst, and to the rest of the team, at Pen & Sword; and to Karyn Burnham, an excellent copyeditor. Thomas Bohm (User Design, Illustration and Typesetting) once again displayed much skill – and patience! – in drawing up the Family Tree and the maps.

Any remaining errors are down to me – or possibly also to my cat, Hedgie, who seemed much more interested in the Che book than the Trotsky one, and 'contributed' by frequently wandering across the keyboard, adding/deleting text in the process!

I would also like to thank, once again, our daughters, Megan and Vanessa – and our grandchildren, Alexander and Emilia – for being there, and for continuing to provide what Coleridge described as 'a sheltering tree'.

And finally, as ever, I owe a huge debt of gratitude to Cyn – *mi única compañera de vida* – who, for my birthday in May 1972, gave me Régis Debray's *Revolution in the Revolution?* This sparked my interest in the Cuban Revolution and, in particular, in the life of Che Guevara.

Allan Todd
January 2024
Keswick

A Note on Usages

Names:

(a) Che's full name was Ernesto Guevara de la Serna; but, as 'Che' is the name by which he's best known to history – and in order to avoid confusion with any other family members with the same first name and/or surname – he is referred to as Che throughout this book. 'Che' is frequently used by Argentinians, meaning: 'Hey, you!' or 'Hey, buddy!'

(b) Many first names have several diminutives which were used by family and friends. Che was often called 'Ernestito'; he also had various nicknames, such as 'Teté', 'Fuser' and 'Chanco'.

(c) Also to avoid confusions, his father – Ernesto Guevara – will be referred to as 'Lynch'.

(d) Fidel Castro – the best known of the two Castro brothers – will be referred to as 'Castro', while his brother will be 'Raúl'.

Seasons:

Because Argentina is below the Equator, autumn and winter last from March to August

Che's writings:

While many of Che's writings have yet to be translated into English, there are several partial but reliable collections in English – though sometimes the translations differ slightly. The main ones used were:

Deutschmann, D., ed., *Che Guevara and the Cuban Revolution: Writings and Speeches of Ernesto Che Guevara* (1987)

Gerassi, J., ed., *Venceremos! The speeches and writings of Che Guevara* (1969)

Hansen, J., ed., *Che Guevara Speaks* (1967)

Silverman, B., ed., *Man and Socialism in Cuba: The Great Debate* (1971)

Tablada, C., ed., *Che Guevara: Economics and Politics in the Transition to Socialism* (1990)

'Sierra vs Llano':

Tensions soon emerged within Castro's 26 July Movement (M26J), between the guerrilla forces and the urban network. The 'Sierra' were the guerrilla commanders fighting in the mountains; the 'Llano' were the urban organisers of the movement.

The *foco* theory:

Che is associated with the *foco* theory of guerrilla warfare. By *foco* is meant an initial centre or base of activity for guerrilla operations. Once established, other groups would split off from this 'mother' *foco*. These developments would then help push existing tensions in a country towards a revolutionary seizure of power.

The Communist Party of Cuba:

In 1959, Cuba's communists organised as the Popular Socialist Party (PSP). In 1961, the PSP merged with the M26J and the Directorio Revolucionario (DR), to form the Integrated Revolutionary Organisations (ORI). In 1963, the ORI became the United Party of the Socialist Revolution (PURS); in 1965, PURS became the Communist Party of Cuba.

'Orthodox' communism:

'Orthodox' communism refers to the ideology that developed under Stalin, and which was subsequently promoted by Stalin's successors. This was opposed by 'classical' communism/Marxism, which drew its ideas from Marx's earlier writings (often more philosophical) and those of Marxist thinkers like Lenin and even Trotsky, as well as Marx's later works.

'Man':

In Spanish, 'hombre' can be translated as 'man' – or as 'mankind'/'humankind'. Che's use of the term in his writings is in the latter, generic, sense. The use of 'man', however, also reflects the patriarchal status quo of the 1950s and '60s.

Law of value:

In simple terms, Marxists argue that, under capitalism, production/exchange of commodities is based on strict profitability, which determines the availability of products/resources. In the 1960s, 'orthodox' communists argued that this would have to operate in post-capitalist societies until human needs were met.

Voluntarism:

This is a pejorative term within the Marxist tradition, applied to individuals/small groups who underestimate objective social and economic factors, and instead overly stress the importance of subjective factors and human will, in attempts to influence the course of history. Essentially, 'voluntarists' are seen as holding that human willpower and the 'right' leadership can play a major role in driving conditions towards a successful revolution – and who thus often engage in adventurist tactics.

Organisation of American States:
The OAS was a Cold War body established by the US in April 1948, with its HQ in Washington DC. Ostensibly, it was to enable cooperation between states in the Americas – but the US used it as a major weapon in preventing the spread of 'communism' (often very loosely defined) in Latin and Central America.

United Fruit Company:
The US-owned UFC was a corporation owning vast landholdings, railways and ports in Latin and Central America, and the Caribbean. It was often referred to as 'The Octopus', and frequently interfered in these 'banana republics'. Allen Dulles (head of the CIA) and John Foster Dulles (US Secretary of State) were both significant shareholders/directors of the UFC – as were many other US government officials.

Che's family tree

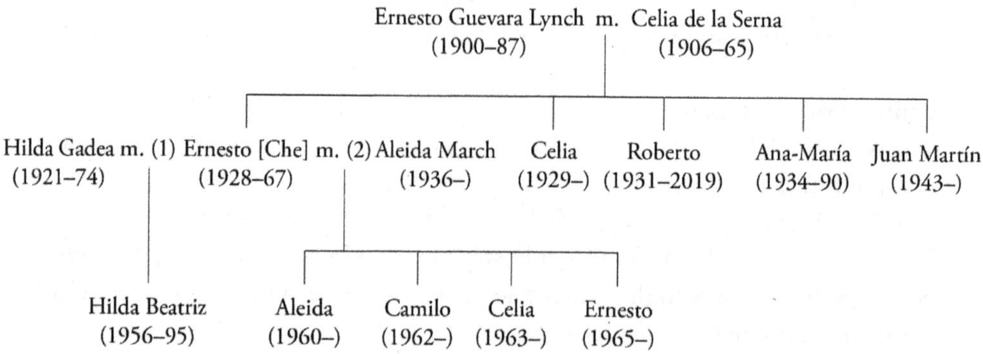

Main Characters

Che's family
Ana Isabel Guevara Lynch (1868–1947) – paternal grandmother
Beatriz Guevara Lynch (1904–86) – paternal/favourite aunt
Ernesto Guevara Lynch (1900–87) – father
Celia de la Serna y Llosa (1906–65) – mother
Celia (1929–) – older sister
Roberto (1931–2018) – brother
Ana-María (1934–90) – younger sister
Juan Martín (1943–) – younger brother
Hilda Gadea Acosta (1921–74) – Che's first wife; a radical activist/revolutionary
Hilda (Hildita) Beatriz (1956–95) – eldest daughter
Aleida March (1936–) – second wife; a M26J activist & supporter of the Cuban Revolution
Aleida (1960–) – daughter; a supporter of the Cuban Revolution
Camilo (1962–) – elder son; a supporter of the Cuban Revolution
Celia (1963–) – daughter
Ernesto (1965–) – younger son

Che's friends
Carlos 'Calica' Ferrer (1929–)
Maria del Carmen 'Chichina' Ferreyra (1933–2021) – first love
Alberto 'Miál' Granado (1922–2011)
Berta Gilda 'Tita' Infante (1924–76)
Ricardo Rojo (1923–96)

Che's M26J/ guerrilla *compañeros*
[guerrilla code-names are shown thus: 'Joaquín']

Juan 'Joaquín' Acuña (1925–67)
Dariel 'Benigno' Alarcón (1939–2016)
Juan Almeida (1927–)
Emilio 'Tembo' Aragonés (1928–2007)

Tamara 'Tania' Bunke (1937–**67**)
Fidel Castro (1926–2016)
Raúl Castro (1931–)
Juan Pablo 'Chino' Chang (1930–**67**)
Camilo Cienfuegos (1932–59)
Osmany 'Tuma' Cienfuegos (1931–)
Simeón 'Willy' Cuba (1935–**67**)
Victor 'Moja' Dreke (1937–)
Alberto 'Pacho' Fernández (1935–**67**)
Moisés 'Moisés' Guevara (1939–**67**)
Manuel 'Miguel' Hernández (1931–**67**)
Antonio 'Ñico' López (1932–**56**)
José Maria 'Papi' Martínez (1937–**67**)
Jorge 'Segundo' Masetti (1929–**64**)
Fernández 'Vinegar' Mell (1931–2019)
Frank 'David' País (1934–**57**)
Guido 'Inti' Peredo (1938–**69**)
Roberto 'Coco' Peredo (1939–**67**)
René 'Daniel' Ramos (1932–**58**)
Ciro Redondo (1931–**57**)
Aniceto 'Aniceto' Reinaga (1940–**67**)
Eliseo 'Rolando' Reyes (1940–**67**)
Roberto 'Vaquerito'/'Little Cowboy' Rodríguez (1935–**58**)
Haydée 'Yeyé' Santamaría (1922–)
Leonardo 'Urbano' Tamayo (1941–)
Lorgio 'Carlos' Vaca (1934–**67**)
Harry 'Pombo' Villegas (1940–2019)

(Dates in **bold** = 'killed in combat')

Che's main political supporters/opponents

Orlando Borrego (1936–2021) – Deputy at INRA, then Vice Minister of Industries; supporter
Mario Monje (1929–2019) – Secretary-General of the Bolivian Communist Party; opponent
Alberto Mora (1934–72) – Minister of Foreign Trade; opponent
Carlos Rafael Rodriguez (1913–97) – PSP/CCP leader; supporter, then opponent

Che's journeys across Latin and Central America

Che's route from the Sierra Mountains to Havana

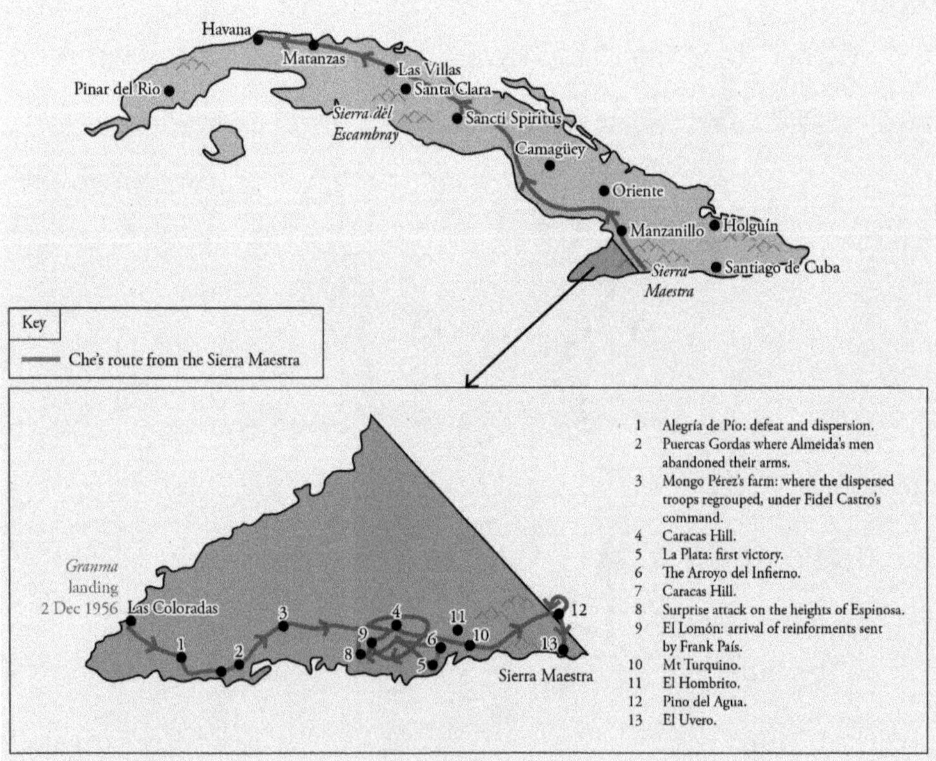

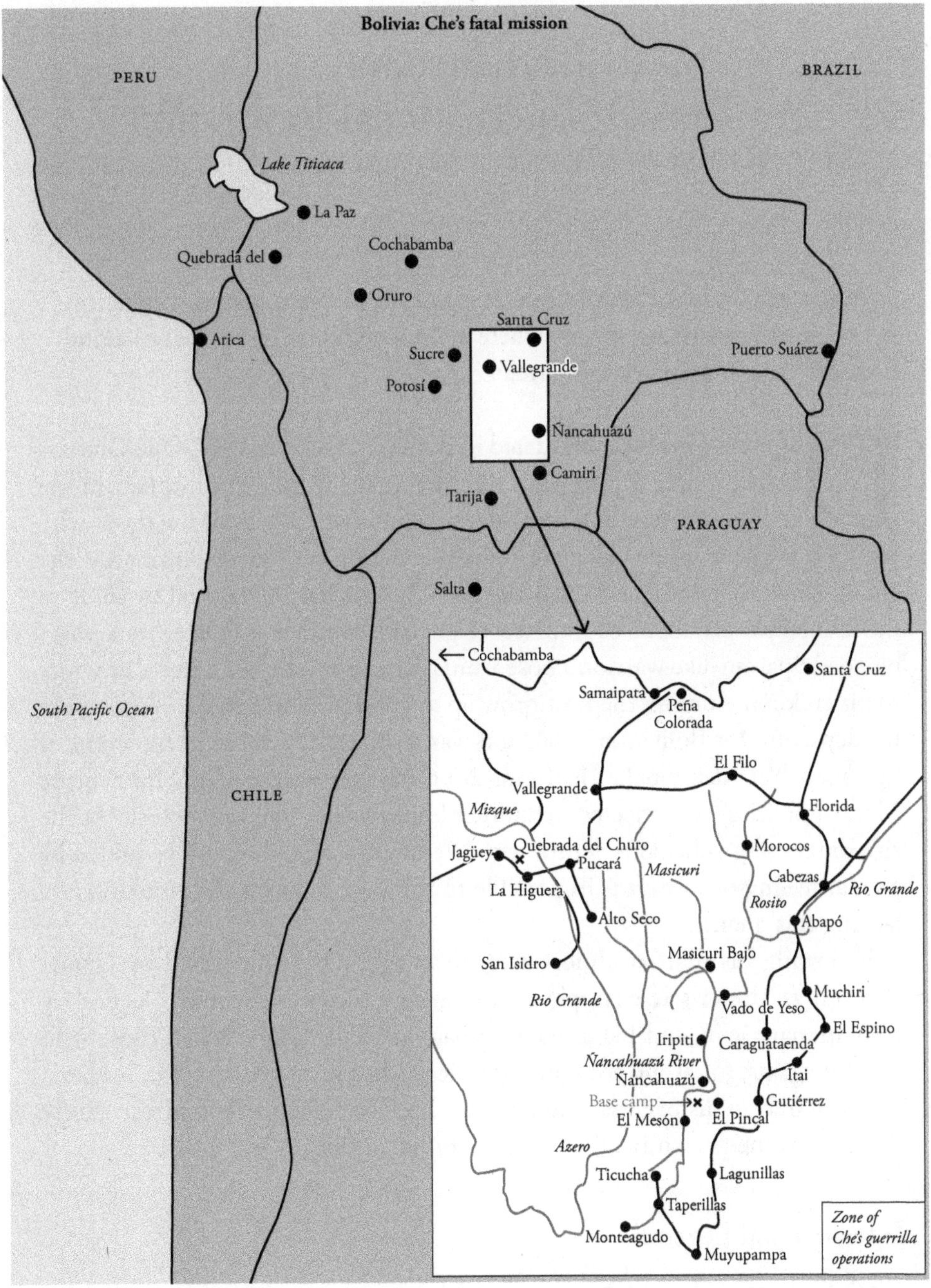

Bolivia: Che's fatal mission
PERU
BRAZIL
Lake Titicaca
La Paz
Quebrada del
Cochabamba
Oruro
Arica
Santa Cruz
Sucre
Vallegrande
Potosí
Puerto Suárez
Ñancahuazú
Camiri
Tarija
PARAGUAY
Salta
South Pacific Ocean
CHILE
Cochabamba
Santa Cruz
Samaipata
Peña Colorada
El Filo
Vallegrande
Florida
Mizque
Quebrada del Churo
Jagüey
Pucará
Masicuri
Morocos
Cabezas
Rio Grande
La Higuera
Rosito
Alto Seco
Abapó
Masicuri Bajo
San Isidro
Muchiri
Rio Grande
Vado de Yeso
El Espino
Iripiti
Caraguataenda
Ñancahuazú River
Itai
Ñancahuazú
Base camp
Gutiérrez
El Mesón
El Pincal
Azero
Ticucha
Lagunillas
Taperillas
Monteagudo
Muyupampa
Zone of Che's guerrilla operations

Introduction:
An Icon Of International Revolution

'Above all, always be able to feel deep within your being all the injustices committed against anyone, anywhere in the world. This is the most beautiful quality a revolutionary can have.'[1]

Despite having been murdered in Bolivia in October 1967, Che Guevara remains for many people – right across the world – the ultimate image of the romantic and idealistic revolutionary. Yet even for those who see Che as more of an idealistic romantic than a serious revolutionary, the above words may come as a surprise. For Che has been described by some as the archetypal exponent of implacable guerrilla warfare – or even as a cold-blooded Spartan-like warrior. Those words come from the last letter Che wrote to his children – urging them to 'grow up as good revolutionaries' – just before his departure for Bolivia in 1966, and was to be read to them in the event of his death. Yet such a belief had long been fundamental to Che's humanistic Marxist politics – as reflected in another letter, written the year before: 'At the risk of seeming ridiculous, let me say that the true revolutionary is guided by a great feeling of love. It is impossible to think of an authentic revolutionary lacking this quality.'[2]

Following his murder almost sixty years ago, Che – described by Daniel Bensaïd as 'the classic example of a man in a hurry' – became a legendary revolutionary icon, and his romantic image came to symbolise all those who struggle against social and economic injustices, wherever they may exist. As Harris states: 'Rarely in history has a single figure been so passionately and universally accepted as the personification of revolutionary idealism and practice.'[3]

International Legend

Che's international reputation began with his increasingly prominent role as a heroic guerrilla fighter in Fidel Castro's Rebel Army that, in less than three years, ousted Batista – Cuba's brutal dictator – in January 1959. He then rose to even greater prominence after 1959, when he took on various government and diplomatic roles in the Cuban Revolution. Along with Castro, he soon became the face of that revolution; and his growing international significance was such that, as early as 8 August 1960, he appeared on the front page of *Time* magazine in the US. Later, on 13 December 1964 – two days after strongly criticising, in a speech at the UN, the US government's continued aggressions against Cuba – he was interviewed on the CBS News programme *Face The Nation*. As ever, he was wearing his green military uniform, and smoking a big Cuban cigar.[4]

World interest in him further increased when, in the spring of 1965, he suddenly disappeared from public view. Then, in April 1967, Castro read out Che's *Message to the Tricontinental.* Written in 1966, before Che left for what would prove to be his fatal mission in Bolivia, it was said to have been sent from a guerrilla base 'somewhere in the world'. Typically – given Che's love of poetry – it began with a quotation from a poem by the nineteenth-century Cuban revolutionary, José Martí: 'Now is the time of furnaces, and only light should be seen.' When, just six months later, on 10 October 1967, the world learned of the circumstances of his death in Bolivia, he became even more of a legend – with the famous red and black poster of him, based on Korda's 1960 photograph, rapidly spreading around the world, and becoming a popular counter-cultural symbol of rebellion.[5]

Che's murder resonated around the world partly because, by 1967, he had emerged as a radical, undogmatic, independent and highly-principled freethinker, whose revolutionary internationalist example and Marxist thoughts had begun to cross over from Cuba – his second homeland – into the politics of countries in Latin America and beyond. Che's political beliefs – increasingly at odds with the restrictive socialism 'actually existing' in the Soviet bloc of the 1960s – were particularly refreshing for Western Europe's rebellious youth.

For the economist Meghnad Desai, Che 'is a romantic figure. He is perhaps the best loved or at least the most paraded global icon that the Revolutionary left can claim. Even more than the bearded founders of the movement, Che Guevara caught the imagination of the 1968 generation.' That 'generation of '68' was looking for a radical politics that was more libertarian, and was attracted by Che's stated belief that: 'The duty of every revolutionary is to make the revolution.'

Consequently, during the late 1960s and 1970s, Che's image – on banners and T-shirts – was present on many demonstrations and protests. At the time, his murder was seen as a bitter blow by young would-be revolutionaries, with many viewing it as: 'the death of a revolutionary, a modern-day warrior chief. The left was in mourning: poets wrote elegies, laments that ended with calls to rebellion.' Even historians critical of him – such as Farber – nonetheless recognise that, for many young people, Che was not just a key leader of one of the twentieth-century's most important revolutions, he was someone who actually remained true to his coherently expressed ideals and principles: 'Even more appealing to many are Che's personal values: political honesty, egalitarianism, radicalism, and willingness to sacrifice for a cause, including his position of power in Cuba.'[6]

In Latin America itself, Che's call – made in his *Message to the Tricontinental* – to create 'two, three, many Vietnams', in order to weaken US imperialism's ability to impose its political and economic interests militarily on underdeveloped countries, resulted in the formation of several guerrilla groups keen to overthrow their repressive and exploitative governments, and to weaken the global reach of the much-hated Yankee empire. For many in Latin America, his willingness to sacrifice his life spoke to a universal belief that the mark of an individual's greatness is their preparedness to dedicate themselves to a cause that is greater than themselves. For Che, and for his would-be imitators, that cause was to end suffering, exploitation and oppression wherever it existed, based on the universal humanistic values of equality, justice and liberty. In many ways, his life – and death – enshrined those values.

While news of Che's murder undoubtedly pleased the CIA – whose file on him, first opened in 1954, eventually became its biggest on any individual – and the various dictators in Latin and Central America, a surprisingly-large number of the world's leading thinkers, writers and artists rushed to pay tribute to him. Among the 'great and good' who did so were Alan Sillitoe, Christopher Logue, Frederic Raphael, John Berger, Italo Calvino, Andre Gorz and Graham Greene. Jean-Paul Sartre – one of Europe's foremost philosophers in 1967 – had this to say on hearing of Che's murder in Bolivia:

> I believe that [Che] was not only an intellectual but also the most complete human being of our age: as a fighter and as a man, as a theoretician who was able to further the cause of revolution by drawing his theories from his personal experience in battle.[7]

A Romantic 'Renaissance Man'

Despite often being dismissed as merely 'the romantic guerrilla fighter or the idealist dreamer', Sartre's comment about Che being 'a complete human being' was surprisingly accurate. For many, though, his travels across Latin and Central America and his later involvement in guerrilla warfare seem to 'have placed blinkers on history, blinding it to other aspects of this multifaceted man'. In addition to his revolutionary activity – and the fact that he was a qualified doctor of medicine – Che was a prolific diarist and writer who left behind an impressive body of work. Even while conducting guerrilla warfare – whether in Cuba or, later, in the Congo and Bolivia – he continued to make notes and diary entries whenever the opportunity arose. He also maintained an extensive correspondence with family and friends. As well as his books on guerrilla warfare, he is also known as a bold traveller with a romantic sense of adventure, and a keen desire for new experience. His various travel diaries, written while in his early twenties, were published after his death, and one formed the basis of the 2004 film, *The Motor Cycle Diaries*.[8]

From an early age, he was an avid reader of a wide range of poetry, fiction and non-fiction – and soon proved able to quickly master new topics. In particular, he developed a real love for the adventure novels of Alexander Dumas and Jules Verne. His favourite novel seems to have been Cervantes' *Don Quixote*, which he read at least six times. During Cuba's guerrilla war, Che made that book part of the literary courses he gave to illiterate peasant recruits to the Rebel Army; and it was also the first book to be printed on a mass scale in Cuba within months of the Revolution's victory in 1959. While in his last letter he wrote to his parents, dated 1 April 1965 – as he was going off to fight in the Congo – he made a reference to that favourite novel: 'Once again I feel beneath my heels the ribs of Rocinante. Once more, I'm on the road with my shield on my arm.'[9]

Che loved poetry, and often quoted extensively from French poetry. He was particularly fond of the Chilean poet and communist, Pablo Neruda, the Cuban Nicolás Guillén, and the Turkish communist poet, Nâzim Hikmet. The latter has been described as a 'romantic revolutionary', whose political outlook was international and reached beyond borders – rather as Che's internationalism was focused on opposing 'Yankee imperialism' across the globe. Volumes by Guillén and Neruda were among the books Che took with him on his last mission. Neruda had met Che in Havana, when Che was a minister, describing him as 'dark, slow-speaking' and whose 'sentences were short and rounded off with a smile, as if leaving the discussion up in the air'. Neruda had been flattered when Che told him 'that he often read my *Canto general* to the … guerrillas in the Sierra Maestra'. On learning that Che – 'the pensive man who in his heroic battles always had a place, next to his weapons, for poetry' – had been murdered, Neruda wrote: 'Che Guevara's official assassination, in poor Bolivia, was a bitter blow. The telegram announcing his death ran through the world like a cold shiver of reverence. Millions of elegies tried to join in tribute to his heroic and tragic life.' Neruda saw Che as 'a great guerrilla and a powerful political mind', but very much 'an exception'. Though, as a more orthodox communist, Neruda didn't support Che's ideas about the usefulness of guerrilla warfare or 'the romantic spirit and the wild guerrilla theories that swept Latin America' in the years following Che's 'heroic death'.[10]

Che also had a deep interest in the ancient civilisations of Latin and Central America. As well as reading about them, he took every opportunity on his travels to visit Inca, Aztec and Maya archaeological sites – and spent much time in museums in order to learn more about an area's ancient history. Even on his delayed honeymoon, with his heavily-pregnant first wife, he insisted on visiting Maya ruins. As a result of all this reading and studying, he proved uncommonly erudite on a wide variety of subjects. He was also an exceptionally-good chess player – a game his father taught him at an early age, and which later became his main pastime. Che once achieved a draw in a simultaneous match given by the Polish-Argentinian International Grandmaster, Miguel Najdorf – who was among the world's top chess players in the period 1939–49, and is best known for his Najdorf Variation of the Sicilian Defence. Finally, despite suffering badly from asthma from early childhood, he was very sporty, taking part in football, tennis, golf and especially rugby. His determination not to let his asthma limit what he did meant that, at times, he experienced serious attacks and sometimes had to be carried back home by his schoolmates.

Marxist Intellectual

Until relatively recently, most books about Che focused almost exclusively on him as an adventurous travel writer, a romantic revolutionary and an exponent of guerrilla warfare; only occasionally was his work as a government minister in Cuba covered. Thus Sartre's description of Che as an intellectual may come as a surprise to those whose knowledge of Che is limited to those aspects of his life. Although few think of him as a significant Marxist theorist on economics and philosophy, Che was, in fact, someone who made original contributions to debates over the best methods of economic management for bringing about the transition to socialism.

When Che first became a Marxist – before Khrushchev's revelations about Stalin's crimes – he was happy to be associated with 'Comrade Stalin'. However, as his reading of the Marxist classics widened and deepened, he increasingly developed ideas that ran counter to the Soviet Union's version of 'orthodox' Marxism. Most crucially, Che's theoretical writings arose from his practical involvement in revolutionary struggle and construction – a real combination of Marxist *praxis* (the unity of theory and practice). Che understood that, while to a large extent people are the product of the conditions of society in which they live, those very conditions can be changed by the *conscious* actions of people. He saw the transition to socialism, via the revolutionary transformation of productive forces and social relations, as being closely linked to the revolutionary education and self-education of people – hence his emphasis on moral, rather than material, incentives.

During his brief time as a minister, Che wrote many articles and made many speeches which attempted to breathe new life into Marxism, in opposition to the ossified version – almost a 'sterile state religion' – upheld by the Communist Party of the Soviet Union and the 'orthodox' communists who supported it. This was especially so as regards the problems of the transition to socialism in developing countries. In addition, his arguments for the need to create 'new' human beings – far from being 'romantic' – were based on Marxism's recognition that humans are capable of real adaptability. This was why he argued – in the face of 'orthodox' communists – that the right production methods would help people develop the new concepts and new ways of thinking vital for creating a revolutionary proletarian class-consciousness, and a qualitatively-different kind of society.

Although 'orthodox' Soviet communists criticised Che's attitude as being too subjective (or 'voluntarist'), Che's emphasis on the 'subjective factor' in history – as the 'conscious, purposeful intervention in the objective historical process' needed to bring about revolution and then the transition to socialism – was 'a decisive component' of early Marxism. For Che – as for Marxists such as the Trotskyist revolutionary Ernest Mandel – this was vital for increasing and developing proletarian class-consciousness; because, to make the transition to socialism, feelings of communality and class solidarity needed to be raised. Thus, for Che, using the correct means and tactics was crucial. Che followed the classical Marxist view that any non-socialist method, even if adopted for 'purely practical' reasons, would 'in the long run detract from the socialist goal, instead of bringing it a step closer'. Essentially, 'the decisive factor in the transition from capitalism to socialism remains the raising of the class-consciousness of the proletariat.' There is 'an ethical component of Marxism' which argues that 'only that which raises proletarian class consciousness and, among other things, promotes a deeper understanding by the workers of the fundamental difference between bourgeois and classless society, can advance the class struggle in the long run.' Che saw this aspect as important as developing an internationalist perspective.[11]

However, some of Che's views have been criticised by several Marxists. One area concerns the role of workers' self-management in the transition to a socialist planned economy. Although, in principle, Che favoured this being carried out through Cuba's trade unions, he actually opposed it while a minister as the trade unions tended to be dominated by the Cuban Communists, who had 'orthodox' pro-Soviet views. However, he may well have continued to change and develop his views – and it is perhaps worth reflecting that Trotsky, in favour of maintaining party unity, at first opposed the first anti-Stalinist groups when they appeared. Trotsky, of course, had many more years in which to reflect and amend his views – but Che was killed at the relatively young age of 39.

Another aspect of Che's views which has been criticised as 'un-Marxist' was his conviction that, by launching armed struggle in Latin America, it would be possible to hasten revolution. Yet Marxism, with its theories of combined and uneven development, had recognised since the Russian Revolution in 1917 that the relative underdevelopment of capitalism in some 'Third World' countries during the epoch of imperialism actually made a political revolution *more* possible there than in more developed countries 'for the very same reasons which make the construction of a classless society exceedingly difficult.' For Che, to ignore this was to condemn such countries 'to remain stuck in barbaric underdevelopment.' Che was convinced that, for Cuba to develop socialism, it would be necessary to end its isolation in the region. In opposition to the 'orthodox' Soviet view, Che argued – as did Mandel – that 'premature' revolutions in the periphery could nonetheless act as 'springboards for the socialist world revolution, which *can* spread by degrees and stages to the most important industrial countries of the world'. As later history would prove, the lack of socialist revolutions in the developed world meant that socialist states on the periphery – including the Soviet Union itself – remained 'arrested and frozen in the transitional period between capitalism and socialism, as a result of the delay of the proletarian world revolution'.[12]

Che also argued against privileges for the upper layers of bureaucracy and skilled workers, as it created divisions when there needed to be unity, in order to develop the class-consciousness and solidarity necessary for the transition to socialism. Once again, this was in line with classical Marxism, which recognised that in order to bring about such a transition, there would need to be 'an enduring change in work motivation and the work ethic which, in turn, is inconceivable without ... the changing of morals and customs'. For Che, this was all part of his desire to aid the development – and self-development – of the 'socialist human being'. As part of that, Che placed great emphasis on international solidarity. Che's dream went beyond changing economic, social and social structures,: he also wanted to transform human consciousness, values and behaviours. In other words – using the patriarchal term that has been used so widely in the past, and was also a reflection of Latin American culture in the twentieth century – to create the 'New Man'. For this aim – as well as for his belief that the methods of guerrilla warfare which had triumphed in Cuba could be 'exported' anywhere else – he has often been dismissed as a being, rather like his hero Quixote, committed to some romantic idealism or utopianism. But, as Löwy commented: 'The dream of all great revolutionaries, from Rousseau to Lenin, has been to change not merely "the world" but also "man": ... A revolution is authentic only if it can create this "new man".'[13]

Che's belief that a revolutionary needed to love to be authentic underwrote his concept of the 'dignity' due to fellow humans, based on what José Martí had said: 'A real man should feel on his own cheek the blow inflicted on any other man's.' More importantly, far from being merely the view of a romantic idealist, it was actually very much in tune with Marxist humanism, which urges revolutionaries: 'to take a positive attitude toward life and human beings and to love them'. Marx himself wrote: 'The proletariat ... needs its courage, its self-respect, its pride, and its sense of independence even more than its bread.'[14]

Che's Marxism also emphasised the importance of freedom – not the individualistic capitalist idea of each against each in the 'freedom' of the market place – but the idea of the rational control of social life by unalienated humans themselves, rather than by capitalism's 'blind' impersonal 'laws'. At bottom, his Marxism reflected a 'yearning for a society of free, equal and associated producers', and his adult life can be seen as being just one example of what Mandel has described as the 'inextinguishable spark of revolt against inequality, exploitation, injustice and oppression, which lights up again and again in the human race ... sometimes only among poets, philosophers and scholars, at other times among great masses of people, according to the tides of history'. History has shown – by an almost 'uninterrupted stream of upsurges, rebellions, revolts and revolutions against the exploitation of the poor and the oppression of the powerless' – that humans have long hungered for equality.[15]

Unrevolutionary beginnings

Yet, before Che became a revolutionary, a famed exponent of guerrilla warfare, and a Marxist theorist – and most unlike the young Trotsky – Che was not interested in politics until his mid-twenties. In his early years, influenced by his parents' politics, he took the side of the Republicans in the Spanish Civil War, and became involved – in a limited way – in anti-fascist activity during the Second World War. However, even when some of his friends became involved in protests before and during the Perón years, he stayed neutral. In fact, in some ways, the young Che was a typical product of his family background – and of the conservative and macho culture which predominated in 1950s Argentina, and in Latin America as a whole. Although his parents were relatively impoverished, they both came from wealthy upper-class families – especially his mother – and many of their relations held important posts in Argentina's military and diplomatic corps. However, Che's parents – and, again, especially his mother – were also unconventional in many ways, and thus Che frequently played with children from lower social classes, which was unusual considering his parents' background.

Nonetheless, as an older teenager and a young man, Che did share the attitudes of his wealthy, upper-class heterosexual male friends when it came to sexual relations with lower-class women. This was particularly true as regards the young female Indian servants their families employed. These *mucamas* seemed to have been treated as a readily-available (and readily-exploited?) source for their early sexual experiences.[16]

Although some of his biographers have noted various questionable incidents with women in Che's early years, none seems to have commented on the considerable social and economic disparities between these white upper-class male youths and their young Indian female (and not necessarily heterosexual) servants. Yet, in the twenty-first century, comments about intersectionality issues are surely relevant here, as are debates about the ability to consent. In addition, the young Che's travel journals indicate that, in common with many Argentinians in the 1950s, he also shared some of the prevailing racist views and negative attitudes regarding black people and gay men.

Throughout his life, many women found Che attractive – despite his poor personal hygiene and lack of interest in his appearance! His attractiveness to women would, at times, cause tensions with both his wives. His original travel diaries occasionally seem to have contained explicit comments about his sexual encounters and thoughts. However, as Anderson noted, these diaries were not published until after his death and had almost certainly been 'cleaned up' before publication, with 'some explicit sexual references … [being] expurgated'. On a diplomatic trip to Japan in 1959, Che revealed to his bodyguard that 'I know what it's like to *putear* – I whored round in my youth, too.' Later, though, as Che matured and became a committed revolutionary, he developed a more austere attitude towards casual sex. Ultimately, Che's life from his mid-twenties onwards seems to prove the veracity of the saying that 'travel broadens the mind' as, both personally and politically, Che's attitudes and beliefs quickly developed in ways much more in keeping with the world's idea of the legendary revolutionary know as 'El Che'.[17]

Of course, Che's development – both as a man and as a revolutionary – was cut short at 1.10 pm on 9 October 1967, when he was murdered in cold blood by the Bolivian army. They may have killed 'only' a man on that day – but, by doing so, they had begun the process whereby that man would be reborn as the legend the world knows as 'Che'.

Chapter 1

The Young Che, 1928–43

'Look out, here comes El Furibundo [The Furious] Serna!'[1]

The above warning was frequently issued by the teenaged Che, just before plunging headlong into rugby tackles. Yet Che's physical recklessness was evident even before he reached his teens. Arguably, such recklessness eventually led to his murder in Bolivia, following his ill-fated guerrilla campaign there. Several of the seeds which led to that tragic end – and his subsequent transformation into an iconic revolutionary legend – were sown during the first fifteen years of his life.

Che's bourgeois family

Che was born (officially) on 14 June 1928. His parents – Ernesto Guevara Lynch and Celia de la Serna y Llosa – belonged to Argentina's upper-classes. His father's ancestors included members of Spanish and Irish nobility, while a great-grandfather had been one of the wealthiest men in Latin America. However, though maintaining their class position, the Guevara family had lost most of its wealth over the years. Che's mother came from a wealthy upper-class Argentine family of noble Spanish descent, which still owned extensive estates.

When Che's parents first met in 1927, his mother was 20, and had just graduated from an exclusive Catholic girls' school in Buenos Aires. Highly intelligent and well-read – and increasingly unconventional – she was due to inherit a significant amount of wealth on reaching the age of 21. Although there was a distant connection between the two families, her family became wary once they realised she and Lynch – seven years her senior – were becoming more than friends: 'when her family realised that there was something more than friendship between us, some of her brothers objected to our relationship'.[2]

In 1927, Lynch – who'd already put his inheritance into a yacht-building business – decided he could make a fortune by growing yerba maté – an indigenous tea, known as 'green gold', which was hugely popular in Argentina and the rest of Latin America. He persuaded Celia that, once they were married, her inheritance would buy an estate in Misiones province, a remote settlement in Argentina's northern jungle. However, as Celia wasn't yet 21, she had to ask her family for permission to marry and to have her inheritance early. According to Lynch, he was a 'Socialist' and moved her to socialism, and thus their social equals soon saw them as 'the Communist Red Devils'. In particular, he claims her family blamed him 'for having taken Celia away from the bosom of the Catholic Church to turn her into a Socialist miscreant.' Whatever the truth of this, her family refused to give their permission.[3]

As Celia was already pregnant, they pretended they were going to elope, so the family reluctantly consented – the marriage taking place on 10 November 1927. Though Celia only succeeded in getting some of her inheritance early, it was enough to buy a maté planation of almost 500 acres in Misiones – sufficiently remote from their conventionally-respectable families for them to hide Celia's pregnancy.

Che's early years

As Celia's pregnancy developed, they moved to Rosario, Argentina's third largest city. It was there, on 14 May 1928, that Che was born. He was christened Ernesto Guevara de la Serna; but was usually referred to as 'Ernestito' ('Little Ernesto') by his family. His birth certificate, however, states he was born a full month later, on 14 June – a doctor friend having agreed to falsify the birth certificate. When Che was a month old, his parents told their families that Che had arrived two months prematurely. As Anderson remarked, it seems fitting – given his later career as a revolutionary – that Che 'should have begun life with a subterfuge'. Che would later have four siblings: Celia, Roberto, Ana-María and Juan Martín.[4]

While in Rosario, however, Che contracted bronchial pneumonia. It's possible that this triggered the respiratory problems that would afflict him for the rest of his life. After a while, they made a quick trip back to Buenos Aires to show off Che to their respective families, before returning to Misiones. Lynch treated his Guaraní Indian labourers fairly: though this made him a very popular employer, it set him apart from other landowners. According to him, he was called 'The Communist' by the other landowners. Although Che was too young to know what his father was doing, Luther surmises that his father's actions 'undoubtedly reflected an attitude … of fairness and justice that Che would live and, eventually, die for'.[5]

Signs of Che's iron determination emerged as he was learning to walk – he would get angry if he stumbled or fell. His father relates how Che often fell over a pipe in a ditch when bringing them a gourd full of yerba maté from the kitchen: when he fell, he got up but 'kept going back for the maté until he learned to jump over the ditch'.

Another possibly formative experience for the young Che was his mother's fearless nature – according to Lynch, she seemed 'attracted to danger' – a characteristic Che would also exhibit. Despite being a strong swimmer, she once almost drowned in the river while six months pregnant. Yet, despite that experience, she had other narrow escapes – at least two of which were witnessed by Che when he was only 5 years old.[6]

In late 1929, with the first crop of yerbe maté planted, and Celia about to give birth to their second child, the family moved back to Buenos Aires. Another reason for the move was that Lynch's yacht-building business was on the point of bankruptcy. They moved into a bungalow – in the grounds of a large colonial residence owned by Lynch's sister María and her husband – in San Isidro, a suburb of Buenos Aires on the R. La Plata . In December, Celia gave birth to a daughter – Celia – who was named after her. When the yacht shipyard burned down, Lynch lost his entire investment. However, they still had an income from Celia's Córdoba estate, and they were expecting to get their first revenues from their yerba maté planation. Plus they had plenty of wealthy relations and friends. Consequently, Lynch was unworried, and spent weekends cruising on the river with friends; or, with Celia and their children, visiting rich family members on their country estates or relaxing on the beach of the San Isidro Yacht Club. Before long, however, his 'playboy ways and financial troubles created an ever-growing distance between his wife and him'.[7]

Che's 'cursed illness'

It was while in Buenos Aires that Che had his first asthma attack – the 'cursed illness' from which he would suffer for the rest of his life. Che's mother often took him to San Isidro's Yacht Club, where they both went swimming. In May 1930, on a particularly chilly and windy day during the Argentine winter, they went swimming as usual. When his father met them later to take them to lunch, he 'found Ernesto in his swimming gear trembling with cold … By the time we arrived at our house Ernesto was not well.'[8]

That night, Che became extremely unwell. He was rushed to a local doctor, who informed his parents that he had asthmatic bronchitis 'without complications'. The doctor suggested it may have been linked to the bronchial pneumonia that Che had contracted in Rosario when just a few days old. The attack lasted several days, with Che not really responding to standard treatments. His father noted: 'Ernesto had scarcely begun to talk when he learned to say, "Daddy, injection" whenever his asthma got the better of him.' This soon became a frequent 'call for medicine when he felt an attack coming on'. Lynch himself found this frustrating: 'Ernesto's asthma was becoming chronic, and for us it was becoming a curse.'[9]

Che's illness soon put an end to plans to return to the plantation in Misiones. As his father wrote: 'It was our intention to return a few months later, but Ernesto's asthma and the birth of our daughter Celia forced us to give up that idea.' In later years, Che's father felt Che's asthma may have been brought on by Celia taking him swimming on such a cold day. However, while the cold air and water may have triggered this first attack, Celia herself was extremely allergic and suffered from asthma; while Che's siblings were also allergic, thought not as severely as Che. This is one of the reasons why Che at one time thought of becoming a doctor to find a cure.[10]

For the next two years, in addition to all the medicines prescribed by doctors, his parents desperately tried various cures – including syrups and burning 'Andrews papers in his room'. But nothing worked. Both parents were anxious, and clearly devoted a lot of care: 'Celia used to spend the nights listening to his breathing. I used to put him to sleep on my chest because it seemed he could breathe better that way, but consequently I hardly slept.' According to Lynch, 'All the doctors who saw him [Che] said they had never seen such an acute manifestation of the illness, and some even said they had never seen it in children … and none of the asthmatic people we talked to had attacks of the intensity of Ernesto's.'[11]

Eventually, their doctor advised that a drier climate might lessen the frequency and severity of Che's attacks. So, in 1931, they moved to central Buenos Aires, near to Lynch's mother Ana Isabel, and his sister Beatriz, who lived with her. Both women fussed over the sickly Che, and showered him with love. This move turned out to be 'the beginning of our lengthy pilgrimage in search of a better climate for our child'. In May 1932, Celia gave birth to Roberto. Although Che – now aged 4 – experienced a slight improvement, his continuing asthma attacks began to frustrate his father: 'By now Ernesto's asthma was shaping all our decision. Each day brought a new restriction to our freedom of movement and we were at the mercy of his cursed illness.'[12]

His father recalled how, as advised by Che's doctors, he kept 'a large balloon of oxygen at hand so that I could give the boy a blast of gas when the worst moment [of the attack] came'. An early indication of the self-discipline, determination – and even stubbornness – that became a hallmark of the adult Che was shown by his refusing the 'blast of oxygen' as long as he could, often turning purple in the face before finally giving in and indicating that he needed oxygen.[13]

During the summer holidays, they spent time on the *estancia* of Celia's brother-in-law, Ernesto Moore; and on Lynch's mother's *estancia* at Portela: a large house that had eleven bedrooms and several bathrooms, where Che became particularly close to his paternal grandmother. However, on doctors' advice, they began to consider moving to places with even drier climates – what Lynch later described as the start of their 'nomadic destiny'. Initially, they spent several months travelling back and forth from Buenos Aires to Córdoba, Argentina's second largest city, located in the central highlands, At first, Che showed signs of improvement. But though he had long periods free from illness, there was no predictable pattern. Eventually, doctors urged them to stay in Córdoba for at least four months. In early 1933, they moved to the near-by spa town of Alta Gracia which, because of its dry climate, had become a popular retreat for those suffering from a variety of lung diseases. Though intended as a short stay, it was here Che spent his childhood, between the ages of 5 and 16.

Alta Gracia

Alta Gracia was a small provincial town and – at least for some time – its pure mountain air proved beneficial for Che's health. Although he continued to have asthma attacks, they became intermittent rather than frequent. To limit his attacks, his parents tried different types of bedding, and certain foods were banned – especially during his attacks. An aspect of Che's personality which emerged during this period was his self-discipline: 'He showed unusually strong self-discipline by adhering to these diets, but once his attacks had subsided, he gorged himself, and became known for his ability to consume huge quantities of food at a single sitting.' Eventually, however, it soon became clear that there was no pattern to Che's asthma: the most they could do was find ways to contain it. In January 1934, Ana-María – the couple's fourth child – was born. Although Che often argued with his other siblings, he soon became very protective of his youngest sister. He would tell her stories, and, as soon as she was able to accompany him, he would take her on walks; when his asthma restricted his breathing and tired him, he would rest his head on her shoulder.[14]

After two years, as Che's health recovered – though Lynch failed to find work and 'We were going through a bad patch financially because it was difficult for me to find work locally and my maté plantation was in crisis, since the price of maté leaves had plummeted. My wife's estancia was enduring a lengthy period of drought.' Because Che's 'condition seemed to diminish after he swam … they joined the Sierras Hotel swimming pool'. Che's improvement meant Celia was able to take him and his siblings on mule rides and hikes to swimming holes in the unspoilt countryside. His mother also began to meet with Alta Gracia's inhabitants. Such physical activities, and his longer periods between attacks, meant he was able to play with the local children and even attend school occasionally. But he also continued to have long spells in bed because of asthmatic attacks.[15]

Che's father, increasingly concerned by their diminishing funds and beginning to feel isolated, wanted to move back to Buenos Aires. As a result, he grew more distant from his wife. However, his devotion to Che was obvious to all who knew the family – he often sat through the night with Che, in case he suffered an attack. Celia herself recalled how Lynch 'became accustomed to sleeping on [Che's] bed, so that the latter, reclining on his chest, could better beat the asthma'.[16]

Che's long periods of confinement to bed affected his physical appearance. At 5 years old, family photographs show him to have been 'full-faced, stocky … [and] with pale skin and unruly black hair.' By the age of 7 though, photographs show a slimmer Che, with a face that looks sallow and drawn. Nonetheless, once recovered from his bouts of asthma, Che seemed determined to make up for lost time, and threw himself with gusto into outdoor activities. He was usually a lively, competitive – and, at times, wilful – child, who delighted in playing with the gangs (or *barras*) of local children. Their exploits included playing trench warfare or 'cops and robbers' – the latter often involved them riding their bicycles at high speed up and down the town's hilly streets.[17]

Though Che had a few middle-class friends, the majority of his playmates were working class. From the latter, Che learned what real misery and deprivation were. According to his father, this was how Che discovered, early on in his life, how the poor lived and were exploited, and how the various injustices gave them only limited chances for improving their lives: 'He had the opportunity of living among the destitute as well as among the wealthy, and he drew a lesson from it that he never forgot.' In addition, Che's family also discussed all types of social problems, including stories of exploitation and misery.[18]

In 1935, when Che was 7, the family moved to Villa Nydia, a more spacious house in Alta Gracia. This house is now the Museo Casa del Che Guevara (Museum of Che Guevara's House). One reason for the move was because the rent was low – an important consideration because the family continued to suffer from lack of funds. Although Lynch won a contract to improve the Sierras Golf Course in 1941, once that contract ended it seems he was unable to get any other paid work for the rest of their stay in Alta Gracia. According to family and friends, it was Celia's remaining money which enabled the family to struggle on.

Although their economic problems were partly due to the expense of doctors and medicines necessitated by Che's asthma, they also arose because his parents were not good at budgeting. In fact, they were both determined to maintain a lifestyle they could not afford – including spending long parts of the summer at Mar del Plata, the exclusive Atlantic seaside resort popular with Argentina's wealthy set – partly because the sea air there was beneficial for Che's breathing. When things were particularly tight, they relied on help from family and friends, who often 'bailed them out.'[19]

A life of reading

Despite the clean mountain air, Che still had asthma attacks – sometimes forcing him to stay in bed for days at a time, meaning he was unable to attend school regularly during his early years. Instead, his mother took on the task of educating him at home, teaching him how to read and write, along with the lessons he was missing at primary school. He became particularly close to his mother during this period and, by the age of 5, it was already clear that Che and his mother had similar temperaments and intellects. Both were rebellious, had strong views which they felt free to express, and had a reckless attraction to danger. The special relationship they forged in this period lasted right through to Celia's death in 1965. In fact, once Che had left home and embarked on his revolutionary career, they regularly exchanged warm and revealing letters.

During those early years, his father – who according to Anderson 'looked across a perceptual divide at his wife and son' – taught him how to play chess. Che soon became an excellent player, and it was a game he enjoyed for the rest of his life. Typically, though, he was furious if he felt his father was letting him win. In 1962, Che's father met the chess grandmaster Miguel Najdorf in Cuba, who told him Che was 'a first-class player'. Later, Najdorf said how Che preferred an aggressive game and liked sacrifices, but prepared them well. Najdorf also related how he had been invited to play ten matches simultaneously at a chess club in Cuba, at which Che – and several other government ministers – were present. Najdorf described his game against Che thus:

> With Che I played well and offered him a draw … He rejected the offer, saying, 'When I was a student of medicine in Buenos Aires I lost against you at a display in which you played fifteen boards simultaneously at the Provincial Hotel in Mar del Plata. Now I prefer to lose or to ask for a return match.' I accepted the invitation to fight it out, but the match ended in a draw.[20]

Che soon became an avid reader, and was influenced in his choice of reading matter by both his parents. His mother stimulated his long-lasting love for philosophy, novels and poetry; while his father introduced him to adventure stories – particularly those of Jules Verne – and to history. Che often spent hours reading alone and, as a teenager, he began making notes on what he had read. As he grew older, Che often recalled that 'these periods of confinement only deepened his love of reading', and it proved to be a love which he never outgrew.[21]

During this period, Che also forged a close relationship with his unmarried aunt Beatriz, who was particularly fond of Che and showered him with gifts. One of Che's first 'letters', written in 1933, was to Beatriz, informing her that his asthma had improved. Although the letter was actually written by one of his parents, Che had scrawled his own signature: 'Teté' – Beatriz's nickname for him, which had quickly been taken up by the rest of his family.

Between periodic asthma attacks, Che liked to spend as much time as possible outdoors. He particularly enjoyed swimming, horse riding, golf, pistol-shooting at targets (Che was just 5 years old when his father began teaching him how to shoot), and biking. His early childhood friends remember him as an energetic, mischievous – and often bold and courageous – child, who loved playing games that required physical endurance, and who often organised long hikes into the foothills of the mountains. Early on, it became apparent that there was often a competitive edge to these physical activities – with Che clearly determined to show that when he wasn't suffering an asthma attack, he could excel at sports such as football and table tennis. He was also a fearless combatant in the organised rock fights between the various local gangs. His father wrote: 'From the time he was a small child, Ernesto felt deeply attracted to danger. He sought it and enjoyed overcoming it. He did this very often and had acquired real control over his nerves, which gave him great serenity so that he could act without hesitation.'[22]

However, the fact that his mother encouraged Che in such physical activities – in part because, as with swimming, they seemed to alleviate his symptoms – led to tensions between her and his father, who tended to frown on such activities. The latter once 'remarked that his son had inherited his "tendency to face danger" from his mother'. His mother, however, considered Che returning to these outdoor pursuits – with renewed vigour once recovered from asthma attacks – as important in allowing Che to have as normal a childhood as possible.[23]

Early on, it soon became clear that Che was determined to defy his father's authority, and, with his mother never really trying to discipline him, he became increasingly unruly and disobedient. One morning Che, then aged 9, answered his mother back when she had reprimanded him; as his father got up, Che realised he was in for a 'good spanking' and so ran off. Although both parents tried to catch him, he out-ran them and disappeared into the hills behind their house. His father then mounted a horse to give chase, but Che still managed to escape capture by running into the bushes. When Che still hadn't returned by evening, his father began to worry. However – showing their difference in temperament – Celia said: 'I know him better than you. Don't attach too much importance to it. I am sure that tonight when he feels hungry he will come back' – which he did. Lynch saw Che's abilities to run and hide in forests as standing him in good stead for his later life 'when, as a guerrilla, he had to attack, hide and escape in the jungles and mountains where he chose to fight. Alta Gracia turned him into a real master of the forests and mountains.'[24]

Both of Che's parents had fiery tempers; and it soon became apparent to both family and friends that fierce arguments were frequent occurrences. In part, these were due to differences in personality: Lynch was 'overly cautious' and thus always worried about Che; while his mother seemed to think being Che's 'confidante and co-conspirator' was the correct parental role. However, these arguments were also no doubt linked to their on-going money problems, which Che's father unfairly began to blame on Celia's 'imprudence'. Yet, according to neighbours and Celia's closest friends, the main reason was Lynch's affairs with other women – in such a relatively small town, these soon became common knowledge.

From hills to school

In early 1937 – when Che was almost 9 years old – the local education authorities became increasingly concerned about his long absences from school. Thus, in March 1937, he had finally to swap his freedom in the hills for regular lessons in the Escuela San Martín, Alta Gracia's state primary school. While most children from Argentina's elite went to private schools, Argentina's state schools accepted children from all social classes. According to Luther this exposure may have helped shape his later beliefs in equality: 'This early experience of academic and backyard equality would come into play as the adult Che interacted with the Cubans he fought so hard to help.'[25]

For the first two terms, he hardly missed a day; though, despite his regular attendance at school, his mother continued his home tutoring: in particular, teaching him to speak and read French fluently. However, during that year's final term, he was absent for three weeks – almost certainly as a result of a particularly lengthy bout of asthma. Nonetheless, Che seemed to take education seriously: 'On days he didn't attend class, his siblings would copy his assignments and bring his school work home to him.' Yet, despite getting high marks in History, he didn't shine as a particularly academic student; although he showed brightness in class, he rarely seemed to study. Thus his report for the 1938 academic year assessed his overall grades as only 'satisfactory'.[26]

While his conduct was judged as 'good' for his first two terms, there was a noticeable change in his behaviour during his final term, with his conduct falling to 'deficient'. The primary school's headteacher noted he was undistinguished in class, but was a 'mischievous' boy, and 'an intelligent and independent person' who 'had the qualities necessary to lead a group', which he displayed in the playground. According to her, 'Many children followed him during recess. He was a leader, but not an arrogant person.' Years later, Che told his second wife, Aleida March, that she was a strict disciplinarian who spanked him frequently – and that he once got his own back by placing a brick in his shorts, so that she injured her hand when she smacked him. He also exhibited a love of theatre and dressing up – as an Indian or an Ancient Greek – possibly inspired by the adventure books he read.[27]

His former classmates remembered him as someone highly competitive, who often loved gaining attention by carrying out hugely amusing pranks that angered adults – such as drinking ink out of a bottle, and eating chalk. Che once threw fireworks through an open window, thus disrupting a neighbour's dinner party; while he and his gang mates also used catapults to break the town's street lamps. Though, as his youngest brother pointed out, the breaking of the street lamps was more than mere high jinks – and in fact was a 'feat of arms which remained enshrined in the annals of Alta Gracia'. Following a massive hike in electricity prices by the Swiss-owned company, Che and Roberto found out that a municipal ordinance stipulated 'that each electric light bulb in a public lamp post was to be replaced by the electric company the same day that it blew. The municipality could also impose a fine of ten dollars per defective bulb on the company.' As the company eventually revised its tariffs, Che 'drew a lesson from all this: action was sometimes the only effective remedy against injustice'.[28]

One characteristic Che inherited from his father was a temper. If Che felt he was being unjustly reprimanded or punished, he often erupted into an uncontrollable fury – and sometimes resorted to using his fists. However, by the time he moved from primary to high school, he had brought his temper under control and thus only rarely resorted to physical violence. Instead, he used his 'razor-sharp' tongue to settle scores. Nonetheless, one of his friends remembered him as a 'real friend when somebody needed him', and 'a charismatic person' who 'never got angry more than two minutes'. Consequently, they 'all respected and admired him for his kindness'.[29]

A bohemian home

While Che's unruly antics had began to earn the Guevara family a certain notoriety, his parents also followed few of the social conventions prevalent among their class – and were soon seen as being 'Bohemians'. Particularly significant were their criticisms of the conservative hierarchy of the Catholic Church and their open anti-clericalism. Che's beloved paternal grandmother was an atheist, and had given his father a secular upbringing. Celia, though, had had a religious upbringing and, on first arriving in Alta Gracia, had taken their children to Sunday Mass. Though, according to Che's father, this was mainly for the ceremonials. Yet, to please Che's grandparents, Che and the other children were baptised while still infants. However, they were never confirmed as a Roman Catholics.

Che's parents' attitude to the Catholic Church was because of its strict moral codes, its frequent hypocrisy and its support of Latin America's wealthy elites. Once Che began school, Celia stopped going to church. Furthermore, his parents requested that Che – and his brothers and sisters – be excused from religious lessons in school. Che's brother Roberto remembered that after-school football matches were between those who believed in God, and the small minority who didn't. Religion was rarely discussed at home and when it was, it was always in a very critical way.

Celia was seen very much as a 'liberated' and 'free-thinking' woman for the times and the socially conservative circles they moved in. She was the first woman in Alta Gracia to wear trousers, smoke cigarettes in public, and to drive a car. She was also 'active in feminist causes. She held many meetings in her home as Argentine women fought for civil rights'. In part, she was able to get away with this in such a provincial town because of her high social status, and because of her generosity. She regularly drove her children and their friends to school, and even started – and paid for – a daily free-milk programme for the poorer children of the town. This was eventually adopted by the local school board.[30]

Socially, their home was always open to a wide variety of people – including Che's friends who came from poorer backgrounds. Celia in particular encouraged her children to mix freely with all and sundry. His father notes that, 'our doors were permanently open to all-comers'. Thus their family was seen as a lively but disorderly household. If friends of their children arrived at mealtimes, they were often invited to join the family, even if food (especially when funds were tight) had to be divided into smaller portions in order to feed the extra mouths – regardless of their social status. According to his father: 'Although we were in financial straits, we never had to refuse anyone a meal.' Luther speculates whether this practical example of loving your neighbours, and sharing what you have with them, led to Che thinking this was the right and fair way to behave: 'The image of a dinner table with room for all was never far from his mind in later years as he struggled to eradicate social inequalities.' Che's father said: 'They were my children's friends and there was no discrimination. They all sat at our table and were treated as equals, and this was something that made us really happy.'[31]

Che and politics

According to Harris, Che's mother 'was a leftist in her political orientation and far more progressive minded in her political views than his father, who was more of a libertarian conservative'. In fact, both of Che's parents were involved in political activities – in particular, opposing fascism and, later, Peronism. Che was certainly aware that his parents supported the anti-fascists in the Spanish Civil War, which broke out in 1936. Che's parents soon became close friends with two Spanish Republican families who'd been forced to flee and seek exile when it became clear that Franco was winning the war. In 1938, the mother and the four children of the González-Aguilar family settled in Alta Gracia; though their father – a doctor, and the Republic's Naval health chief – remained until the fall of Barcelona in January 1939. The González-Aguilar children were similar in age to the Guevara children, and thus went to the same school. According to Che's father: 'Ernesto became very close to their eldest children. It was at their home that he met many Republican combatants and that is why, although he was only a child, he supported the Spanish Republic with great enthusiasm.'[32]

For a time, the Guevaras also shared their home with Celia's eldest sister Carmen and her two children while their father – Cayetano 'Polich' Córdova Iturburu – was in Spain, reporting on the civil war for the Buenos Aires newspaper *Crítica*. As well as a journalist, he was also a Communist poet, and when his letters arrived in Alta Gracia, Carmen read them aloud to the household. Che would have been present at such times – and when discussions took place around what was happening.

Che's father helped establish a Committee to support the Spanish Republic. He also became close to another refugee, General Jurado, the victor of the Battle of Guadalajara of March 1937. General Jurado, a hero of the Spanish Civil War, often dined with the Guevaras, and regaled the family with accounts of the war. According to his father, Che 'saw in General Jurado the model for a military man … I have often asked myself if the stories of this Spanish general turned out to be valuable lessons for Ernesto in his revolutionary struggles.' Che – by then, aged 10 – had a map on which he placed flags to indicate the changing positions of the Republican and fascist forces. The children began to play war games, with Republican and fascist sides. According to the family, Che also decided their dog should be called 'Negrina' – not just because she was black, but also in honour of Juan Negrín, the Spanish Republic's prime minister. Thus it was probably the Spanish Civil War which was the first political event to influence Che's political development. His father said: '[Che] was of an impressionable age and I believe this was the beginning of his need to rebel and develop his combative character.'[33]

An additional influence on Che was his parents' general concerns about the rise of fascism around the world. As the Second World War began, his parents became active anti-Nazis. His father belonged to Acción Argentina, which supported the Allies. Che, aged 11, joined its youth wing and was issued with an identity card which he 'would exhibit ... with enormous pride', and 'was proud of his role within the youth of the organisation'. Once, despite a severe asthma attack in the morning, he was to accompany his father to a meeting at which Lynch was to speak; his mother – unusually – said he was too ill to go. Che remonstrated and his parents took him – along with all his various medicines. His father states that: 'This episode showed me two things: that Ernesto took his commitments seriously and that he was very fond of me.' It certainly seems his father's claims that Che spent all his free time – outside playtime and study – working with that youth section were valid; and, as he noted, Che 'always listened to the discussions of the grown-ups within the organisation'. While Che and his father carried out their activities for Acción Argentina, his mother was also involved in anti-fascism. After Nazi Germany's invasion of France, she formed a committee to send clothes and food to de Gaulle's Free French forces.[34]

Moving on

In March 1942, just before his fourteenth birthday, Che began attending the Colegio Nacional Deán Funes in Córdoba – there being no high school in Alta Gracia. This school was considered one of the best state schools; but, as Córdoba was just over twenty miles away, Che had to travel there each day by bus. Still relatively short for his age, and still wearing short trousers, he was nonetheless clearly intellectually-curious and questioning – and already confident enough to disagree openly with his elders if he thought he was in the right.

He soon impressed his new schoolmates by his intelligence – and by the speed with which he absorbed new lessons. However, he remained an unexceptional student, seemingly unconcerned about achieving high grades. Instead, as in Alta Gracia, he put more effort into sports, hiking and chess. After a year, in early 1943 – with his sister, Celia, about to start at a girls' high school in the same city – Che and his family moved from Alta Gracia to Córdoba. There a new chapter in his life would unfold.

Chapter 2

Learning And Love, 1943–50

'I dreamed about being a famous researcher … of working tirelessly to achieve something that could really be put at the disposal of humanity…'[1]

In 1943, when Che was 15, the entire family moved to Córdoba. The period 1943–50 would prove to be an important phase of his life. It included his parents' separation, and – following the death of his beloved grandmother – an unexpected decision to study medicine. At the time, Che didn't really explain that sudden change of direction. Though, in a speech to medical students in Cuba, on 20 August 1960, he revealed that one factor was the desire to achieve a 'personal triumph'.

Although Che read books on politics during this period, and enjoyed discussing political topics with family and friends, most of his classmates remember him as '"politically disinterested" during his secondary school years'. He himself later said: 'I had no social preoccupations in my adolescence and had no participation in the political or student struggles in Argentina.'[2]

'Open House' in Córdoba

The family's home in Córdoba was a new two-storey house: 288, Chile Street. It was near Parque Sarmiento and the Lawn Tennis Club – and not far from the University of Córdoba. Across from their house, were several vacant building plots, on which were some 'very poor people who lived in real hovels.' These were often Aymara Indigenous and *mestizo* people.[3]

The Guevaras' 'open house' and bohemian lifestyle continued in Córdoba. According to Che's father, even though he felt their new home couldn't be called 'the house of the people', as the one in Alta Gracia had been known: 'Our house continued to open its doors to the friends of my children, just like the one in Alta Gracia had always done.' Books and magazines were all over the place, and there were no fixed mealtimes. One friend was fascinated by the way family members would, without hesitation, divide up their meals if extra friends arrived at mealtimes. However, although their new home 'had a friendly and popular atmosphere', the family wouldn't tolerate 'pomposity, pedantry, or pretence' – those guilty of such offences would be teased mercilessly, with the young Che often leading such attacks.[4]

While growing up, Che continued to 'come in contact with painters, poets, and professors, a creative bunch that seemed to embody the egalitarian ideal'. As neither of his parents believed any topic was off-limits – and, instead, encouraged 'critical thinking', believing everything should be 'vigorously debated' – mealtimes would often end in heated arguments. His youngest brother, Juan Martín, held that Che 'was the best debater in the family, the most intelligent in terms of thought, analysis and the capacity for provocation. He always developed the deepest, clearest and most precise critiques.'[5]

But the move to Córdoba didn't mean Che lost touch with his Alta Gracia friends. For holidays, the Guevaras frequently returned to Alta Garcia – allowing Che to meet up with his *barra* friends. Che's father also bought a weekend house, close its popular golf club – Che, who'd begun to play at the age of 6 in Alta Gracia – was already a good player by the time they moved to Córdoba: 'he could show off his skill in front of good players. He loved the sport.'[6]

Teenage Che

As Che moved into adolescence, he was still relatively short for his age, but no longer stocky – his unfashionable crew-cut earning him the nickname of El Pelao (Baldy). He increasingly asserted himself, assessed his parents' values, and showed the first tentative signs of his developing political philosophy. Among the various new friends Che made at his secondary school, was Tomás Granado, the youngest of three sons of a Spanish émigré. It was through Tomás that Che met his older brother, Alberto Granado. Granado, aged 20, was already in his first year at university, studying biochemistry and pharmacology. He was a keen rugby player, had a good sense of humour, loved literature, and was fond of wine and women. When Che discovered that Granado was the coach of the local rugby team, he was desperate to join. Although Granado thought Che's asthma and slight build made him unsuitable for rugby, he agreed. It was during training sessions, with Che running headlong at players in possession of the ball, that Che himself coined another of his nicknames: 'El Furibundo'. Granado shortened it to 'Fuser', and adopted 'Miál' as his own (short for 'mi Alberto'). This game, later on, may have been 'instrumental in shaping [Che's] personality as a daring leader'.[7]

Chess remained one Che's main hobbies, and he became an excellent player. He also developed passions for football and table tennis – and, on Sundays, he frequently did pistol target practice with his father, with the two of them 'taking turns shattering bricks with their displays of accuracy'. In addition, Che was introduced to motorcycles at an early age when his father bought an old one and proceeded to teach Che, and his brother Roberto, how to ride it. This gave Che 'the opportunity to visit new areas, and ... It was the beginning of his curiosity for new horizons ... That small motorcycle was no doubt the start of the experiences that turned him into a master in the art of being on the road.'[8]

Some of the adult Che's personality traits – already present in Alta Gracia – which would become legendary after 1956, were well in evidence by this time: 'His physical fearlessness, inclination to lead others, stubbornness, competitive spirit and self-discipline – all were clearly manifest in the young "Guevarita".' In addition to a certain recklessness, Che displayed a dislike of formality, had an argumentative intellect, delighted in shocking people, and had a sense of humour which could be confrontational. According to Granado, people were soon referring to Che as 'El Loco Guevara' – or, because of his dislike of washing, 'El Chancho' (The Pig). Though, as pointed out by Harris, Che's reluctance to bath or shower may have had something to do with the fact that, if the water was cold, he often experienced asthma attacks afterwards.[9]

Che was somewhat disruptive in class: smoking one of his 'anti-asthmatic' cigarettes, and frequently challenging his mathematics and literature teachers if he spotted any inaccuracies. Yet, on the whole, his grades were good – especially in Mathematics, History, Geography and Natural History. He also made steady improvements in his grasp of French, Spanish, writing and music. However, he had no ear for music, and was a poor dancer. At weekends, he often organised expeditions with his friends in the mountains or in Alta Gracia – where he continued with his daredevil stunts, including clinging to a railway track above a chasm, exploring a dangerous mine shaft, acting as a matador in a field with an angry ram, leaping from high rocks into rivers, and bicycling along railway tracks.

Political developments

On 4 June 1943, shortly after the Guevaras had arrived in Córdoba, the pro-German President was overthrown in a coup. The new president was an ultra-nationalist and proceeded to suppress all opposition. Elections were cancelled indefinitely, and the universities purged – including in Córdoba. Later that year, all political parties were banned, religious instruction in schools was made compulsory, and the press controlled even more. As a result, protests by teachers and students took place, including in Córdoba.

In Alta Gracia, Che had been involved in his parents' anti-fascist political activities. Although this may well have helped form his political consciousness, ideals and worldview, Che nonetheless seemed much more interested in physical activities and reading the adventure stories of Jules Verne and Alexandre Dumas than in politics. In November 1943, Granado was one of several students arrested in Córdoba, and held for several weeks with no indication of a trial date. Yet, although Che visited Granado in prison, he did not take part in protests by secondary school students demanding the release of those arrested – despite Granado asking him to. Che's response was that he would only do so if he was given a revolver – seeing a mere demonstration as a futile gesture. Nonetheless, after Granado was released, his friendship with Che resumed, with no bad feelings.

In July 1944, Perón – an admirer of Mussolini's Fascist Italy – became Vice-President, heading a new ministry: the Department of Labour and Welfare. Che's mother – who had joined Córdoba's Comité Pro-De Gaulle, which helped the Resistance in Nazi-occupied France – soon became a fervent *antiperonista*. Che's father, meanwhile – as well as joining his wife in the Comité – also continued as an activist of Accíon Argentina. Unknown to them at the time, Che also continued his anti-Nazi activities. With a friend, he checked out a hotel suspected of being the HQ for Nazi operations in Argentina – despite his father having warned him previously that a government investigator had gone missing, presumed murdered, while investigating that hotel. One night, Che and his friend were spotted snooping around and shots were fired: 'They heard us, someone came out with lanterns, and they fired two shots at us. We left and never returned.'[10]

Although he and his Spanish refugee friends had frequent heated discussions about why the fascists had won in Spain, Che was not really interested in political developments in Argentina itself. When he did show some interest in such matters, it was usually to shock his parents and friends. For instance, when Córdoba's *peronistas* were rumoured to be planning an attack on the local Jockey Club – a symbol of the conservative landed oligarchy – according to friends, Che apparently said: 'I wouldn't mind throwing some stones at the Jockey Club myself.' In June 1946, Perón won the presidency in a general election. That year was Che's final year in high school. Unlike his parents – who opposed Perón's populism, despite his help for the poor – Che's views about Perón have been described as 'a-Peronism', meaning he didn't care much one way or the other.[11]

However, when a local pro-Nazi group began to intimidate those who supported the Allies, Che was actively involved with a branch of the Federacíon Estudiantil Socialista (FES), to form units to defend pro-Allied students. Raúl Melivosky, the son of a Jewish university professor, recalled that Che had been pointed out to him as 'the only student in school who had stood up in class to a notoriously pro-Nazi history professor over a factual inaccuracy'. When, one afternoon, some of the pro-Nazis blocked Raúl and some other students from leaving the school grounds, threatening them with penknives, Che fearlessly 'hurled himself at the throng, whirling his school satchel around his head'.[12]

This, however, was not typical of Che's attitude to political issues: for most of his high school years, he was essentially politically inactive. More bizarrely, when – under US pressure – Argentina finally broke off diplomatic relations with the Axis powers, Che attacked this decision. This seems to have been because it came as a result of US pressure, rather than being a principled anti-fascist act. If so, this was possibly the start of the firm 'anti-Yankee' politics Che was soon to develop.

However, there was no real sign of the militant socialism that Che would adopt over the next ten years – most of his friends in Cordoba recalled him as having no 'defined political ideal'. While his friends recall that they loved to argue over politics, Che rarely got seriously involved.

An avid reader

During his time in Córdoba, Che kept up his wide extra-curricular reading – which his friends noted was both varied and, considering his age, advanced. Even while waiting for his team to get on the rugby field, Che would often be found reading a book. His reading matter by then included the poetry of Baudelaire, Verlaine and Mallarmé; and novels by Zola and Dumas, most of which he read in French. In addition, he also read Freud, the latest novels by William Faulkner and John Steinbeck, and the poetry of Chile's famous poet, Pablo Neruda. Granado, an avid reader himself, was amazed that Che had read so much – Che explained this by telling him how often he'd been confined to bed by his frequent asthma attacks. According to Che's first wife, Hilda Gadea, Che told her he'd read everything in his father's library as a teenager, pointing out that 'the books were not classified and next to an adventure book he would find a Greek tragedy and then a book on Marxism'.[13]

From 1945, at the age of 17, Che also became seriously interested in philosophy – and took a course in it, gaining grades that were either 'very good' or 'outstanding'. He began to annotate his books – including Marx's *Capital* – and to make notes on what he read. In particular, he began the first of seven handwritten and carefully-indexed notebooks – which he called his 'philosophical dictionary' – recording the main ideas of those he read. He continued this habit for ten years – often going back and revising, or adding to, what he'd written previously, as his knowledge and understanding deepened. 'Love, immortality, death, and morality were just a few of the subjects covered within its pages.'[14]

As well as non-fiction, Che also began to concentrate on novels that dealt with social issues, including Latin American writers, some of whom dealt with the inequalities suffered by the marginalised and poor Indians and mestizos – something that Che would soon witness for himself. A friend believed that everything for Che 'began with literature'. One habit Che increasingly developed was reading, for hours on end, in the bathroom, in order to find some peace from the interesting but noisy family home.[15]

Sex and servants

As a typical teenager, Che soon developed an interest in sex. At this time, the prevailing attitudes in Argentina around sex were very 'traditional' – with girls from respectable Catholic middle-class families expected to remain virgins until marriage, and boys from similar backgrounds expected to 'respect the virginity of the girls they dated'.

Consequently, for boys of Che's upper-class background, their first sexual experiences were usually in brothels – or with working-class girls. The latter included the female servants who worked in their homes – most frequently the family *mucama*, or young servant girl, who was usually Indian or *mestizo* from Argentina's poorer rural areas. In all of this, Che's attitudes and behaviour were typical of a 'child of [his] environment'.[16]

Sometime around his fifteenth birthday, Che had sex for the first time – with the servant girl employed in the house of his friend Carlos Ferrer, who 'arranged' the sexual encounter for him. Several of his friends spied on the encounter through the bedroom door's keyhole – and were amused to see that Che 'periodically interrupted his lovemaking to suck on his asthma inhaler'. Che went on to have frequent sessions with this servant girl. Given the huge class and racial inequalities involved in such 'relationships' – and especially the need of poor servants to keep their job – such sexual encounters may not always have been fully consensual, thus raising intersectionality issues around teenage boys of Che's class 'bedding the family *mucamas*'.[17]

With girls from his own class, Che mainly limited himself to reciting extracts from bawdy poems. During the summer holidays of 1945–46, he became reacquainted with Carmen Iturburu, the daughter of his communist uncle and aunt. Three years younger than Che, she shared a love of poetry with him – one time, Che recited to her part of Pablo Neruda's *Twenty Poems of Love and a Desperate Song*. She developed a crush on him, and later recalled that they 'were a little more than friends', and that Che had once asked her if she was 'now a woman'. A lover's tryst followed, and they continued to meet up when the Guevaras eventually moved back to Buenos Aries. She recalled 'romantic interludes' in the stairwell when she stayed in the Guevara house, and how they talked of 'literature and love'.[18]

By the time he was 17, Che had become an extremely attractive young man: 'slim and wide-shouldered, with dark brown hair, intense eyes, clear white skin, and a self-contained, easy confidence that made him alluring to girls'. Carmen once commented that 'Ernesto was so handsome!' – while another upper-middle class girl, Miriam Urrutia, stated that: 'The truth is, we were all a little in love with [Che].' According to his brother, Juan Martín, Che 'was … extremely attractive, with large expressive, laughing eyes, a thick black mop of hair, and an easy smile'. Apparently, Che 'didn't seem aware of his sex appeal. Yet girls had flocked around him ever since adolescence, obviously attracted by his charm and personality.'[19]

Family relationships

The move to Córdoba initially saw an improvement in the family's economic situation. Yet, according to Che's sister Celia, their parents spent without saving. His father enrolled the family in Córdoba's exclusive Lawn Tennis Club, where Che and his siblings swam and played tennis. But the relationship between his parents continued to worsen because of Lynch's affairs – especially as he 'often spent much of the money he did make, not on his family, but on the young women he spent time with'. According to a friend of the Guevara children: 'The father had pretensions of being a playboy. But he was a disorderly playboy, because when he worked and earned money, he spent it all … on going out with "young ladies," on stupidities, nothing concrete … and the family would get nothing.' Although they still slept in the same house, Che's parents led increasingly separate lives.[20]

By then, as well as continuing his studies, Che had also got his first job, in Córdoba's public works' office dealing with road construction in the provinces. Working with him was his friend, Tomás Granado. One reason for taking this part-time job was that both of them were considering studying engineering at university, and the job would give them valuable work experience. After leaving school, the two began working full-time, but were assigned jobs in different parts of the province.

Che continued to be more of a social rebel than a political one. Unlike most young males of his class, he made very little effort over his appearance, often wearing old, dirty and ill-fitting clothes. According to his youngest brother, Che 'was the shabbiest, most fashion-resistant man ever!'; while Dolores Moyano claimed his appearance was much discussed by his friends. His favourite item of clothing was a nylon shirt: originally white, but soon turning grey from constant wearing, which he called 'La Semanera', because he claimed to wash it only once a week – often wearing it as he went through the shower. The infrequency of his bathing – even after a game of rugby – earned him the family nickname

'Mr Once-Weekly'. Che seemed to revel in the impact all this had on his friends when he turned up for social events – for instance, not bothering to change into new clothes before going to a dance. He was similarly uninterested – or in any way gifted – in music or dancing; according to his father: 'He did not care for music and was a very poor dancer'; though, according to one friend, he made an effort – but simply to increase his chances of seducing girls.[21]

He often boasted to his parents about how long it had been since he had washed his clothes; he never wore a tie; and his footwear was 'usually a pair of old boots, sometimes not even a matched set'. Whether or not such appearance was the first tangible expression of blossoming political outlook is debatable, but Che clearly enjoyed his nickname 'El Chanco' – 'the pig'. Particularly so when he realised it upset his father, who was more conventional. Luther sees such behaviour as 'his way of separating himself from his social standing and the beginning of a philosophy that would come to guide his life'. Typically, when Che later founded a rugby magazine called *Tackle*, he signed his articles 'Chanco' – when his father objected, he changed it to 'Chang-Cho'.[22]

In some ways, this was because of the nature of his relationship with his father, which was increasingly combative. Che teased him 'continuously' and they argued constantly – with Che 'goading' his father 'with arguments of a political character'. This was a contrast to his relationship with his mother; already close, they became even closer when she had been diagnosed with breast cancer in 1946. His siblings – especially Roberto – at times felt excluded from their close relationship. His mother continued to run the house like a bohemian salon, playing cards, smoking and welcoming young visitors for their conversation and ready to give them advice. Friends and visitors noted the abundance of books – and the lack of furniture, ornaments and even paintings on the walls.

During this period, Che also continued his custom of having sex with Indian and *mestizo* servants. His cousin Saravia was one of the few of Che's friends who knew of this – he recalled Che regularly having sex with his family's Bolivian maid, a poor Aymara woman in her late thirties, from the Altiplano, who spoke Quechua but only a little Spanish. According to Saravia: 'She was the ugliest woman I have ever seen. But when she invited him, he would go to her room.' However, Che's brother Juan Martín, claims Che was able to understand her, and was:

> curious about her life, her origins, her people … It was extremely rare for Argentinians of our social class to be so interested in a person's background … In retrospect, I came to understand her influence on him, as thoughts of revolution started to germinate within him. She was the person who made him decide he wanted to go to visit Bolivia.[23]

All change in Buenos Aires

In March 1947, while Che was working away from home, his family moved back to Buenos Aires. This was mainly because his parents had finally decided to split up – and, once again, were also short of money, as his father's building enterprise had folded. Before too long, he was also forced to sell his Misiones plantation.

Once back, the family moved into an apartment owned by Che's beloved paternal grandmother, Ana Isabel, then aged 96 – and still an atheist. In May she became ill, and Che received a telegram from his family advising him how serious it was. On 18 May, Che wrote back, requesting more details – and making it clear that if her condition worsened, he would give up his job and return immediately to Buenos Aires. After just a few days, he was told she'd suffered a stroke – and Che rushed back. According to his father, Che tried with great patience to get her to take some food: 'He looked after her without leaving her bedside for seventeen days when her illness was in its most critical phase … until my mother left this world.' Che was grief-stricken – his sister Celia had never seen him like that: 'He was very sad. It must have been one of the great sadnesses of his life.' Che then moved back into the family home.[24]

His grandmother's death led Che to make a dramatic change of direction. Almost immediately, he informed his parents that he was going to study medicine instead of engineering; and was accepted by Buenos Aires University's Faculty of Medicine. His family thought this sudden switch was because of his pain at the inability of Ana Isabel's doctors to ease her suffering – his youngest brother stating: 'it was also due to her death that he decided to abandon his engineering studies and take up medicine'. However, Anderson believes Che's decision had as much to do with wanting to find a cure for the asthma that continued to plague him. Certainly, his choice of specialisms seems to confirm that view. Additionally, in 1947, his mother had to undergo a mastectomy – with another mastectomy in 1950, when the cancer had returned. This, too, may well have inspired him to continue with his medical studies, in the hope of being able to save her.[25]

While studying medicine, Che had several part-time jobs, but particularly significant – and long-lasting – was his choice to work at the Clínica Pisani, which focused on allergy treatments. Dr Pisani was impressed by Che's intelligence and curiosity, so he was taken on as an unpaid research assistant. Che therefore decided to specialise in allergies. Dr Pisani's sister and mother soon grew fond of Che; sometimes, when he suffered an attack, he was put to bed there. Typically, Che began to conduct medical experiments – including on himself and his friends. On one occasion, though, he made himself seriously ill.[26]

As he was so busy with his studies and his part-time jobs – taking his exams in 1948 – Che saw increasingly less of his father in this period. Following Ana

Isabel's death, the Guevara family initially stayed on in her apartment. When his father sold his Misiones plantation, he gave the money to Celia, which she used to buy an old house, at 2180 Calle Aroaz. Because of the money problems, the older children had to find jobs. When Che was called up for military service, he was rejected on grounds of 'diminished physical abilities' because of his asthma. Though not ideal for the guerrilla fighter he would become, Che was pleased at the time, and told friends that he 'thanked his shitty lungs for doing something useful for a change.'[27]

Che the student

During his first year at the university, Che met Berta Gilda 'Tita' Infante – she was also a medical student, and they soon became firm friends, and remained so for many years. Che wrote to her frequently after he'd left Argentina, almost as much as he did to his mother and aunt. Tita, as she was known, was attracted to Che. Writing a year after Che's murder, she said he was 'a beautiful and confident young man', and how 'a mixture of timidity and haughtiness, maybe of courage … masked a deep intelligence and an insatiable desire to understand and, deep inside, an infinite capacity for love'. Although their relationship remained platonic, Che clearly appreciated being able to confide in an intelligent woman during this period of turmoil and change in his life. Apart from attending the same lectures, they met frequently in cafés or in her family apartment, where they talked about personal problems, philosophy and politics; swapped and discussed books; and recited their favourite poems to each other.[28]

Apart from his mother, Che's aunt Beatriz – who lived in an apartment not too far from the Guevaras' new place – was also a very important woman in his life. Although Che was close to his mother, she had never really 'mothered' him in the way that Beatriz did. Che thus spent a lot of time at her place, where she made him meals and generally fussed over him, and the two formed a special relationship. Juan Martín said: 'She worshipped [Che]. After the victory of the Cuban revolution,' she'd often exclaim indignantly: 'I have no idea why they all accuse Ernestito [Che] of being a communist. He's so nice, so nice and so kind!' This was despite the fact that he'd often signed his letters to her as: '"Your communist nephew", "Your proletarian nephew", or "Stalin II"!'[29]

Although he liked to shock her with his views, he didn't reveal that he had seduced 'the maid she so carefully locked into her room at night'. One of Che's cousins also often visited when Che was there and once – in what may possibly have been yet another example of unequal sexual power relationships – 'watched in astonishment from his place in the dining room as [Che] had quick sex with the *mucama* on the kitchen table'. According to this cousin, Che 'was like a rooster. He mated and then continued with his other functions.'[30]

Although Che's grades were good, and he took a large number of courses, he continued not to excel – as had been the case when a school student. Che had little to do with most of his fellow students, and – as well as spending much time with Tita and his aunt – he also used many weekends and holidays to hitchhike back and forwards to Córdoba. Occasionally, he began to go further away, and for longer periods. To many, he seemed a young man in a hurry – though not very clear about what he wanted to do or where he wanted to go.

Some things, however, were more constant: he still suffered asthma attacks; and rugby – and especially chess – remained favourite pastimes. His parents – and his doctors – thought rugby too strenuous an activity, given his asthma. His doctor thought it would strain his heart too much; yet, when his father mentioned this, Che replied, 'I like playing rugby and I will continue to do so even if it kills me.' When his father went so far as to get the president, a brother-in-law, to remove Che from the team, Che was furious – but then 'simply joined the neighbouring club Atalaya and continued to play rugby'.[31]

In 1949, Che took part in the University's 'Olympics', for both rugby and chess. In addition, he continued to read widely, to complete further philosophical notebooks, and to write poetry. His reading remained varied – apart from medical texts, he also read modern novels, literature classics, poetry, biographies, philosophy, social philosophy and psychiatry. He also continued to devour adventure stories – one of Che's most prized possessions was a three-volume set of Jules Verne's collected works. He didn't enjoy 'large social gatherings, as he was rather reserved ... but when it came to mixing with intelligent and knowledgeable people, he mingled with them and showed how well read and cultivated he was'. For instance, he liked to visit Carmen de la Serna and her husband, the poet Cayetano Cordova Iturburu – both of whom were active Communists, until the latter was expelled – in their summer house outside Córdoba, as many artists and writers attended their gatherings.[32]

'Yankee' imperialism and socialism

Despite his medical studies, Che began to devote even more time to private study and reflection. His brother Roberto was amazed to find Che systematically going through their father's twenty-five volumes of *Contemporary History of the Modern World*. As well as making copious notes on what he found in his notebooks, he also began to compile an index of all the books he'd read, as well as continuing to make comments in the margins of the books he read; his sister Celia (also a voracious reader) often did the same. The books in his father's library even included Trotsky's works, and many French books that hadn't been translated into Spanish – his brother Juan Martín noting that Che: 'read a lot in French.' His father later commented that 'he always found time to be on his own in order to concentrate on his books'.[33]

However, one area to which he now devoted an increasing amount of time was the subject of socialism and communism. As with his other reading, he covered an eclectic mix: including a French biography of Lenin, Stalin's views on Marxism, and novels by Zola and Jack London. In particular, he began to devote more and more time to a study of Marx – as well as *Capital* (with which he later admitted he'd struggled), he also read *The Communist Manifesto*. Even while living clandestinely in Africa in 1965, he actually sketched out plans for a biography on Marx. One particular description of Lenin captured Che's attention: this stated that Lenin '"lived, breathed and slept" socialist revolution and sacrificed all else in his life to its cause'. As Anderson comments, that passage 'presages to an uncanny degree the way Che Guevara would be described by his revolutionary comrades'. However, as Luther notes: 'the presence of these men most likely was the result of [Che's] interest in philosophy rather than politics'.[34]

Yet this growing interest in revolutionary socialist and Marxist politics still did not lead Che to join any of the left groups which existed in the university, or in the city itself. Later on, he admitted that 'his earliest readings of Marx and Lenin made little sense to him'. Instead, he stayed outside formal political involvement, preferring to observe and, occasionally, to debate rather than to get involved with political activism. He avoided expressing sympathy for either the *peronistas* or the *antiperonistas*. According to Juan Martín, when his cousin, Guillermo Moore de la Serna, asked him to join the anti-Peronist movement, Che replied, 'No, no, I'm not interested.'[35]

In a way, this wasn't too surprising: the Argentine Communist Party was doctrinaire (and thus not likely to appeal to a free-thinker like Che), and had also been weakened by Perón's policies. Tita's brother Carlos was a Communist and described Che at that time as a 'progressive liberal' – more interested in medicine and literature than in politics. Although they discussed the writings of the Argentine Marxist writer, Aníbal Ponce, Che was very critical of the Communist Party's sectarianism. Che also knew some of the militants in the Federacíon Juvenil Comunista (Communist Youth) at the university. But their discussions with Che were often sharp; one of those militants said of Che at this time that: 'He had very clear ideas about certain things. Above all from an ethical perspective. More than a political person, I saw him at that time as someone with an ethical posture.'[36]

Nonetheless, Che's interest in Marxist politics continued to develop – sometimes leading to arguments with family members, as he began adopting an anti-imperialist and, increasingly, an anti-Yankee position. This was especially marked during the Korean War, with Che being very critical of what he came increasingly to see as the role of US imperialism, and of his father's support of the US (what Che later called 'your Yankee friends'). In fact, his brother Juan Martín makes it clear that, politically, their father – despite being anti-Francoist, anti-fascist, pro-republican and anti-Peronist – was not 'revolutionary, proletarian or socialist. He was a weather vane … He spent years being pro-Yankee and then anti-communist before ending up as an arch-communist in Cuba, playing the role of Che's father, living off the Cuban state and singing the *Internationale*!' Yet neither Che, nor his family or friends, identified him as a thorough-going Marxist. Instead, they tended to put his outspoken views down to his contrary nature and the bohemian upbringing he'd had;: this they felt, explained his political views, his unconventional dress, and his wanderlust.[37]

Che would increasingly come to oppose 'Yankee' interference in the weaker countries of Latin America – what the US had seen as 'its backyard' since the Monroe Doctrine of 1823, and where it had acted politically, economically and militarily to oppose developments it felt threatened their interests. In Argentina, the US had openly campaigned against Perón in the lead-up to the 1946 general election, and Truman's administration began to pressure Latin American states to join what it called 'pan-Americanism' and its 'mutual defense treaty', as part of the USA's anti-Communist Cold War 'Truman Doctrine', announced in Rio de Janeiro in 1948. In the Cold War, the US usually interpreted 'communism' as any movement or government that wanted redistribution of wealth in what were often poor countries. The Truman Doctrine also made it clear that the US felt it had the right to intervene militarily in any neighbouring state where 'communism' threatened to take a foothold.

This would prove to be a big influence on Che's developing politics – at the time of the Rio Conference, he commented on this and '*panamericanismo*' in one of his notebooks. This was the real start of Che's developing and deep-seated hostility towards US imperialism during the 1950s. He increasingly saw the US pursuing a conscious foreign policy designed to protect its extensive economic interests in the region. His friend Dolores Moyano noted that: 'He was convinced of the dark princes of evil who directed every United States move abroad.' This was not very surprising, given the USA's increasingly aggressive interventions in the affairs of its neighbours – and its active support of right-wing military dictatorships in the region. The CIA even feared that Communists would 'exploit' liberal democratic hostility to dictatorship![38]

However, when Perón began to crackdown on the Communists and the left generally in Argentina, one of Che's Córdoba acquaintances, Fernando Barral (a Spanish Republican refugee), was one of those arrested – for 'Communist agitation'. Che, by then in his fourth year of medical studies, had had little contact with Barral since the move to Buenos Aires. He never visited him in prison (where he remained for seven months) and, as with Granado's earlier imprisonment, did not get involved in the campaign to secure his release. Anderson, though, wonders if this was also due to Che resenting the close friendship between Barral and his cousin, Carmen Cordova Iturburu.

As regards Che's attitude to Perón, one friend recalled him advising his family's maids to vote for Perón, because his social policies favoured their class; while another says he joined a Peronist youth movement – though only to gain access to its extensive library. Che himself described his views at this time thus: 'When I started out as a doctor, when I began to study medicine, the majority of the concepts I hold today as a revolutionary were absent from the storehouse of my ideas.'[39]

Wanderlust

Che's great need for adventure soon found an outlet in travel. According to his father, Che's 'obsession with travelling was just another part of his zeal for learning.' At first, starting in 1949, Che's thirst for adventure was filled by hitchhiking – often with his friend, Carlos Figueroa, whom he'd first met in Alta Gracia. Their destination was frequently Córdoba. During these jaunts, they sometimes slept in abandoned railway carriages, or even in the open. Occasionally, they had to 'pay' for their rides on trucks by helping to unload them. Figueroa thought Che 'was the most generous person in the world' – once, when they were both broke, he told Che about a debt he had, so Che 'went to get his savings book and gave Carlos all he had, saying, "Here are all my funds. If you can return them, fine. If not, too bad."'[40]

These escapades, however, were not enough; Che's first big adventure alone began on 1 January 1950, after he'd completed the third year of his medical studies. He decided to explore northern Argentina's interior – which at that time was 'exotic … magnificently backward … neglected and ignored. It reminded the citizens of the capital that Argentina, far from being European, was South American' – not by foot and hitchhiking this time, but by getting his uncle Jorge de la Serna to fit a small engine to his bicycle. Juan Martín, though still very young, remembered the 'hubbub caused by his departure'. This trip turned out to be one of the most formative trips of his young life. He later recalled this trip as being 'intoxicating', in part because of its hardships: 'As the days went by, my flesh was weak and cried out for a mattress, but my spirit was willing and the ride went on.'[41]

The plan of his first 'motorcycle' journey was to get to Córdoba and, from there, to travel to where Granado was working at a leprosy clinic. His first destination was Pilar, a town outside the capital. Some of his family and friends predicted he'd get no further, but Che later said that on arriving he'd felt 'the first happiness of one who triumphs'. For him, there'd be no turning back from his first real adventure – which would last six weeks. In all, he covered around 2,500 miles, and visited twelve provinces in central and northern Argentina, 'but the distance traversed internally was far greater'.[48]

Although only 22 at the time, this trip was to establish two key and long-lasting aspects of Che's life: travelling – and regularly writing a diary, in which he recorded his daily experiences, exploits and thoughts: 'his thoughts, resonant and romantic, provide a snapshot of what his life on the road was like'. After Che's death, this first 'motorcycle' diary – actually, a series of notebooks, written in pencil – was discovered by his father in 1972, who transcribed it. Although Che's comments were almost impossible to read in places, he published it in one of his memoirs of Che: 'I owe it to chance, to pure luck, that I recovered these diaries.'[43]

During that trip, Che passed through scores of small towns, met all sorts of people, and scrounged beds (in hospitals and vacant police cells) and meals along the way. He spent the second night in Rosario, where he'd been born. Along the way to Córdoba and the Granado family home – reached 'in forty-one hours and seventeen minutes' after leaving Buenos Aires – he'd been pulled behind a car travelling at 40mph. This ended when his rear tyre burst and he fell in a heap on the road, waking up a tramp in the process: 'We started chatting and when I told him I was a student he took me under his wing. He produced a dirty thermos and made me a maté with enough sugar to sweeten an old maid.'[44]

After 'eating, taking a bath, eating and then sleeping' at the Granado home, he spent several days in Córboda, meeting up with friends, and going on camping trips with Granado's brothers – with Che and the others resuming their habits of rock-climbing and diving from great heights into shallow rockpools. Eventually, they parted company and Che continued his journey. By then, both Che and Granado were actively interested in allergies and medicine in general. Che was keen to accompany Granado on his rounds – but one day fell out with him over an attractive young girl who'd been interned in the clinic, and whom Granado was treating. As she had few obvious symptoms of leprosy, Che felt she shouldn't have been interned. To prove that she was infected and thus contagious, Granado plunged a needle into the girl's back, where there were some areas of dead skin. Che became angry at what he felt was Granado's lack of compassion, clearly believing that a more friendly approach could be as beneficial as medicines: 'He [Che] repeated again and again the need to treat the patients more humanely; they were people, after all, just like the doctors and nurses who cared for them … For [Che], a man who would dedicate his life to those in need, it not only mattered what was done for people, but also how it was done.' They soon made up however.[45]

After a few days, Che – anxious to be off again – persuaded Granado, who had a motorcycle, to travel with him to Argentina's remote northern and western provinces. They set off, with Granado pulling Che behind him on a rope. The rope kept breaking however, so Granado returned to the clinic – after the two had agreed to make another trip together soon. As Che wrote later in his diary: 'We gave each other a not very effusive hug, as between two machitos, and I watched him disappear like a knight on his bike, saying good-bye with his hand.' Che then travelled on alone.[46]

Arriving in Loreto, a small town, the local police gave him lodgings for the night. On realising he was training to be a doctor, they tried to persuade him to stay, as Loreto had no doctor. Che records, in his second notebook: 'I told him that I would think about it, but I have not decided yet. I really don't know what to do.' It was in Loreto that he was 'interviewed for the first time in my life' by the local correspondent of *El Tropico*, a Tucumán daily newspaper. The one paragraph was headed: 'Guevara, a young globe-trotter, sets off on a big trip.' Che then decided to continue with his adventure. When he reached the provincial capital, Santiago del Estero, he met up with relatives of friends.[47]

He then continued on to Tucumán itself. On the way, he met another 'tramp' – this time, an itinerant worker moving from the cotton harvest in one area to the grape harvest in another. The tramp was mystified by Che travelling so far merely for reasons of personal satisfaction. This made Che introspective, as is shown by this diary entry, made after experiencing a sublime moment in the forested area north of Tucumán: 'I then realise that something has matured in me, something that had been growing inside me for some time … and it is a hatred of urban civilisation'.[48]

At one point, he visited a farm where is aunt Maruja was spending the summer holidays. Che enjoyed telling his parents that 'she did not recognise [me] because [I] was covered in dirt and had long hair and a beard'. His aunt took charge – sent his clothes to be washed, arranged for his bike to be repaired, and gave him a 'succulent and plentiful lunch', before sending him on his way with some money that, despite being almost penniless, he was reluctant to accept.[49]

One day he was offered a pull by someone riding a brand-new Harley-Davidson, but he declined. He had a narrow escape – a few hours later, after arriving in the next town, Rosario de la Frontera, he discovered the rider had been killed in a crash. On reaching Salta, he went to the local hospital and, as a medical student, begged a place to sleep – and was offered a seat in a truck 'with soft cushy seats … worthy of a king'. On arriving in Jujuy, Argentina's most northerly city, he tried the same trick for obtaining accommodation: this time, he was asked to pick the lice out of the hair of a 2-year-old Indian boy, in return for a bed in one of the wards. However, when the boy's mother smiled her gratitude, Che describes how the 'laughter of sex … goads me on to take her. My hands stretch out, avid for the delicious morsels of her breasts, but the appearance of a nurse startles me,' thus preventing things going further.[50]

Although he'd wanted to go all the way up to the border with Bolivia, he had to return. His fourth year of medical studies was about to begin, so he began to journey home. Che showed for the first time how his travels were leading him in a more political direction: 'the soul of a people is reflected in the sick in the hospitals, the men in custody at police stations'. For the first time in his adult life, he'd really seen the gap between his privileged European culture and the poverty, exploitation and injustices inflicted on the poor and socially-marginalised majority of Argentina's population (mainly the Aymara Indigenous people). It was for such despised people that Che would later risk, and ultimately lose, his life. On his journey, he'd shared 'their dwellings and their meagre pittance', and now 'knew they deserved to be treated better, especially as others were living so well, often at the expense of the poor'. Che soon came to see 'Yankee' imperialism as being behind, and largely to blame for, poverty in the Americas and beyond, by propping up the often semi-feudal landed elites in remote areas, dictatorships, and exploiting the region's resources and people. It was an outlook that finally led him to his death in Bolivia just seventeen years later.[51]

Love's 'lightning bolt

Back at university – although his taste for adventure had been well-and-truly awakened, leading him to start planning, almost immediately, new trips – he settled down to study and passed another five exams towards gaining his medical degree, and also continued working on allergies at the Clínica Pisani.

However, in October 1950, Che – unexpectedly, and for the first time – fell in love. One of the guests at a wedding he attended was María del Carmen 'Chichina' Ferreyra – according to Juan Martín, she was 'the great love of his youth'. She was a daughter of one of Córdoba's oldest and wealthiest families – a family Che had known when his family lived in Córdoba. In 1950, she was 16; as well as being attractive, she was also extremely bright and imaginative. She made a big impression on Che, who was soon deeply in love. Che made a similarly big impression on her: both his physicality and his playful, unstuffy behaviour – and even his unconventional attire. However, the relationship was not so serious on her part. Her family was conventional and religious, and she was destined to inherit substantial property. Whereas Che was from a family of relatively-impoverished, unconventional and secular former aristocrats – whose name, nonetheless, 'was still able to open the doors of high society'. Although Che by then apparently despised such wealth and privilege – according to Juan Martín, it was 'everything he already hated' – he nonetheless 'had unwillingly fallen deeply in love'. As Luther comments, 'the heart is unpredictable, and [Che's] was no exception'.[52]

Yet, although Che was not anywhere near the type of son-in-law her family wanted, they did not immediately prevent him socialising with her. Like many others, despite his scruffy appearance – according to Juan Martín, usually 'looking like something the cat had brought in' – they were initially charmed by his eccentricities, his wide cultural knowledge and his obvious intelligence. Soon, Che was making frequent trips to Córdoba to see Chichina, staying at the family home or their *estancia*.[53]

Soon, however, Che began to put pressure on Chichina to marry him – proposing for their honeymoon a trip around Latin America in a 'mobile caravan'. Not only was she reluctant to commit, but her family now began to have serious doubts about the relationship. Che's own family was also worried by the relationship, as she 'had been educated in a totally different way from the way we had brought up our children and I could see that, if they got married, it would be very difficult for it to work, since for Chichina it would represent a sharp contrast with her own upbringing.'[54]

At this time, Che was still a 'hippyish and sickly' figure who often wore his dirty nylon shirt at formal family dinners, and seemed to delight in saying provocative things. Consequently, Carmen's family became increasingly opposed to the relationship – in part because 'At any social gathering, the directness, the candor, the mocking quality of his opinions made his presence dangerous.' From then on, Chichina only saw Che secretly – once 'hiding' him in a car with some of her girlfriends, so they could meet up as the family had gathered to watch her father play in a polo match. Chichina's mother was devoutly religious and thus horrified at the idea of her daughter marrying someone like Che. Che's brother Juan Martín wondered if, after Che had become famous, she regretted turning him down – but concluded: 'Politically, I doubt it; she didn't share his ideas at all, and would certainly not have liked to be the wife of a revolutionary.'[55]

Yet, when the school term ended at the end of December 1950, Che didn't rush to Córdoba to be with Chichina. Instead, partly because he needed to earn some money, he applied to work as a 'doctor' with the shipping line of the state petroleum company. Anderson wonders if this was an attempt by Che to appear more adventurous to Chichina – similar to her adventurous father and uncles – rather than that Che's love of adventure had won out over his love for Chichina. Whatever the truth, the next three years would see Che develop a more coherent – and radical – political outlook.

Chapter 3

Motorcycles, Medicine and Marxism 1951–53

'All this wandering around "Our America with a capital A" has changed me more than I thought.'[1]

At the end of 1950, Che's application to become a 'doctor' (actually, a nurse) on an oil tanker was approved. He did this partly to earn money, and partly to have some time to study for his next medical exams. However, Che's romantic wanderlust – which his father put down to 'his zeal for learning' – was not quenched by those sea travels, which ended in June 1951. Only six months later, he began the famous journey recorded in *The Motorcycle Diaries* – although most of that journey was done without the motorbike. These *Diaries* provide insights into Che's personality and political development during a relatively-unknown period of his early adulthood.

Nonetheless, his experiences during those years proved extremely formative for the charismatic and globally famous guerrilla fighter and revolutionary he eventually became. In particular, it's clear how he gradually developed 'a critical social consciousness based on the many instances of social injustice, human exploitation, and racial and ethnic discrimination he witnessed in all the countries he visited'.[2]

Wanderlust

Che's first sea journey began in February 1951, on the tanker *Anna G*, owned by the state oil company and bound for Brazil. In all, he served on four trips, calling at several ports along Latin America's Atlantic coast, visiting Brazil, British Guiana and Venezuela, and Caribbean islands such as Trinidad and Tobago. However, these trips were not as satisfying as his earlier land travels – his letters complained that they rarely docked long enough for him to be able to undertake any real explorations of these new countries. Whenever he returned to Buenos Aires' port he called his sister Celia, asking if there were any letters from Chichina: 'He asked me to go running to the docks, and I ran and ran like he asked and I took him the letters.'[3]

Thus, at the end of June 1951, Che – now aged 23, and with two more years to go before he became a fully-qualified doctor – gave up his job to resume his medical studies. However, he did so with less enthusiasm, because of his two loves: Chichina and travelling. Despite feeling lovelorn and restless, Che thought he would eventually be able to marry Chichina – despite the opposition of her family. Although he worked hard at his medical studies, he 'really had only one idea in mind: to decamp'. Che was thus pleased when Granado, still working in Córdoba, proposed a trip across the whole of Latin America. Che quickly accepted the offer, and the two friends began planning their itinerary – though, as Che recorded, the trip's general principle was 'improvisation'. Very soon, they decided to extend their big journey by also visiting North America.[4]

On 4 January 1952 – during Argentina's summer, and almost two years after Che had undertaken his first trip – the two friends left Buenos Aires on an old 500cc Norton motorbike which they called 'La Poderosa II' – 'The Mighty One'. Che's parents begged the older Granado to look after their son, and stop him getting into any danger. But, as his brother Juan Martín later noted: 'as the journey unfolded [Che] became the master', and eventually 'the leader and guide'. Che's father was furious with him for apparently abandoning his studies, even though he'd promised to complete them on his return. Che's mother was sad and 'suffered from the separation'. Along with their father's infidelities and on-going money worries, 'the absence of her beloved son' was 'more than she could bear. The only thing that brought her any comfort was [Che's] letters.'[5]

His father was surprised Che was prepared to contemplate such a long separation from Chichina – Che replied that: 'She'll wait for me if she loves me.' Nonetheless, before starting their explorations, Che decided to give her a young puppy which he named 'Comeback', to symbolise his determination to come back to her. So they travelled first to Miramar, the beach resort where she was holidaying with an aunt and some friends. Despite some falls from the somewhat unstable motorbike, they reached Miramar on 6 January – and Che pleaded with her to wait for him. Initially, they'd planned to stay for just two days, but Chichina's reluctance to commit meant they stayed for eight days instead.[6]

Yet, despite his pleadings, Che failed to gain a definite promise from her – or her gold-bracelet, which he asked for as a keepsake. However, she didn't turn him down flat, and accepted the puppy, which Che felt meant he had been 'victorious, or so I thought'. In addition, she gave him US$15 to buy her a scarf in the US. Some forty years later, Chichina was tracked down in Córdoba by the author Patrick Symmes. Though initially reluctant to talk about her first love, she made it clear that there was a big difference between the young man she'd known and the legend that Che had later become: 'They don't even know who he was.'[7]

On 14 January, clearly disappointed, Che nonetheless set off with Granado on a trip that would last eight months. In that period, they travelled down the

Atlantic Coast of Argentina, through the Andes, and then into Chile, Peru, Colombia and finally into Venezuela. As on his earlier solo trip, Che kept a journal. When he later reworked this, he noted that he did so with a different perspective from the young Che who'd jotted down his immediate thoughts: 'The person who reorganizes and polishes them, me, is no longer, at least I am not the person I once was.' Che's account was later transcribed by his widow, Aleida March, and published posthumously in 1967 as *The Motorcycle Diaries*.[8]

Che's father later said that Che's wanderings were his attempt to understand the poor of the Americas – a kind of social research. However, these *Diaries* show that, at this stage in his life, Che was still mainly motivated by a romantic sense of adventure, personal fulfilment and poetry, rather than by any political factor or social awareness. Nonetheless, they provided him with material that, within just a couple of years, set him on the road to becoming a Marxist revolutionary.

Under the stars

As the two friends journeyed on, they often struggled to control La Poderosa on the rough roads. One day, they had no less than nine falls, some of which happened while Che was steering. In addition, Che was plagued with health problems from time to time during their trip. He caught flu early on, which eventually required a few days in hospital: 'Alberto photographed me in my hospital gear. I made an impressive spectacle: gaunt, flushed, enormous eyes.' They often slept out in their tent, on camp beds under the stars – which appealed to Che's love of adventure: 'Distant countries, heroic deeds and beautiful women spun around and around in our turbulent imaginations.' Interestingly, even while he was thinking of 'beautiful women', he was also reminded of Chichina and her green eyes: 'My tired eyes refused to sleep and in them a pair of green spots swirled, representing the world I had left for dead behind me and mocking the so-called liberation I sought.'[9]

On their way to San Martín de los Andes, they had another fall – yet again, it was Che who'd been driving. After repairs, they stopped at a ranch owned by a German family who'd known one of Che's uncles. After fishing for their supper, they spent the night in the farm labourers' kitchen. Although Che attempted to find out about their life, 'In general, they didn't try to communicate with us, as is typical of the subjugated Araucanian race who maintain a deep suspicion of the white man who in the past has brought them so much misfortune and now continues to exploit them.' On reaching San Martín de los Andes, the beauty of Lake Lacar tempted Che to think, eventually, of settling there. Typically, the thought of a permanent home didn't last long: 'I now know, by an almost fatalistic conformity with the facts, that my destiny is to travel.' As they continued their journey, along what was known as the 'Seven Lakes Route', Che wrote to his mother (addressed as 'Dear Mama'), describing the beauty of the Andes. After asking her to send him a letter 'poste restante', he mentions that he will next be writing to Chichina.[10]

However, while they waited in the ski resort of San Carlos de Bariloche for a boat to take them to Peulla, on the border with Chile, Che received a letter from Chichina. Although he doesn't reveal the contents in his diaries, it was clearly a letter – perhaps written under family pressure – stating that she wouldn't wait for him, and indicating she'd begun seeing someone else: 'Just like that, all my dreams of home, bound up with those eyes that saw me off in Miramar, came crashing down for what seemed like no reason.' Although he began to write 'a tearful letter' in reply, he didn't finish it; when he tried to dream of her, '"she" wouldn't appear. I still believed I loved her until this moment, when I realized I felt nothing.' To what extent Che was devastated by the news from Chichina is not clear – but the next few diary entries suggest what Luther describes as 'a melancholy sense of freedom'. When an American doctor they met on the boat said: 'I think you'll get where you're heading, you've got guts. But I think you'll stay a while in Mexico', Che suddenly felt himself 'flying off ... to far-off lands, far from the current drama of my life'. Although he didn't know it at the time, it would be in Mexico that, just three years later, Che would meet Fidel Castro – and make the fateful decision to join him in his plans for carrying out a revolution in Cuba.[11]

La Ponderosa expires

Arriving in Chile, Che and Granado decided to pass themselves off as leprosy doctors, which resulted in gaining them coverage in the local newspapers – one of which described them as 'key figures in the field of leprology'. These misleading articles made it much easier for the cash-strapped adventurers to get meals and accommodation for nothing: 'we were now "The Experts", and we were treated accordingly'. When another accident necessitated yet more repairs to La Poderosa, in Lautaro, the two 'leprosy experts' were 'treated like kings' by a railway worker, who took them to his house. The two travellers were then invited to a village dance. However, having drunk a fair amount of wine, Che's macho double-standards attitude to working-class women reasserted itself. After being asked by one of the mechanics who'd been repairing their bike, to dance with his wife, Che 'started pulling her towards one of the doors'. When she declined, Che was 'in no state to listen to reason'; although she tried to kick him, he kept pulling and she 'fell crashing to the floor'. As a result, 'a furious swarm of dancers' chased Che and Granado out into the night.[12]

On the road again, they had yet more accidents, requiring further repairs and lifts in trucks – until, on 26 February, La Poderosa finally 'expired' outside Los Ángeles. For nearly two months, the bike had taken them almost to the southernmost tip of Latin America, and then up north, and finally to the west of the continent. Che's diary recorded that: 'It was our last day as "motorized bums", and that they were now "bums without wheels".' They stayed in Los Ángeles for three days – two of which were spent in the house of the fire station's caretaker. There, they were 'lured by the charms of the caretaker's three daughters'. Although Che's diary entry merely records how he was captivated by their 'spontaneity' and 'freshness', Granado later wrote that they went out with the girls – who seemed less inhibited than Argentine girls – stating that, when they got back, Che was 'really agitated, I don't know if from asthma or the girl'.[13]

Social awareness in Chile

At the end of February, they – and 'the corpse of La Poderosa II' – left for Santiago on a truck. Arriving in Santiago on Sunday, 2 March, they contacted the Argentine consul, and were permitted to sleep for the night on the patio of the office. During their stay in the city, they obtained visas for Peru, and also met up with some friends from Córdoba, who were there as part of a water-polo team. Accompanying their friends were some female 'good lookers from the host club'. However, their friends were clearly embarrassed by the two adventurers' 'unorthodox attire', and were at first uncertain about introducing them to 'these "distinguished ladies of Chilean society".' Luther sees Che's reaction to that embarrassment as reflecting 'a subtle change in societal awareness. His time on the road was already beginning to heighten his sensitivity to the divisions between the haves and the have-nots.'[14]

From Santiago, they managed to get a lift in a truck going to Valparaíso. Having found very basic 'accommodation', the next day they made the acquaintance of an Argentinian who invited them to a cheap restaurant next to the truck park – La Gioconda. Although they never saw their compatriot again, they became friends with the owner – a generous man who didn't charge them, or his poor customers, making the difference up by overcharging those who could pay. The owner also let them sleep in the kitchen. As they began exploring the city, Che really began to experience the true level of poverty in Latin America. They spent more and more time in the city's poor areas: 'we pry into dirty stairways and dark recesses, talking to swarms of beggars; we plumb the city's depths … Our distended nostrils inhale the poverty with sadistic intensity.' This experience was deepened when, hearing Che's boasts of being a doctor, he was asked by the owner of La Gioconda to visit a poor old woman suffering from severe asthma and a heart condition. Che was appalled – both by her pain and by her poor surroundings, and, once again, his humanity was engaged. This led him to make his most political statement to date:

> It is at times like this, when a doctor is conscious of his complete powerlessness, that he longs for change: a change to prevent the injustice of a system…; it's time that those who govern spent less time publicizing their own virtues and more money, much more money, funding socially useful works.[15]

They then decided to continue their travels and, rather than walk across the Northern Chile desert, they sneaked on board a boat that was going north to Antofagasta. At first, they hid in the latrines in the officers' quarters, but eventually sought out the captain, and confessed they were stowaways. The captain put them to work – Che was given the task of cleaning the foul toilets; later, they were given a cabin to sleep in. Yet, despite his job, Che's love of adventure came to the fore once again: 'There we understood that our vocation, our true vocation, was to move for eternity along the roads and seas of the world, Always curious, looking into everything that came before our eyes … not setting down roots in any land.' At this point, politics still clearly came second to the romantic lures of travel. However, politics would soon appear increasingly prominent in Che's *Diaries*.[16]

First intimations of communism

Once landed in Antofagasta, after a failed attempt to stow away on another boat going further north, they decided to visit Chuquicamata: the largest open-cast copper mine in the world, owned by a US mining monopoly. While waiting for permission to visit the mine, they met a communist couple huddled together without even a blanket to keep them warm during the cold desert night. They were desperately searching for work in the sulphur mines in the mountains, where the conditions were so bad employers didn't worry about the politics of their workers. Che, who gave them one of his and Granado's blankets, listened to their story: the husband had been imprisoned for three months for going on strike and for his membership of the Chilean Communist Party. The US – fearing the copper mines might be nationalised – had pressed the Chilean government to break up the mine workers' unions and ban the Communist Party

Che concluded the couple 'were a living representation of the proletariat in any part of the world'. He went on to write: 'It was one of the coldest times in my life, but also one which made me feel a little more brotherly towards this strange, for me at least, human species.' He noted that for people like this couple, communism 'was no more than a natural longing for something better, a protest against persistent hunger transformed into a love of this strange doctrine'. According to Luther, this meeting 'gave Guevara a harrowing glimpse at their world, a world he found upsetting.' These thoughts were increased by what they saw at the mine. As well as noting the conditions of the workers and the poor medical treatment provided by the company:

> The cruel reality of human suffering as an accepted consequence of corporate greed was all too evident. Guevara's exposure to the people and hardships on this trip grew his political awareness at an alarming rate. He began to fully understand that the exploitation of the worker was a widespread problem.[17]

Politics and archaeology in Peru

From Chile, they headed for Peru; as they travelled to the next country, Che 'synthesized his experience into a political, emotional, and aesthetic assessment of [Chile]. He recorded predictions about Chile's political and economic future, predictions every bit as revealing of their author's intellectual insight as they were accurate forecasts of political and economic events to come.' Later, he noted that the standard of living was lower in Chile than in Argentina; and, in particular, that: 'The hospitals have no money and they lack medicine and adequate facilities. We have seen filthy operating rooms with pitiful lighting, not just in small towns but even in Valaraíso.' Interestingly, when redrafting his *Diaries*, Che decided not to give his current views – instead, he preferred 'to review what I wrote then': 'an economic and political battle is being waged in Chile between a coalition of nationalist and left-wing groupings that advocate nationalizing the mines, and those who, in the cause of free enterprise, prefer a well-run mine (even in foreign hands).' He went on to mention 'Salvador Allende, who is supported by the communists.' Noting how the US 'flexes its economic muscle whenever its interests appear threatened', he then made his first comment about the pernicious influence of the US, concluding that: 'The biggest effort Chile should make is to shake its uncomfortable Yankee friend from its back.'[18]

On 25 March 1952, having marvelled at the ancient Incan canals, they reached the Peruvian town Tarata on foot, after declining to spend money for a lift. Once in the town, they discovered it – like Peru itself – was essentially an Indian town, where the bulk of the population still seemed to be exhibiting the effects of the Spanish conquest. As they travelled through the Andes over the following weeks, they came into close contact with the poor and exploited Aymara Indian masses, and Che was reminded time and time again of the inequalities suffered by the indigenous population. The local Indians were especially keen to hear about Perón's Argentina, where they'd heard that the poor had the same rights as the rich. Rather than destroy their hopes and dreams, 'Like doctors lying to terminally-ill patients', Che and Granado often went along with their erroneous impressions. They left Tarata on another truck, this time sharing their lift with a schoolteacher who'd been fired because he was an Aprista – a member of the left-wing American Popular Revolutionary Alliance (APRA). Che would eventually meet another Aprista in Guatemala – she later became his first wife.[19]

On reaching Cuzco at the end of March, Che's interest in the temples and palaces of the region led them to visit the Valley of the Incas and Machu Picchu – at one time travelling on a third-class train used only by the local Indians, which Che compared to the 'cattle transportation wagons' used in Argentina. Che's love of archaeology led him to write a whole section – entitled 'The land of the Incas' – about Peru's history and architecture. Significantly for his future direction, he also increasingly commented negatively on the impact of the US – noting how North American tourists were 'plundering' the ruins for 'mementos'. Che derided them as 'unaware of the moral distance separating them' from the living remnants of the Incas, 'since only the semi-indigenous spirit of the South American can grasp the subtle differences'. According to Luther, Che was 'feeling a kinship with these indigenous "conquered races" … He knew that, no matter the differences, he was closer to them than the Northern Anglo-Saxons would ever be.' More significantly, and in line with the comments he'd made earlier as they were about to leave Chile: 'At the heart of the problem, Guevara saw the awesome economic power of the United States.' As yet, though, Che had not decided that communism – the 'red flame dazzling the world' – was the answer.[20]

Che continued to suffer from periodic asthma attacks; a particularly bad one hit him on 11 April 1952, leaving him virtually unable to stand. They scrounged free bed and board in the local hospital, in return for which, they gave some lectures on leprosy and asthma – as well as flirting with the nurses. After the two days needed for recovery – including three adrenaline injections by Granado – they moved on to Huambo, in order to visit a remote leper colony. On the way, they stopped at the town of Hancarama, and asked the lieutenant governor for help in getting horses – by then, Che's asthma was so bad he could barely stand and they were out of adrenalin. Unknown to them, the two horses the official had 'obtained' for them had simply been commandeered for the Argentinian doctors from an Indian woman. Che and Granado left, accompanied by an Indian guide who spoke no Spanish. Eventually, they were caught up by the horses' owner and her son, who grabbed the reins and began shouting. Eventually, Che and Granado realised what had happened: the two travellers apologised and doing 'what any decent person would do', they returned them, proceeding the rest of the way to Huambo on foot. Their Indian guide then carried all their gear on his back![21]

Once there, Che yet again complained about the sanitary conditions – and the manner in which patients were treated, reiterating his stance on the need for humane, not simply medical, treatment for patients. While there, they were put up by a wealthy *hacendado*. However, Che's asthma was acerbated by heavy rains so, after two days, they moved on, having decided Che needed treatment in a hospital. The *hacendado* sent one of his Indian servants to go with them and carry their baggage back to Huancarama, where they could get a truck to the hospital in Andahuaylas. In his entry for that time, Che recorded that: 'In the mentality of the district's rich people it's perfectly natural that the servant, although travelling on foot, should carry all the weight and discomfort.' This time, though, once out of sight of the rancher, they took their bags from the guide – though it wasn't clear whether the gesture was appreciated.[22]

Che spent two days in the hospital; then, after being 'hosted' by the local Civil Guard for three days, got a truck to Ayacucho – which was just as well, as Granado had 'violently' expressed his anger at how the police had 'lewdly' treated an Indian woman bringing food for her imprisoned husband – as Che noted: 'His reaction must have seemed completely alien to people who considered the Indians were no more than objects, who deserve to live but only just.' The next day, they left for Lima. Their journey through the Andes to Lima took ten days; by the time they finally arrived, on 1 May, their funds were depleted.[23]

Latin American Marxism

Fortunately, through the good offices of Dr Hugo Pesce – a university professor, the director of Peru's leper treatment programme, and the founder of the leper clinic in Huambo – they found accommodation in a leper hospital. He also invited them to have dinner with him – which they did most nights during their stay in Lima. In addition, their respective families sent them some much-needed money. Significantly for Che's political development, Pesce was a prominent communist, much influenced by the Peruvian Marxist philosopher, José Carlos Mariátegui (1894–1930) – seen as 'the true founder of Latin American Marxism'. Mariátegui had founded the Peruvian Communist Party in 1928 and, though never fully aligned with Trotskyism, had refused to support Stalin. Mariátegui had written a book – still referred to today – which 'outlined the revolutionary potential of Latin America's disenfranchised Indians and peasantry'.[24]

Che had many talks with Pesce, and formed a long-lasting bond with him – it seems that this was when Che first began seriously reading Marx. He was particularly impressed that he'd at last found a doctor who was dedicated to the 'common good' – the sort of life Che was beginning to see as his future. In 1962, Che sent him a copy of his first book, *Guerrilla Warfare* – writing an emotional inscription: 'To Doctor Hugo Pesce: who, without knowing it perhaps, provoked a great change in my attitude toward life and society.' As yet, however, although Che was increasingly interested in communism as a possible solution to the problems of Latin America, he had yet to fully commit philosophically and ideologically to Marxism itself.[25]

As well as Che continuing his interest in Latin American archaeology during their stay of almost three weeks – he paid several visits to the city's National Museum of the Archaeology, Anthropology and History of Peru – they also decided to visit the San Pablo leper colony – the largest of Pesce's three treatments centres, located in Peru's Amazonian region. To get there, they hiked and bussed to Pucallpa, and then travelled down the Río Ucayali by boat. The Indian passengers, who travelled third-class, were placed – along with a cargo of pigs and timber – in a barge that was towed by the boat.

According to Granado's account, they both had several sexual encounters with a young prostitute during the one-week journey – despite them not having spare money. Che's account, though, suggests their lack of money meant it was only flirting. However, he noted that: 'A careless caress from that easy girl who showed sympathy for my pathetic physical state penetrated the dormant memories of my pre-adventurer life.' This incident led him to dream of Chichina. As they journeyed down the river, Che thought again of Chichina – and imagined her with a new boyfriend – finding his dream had more of 'honey' about it than 'bitterness'. Yet, in the end, he concluded his adventurous journey was worth losing her: 'I sent her a soft and unhurried kiss, that of an old friend.' During the journey, Che had yet another prolonged asthma attack: 'My asthma showed no sign of abating and I had to take the drastic measure of getting asthma medicine by the banal method of paying for it.'[26]

Once arrived in Iquitos on 1 June, they had to wait another six days before being able to get a boat to the San Pablo clinic. During those days, he had to have four injections of adrenalin a day, and spent considerable time in bed. He wrote to his beloved aunt Beatriz, asking her to send a new asthma inhaler and some anti-asthma medicine in Bogotá – but stressed he wasn't ill and didn't have asthma! By the time they arrived at the clinic, it was Che's twenty-fourth birthday. When the staff threw a party for him, Che turned his 'thank you' toast into a political speech, in which he talked of how their journeys had shown him that the peoples of Latin and Central America were: 'a single mestizo race, which from Mexico to the Magellan Straits bears notable ethnographic similarities. And, so … I propose a toast to Peru and to a united Latin America.' In that speech, Harris sees 'the stirrings of his political oratory skills as well as his ultimate political mission – the political unification of Latin America.'[27]

One incident while there illustrates how Granado was unable to 'control' Che as requested by his parents. This was when Che decided to swim across the Amazon. Although Granado remonstrated – 'You're stark raving mad. The river is full of piranhas! They'll eat you alive!' – Che 'turned a deaf ear, dived in and swam to the other bank', taking two hours. Such recklessness was similar to his mother's love of danger. As Che said to Granado: 'I vowed to myself that I was going to do it. I had to respect my promise.' While there, they once again treated the patients with humanity and dignity – playing football with them, and organising hikes and hunting expeditions. According to Symmes, Che's visit was still remembered and talked about: 'For millions of the dispossessed all over Latin America, there were no other heroes … The point of the legend was always the same, and as powerful as it was simple: Che lived and died for us.'[28]

The end of the journey

After an emotional leave-taking, they left the clinic on a raft, built for them by the staff and patients, and named 'Mambo-Tango' – which Che referred to as 'our little *Kontiki*' – down the Amazon to Leticia in Colombia, where the borders of Colombia, Peru and Brazil meet on the upper Amazon. From there, on 2 July – in what was Granado's first flight – they flew to Bogotá in an old twin-engine hydroplane that Che described as a 'cocktail-shaker'. By the time they got to Bogotá, they were exhausted from their long journey. Thanks to a letter from Dr Pesce, they were given lodgings at a hospital; and ate their meals at the university, where they made friends with some students. Che's growing interest in politics is shown in a letter to his mother, dated 6 July, in which he commented that 'there is more repression of individual freedom here than in any country we've been to'. This government repression was part of what was called 'La Violencia', which had been raging – mainly in rural areas – since 1948. Interestingly for Che's later political development, this had begun when anti-imperialist Latin American students had gathered in Bogotá to protest against a conference arranged by the US, to finalise the establishment of their Cold-War Organisation of American States. The students had seen this as an example of US imperialism – when police repression led to fighting, one of the students who took up arms was none other than Fidel Castro.[29]

While in Bogotá, a disagreement with the local police – over a knife which his brother Roberto had given him – led to 'an altercation with the police who harassed us so badly that ... both of us decided to leave for Venezuela as soon as possible'. Typically, Che had warned the police that his asthma inhaler was a 'very dangerous poison'. As a result, they were arrested, taken to various police stations, before being taken before a judge – accused of '"making fun" of the authorities'. After the production of identity papers, they were released – and Che eventually had the knife returned to him. However, their student friends advised them to leave Colombia immediately – and even made a collection to help pay their travel costs. Che's letter of 6 July also shows his closeness to his mother – 'A huge hug from your son, who misses you from head to toe,' – and his mockery of his father's love of the USA: 'By the way, if after living up here for a while he's still in love with Uncle Sam.'[30]

They left Bogotá by bus, and crossed the border into Venezuela on foot on 14 July (Che successfully concealed his revolver in 'a bundle whose stench scared off the customs officers'), and caught a van to San Cristóbal. After some haggling, they continued their journey to Caracas. On the way, Che once again began to suffer with his asthma – consuming his last two tablets that night, and Granado giving him 'a substantial adrenalin injection' – with the attack continuing the next day as they finally reached Caracas on 17 July; with Granado worrying that Che was having too much adrenalin. Once there, their earlier plan to continue on to Central America and Mexico was abandoned, as their funds were exhausted. Initially staying in a cheap pension, Che contacted the aunt of one of his friends, and she got them into a Catholic Youth Hostel, and provided them with food. Granado, having a letter of introduction from Dr Pesce, found a job at a leprosy clinic near Caracas, while Che – the worst of his latest asthma attack now over, and in possession of a 'French inhaler' – began to make preparations for his return to Argentina.[31]

Not surprisingly, after so long on the road together, their parting – at the end of July 1952 – wasn't easy. But, as Che noted, he'd obtain his degree the following year, and once obtained, he said he'd rejoin Granado to work with him in Venezuela, and the two then began to make plans for another adventurous journey. Nonetheless, Che later commented, towards the end of his *Diaries* that: 'I feel Alberto's absence so sharply ... At every other moment I'm turning around to share an observation with him only to realize he's not there.'

During his time in Caracas, Che noted the presence of black people – a rarity in Argentina, but common on Latin America's Caribbean coast. His comments in the *Diaries* reveal typical white Argentine arrogance and racist prejudices: after commenting on how 'the blacks have maintained their racial purity thanks to their lack of affinity with bathing', he went on to say they were 'indolent', and spent their 'meager wage on frivolity or drink'. Given that he revised these before publication – and given the number of black people in Cuba – it seems strange these comments were not removed, either by Che himself or, later, by his widow.[32]

In the 'Belly of the Beast'

On 26 July, Che managed to get a seat on an old cargo plane which needed to refuel in Caracas. The plane was transporting several racehorses belonging to one of his uncles, from Buenos Aires to Miami. Once the horses had been unloaded, the plane would return to Buenos Aires. However, on landing in Miami, it was discovered that the plane had an engine problem, so Che had to stay over while the repairs were made. Although he had no money – and, according to his father, because of 'his exaggerated pride he did not ask us for help' – he was able to stay in a small hotel by promising to pay the bill once back in Buenos Aires, which he honoured. Chichina's cousin, Jaime Roca, was completing his architectural studies in Miami, and the two spent their time on the beach and exploring the city. Roca also got Che a job, cleaning the apartment of a Cuban stewardess that he knew. Che was so clueless, she told Roca not to send him again, claiming he'd left it in more of a mess than before! However, she did help him get a job as a dishwasher in one of Miami's restaurants. Despite being encouraged by Roca to spend the $15 Chichina had given him for a scarf, Che refused. It seems he did buy her that scarf – but posted it to her, rather than face seeing her again.[33]

Che's *Diaries*, rather surprisingly, don't mention this stay in the US; and Roca claims they didn't talk politics. But, later, Che said these were 'the worst weeks of his life', and commented on witnessing white racism against African Americans – and how the police had hassled him about his political affiliations. Not surprisingly, this brief stay in what would soon be seen by him as the 'evil empire', 'did little to improve his impression of the United States'. While, according to Harris, the *Diaries* are notable for revealing Che's 'growing political consciousness and his early leanings toward socialism' as a result of the poverty and oppression he witnessed. Yet his growing desire to help the 'Wretched of the Earth' did not display 'self-righteousness or exaggerated piety that one often associates with zealous do-gooders and missionaries'. These *Diaries* can be seen as showing how travelling for days on end with little or no money, few chances of washing or changing clothes, and often sleeping outdoors, was preparation for 'the life he would lead much later as a guerrilla fighter when he often had to survive without food, water, bathing, or adequate clothing'.[34]

Back home

Che reached Buenos Aires in September 1952, and was met at the airport by his whole family. There was a family celebration and, according to his youngest brother, 'My mother seemed to regain some of her strength and spirit. Her son's presence was enough to make her happy.' But after eight months of travelling, Che – who'd continued his 'passion for archaeology, not only by visiting many sites, but also reading about them in the local libraries' – was aware now that the poor he had seen on his wanderings 'continued to huddle under blankets on frigid nights as they fled from persecution, work for unfair wages in unsafe conditions, and suffer from poor medical care'. In fact, Che's motorcycle journeys had fully demonstrated the saying that 'travel broadens the mind'. In his case, it was very much a social and political widening. His brother Juan Martín noted that during Che's eight-month journey, his family 'noticed a change in his correspondence. Gradually, as he continued on his journey, he was transformed. The tone became more … engaged in … the social problems he was discovering along the way. He talked more and more about politics and embarked on economic analyses.'[35]

Che wasted no time in returning to his medical studies – he had over a dozen exams to pass before qualifying as a doctor. Typically, he studied in an extremely self-disciplined way – sometimes studying up to fourteen hours a day, often at his aunt's, or in his father's studio. Even so, he still found time to help Dr Pisani – and was listed, along with several others, as co-author of a research paper on allergic reactions to pollens. In addition, he began to add to his *Diaries*. In November 1952, he became seriously ill after carrying out some research involving the entrails of patients who'd died from infectious diseases. Nonetheless, after only two days in bed, he got up and sat – and passed – several exams over just a few days.

Over the next few months, he passed the remaining exams – becoming a fully qualified doctor in April 1953. He notified his family of his qualification by phoning from his aunt Beatriz's house, saying; 'Call me doctor.' His proud father – who said Che phoned him at his studio, and said, emphasising the word 'doctor': 'This is Doctor Ernesto Guevara de la Serna' – 'told everybody that even if [Che] was not the best student in the medical school, he had still broken all records for the speed with which he was graduating.' But according to his brother, Juan Martín, by then, Che simply 'wanted the diploma that would buy his freedom'.[36]

Now aged 25, Che clearly had no intention of settling down – he wanted to visit Europe and Asia, and was soon planning his 'second Latin American odyssey'. At the same time, Che's friends noticed a change in him: he became more politically vocal, now adopting clear anti-Peronist politics, and vehemently objecting to a study of Peronism being made part of his university studies. More significantly, he made it increasingly clear that he saw the social and economic problems of Latin America as mainly down to 'Yankee imperialism'. Over the following twelve months, this particular development would be confirmed by his experiences in the countries he visited next – especially in Guatemala, where his travel adventures would end. It was also there where he would meet the woman who eventually became his first wife.[37]

Chapter 4

Revolution and Romance in Guatemala, 1953–54

> 'It was in 1954 ... when the last revolutionary American democracy ... in the area – that of Jacobo Árbenz Guzmán – succumbed before the cold, premeditated aggression of the USA...'[1]

As with his previous trip, Che once again kept a diary – published posthumously as *Back on the Road: a Journey to Central America.* In part, this journey was a result of his continuing desire for romantic wanderings, and his strong interest in the ancient indigenous civilisations and archaeology of the Incas, Mayas and Aztecs. During these travels, his political views become increasingly radicalised by the economic and social conditions – and the political struggles – he observed. This second journey consolidated his 'political knowledge' and created a desire to understand 'why and how a struggle must be waged that will culminate in a genuine revolution'. This was especially true of his experiences in Guatemala – Che later said in a speech in Havana: 'I began to be a revolutionary in Guatemala.'[2]

As Richard Gott notes, Che's political outlook dramatically shifted during this second journey: 'He moves from being a detached and cynical observer to becoming a fully fledged revolutionary ... ardent in his desire to take immediate action.' These changes were revealed in letters sent to various family members; his mother or father usually read them aloud, with 'each letter ... an event around which the whole family gathered'. As Che got to find out more about the lives of poor people, 'his political awareness grew... his outrage at injustice exploded ... [and] his humanistic concerns developed'. This journey saw him shift to a communist position, becoming someone who increasingly saw himself as a Latin American. He thus refused to call the United States 'America' – instead seeing 'America' as 'the whole continent'. Within just a few years, he would develop the revolutionary internationalist perspective that would lead, ultimately, to his death in 1967.[3]

To Bolivia

For this journey, Che was accompanied by Carlos 'Calica' Ferrer, another of his childhood friends from Alta Gracia. As would soon emerged, Ferrer – unlike Che – was not really interested in politics or archaeology. Their plans were rather sketchy – with Che initially still thinking he'd join Granado in Venezuela, as well as having vague ideas of travelling on to Europe and even Asia. The evening before they left, the Guevara house was 'full of guests' to say farewell to Che, and his mother presented him with a suit she'd made for him. There was 'music to dance to, with laughter filling the house' – though Che 'jigged around without harmony or grace'.[4]

They left Buenos Aires by train on 7 July 1953, bound for Bolivia's capital, La Paz. They were seen off by their respective families, with both young men feeling embarrassed by the amount of food given them as they boarded the train, as it emphasised the differences between them and their poorer Indian fellow passengers. According to his father, Che said, prophetically: 'Here goes a soldier of the Americas' as they left. The send-off was an emotional one for Che's parents – in part because of their concerns over his continuing health problems. It was particularly difficult for his mother, who ran after the departing train, 'tears running down her face, her handkerchief fluttering in the air, certain she would never see her beloved son again'. In fact, it would be another six years before his parents saw him again, by which time he'd become a seasoned guerrilla fighter, and one of the most important leaders of the Cuban Revolution.[5]

The train crossed into Bolivia at La Quiaca – near to where Che would meet his death in 1967. They spent three days there, as Che's asthma was once again causing problems. They then continued to La Paz, arriving on 11 July, where they stayed for around six weeks. There, they experienced the aftermath of the 1952 Bolivian Revolution, following which the Revolutionary Nationalist Movement (MNR) government had nationalised the country's foreign-owned mines, disbanded the army, and introduced universal franchise – giving the vote for the first time to Bolivia's illiterate poor, including women. During Che's stay, on 2 August 1953, the government announced an ambitious land distribution to the mainly indigenous peasants. Predictably, the US made it clear it didn't want this revolution to go too far.

Revolutionary fervour was still very much evident in La Paz, but there were also rumours of reactionary coups, and Che noted how the privileged classes were finding it difficult to adjust to the new situation: 'The "well-to-do", refined people are shocked at what has been happening and complain bitterly about the new importance conferred on Indians and mestizos.' On 15 July, they'd witnessed a torchlight procession, which Che thought was 'long and boring'

– though he was interested by how people in the armed militias showed their support 'by firing off a Mauser or a "Piri-Piri".' When he went to the Ministry of Peasant Affairs, he was shocked to see peasants being sprinkled with DDT to rid them of lice before meeting government officials – similar to his earlier reactions at seeing how leprosy patients were often treated.[6]

In a letter to his father, he described himself a 'neutral observer' – despite his general sympathy with 'the downtrodden masses'. However, in a letter to 'Tita' Infante, he is more political, writing about 'the highly absorbing political panorama' in Bolivia, and stating that the Bolivian Revolution 'has given a really major example to the American continent'. However, Che speculated – correctly as it turned out – that the centre and right might unite against the left and weaken the reforms. As noted by Gott, Che also 'guessed rightly, that this was not a revolution that would challenge the hegemony of the United States in Latin America'. While there, he dragged Ferrer to see some of Bolivia's tin mines in an area where, before the Revolution, mine-guards had machine-gunned miners and their families. Che's reaction was similar to when he'd seen the conditions in the Chilean mines. According to Luther, once again Che 'saw evidence that as long as Latin America was dependent upon the United States, independence was but a dream'.[7]

While in La Paz, they also met a group of wealthy anti-Perón Argentine exiles. Through them, Che and Ferrer spent a lot of time with Bolivia's 'well-to-do refined people', despite Che's sympathy with Bolivia's poor. Luther speculates that while Che 'may have had some pangs of remorse about this dichotomy, his companion, [Ferrer], had none', and wasn't offended by the elitist and racist views expressed by their privileged new acquaintances. One member of this group was Ricardo Rojo, a young lawyer and *antiperonista* of the Radical Party, who'd escaped from police custody in Buenos Aires – they would met up again in other countries. According to Rojo, Che was staying in a very basic room in one of the oldest parts of the city, and when he wasn't having discussions in the noisy cafés along the city's main street, he was exploring ancient Incan ruins. In a letter to his mother, Che wrote that while on the island of Isla del Sol, 'one of my most cherished hopes as an explorer was fulfilled: I found – at an ancient indigenous cemetery – a small female statue … made from the famous chompi, the alloy of the Incas.' This interest was not shared by Rojo, who thought Che didn't seem overly-political. According to Harris, although Che was a 'political nonconformist with a keen sense of justice', he hadn't yet become either a Marxist or a revolutionary. However, Che would soon commit to that political ideology.[8]

Onwards to Peru and Ecuador

On 7 August, Che and Ferrer left Bolivia and headed for Lima in Peru – then ruled by the dictator Manuel Odría. Che noted that 'Each of us had his amorous connection to leave behind', believing 'there is something between us – between her and me' – though no name was given. An indication where Che was heading politically was that, at a customs' border post, two of his books were confiscated: '*El hombre en la Unión Soviética*, and a Ministry of Peasant Affairs publication, which they loudly accused of being "Red, Red, Red".' On the way, Che insisted on revisiting the Incan sites of Machu Picchu and Cuzco. In his diary, Che noted he was missing Granado; and in a letter to his mother, he commented on how Ferrer 'keeps cursing the filth' and is more bothered about watching out he doesn't stand on 'one of the innumerable turds lining the streets' than looking at 'the sky or a cathedral ... It's a question of temperament'. Che also wrote: 'I still miss [Granado's] company. The way in which our characters were so suited to each other is becoming more obvious to me here in Machu-Picchu.'[9]

As well as visiting Incan sites, Che met up again with Dr Pesce in Lima, the communist who'd so impressed him during his first visit. They had many 'thorough chats ... about ... varied subjects'. Che also crossed paths again with Rojo, and made plans to meet up soon in Guayaquil, Eucador. On 3 September he wrote to Tita, referring to a political strand that became increasingly important to him – the negative impacts of 'Yankee domination' which he saw in Peru: 'for Peru Yankee domination has not even meant that fictitious economic prosperity which can be seen in Venezuela'. Significantly, as a further pointer to Che's increasing drift to left-wing politics, he and Ferrer were later detained by the police, and their hostel room was searched – which Che thought may have been linked to the earlier confiscation of his two books, as well as his meetings with Pesce.[10]

On 28 September 1953, after a three-day bus journey, during which Che's asthma was once again a problem, they arrived in Ecuador – where Che's mother had used her connections with Ecuador's president, to arrange accommodation for them in Quito. They moved on to the port of Guayaquil by boat, where they met up with Rojo – and three of his leftist Argentine friends. All six stayed in the same pension, and had many discussions – in particular about the revolutionary situation developing in Guatemala, which they said 'was more radical than anything they had witnessed in Bolivia'. In a letter to his father, dated 4 October, Che mentioned the 'good climate of personal freedom' in Eucador – in contrast to Peru's unpopular government, which only held on to power 'Thanks to the bayonets of its [US] friends.'[11]

Che stayed in Ecuador for around three weeks, although the tropical climate triggered several asthma attacks. While there, Che met two leprosy doctors

– perhaps significantly, both were 'bolches' – or communists. Che's asthma gradually improved, and he enjoyed himself playing chess. During their stay, Che told one of Rojo's friends that he'd never before known such 'unconditional comradeship, where everyone shared what they had without misgivings'; and that such 'camaraderie had been missing from his life, even within his own family'. In a letter to his mother, Che mentioned that he and the others – described by him as 'four new candidates for Yankee opprobrium' – were making preparations for going to Guatemala. However, he also admitted that he was a 'total adventurer'. Clearly, Che's initial plan of eventually joining Granado in Venezuela was seriously wavering – his twin desires for adventure and political study were too strong.[12]

Problems with visas, boat tickets and lack of funds caused several delays, and Ferrer went off separately to Quito, to wait for the others. In the end, further problems meant the two friends never met again. During the delay, Che again suffered an asthma attack – made worse by a bout of diarrhoea. Eventually, the necessary visas were obtained, and tickets were purchased on an Argentine boat – partly paid for by Che selling the suit his mother had made him. At the end of October, Che and one of Rojo's friends left for Panama, with Che noticing that 'the soldiers watching over the enrolment offices have the initials "US" on their backs'. One friend remained behind, to help pay off their debts; but, in the end, he never made it to Guatemala. When they parted, Che's journal described their farewell as 'cold, always less than you expected'. Yet, according to the one left behind, Che 'cried "like a child", telling him how much his friendship meant to him'.[13]

From Panama to Costa Rica

On arrival in Balboa, they moved on to Panama City, from where they'd continue their journey to Guatemala. When they arrived, they found that Rojo and his friend had already left – but had left contact details of some students at Panama University. While there, Che had his first non-medical writing published: an account of his and Granado's raft journey, and a piece on Macchu Picchu. The publication of the latter was delayed however, because of Che's criticisms of how the US had plundered Machu Picchu to fill 'the museums of North America', and the ubiquitous 'Coca-Cola propaganda'. Also controversial was his call to the peoples of Latin America: 'Citizens of Indoamerica, reconquer the past!' In addition to the fees he received for them, his student contacts arranged for him to deliver a lecture on allergy at the university – to an audience of twelve, but with a useful fee of $25. One of the staff he met afterwards was Dr Carlos Guevara Moreno: a supporter of Perón, 'an intelligent demagogue', but not very knowledgeable about 'the dialectics of history' – i.e., Marxism. According to Che, he wouldn't 'take a revolution beyond what is strictly necessary to keep the masses content'.[14]

By late November, they'd obtained visas for Costa Rica, and initially travelled north by truck. After several problems and delays, and using trains and hitchhiking, they reached the port of Golfito. Che soon discovered the port was owned by the United Fruit Company (UFC), and that hospital treatment depended on 'the grade of the person working in the company ... "as always, the class spirit of the gringos makes itself felt"'. It was in Costa Rica that Che became fully aware of the influence of the US and the UFC. His favourite author, the Chilean Communist poet Pablo Neruda, had written a poem about the UFC a few years earlier, condemning the way they'd turned Central American countries into subservient 'banana republics' ruled by corrupt dictators.[15]

On leaving Golfito for San José – having missed a train – they travelled on a boat that transported down-and-outs. The sea became rough; while his friends suffered from sea-sickness, Che stayed on deck with 'a negress who had picked me up – Socorro, as horny as a toad, with 16 years spent on her back'. He also noted that the Chief of Police in Costa Rica was 'a Cuban colonel and FBI agent imposed by the United States'. According to Luther, Che's response to the influence of the UFC was 'typical of his growing hatred for capitalism and foreign domination. His past observations had set him on a path to communism that this experience only solidified.' This growing revolutionary fervour against the 'capitalist octopuses' now began to feature in his letters to his family and friends for the first time.[16]

In San José, Costa Rica's capital, there were several exiled politicians. Che's growing interest in politics resulted, over several days, in meetings with a number of these individuals, whose strengths and weaknesses he noted in his journals. These included Juan Bosch, the revolutionary nationalist leader of the Dominican Republic; Rómolo Betancourt, the exiled Venezuelan political leader; and Manuel Mora Valverde, the leader of the Costa Rican Communist Party. Che found Bosch a 'first rate guy' and 'very interesting', with 'clear ideas and left-wing tendencies', and noted that they didn't talk about literature (even though Bosch wrote short stories) but 'just about politics'. Interestingly, they touched on Cuba, with Bosch describing Batista as 'a thug surrounded by thugs'. Later, though, Che revised his opinion, dismissing Betancourt as being: 'solidly on the side of the United States. He gave a false idea of the Rio Pact and spent most of the time raging about the Communists.' Valverde gave them a run-through of Costa Rican politics – which left Che wondering what would happen when the current president of Costa Rica 'sees the light and stops having any illusions about the goodness of the United States? Will he fight or give up? We shall see.' This shows Che as already strongly anti-Yankee – and seeing the need to fight against its influence.[17]

While in San José, Che also met some Cuban rebels who'd taken part in Castro's attack on the Moncada Barracks in on 26 July 1953. In a letter, dated 10 December, to his beloved but conservative aunt Beatriz – addressing her as 'Auntie-auntie-mine' – he updated her on his physical journey so far. Significantly, he also made clear his political journey, by announcing his:

> shining faith in a Socialist future ... I have sworn in front of an image of the old and much-lamented Comrade Stalin that I won't rest until I see these capitalists crushed. I will perfect my skills in Guatemala and I will achieve what I still lack in order to be an authentic revolutionary.

He signed off as 'Chanco.'[18]

They hitchhiked from Costa Rica into Nicaragua; after obtaining visas in Managua, they ran into Rojo and his two anti-Peronista friends again. That night, the five of them discussed Argentine politics. According to Che: '[three] were intransigent radicals, [one] pro-Labour, and myself an independent – or at least that was how Big Rojo saw it.' The next day, Che and two friends set off for Guatemala by car – with plans to sell the car for funds on reaching their destination. After travelling across Honduras and El Salvador – on a journey which included punctures, lack of money, sleeping outdoors and problems crossing borders – Che eventually arrived in Guatemala City just before Christmas Eve.[19]

The Guatemalan Revolution

The reason why so many Latin American leftists wanted to go to Guatemala was because of what became known as the 'Guatemalan Revolution' – and their desire to see a socialist experiment in action. Many thought the future of Latin America would be decided by whether this revolution was victorious or defeated. The Revolution had begun in October 1944, when Guatemala's dictator – who had ruled Guatemala as a banana republic serving the interests of the local landed oligarchy and of the UFC – had been overthrown in a popular uprising. In 1951, Árbenz had been elected president, and had continued reforms that benefited the majority Indian population. By the time Che arrived there in late 1953, thousands of hectares of uncultivated land had been transferred to over 100,000 landless peasants. Most of that land had been taken from Guatemala's large landowners – but 11,000 hectares were uncultivated lands belonging to the UFC. The events that unfolded in Guatemala would soon set Che on the road to becoming a revolutionary Marxist.[20]

Finding Hilda

On arrival in Guatemala City, Che and the others were without funds, but managed to find a boarding house which didn't require advance payment. Within a week, Che was struck down by a bout of asthma. It seems it was then that he was first introduced, by Rojo, to Hilda Gadea Acosta – the woman who would eventually become his first wife. Gadea was a Peruvian exile who'd been given political asylum in Guatemala. She'd been a militant activist of APRA, Peru's leftist party, and one of the leaders of its youth wing. She'd been forced to flee from the military dictatorship which had seized power in 1948. She was of mixed Indian and Chinese parentage, and was seven years older than him. At the time Che met her, she was working for the Árbenz government; importantly, she was certainly his intellectual equal, and well able to hold her own in discussions of politics and philosophy, the two topics that were by now Che's main interest.

Gadea described her first impressions of Che as follows: 'Guevara had dark brown hair … striking black eyes … and a commanding voice … I noticed his intelligent and penetrating look and the preciseness of his comments.' Initially, though, she concluded that he seemed 'superficial, egotistical and conceited'. But, on finding out he'd been suffering from an asthma attack at the time, she began to modify her opinion of him. She soon came to be concerned about his health, doing many things to help him through his bouts of asthma, and also helping him out financially.[21]

Politics to the fore

It was largely through Gadea that Che came to meet a wide circle of intellectual and politically active people. These included the Peruvian student leader Juan Pablo Chang, who'd later fight alongside him in Bolivia. Some of Gadea's friends were Guatemalan government officials, while others were members of left-wing parties from various Latin American countries living as exiles in Guatemala. During those meetings, Gadea and Che became increasingly close – and Che confided to her that, although his initial plan had been to join his friend Granado in Caracas, he'd changed his mind after his experiences in Bolivia, and now wanted to learn 'as much as possible about the revolution in Latin America'. Gadea was also impressed by his obvious love of his family – especially of his 'old lady'. He even told her about his relationship with Chichina and how it had failed because he couldn't lead a bourgeois life. In particular, Gadea was favourably impressed by his ideas about how doctors in Latin America should work to end the malnutrition and illnesses associated with the extreme poverty and filth in which the majority of Latin Americans were forced to live. According to her, his openness and warmth made her appreciate his underlying humanity.[22]

However, as well as contributing to Che's political development by introducing him to her political friends, Gadea also 'advised him to read' Mariátegui – the Peruvian Marxist so much admired by Dr Pesce. She later loaned him some of her copies of his writings. Whether or not this included Mariátegui's 1928 article 'Aniversario y balance', Che's form of socialism would eventually become much closer to Mariátegui's communism than to the official 'Marxism' of the Soviet Union. Another person Che met was Helena de Holst, a Honduran exile married to a German businessman. She was well-informed about Marxism, and had visited both the Soviet Union and China. They had a 'serious chat', and Che commented that she was 'close on many points to the Communists and struck me as a very fine person'. Increasingly, Che's entries show he was looking at communism – and can be contrasted to an earlier one where he spent the evening talking to Ricardo Temoche, a former APRA deputy. Che clearly disagreed with his views on Communism: 'If you listen to him, the only enemy of the APRA is the Communist Party: there's no imperialism and no oligarchy of any significance; the bolshies are the irreconcilable enemy.'[23]

Another breath of Cuba

Particularly important for Che's future and his political philosophy – and something which eventually ended the relationship between Che and Gadea – was that, among those to whom Gadea introduced him, was a group of Cuban exiles who'd been involved in Castro's unsuccessful attack on the Moncada Barracks. They'd been in the city for several months, having been granted asylum by the Árbenz government. Both Che and Gadea were impressed by the Cuban exiles' 'honest simplicity and the strength of their convictions', and the fact that they had risked their lives to put theory into practice.

Especially inspiring was Antonio 'Ñico' López: the first to give Che his nickname, and who would be with him when they sailed from Mexico to Cuba – and who would be killed in the struggle. Gadea admired his conviction that 'one had to make a revolution, and that in Cuba this revolution was going to be made by Fidel' – even though he'd been sentenced to fifteen years in prison. From then on, Che met with the Cubans virtually every day. For Che, the impact of these Cubans was especially deep: 'Nico left his heart and soul in the microphone and for that reason fired even a sceptic like myself with enthusiasm.'[24]

More immediately, Gadea managed to get Che some much-needed paid work with another of her acquaintances, a US professor called Harold White, who wanted help in translating his book on Marxism into Spanish. He had initially asked Gadea to help him; but as she knew Che had several debts, she persuaded him to hire Che instead. Before long, Che was also giving this 'gringo' professor Spanish lessons, and the three of them became close friends, having many political discussions that ranged from 'the international situation to Marxism, Lenin, Engels, Stalin, Freud, science in the Soviet Union, and Pavlov's conditioned reflexes'. Although Che's diary makes only a brief mention of this professor, according to Gadea, these discussions had a significant influence on his thinking during this period. She stated that Che told her: 'This is a good gringo. He is tired of capitalism and wants to lead a new life.' After the victory of the Cuban Revolution, Che invited White to Cuba, where he stayed until his death in 1968.[25]

Gadea and Che were not yet lovers at this stage – and Che sought physical fulfilment elsewhere. In fact, Che had earlier noted that he'd had 'a little adventure with a plumpish schoolteacher'. According to Gadea, Che had hinted he was romantically interested in her, but she hadn't encouraged him. Yet Che's entries suggest it was she who first showed any romantic interest. In fact, Che's journal entries are 'often cold and callous about her appearance'. Nonetheless, his friends began to tease him about what they saw as early signs of a romance – and Gadea noted that he began to be protective of her. Politically, though, as the months went by, Che increasingly moved to an explicitly revolutionary Marxist position, while Gadea remained wedded to a more moderate electoral socialism. He tried increasingly to get her to drop her membership of APRA. According to Gadea, Che often spoke of his admiration of the revolutionary achievements of the Soviet Union – and that, in contrast to Rojo's electoralist approach, Che argued that the only way 'was a violent revolution: the struggle had to be against Yankee imperialism and any other solutions ... were betrayals.'[26]

When Rojo decided to leave Guatemala at the end of February 1954, Che stayed on, as he was excited by the Guatemalan government's revolutionary programme. Whatever his romantic interest in Gadea at this time, Che was now having an affair with a nurse. Letters to his family show he was increasingly identifying with Árbenz's radical reform programme which he believed had to be defended. According to him, Guatemala had the 'most democratic air' in Latin America; and that 'This is me, the real me, like it or not; you can't do anything about it, so you'd better get used to the idea.' As rumours of an impending coup increased, Che argued that Árbenz was being too complacent and should organise an armed peoples' militia. In a letter to his aunt, dated 5 January 1954, he'd spoken of how several papers in Guatemala were funded by the UFC – and which, if he were Árbenz, he 'would have closed down in five minutes'. He hoped that when the crisis came, Árbenz would eventually arm the members of the Guatemalan Communist Party, and that a successful resistance would allow a socialist revolution to take root in there.[27]

Virtually penniless, Che tried hard to find some kind of employment – including trying to get a job as a doctor in one of the government's public health initiatives. He was particularly interested in a programme centered on the indigenous population in the remote El Petén region. There was also the added attraction of the ancient Maya ruins in the area – archaeology still clearly a continuing passion. Unfortunately, the government insisted he needed to complete another year's medical training in Guatemala before they would validate his medical qualifications. His situation was further complicated by the fact that he wasn't officially a political exile, didn't have a residence visa, and wasn't connected in any way to any of the parties making up the government. In addition, his constant ill-health – mostly recurring asthma attacks, but also stomach infections and headaches – was also a problem.

One of Gadea's friends, an influential member of the communist Workers of Guatemala Party (PGT), tried to get him a job in the government's Statistics Department. This came to nothing when Che was informed he'd have to join the Communist Party first. According to Gadea, Che refused, saying 'when I want to join the party I will do so on my own initiative, not out of any ulterior motive!' He later told her: 'It's not that I disagree with the Communist ideology, it's the method I don't like. They shouldn't get members this way. It's all false.' Nonetheless, his letters from early 1954, whether to his parents or to his friend Tita, make it clear he was already very much aligned with the Communists, who 'comply with a programme in which personal interests do not count' – unlike the other parties in the government.[28]

According to Gadea, in mid-March 1954 Che finally asked her to be his girlfriend, suggesting they might eventually get married – though he'd prefer sooner rather than later. His romantic side came out in the form of a handwritten poem as a formal proposal, which she said was 'beautiful and forceful'. In it, he wrote that 'he did not desire beauty alone but, more than that, a comrade'. But, although she told him she loved him, she said she wanted to 'be free' to 'accomplish something for society', and to focus on the political struggles in Guatemala and Peru. Che apparently blamed her refusal on wrong-headed Aprista views – and pointed out that neither Marx nor Lenin had been impeded by marriage. Perhaps tellingly – given macho Latin American values – he commented that their wives 'supported them'; though in fact Lenin's life companion was a revolutionary in her own right. Interestingly, according to Anderson, Che's original diary entry claims it was she who declared her love via a letter, but as he was experiencing another asthma attack, nothing happened: 'I was very sick or I might have fucked her. I warned her that all I could offer her was a casual contact, nothing definite … Too bad she is so ugly.'[29]

By the end of March, Che had moved into a boarding house with the Cuban exiles. In April, right at the end of a letter to his mother, he makes the first mention of Gadea, referring to her as a '*compañera*': 'I engage with endless discussions with the comrade Hilda Gadea, an *aprista* … She has a heart of platinum, at least. Her help is felt in everything to do with my daily life.' It also alludes to his view that 'the American continent will be the theatre of my adventures much more than I would previously have thought'. Later, his father saw this as alluding to the maturing of his political thoughts, leading to 'his decision to become a man totally devoted to the liberation of the oppressed'. When, in May, Ñico and most of the others moved on to Mexico City, Hilda arranged for Che to stay with Helena de Holst. She treated Che almost like a son, and would have given him free accommodation and food. Che's pride, however, led him to refuse. Instead, he started sleeping on the grounds of a nearby country club, coming to Hilda's boarding house for hot water for his maté. The landlady and Hilda made sure there was fruit and salad about, which were the main components of the strict diet he followed in order to reduce the number of asthma attacks.[30]

While in Guatemala, he began – but didn't complete – a book, which he planned to call *The Role of the Doctor in Latin America*. This was an attempt to combine his twin-interests of medicine and politics into a kind of social medicine, with doctors needing to support social change in order to really help the poor. Yet he spent much more time reading works by Marx, Engels and Lenin, and discussing them with Gadea – who lent him her copy of Mao Zedong's *New China*. According to her, they both saw the Chinese road to socialism as closer to the situation of most Latin American countries with their Indian and peasant majorities. Medicine thus soon came to take second place to politics, although he continued to try to find medical work in Guatemala.

Che was eventually offered work by the Ministry of Education, as an intern in a teacher-training centre. However, in mid-May, he was told that in order to work legally in Guatemala, he'd have to leave the country to renew his visa. Apparently, Gadea again pressed for commitment, and Che once again declined. However, shortly before he left temporarily for El Salvador in order to renew his visa, it seems that Che and Gadea spent their first night together and became lovers. Once in El Salvador, he succeeded in getting a six-month visa for Guatemala, though Honduras refused to issue him one. Che wondered if the Honduran refusal was because he'd come from Guatemala – now seen as a 'hotbed of communism'. The US – which had stopped selling Guatemala weapons because of its new radical government – had recently used Árbenz's decision to seek weapons from Czechoslovakia to declare that that was 'proof' he was a 'communist'. As Che noted, the UFC 'is in a fury, and of course Dulles and the CIA want to intervene in Guatemala because of its terrible crime in buying weapons from wherever it wishes'. Che's comment turned out to be extremely prophetic.[31]

While in El Salvador, Che visited the pre-Columbian Maya ruins of Tazumal, noting they weren't as impressive as Incan ones – and visited another Maya site at Quiriguá. In letters to his mother, he also wrote that he'd earned some much-needed money by working for a couple of days on an Atlantic highway project at Puerto Barrios – working twelve-hour shifts from 6.00 pm to 6.00 am. More significantly, he still seemed uncertain of what to do; he mentions the possibility of archaeology ('anthropology'), though said it seemed 'rather paradoxical that the lodestar of my life could be the study of what is now dead beyond recall'. He then went on to speculate that, if he reached the age of 35, he thought his main areas would be 'nuclear physics, genetics or another area that combines some of the most interesting subjects with which I am familiar'; before going on to say he wanted to visit 'the rest of the world'. Gadea was pleased – and surprised – when he returned to Guatemala City, as she'd feared he wouldn't return.[32]

Birth of a revolutionary

A letter of 10 May 1954 showed him still uncertain of his future. He rejected the prospect of becoming 'very rich' in Guatemala by getting his Argentine medical degree ratified and setting up as an allergy specialist, because he felt that 'would be the most horrible betrayal of the two I's struggling inside me: the socialist and the traveller'. Yet he was still torn between political activism and the romance of foreign travel. However, in June 1954, his uncertainty was ended by the coup – organised and backed by the CIA – against Árbenz's radical government. In March 1954, the US had declared that the Árbenz regime was 'Communist-infiltrated' and was intending to align Guatemala with the Soviet bloc. This had persuaded the OAS to pass Resolution 93, stating that member states had the right 'to take the necessary measures to protect themselves against Communist intervention' in the hemisphere – which the US had declared to be their 'backyard' via the Monroe Doctrine of 1823.[33]

On 18 June, four days after Che had celebrated his twenty-sixth birthday, some aircraft machine-gunned and bombed the streets of Guatemala City, as well as military objectives. Immediately after, CIA-trained mercenary troops under the command of Colonel Castillo Armas crossed into Guatemala. Initially, it looked like the coup would fail. However, the first response of Árbenz – determined to avoid direct US involvement – was merely to protest to the UN. Letters to his mother, dated 20 June and 4 July, show Che responded by enlisting in the emergency health brigades – but, significantly, also in the youth brigades, organised by the Communist Youth, 'to receive military instruction for any eventuality'. Although Che hoped to be sent to the front to resist the invasion, he was ordered by the public health minister to report to a hospital. According to his brother, Che told Gadea that 'he had a "fool-proof plan": he would "seize strategic points in the city, take possession of communications, and ambush those trying to enter".'[34]

The later letter showed him, 'a little shamefully', being excited by the prospects of armed resistance, and feeling a 'magical sense of invulnerability'. Initially, he thought these attacks would unite the Guatemalans – and foreigners like himself – behind the government and repel the invaders. He also made a specific comment about the role of the US and the UFC: 'The Yankees have finally dropped the good-guy mask ... and are now committing outrages in these parts.' However, Che's optimism was soon dashed by what he called 'a terrible shower of cold' – when, on 27 June, Árbenz announced he was resigning, denouncing 'the fruit company and the United States as being directly behind all the bombing and strafing of the civilian population'. The army had ultimately betrayed Árbenz, leading Che to write to his mother that 'once more the aphorism is confirmed that sees the liquidation of the army as the true principle of democracy'. He also noted that Árbenz could have given arms to the people – but hadn't done so. The coup merely confirmed Che's growing opposition to the imperialistic 'Yankee octopus' that was strangling attempts by Latin American countries to address the problems of poverty. In a letter to his aunt, dated 22 July, he mentions his intention to go to Mexico – and how he'll be prepared 'for the next flare-up'. While in a letter to Tita, dated 8 October 1954, he wrote: 'We are like the Spanish Republic, betrayed from within and without, but we did not fall with the same dignity.' As his father commented, it was evident that Che 'had by now become aware that underdeveloped countries could only liberate themselves from the exploitation of imperialism by means of armed struggle'.[35]

A political refugee

These events were significant for Che; the military dictatorship under Armas, as well as reversing Árbenz's reforms, declared martial law and began rounding up all those groups and individuals who'd supported Árbenz. A special 'liberation force' began executing government officials and supporters, as well as turning their attention to political exiles from other Latin American countries – especially those suspected of being communists. The seriousness of Che's situation was brought home by the Argentinian attaché d'affaires in Guatemala City, who warned him to 'Leave immediately. They intend to kill you', and telling him 'the US embassy is aware of your every move. You are a marked man.' Che was now a political refugee, and initially found shelter in the house of two El Salvadoran women. When they left the country in mid-July, he moved to Helena de Holst's house – although she too had been arrested. He then sought shelter in the Argentine embassy, while Gadea changed her lodgings. According to Gadea, in the confused situation, Che initially was able to wander in and out of the embassy, carrying messages for those already there, helping others seeking asylum, and even relocating arms.[36]

Che then told Hilda that he wanted to go to Mexico, where they could marry, and then go to China. According to her, Che said that 'we would one day meet again in Mexico and marry'. But she wanted to return to Peru – or go to his family in Buenos Aires. A few days later, she stopped visiting Che in the embassy, and he learned she'd been arrested. The first question the police asked her was whether she knew where Che was; clearly, he'd already made his revolutionary views and actions known to the authorities. Although she said they should enquire at the Argentine embassy, she refused to give a description of him, or identify him in the photos in her possession. Her possessions were then confiscated and she was imprisoned. When Che found out, he wanted to give himself up in order to secure her release, but the embassy's chargé d'affaires, and the other refugees, convinced him that the police would merely imprison him and not release her. Gadea was eventually released and given a safe conduct out of the country.[37]

Meanwhile, Che – who'd received clothes and money from his family – refused to return to Argentina, despite suffering from several asthma attacks. Though he frequently played chess, being cooped up left him bored. To relieve the boredom, he made notes about his companions, often making perceptive assessments on whether they'd a good understanding of Marxism; realised 'the only ideal path for the working class is Communism'; and whether they'd be good militants or activists. But some of his comments also showed some typical Latin American 'macho' prejudice against members of the LGBT+ community. Although he thought a Guatemalan photographer and dancer 'would be in there when the time came for action', he also noted that 'he has virtually none of the effeminate characteristics of a ballet dancer'. He was particularly impressed by Ricardo Ramírez who, in the 1960s, went on to be the leader of a Marxist guerrilla force in Guatemala. However, one judgement – concerning the Peruvian Hugo Blanco (described by Che as a 'young poet') – was way off the mark. Although Che felt he was not 'an intelligent person', Blanco went on to become a Trotskyist and a 'legendary figure' in the struggles of workers, peasants and Indigenous peoples, and his later support for ecosocialism. Though nine years later – in an interview Che gave in Algiers on 23 July 1963 (later reprinted in the US Trotskyists' paper) – he significantly revised that initial judgement, commenting on Blanco's arrest and possible execution, as a result of his leadership of a peasant-based guerrilla group in Peru, saying: 'He struggled stubbornly but the repression was strong ... Hugo Blanco has set an example, a good example, and he struggled as much as he could.' Some have even called Blanco 'the Che of Peru'.[38]

After the Communist leader Victor Gutírrez managed to get into the embassy, Che – along with twelve others who were seen as 'troublesome Communists' – were confined to the embassy garage; this group became known as the 'Group of Thirteen'. Che eventually asked for a safe conduct to Mexico, where Árbenz and many other refugees had already fled. However, Che's position – and that of the other asylum-seekers – was more perilous than they realised. US Secretary Dulles tried to force Armas to go after the estimated 700 asylum-seekers, as he 'feared that they might "recirculate" throughout the hemisphere if they were allowed to leave Guatemala'. Which is precisely what many did eventually do – often assisted by Che and the Cuban government after the victory of the Cuban Revolution in 1959. As regards Che himself, the CIA soon opened a file on him, because of his earlier attempt to organise resistance against the US-backed coup. Eventually, that file became one of the thickest in the CIA's records. Fortunately for Che – and the others – Armas refused to break international law; and, despite US disapproval, from mid-August began issuing many more safe-conducts to the embassy refugees.[39]

In late August, while still waiting for his safe-conduct pass and visa, Che left the embassy to find Gadea. He also visited Lake Atitlán – which, despite being the deepest lake in Central America, didn't impress him – and then returned to Guatemala City. In a letter to Tita, Che mentions an outing with Gadea, to San Juan Sacatepéquez – where there were 'a lot of passionate embraces and a little quickie'. Gadea later said about their recent experiences that 'in trying to defend the goals of the Guatemalan people we had become closer than ever'. More significantly for Che's future, she says they had 'concluded that the right way for a revolution to maintain national sovereignty, free of the influence of imperialism, would be for it to arm the people to defend their gains'.[40]

On a personal level, Che told her that 'in Mexico we will get married. Have no doubt about it.' Gadea – still intent on returning to Peru – said she was surprised by the strength of his conviction. According to Luther, though, Che expressed 'little dismay over leaving her', while according to Anderson (who saw the diary before it had been revised by Che's widow) he went on to say 'I believe I'll take advantage of the fact that she can't leave yet to split indefinitely.' A few days later, in mid-September, she waved goodbye to Che, as he left by train for Mexico – accompanied by a young Guatemalan called Julio 'El Pajoto' Cáceres.[41]

On her return to the house where she'd been staying, Gadea was once again arrested – and told that she was being deported to Mexico. An interesting insight into Che's politics by then was provided by Dr Alfonso Bauer Paiz in October 1977. In 1954, Bauer – in charge of Guatemala's Agrarian Bank, and a friend of Gadea's – had had a long discussion with Che about politics. He felt Che's politics was a mixture of Marxism and populism – something Che's father disputed – and then commented: 'How could I have imagined that evening ... that that young man, Ernesto Che Guevara, Che, would become the Heroic Guerrilla.' The two years Che would now spend in Mexico would see him commit to becoming just such a 'Heroic Guerrilla'.[42]

Chapter 5

Committing to Revolution, 1954–56

'I met him [Fidel Castro] on one of those cold Mexican nights, and I remember that our first discussion was about international politics. Within a few hours – by dawn – I was one of the future expeditionaries.'[1]

Che's political experiences in Guatemala had seen him move from being a rather detached observer with a social conscience, into someone adopting a firmer revolutionary position. In a letter to Tita, dated 29 September 1954, and sent from Mexico, he said how wrong it was for 'one of the best poets in Mexico' to blame the Communists for what had happened in Guatemala. For Che, the blame for the coup lay firmly with those 'who paid for the aircraft and who placed the puppet they now have' – i.e. Yankee imperialism. During his two years in Mexico – a safe haven for political refugees – he read extensively on Marxism and 'books dealing with military strategy in the Spanish Civil War' – eventually making a total commitment to bringing about a revolution in one of Latin America's countries. His youngest brother noted how, during this period, his letters now became 'more aggressive, angrier than before'. Nonetheless, Che also affirmed to Tita that his romantic aspirations for travel hadn't changed, and that his 'immediate goal' was 'Europe and then Asia'.[2]

Arriving in Mexico

Che arrived in Mexico City in mid-September 1954 – a cosmopolitan city which in the 1930s had welcomed the world's most famous political refugee, Leon Trotsky. In the 1950s, like Guatemala under Árbenz, Mexico City had become a refuge for political exiles from countries across Latin America. As well as those newly arrived from Guatemala, there were many from Cuba. These political exiles mostly lived in the same neighbourhoods, frequently meeting up in the same bars and cafés.

Because he only had a visitor's visa, he once again experienced problems in finding work. However, he soon established contacts among the exiled communities – including with Helena de Holst, now also a political exile – and initially began raising some much-needed cash by working as a nightwatchman, a street photographer, and as an occasional reporter for the Mexican office of the Argentine News Agency, *Agency Latina de Noticias.* Towards the end of September, Che also visited the Aztec pyramids of Teotihuacán, one of Mexico's important archaeological sites. Later, continuing his usual habit, he visited the Museum of Mexican Art, where he was interested in 'the displays of archaic culture'.[3]

Che and Gadea were not reunited until late October, as she'd had a more difficult journey. She quickly obtained full political asylum, thus there were no obstacles to her finding employment. However, their reunion was not a particularly happy one. According to her, Che once again raised the question of marriage, while she wanted to put it off until she could find a job. This 'created a certain tension', with Che saying 'we would just be friends'. This reveals yet another discrepancy between Che's diaries and Gadea's own account: Che's journal made no mention of his proposal, and simply noted that: 'Hilda and I seem to have reached a status quo – we shall see.'[4]

Nonetheless, despite apparently reverting to a platonic relationship, they saw each other regularly over the following months, spending much time discussing their experiences of, and thoughts about, what had happened in Guatemala. One area of agreement was that, by then, both were convinced of the USA's negative, anti-democratic influence across the continent. In the meantime, Che eventually found some low-paid work as an assistant in the allergy ward of Mexico City's General Hospital – and then got a scholarship to carry out research in another hospital.

Che's 'terrible struggle'

Che soon told Gadea that he'd already made contact with the Cuban revolutionary 'Ñico' López, whom they'd first met in Guatemala. From López, he learned that Fidel and Raúl Castro – about to be released from Batista's jails – were expected to join them soon. Despite predicting that the US coup in Guatemala would be merely the first of the global struggles between US imperialism and revolutionary socialist movements and countries, Che hadn't yet committed to getting involved with the Cuban revolutionaries. At this time, Che's growing revolutionary commitment was still in competition with the romance of global travel.

This uncertainty is revealed in letters to his mother in the autumn of 1954, which 'betrayed a certain discomfort. He seemed torn between two contradictory impulses: to engage in struggle, or to continue wandering.' On 10 October, Che wrote: 'I'm an incorrigible vagabond ... My faith in the ultimate triumph of what I believe in is total; however, I don't yet know if I will be an actor in it, or a mere spectator interested in the action.' A month later, he indicated he was still thinking of moving on to Europe – including visiting the countries of the Soviet bloc. He even thought of going to New York – though he was convinced he'd still leave as a strong opponent of Yankee imperialism. He also expressed his admiration for the Guatemalan communists – and had earlier expressed the desire to visit Communist China. He then speculated that he would probably eventually end up joining a communist party, but probably not until he'd travelled to Europe, as he would not be able to travel 'if [he] was subject to rigid discipline'.[5]

A letter to Tita, on 29 November, also showed this uncertainty – and a fair amount of self-criticism. After mentioning the possibility of joining the political struggle in Argentina, he adds: 'I have this terrible struggle between chastity (there) and desire (above all to wander around Europe).' His brother summarised this dilemma as: 'To discover the world or change it, to live his life or sacrifice it, these were the fundamental questions that tormented him.' In the end, he chose to fight to change the world, and would die for his beliefs.[6]

Yet after only a short time in Mexico, Che's dilemma was eventually resolved by evidence he saw of the pernicious influence of the US. In a letter to his mother, at the end of 1954, he explained his growing attraction to Marxism: 'The manner in which the gringos treat the American continent (remember that the gringos are Yankees) aroused my growing indignation, but at the same time I studied the theoretical explanation for what they do and found that it was scientific.' In early 1955, Che tried to persuade his father – who remained opposed to Perón – that USA moves against him should be resisted. While in a letter to Tita, dated 10 April 1955, he referred to the US as the 'Blond Octopus', and wrote about how Nixon's visits to Latin America intended to conclude unfair trade deals to help fund the USA's ability to wage 'new Koreas'. On 9 April, he'd written to his favourite aunt, calling himself 'a Red', and signing off as 'Stalin II'. Nonetheless, a poem he wrote while in Mexico reveals he was still split between travel and political commitment: with Europe calling him with 'a whiff of pale flesh, of art treasures', while also increasingly feeling the 'the soft impact of the song of Marx and Engels'.[7]

The marriage question

Meanwhile, Che and Gadea grew closer together and, according to Anderson, towards the end of December 1954 – despite some ups and downs – they had once again become lovers, though the original diary has Che saying he needed her for 'the occasional loan' – and to satisfy his 'urgent need for a woman who will fuck'. On New Year's Eve, however, there was a serious disagreement when Che said he couldn't go with her to a party, but would be working instead.

Gadea was understandably hurt and felt he was treating her very indifferently. She 'firmly resolved to break' with him – and spent the night dancing with a Venezuelan who asked her to go out with him next day. Che merely noted in his journal: 'As always, Hilda got angry because I didn't want to go with her to a party: I spent New Year's Eve on watch at the OAS building.' Later on, he wrote: 'I think I have broken with Hilda for good after a melodramatic scene. I've started to fancy a girl who's a chemist: ... she has very appealing freshness and fantastic eyes.'[8]

Yet, early on New Year's Day, Che asked Gadea to go on a trip to Toluca – all Gadea's 'resentment of the previous day evaporated' and they made up. Later, on 20 January 1955, Che gave her a poetry book – one of his favourites – as a late New Year present, which according to her, he inscribed as follows: 'To Hilda, so that on the day we part the substance of my hopes for the future and my predestined struggle will remain with you.' Again, she insists it was Che who kept bringing up the question of getting married, and that she continued to resist. Anderson, however, says she offered to marry and support him, but he refused – writing in his diary: 'We should stay as little lovers until I beat it to hell.' Either way, in May 1955, they began making plans to get married. As they were not Mexican citizens, and were even different nationalities, administrative problems emerged regarding obtaining official permission. They decided to live together until they could get the necessary permission, renting a small flat in one of the areas where other political exiles were also living. In mid-May, to consecrate their commitment, they made a weekend trip to the resort of Cuernavaca, and began exploring ancient sites around Mexico City. Soon, according to Che in a letter to his mother on 17 June 1955, they'd settled into a 'monotonous Sunday rhythm'.[9]

Despite that monotony, Che continued his love of arduous and risky physical adventure. With his Cuban friends, he made several attempts to climb Mt. Popocatépetl, a volcano 17,800ft above sea level – described by Che as 'the tonsils of Pacha Mama' (the Incas' 'Mother Earth'). Despite causing real problems for his asthma-weakened lungs, Che's 'mind-over-matter' approach meant he kept up with the others and reached the lower-lip of the crater. In a letter to his father, 20 July 1955, he reveals they climbed in snow – struggling 'for six hours in a blizzard that buried us to the groin with each step we took'. This letter mentioned, for the first time, the presence of Cubans on the climb – his father concluding that 'these climbs were no mere sport, but the physical exercise required to stay agile and strong' for guerrilla warfare. Che reported that his face and neck were burned 'as if I had spent an entire day in the sun in Mar del Plata'. Though his competitive spirit meant he was annoyed that 'an old man of fifty-nine climbed with us ... and climbed like a goat'.[10]

Cuba beckons

Meanwhile, in May 1955, the Castro brothers and eighteen other rebels had been released. Straightaway, Castro secretly formed the 26 July Movement (M26J) – named after the date of their attack on the Moncada Barracks in 1953 – and began recruiting members. One evening in late June, Che brought Raúl Castro (who'd arrived in Mexico City on 24 June) back to their flat. Che had already been introduced to him by López – or possibly by Gadea, who 'moved with ease in circles of political exiles'. Gadea later wrote how 'his ideas were very clear as to how the revolution was to be made', and that he 'had great faith in Fidel … because of his political leadership'. Significantly, Che and Raúl – who was three years younger than Che, and had joined the Cuban Communist Party's youth section at Havana University – began to see each other almost every day from then on, becoming inseparable. As Gadea observed: Raúl had communist ideas, was clearly an admirer of the Soviet Union – and believed the struggle against imperialism was relevant for all of Latin America.[11]

Raúl's ideas on revolution appealed to Che: the need for armed struggle that was closely allied with the support of the people. This last was essential if the revolution was to succeed, given that the US always reacted militarily to topple any elected governments that tried to introduce 'communist' reforms. These two young men thus believed that the struggle to achieve socialism in Cuba – and elsewhere in Latin America – would have to be done in the face of opposition from Yankee imperialism. As early as 27 May 1955 (before he'd met Castro) in a letter to his father, Che made cryptic comments about his political plans: 'I am waiting for some recommendation to march to the fields where dawn is maturing. Havana in particular attracts my attention to fill my heart with landscapes well interspersed with quotes from Lenin.'[12]

Around this time – through Raúl – Che also met Nikolai Leonov, an official of the Soviet Union's Foreign Ministry. Che showed a real interest in finding out about life in the Soviet Union, so Leonov gave him some books and pamphlets, while Che joined the Russian-Mexican Cultural Relations Institute. Leonov would meet Che again several years later.

Following Fidel

On 7 July 1955, Fidel Castro eventually arrived in Mexico – with Che meeting him for the first time a few days later, in the home of Gadea's friend Maria Antonia, a Cuban married to a Mexican. When Gadea asked him why he was in Mexico, Castro made it clear that they'd only come to Mexico to organise and train a group of fighters that would urge the Cuban people to rise up and overthrow Batista's US-supported and corrupt dictatorship. The group ended up talking for almost ten hours through the night – for a time, Che and the Castro brothers went to a near-by restaurant. They mostly talked about Latin American and international politics, in particular of Che's experiences in Guatemala, and Castro's plans for Cuba.

Castro believed that Latin America countries should – and could – achieve real independence from US imperialism. At last, Che had solved his conflicting desires: there would be no more 'procrastination or dilemmas. He had at last found his vocation.' Castro later said that he asked Che that very night to join their movement as their field doctor: 'in a matter of minutes Che decided to join [our] small group of Cubans'. Gadea noted that Che began to see that by aiding the Cuban Revolution – which both Castro brothers had so much faith in – he'd also be struggling against the imperialist tentacles of the capitalist octopus.[13]

In his journal, Che described Castro as 'a young, intelligent, guy, very sure of himself and extraordinarily audacious: I think we hit it off very well.' According to Gadea, Che later told her that López 'was right in Guatemala when he told us that if Cuba had produced anything good since Martí it was Fidel Castro. He will make the revolution. We are in complete agreement ... I could only fully support someone like him.' However, at this time, Castro – unlike both Che and Raúl – despite being strongly opposed to US imperialism, was not a communist. His aim was to replace Batista's dictatorship with a democratic constitution, and to carry out certain radical reforms in Cuba, while trying not to antagonise the US.[14]

Nonetheless, from then on, Che and Castro began meeting regularly, three to four times a week. Significantly for Che, Castro made it clear that 'The struggle in Cuba was part of the continental fight against the Yankees, a fight that Bolívar and Martí had foreseen.' Castro was soon aware that Che shared that outlook. On 18 October 1967, when delivering his eulogy for Che, Castro said that when he met Che in Mexico, 'he was filled with a profound spirit of hatred and loathing for imperialism' – in part because of what he'd witnessed in Guatemala.

Gadea, too, became convinced that Castro would succeed – and even asked Che if Castro would take women fighters. It soon became clear that Che was asking her, in a roundabout way, whether she thought he ought to join this Cuban invasion force. When she gave her approval – even though it would mean their separation – Che then revealed he'd already agreed to go along with them as their doctor, one of the very few non-Cubans Castro was prepared to accept. However, a few days later, Gadea realised she was pregnant and told Che, who was pleased and said they should push ahead with their marriage and inform their respective parents. According to his brother, Che wrote to say the proposal was 'a gesture of absurd chivalry' after he'd 'overdone the tequila'.[15]

Married at last

By then, however, the US was interested in the Cuban exiles in Mexico: the FBI – as well as Batista's agents – were watching the Cuban revolutionaries. Thus meetings had to be kept as secret as possible, in case they were arrested or even imprisoned. On 26 July, after a ceremony to mark the second anniversary of the Moncada attack, Castro organised a large dinner party – for which he cooked. Che was quiet, which prompted Castro to ask whether it was because Gadea – 'his controller' – was there. But it was much more likely because of the difference in personalities between Che and Castro. As Gadea commented, Che was always quiet in large groups, preferring smaller ones. However, Anderson suggests his quietness was because he was pondering his personal dilemma as regards marrying Gadea. According to him, the original journal shows he didn't believe it would be a long marriage: 'I am going to have a child and I will marry Hilda in a few days ... In the end, she gets her way – the way I see it, for a short while, although she hopes it will be lifelong.'[16]

Initially, the marriage was to take place in the Argentine embassy; but Che then changed the plan. Instead, on 18 August 1955, they were married in a civil registrar's office in the town of Tepotzotlan, just outside Mexico City. Raúl was among those present, but didn't sign; while Castro didn't even attend, as he already suspected – correctly – that he was under surveillance. Back in their new flat, Che prepared an Argentine-style roast dinner, which Castro attended. Over the next few days, family and friends were informed – with Gadea's parents sending some much-needed money. Che dictated a 'thank-you' letter, and hinted that their plans were quite fluid, as their 'wandering life' clearly wasn't over yet. Cuba, France, or possibly Peru or Argentina, were on the cards – or even India and China, 'depending on Hilda's ability to travel around'. The letter also claimed that, as both of them worked long hours, their home was 'a free association between two equals'. It also stated that their kitchen was a mess – which was what he was used to from his mother: 'So a sloppy house, mediocre food, and a salty mate, if she's a true companion, is all I want from life.' Yet Che's letter to his parents, dated 24 September 1955, was very low-key about the marriage – giving the news in the final short paragraph of his letter.[17]

However, even at this stage – in that same letter to his mother – Che also wrote of his continuing uncertainly: 'Perhaps [a] bullet will put an end to my days ... Perhaps I'll simply keep wandering long enough to complete a solid education ... before seriously devoting myself to the pursuit of my ideal.' Nonetheless, Che's growing belief in the need for revolution is shown by a poem he wrote after one of his poor elderly patients – suffering from asthma – died. In the poem – 'Old Maria, You're Going To Die' – Maria had become 'the old woman in Valparaiso [Chile], the fugitive couple in Chuquicamata [Bolivia], and the browbeaten Indians of Peru' – yet another representative of the poor downtrodden masses of Latin America, exploited by Yankee imperialism.[18]

In mid-November, Che and Gadea went on a delayed week's honeymoon in Chiapas and the Yucatán peninsular to see the Maya ruins. As they travelled south to the Maya temples at Palenque, the tropical climate brought on several severe asthma attacks. When Gadea offered to give him an injection, it led to a row, and she later wrote that: 'I realized that he didn't want to feel protected, to be helped when he was sick. I kept quiet in the face of his brusqueness, but I was hurt.' Yet, despite his asthma, Che urged her to climb up and down the many Maya ruins and temples in the area, while Che also took photos and recited poetry. He seemed oblivious to her pregnancy – and there was another row when, on the last temple, she stopped half-way from tiredness and refused to go further. This perhaps accounts for the photograph of them which shows her looking somewhat sulky. She herself wrote: 'Tired and impatient from the heat, I ended up feeling and looking thoroughly cross.' Although she later wrote of the honeymoon that they'd been 'fifteen unforgettable days of travel, with immense satisfaction in each other's company at all times', Che's journal has six pages of notes on what interested him archaeologically; but, perhaps significantly, has no mention of her: he even described the trip, not as his honeymoon, but as being his 'much-awaited farewell trip around the south-east of Mexico'.[19]

Preparing for armed struggle

Castro had quickly set up a network to raise money for weapons, and establish 'safe houses'. In Mexico, it was often women who made their homes available for meetings. In late November, he briefly left Mexico for the US on a speaking and fund-raising tour, returning just before Christmas. On Christmas Eve, Che and Gadea attended a traditional Cuban dinner, once again cooked by Castro, who spoke about what projects they would carry out in Cuba, once their revolution had succeeded in overthrowing Batista. According to Gadea, he 'spoke with such certainty and ease that one had the feeling we were already in Cuba, carrying out the process of construction'. She was as excited as Che; though, perhaps for the first time, she realised Che still fully intended to go with the Cubans to help these plans succeed. Thus she would have to see her new husband, and the father of their soon-to-be-born child, leave her to go on a very risky 'adventure'. She wrote: 'For me the challenge was terribly painful: to be separated from [Che],' Nonetheless, she agreed with their plans to begin guerrilla warfare in Cuba, seeing that as 'the first stage in the liberation' of Latin America.[20]

The Cuban revolutionaries also obtained the services of Colonel Alberto Bayo, a Cuban then aged 63, who – brought up in Spain – had served as an officer in the Republican Army during the Spanish Civil War. There, he'd gained experience in guerrilla warfare – and lost an eye! He was soon known as the 'Old Man'. Towards the end of 1955, Che's meetings with the Cuban revolutionaries became more frequent – often at his and Gadea's flat. Castro even arranged for all his post from Cuba and the US to be sent there, addressed to Gadea under her maiden name. In order to get fit for the struggle, Che started eating lightly – though, in fact, his diet of meat, salad and fruit was his favourite diet, and was part of the way he tried to control his asthma. He also continued his mountain climbing. In the second week of October, he made his third attempt to climb Popocatépetl: this time finally reaching the summit after a climb of nearly seven hours – though returning with frozen feet. They also attempted to climb the Ixtacihuatl volcano, near to Popocatépetl. On 15 December, he wrote to his aunt, mentioning these further climbing exploits. There were several failures to get to the top – sometimes losing the route because of snow – before they finally reached the summit.[21]

Although he told his parents he'd been offered a lectureship in physiology at the National University of Mexico, he told them later that he'd never had any intention of accepting it. As well as turning it down, he had even given up his allergy research. Now a 'devoted convert' of 'St Charles' [Marx], he used his free time to join the Cubans in a gym, where they practised judo, wrestling and karate, in preparation for unarmed combat. His innate self-discipline and competitiveness meant he refused to allow his asthma attacks to stop him from keeping up with, and even exceeding, his Cuban friends. Che – probably mistakenly – seems to have assumed they were not aware of his frequent need to use inhalers. Bayo also instructed them on aspects of guerrilla warfare, and, in February 1956, hired a firing range – Che was among those selected by him for this. They also undertook long walks around Mexico City's streets, and demanding hikes up the heights in the city's suburbs – with instructions to climb backwards and sideways, in order to strengthen all their legs muscles. They also continued mountain climbing.[22]

Che also started reading extensively about, and making copious notes on, economics – in particular, works by Marx, Engels, Lenin and Mao. Some of these were borrowed from the Russian-Mexican Cultural Institute. He then had serious discussions with Gadea who, as an economist, had read most of the books he was now reading. On his request, she also taught him to type. In order to deepen his understanding of Marxism even further, he also began attending meetings of the Mexican Communist Party. Interestingly, in view of Che's later exploits once the Cuban Revolution had succeeded, she too realised that the liberation of Latin America would mean that 'the struggle would have to be continued in the other countries' if the 'fight against Yankee imperialism' was going to succeed.[23]

Che the father

On 14 February 1956, Che and Gadea had moved into a larger flat; and, the following day, Gadea gave birth to a girl – with Che present, and saying 'She makes me happy twice over.' Their daughter, Hilda Beatriz, was named in honour of Gadea and Che's favourite aunt – it having been agreed that if the child was a boy, Gadea would choose the name and, if it was a girl, Che would choose. Though in later letters to his mother, he said she was 'rather ugly', he also said he was 'very happy with her, my Communist soul swells with pride as she is identical to Mao Tse-Tung'. Their first visitor in the hospital was Castro, who said: 'This girl is going to be educated in Cuba' – with such conviction that Gadea 'felt sure it would happen'. Che proved a doting father, rushing home to play with 'Hildita', as she was soon called. When Gadea came down with a feverish cold, Che stayed home to look after his daughter and wife. During this period, they read many books about the Chinese Revolution (then only seven years old) and other wars of liberation – with both concluding that guerrilla warfare was probably the best method for bringing about revolution in Latin America.[24]

Yet in a letter to a friend, he revealed that, despite his great pleasure in being a father, Hildita's birth had only 'reinforced his inability to live with her mother'. In late October, in a letter to Tita, he makes it clear that their marriage is nearly over:

> my married life is almost totally at an end and … this will become final next month when my wife leaves for Peru to visit her family … There is a certain bitter taste in this break-up because she was a loyal *compañera* and her revolutionary behaviour was beyond reproach during my enforced holiday.

He concluded by blaming this on his 'anarchic spirit that leads me to dream of other horizons', – making reference to Neruda's poem 'A Song of Despair', which contains these telling lines: 'Ah! Woman I do not know how you could contain me in the earth of your soul, in the cross of your arms.' In the final paragraph of this journal, Che noted that his 'plans for the future are pretty vague', and thought 1956 'may be an important year for my future'.[25]

Military training in earnest

On 17 March 1956, Che's determination and commitment was noted by their shooting instructor: 'excellent shooter ... Excellent discipline, excellent leadership abilities, physical endurance excellent.' Che's esteem among the Cubans thus increased, and he was made leader of one of their safe houses. However, Che occasionally felt his nationality was a problem – and some of the Cubans did have reservations about him, referring to him as 'El Argentino' rather than 'Che'. Castro, though, made it clear that, because Che was prepared to risk his life to liberate Cuba, such tensions were unwarranted.[26]

In April 1956, Colonel Bayo had identified a large *hacienda* – the Rancho San Miguel – as a guerrilla training base for the Cubans. This was located about thirty-five miles east of Mexico City, in the mountainous Chalco region – and Che had played the role of a wealthy colonel wanting to buy the ranch. As some alterations were needed, he offered to rent the ranch, at just $8 per month, until these were completed. Once agreed, it became a secret military training camp for eighty recruits. Che was one of those recruits; before too long, he'd been singled out as 'the best guerrilla of them all' by Bayo, who made him 'chief of personnel'. Bayo was also a good chess player – Che later told Gadea that 'We had some memorable games when we finished working. At first the Old Man didn't want to admit that I could beat him. He plays very well – really the only good adversary I've had in a long time.'[27]

In late May 1956, Che moved to the ranch semi-permanently – and was amused by the Cubans, who tried to maintain their urban smartness by bathing every day and changing their clothes. As he commented in a note to Gadea: 'That's fine, but what will they do in the hills? I doubt we'll ever be able to take a bath or change clothes.' Thus, when they formed rudimentary camps in the hilly countryside, and went on long night-time marches, Che's earlier reputation for poor personal hygiene meant he coped better than many of the others when they had to go days without washing. He also began to get a reputation for being a strict disciplinarian – though he never asked others to do what he didn't also do. Che only came home at weekends – and then, in late May, he informed Gadea that they were going 'somewhere' to do some field training – from where they might then depart for Cuba.[28]

By early June 1956, the bulk of their training was complete, and Castro was anxious to launch his revolution – partly because there were growing signs of revolt in Cuba; and partly because he'd said his action would begin on 26 July, the third anniversary of the Moncada attack. While at the ranch, Che continued to read extensively about Marxism in general, political theory and economics, and the problems of Latin America. For him, it wouldn't be enough to depose Batista:

he wanted to help bring about a socialist revolution. However, six days after Che's twenty-eighth birthday, Gadea was alarmed to read a report that Castro and four of his Cuban recruits had been arrested on 20 June 1956 – ostensibly because their immigration papers were not in order. Within a matter of days, most of the safe houses were raided, documents were seized, and almost all of the Cubans were arrested. They were accused of plotting Batista's assassination, in collusion with Cuban and Mexican Communists – and Batista demanded their extradition. Castro speedily denied any communist connections.

Gadea quickly gathered together all incriminating letters and papers in their flat, and left them with a friend – just in time, as she was soon visited by two men who said she had received a 'compromising' telegram. In the end, because she was nursing 4-month-old Hildita, she wasn't taken to a police station. She then rapidly got a message out to the Cubans that she was being watched by the police. Later, though – along with Hildita – she was taken to the federal police offices, and interrogated about the telegram and Che's whereabouts. It quickly emerged the police were wanting to establish that Che and the Cubans were communists. According to Gadea, she felt one of the interrogators was a CIA or FBI agent. After failing to get the information they wanted, she was taken back to her flat, with two police officers staying with them all night. The following morning, she was again taken for interrogation. She was taken to see Castro, who advised her to tell the police what they wanted to know, saying: 'I can't let you and the baby go through these discomforts and dangers.' She thus signed the statement the police wanted, and was released.[29]

Che wasn't arrested at first, however, and stayed at the ranch while Bayo and Raúl went into hiding. It later emerged that Mexico's President, Lazaro Cardenas – the one who'd given asylum to Trotsky – had intervened on Castro's behalf, and, in order to avoid a battle, agreed to take the police to the ranch where Che and the others were hiding. When they arrived, on 24 June, it emerged that Raúl and about half the group had already left – after hiding the weapons. Che was then arrested – along with twelve others – and taken to the Miguel Schultz Immigration Detention Centre in Mexico City. They were then imprisoned and interrogated.

Initially, Che only volunteered information he thought the authorities already knew. Soon, however, the main Mexican daily reported that Mexico's security police saw '"the Argentine doctor Ernesto Guevara Serna" as "the principal link between the Cuban plotters and certain Communist organizations of an international nature"'. Some of those detained were tortured to extract information – Che and Castro were not. In addition, some of the newspapers mentioned Che's membership of the Russian-Mexican Cultural Relations Institute – and that the police had found a card belonging to Nikolai Leonov; as a result, Leonov was quickly recalled to Moscow. All this was much to Castro's consternation, who didn't want the US to see his movement as a communist one. In the end, though, the authorities simply charged them with not having the right immigration papers.[30]

When Gadea visited Che, he told her he was certain the FBI were behind all these arrests, and that they were acting on behalf of Batista: 'It's those Yankee *hijos de la chingada*, sons of bitches, as they say who are behind this whole affair.' After several weeks of detention, Che joined the others in a protest hunger strike. After only a few days, beginning on 9 July, all but three of the twenty-three who'd been arrested were released over several days. The three who remained in detention included Che, apparently because his immigration papers were not in order. Typically, when questioned further, Che was the only one to admit to the aim of overthrowing Batista's dictatorship. He also proudly acknowledged his communist beliefs, and his determination to engage in armed struggle in order to liberate the whole of Latin America, once Cuba had been freed. When questioned, he stated his ideology was unreservedly 'Marxist-Leninist' – which wasn't appreciated by Castro, who emphatically denied any communist links.[31]

During his detention, Che wrote to his family and revealed just how involved he was with the Cubans. On 6 July 1956, he told them how he'd been asked to join 'a movement for the armed liberation of Cuba, and that he'd accepted: 'I must tell you that my future is linked to the Cuban Revolution. Either I succeed with it or I die there,' The letter closed with a line by one of his favourite poets, the revolutionary Turkish poet, Nâzim Hikmet: 'I will take to the grave only the sorrow of an unfinished song.' On 15 July 1956, he revealed his current positions to his mother: 'During these prison days and the period of training that preceded them, I have identified totally with my comrades in the cause.' He also confirmed his 'Communist morality', and asserted how 'the revolution requires passion and audacity in large doses' – not the moderation which his mother had tried to counsel him on in a previous letter.[32]

What is really significant about this letter is that, after sympathising with her current 'bad depression', towards the end, he makes it clear that he would not betray his 'sacred flame'; and how a conventional career, 'shut up in some bureaucratic office or allergy clinic', would be the death of him. He also said that, once the Cuban Revolution has triumphed, he would move elsewhere to combat Yankee imperialism: 'Moreover … after I have set wrongs [right] in Cuba, I'll go somewhere else.' While in another letter to his family, he wrote: 'I will triumph with it [the Cuban revolution] or I will die in the attempt … From now on, I will not consider my death as any kind of frustration.' Just over eleven years later, his commitment to revolutionary internationalism would see him captured and shot in cold blood in Bolivia, after having already fought against US imperialism in the Congo.[33]

Castro was finally released on 24 July – but told to leave Mexico as soon as possible. Che, however, remained in prison, although Castro made it clear to Che that he wouldn't launch his invasion until he was able to join him. Che's father then used his diplomatic connections to get him released – much to Che's annoyance, who wrote to his father, asking him to stop sending 'these undesirables', as he did not want to be released without his Cuban comrades. Castro informed Gadea that he would give the Mexican authorities 'a sum of money' to resolve those issues. In mid-August, after almost two months in detention, Che was finally released – with orders to leave Mexico within a few days. During his fifty-seven day detention, Gadea had regularly visited Che, and had brought their daughter along. She later wrote that she loved to see Che play with Hildita, whom he took to calling 'love's petal most profound' and that 'Che played for long periods of time with Hildita until she fell asleep'.[34]

By the time Che was released, Hildita was 6 months old. Yet, once back in their flat, Che told Gadea that he would only be able to spend brief periods with them, as he would have to go into hiding and finish his training. Initially, though, they spent three days together – with Che spending hours reciting poetry to their Hildita, or simply watching her. Thereafter, over the next three months, he occasionally slipped back, usually for just a few days, while Gadea paid visits to him whenever possible, bringing Hildita with her. During these visits, he continued to spend as much time looking after their daughter as possible. According to Gadea, he began to call her 'my little Mao'. On one occasion, he said to her: 'My dear daughter, my little Mao … When you grow up, this whole continent, and maybe the whole world, will be fighting against the great enemy, Yankee imperialism … I may not be here any more, but the struggle will inflame the continent.' The seriousness of the fast-approaching mission was underlined when the rebels were asked to provide contact details of those who should be informed of their deaths.[35]

Leavings

In late October, during what turned out to be Che's last weekend visit, they began making plans for a brief holiday in Acapulco. However, early on the Sunday morning, one of the Cubans came to say the police were on their trail – and that Che would have to leave immediately. Gadea was disconcerted, suspecting there was something Che wasn't telling her – but Che remained calm and tried to reassure her. After a parting kiss and embrace, he left, saying 'Sorry, but we'll have to leave our Acapulco trip until later.' That was the last time she saw him until after the triumph of the Cuban Revolution in January 1959 – by which time he was already in a relationship with the woman who would eventually become his second wife.[36]

For several days, Che stayed in a small servant's room in a flat belonging to Dr Alfonso Bauer Paiz, a Guatemalan and Arbenz supporter Che had met in 1954. Bauer, then in exile, had bumped into Che in Mexico City, when Che was taking photographs in Chapultepec Park. Bauer revealed later in an interview that Che, typically, had left without saying goodbye – leaving his bedroom 'in total chaos, the bed unmade ... his clothes all over the place and half a dozen books opened as if he had been reading them all at the same time'. These books included Lenin's *The State and Revolution* and Marx's *Capital* – along with a book written by Bauer, *How American Capital Operates in Central America*.[37]

In a letter to his mother – probably dated 15 November – he outlined his earlier hopes, which had included a 'life plan that included ten years of wandering' to be followed by medicine and then physics, and announcing Gadea's intention to take their daughter to spend New Year with her parents in Peru. He then made it clear that he has – at least for now – put aside visits to Europe and elsewhere. Instead: 'Now, when I get to a new country, it won't be to look around and visit museums or ruins, but also (because that still interests me) to join the people's struggle.' His first step to that goal was soon to be irrevocably taken.[38]

Since his release, Castro had been busy: some forty new recruits had arrived from Cuba, and he'd persuaded the Directorio Revolucionario (DR) to cooperate with his forces once they landed in Cuba. Also – possibly under Che's Marxist promptings – Castro now called on all Cuban parties, including the Cuban Communist Party, to support his rebellion. By late September, Castro had obtained around $50,000 during a secret trip to Texas. However, he was only able to obtain one boat for their 'invasion'. This was the *Granma*: an old, not very seaworthy, yacht – only capable of carrying twenty passengers. Nonetheless, this yacht would soon become one of the most famous boats in history. Once purchased, the yacht was overhauled so that it would be better able to survive the waters. Although Frank País – and the Cuban Communist Party – warned Castro that the Cuban people were not yet ready to rise up against Batista, Castro insisted that plans were made to begin armed uprisings to coincide with their landing in eastern Cuba.

On 23 November, Castro ordered the rebels to travel the next day to a town just south of Tuxpan, where the boat would be loaded up. Che was picked by some of the Cubans and taken to their destination. Finally, late at night on 25 November 1956, Che was one of eighty-two revolutionaries of the M26J who arrived to embark. Apart from the Castro brothers, the other Cubans included Camilo Cienfuegos, Juan Almeida and Ramiro Valdés. At just after midnight, the *Granma* – with all lights extinguished – slipped out into the Gulf of Mexico on what was assumed would be a five-day journey to Playa las Coloradas in Oriente province. A coded message was sent to País that 30 November would be the arrival date. In a 'farewell' letter to his mother, Che wrote that this letter would only reach her when 'things are really getting hot'. By then, he would be fighting 'in a sun-drenched land of the Americas … with our backs to the wall … until victory or death'. It ended: 'Again kisses, with all the affection of a farewell that refuses to be a final one.' His mother read this letter 'out loud in front of the whole family, with a serene and firm voice'. Thus Che began the journey that would, in the space of just a few years, turn him into the iconic global hero known to millions.[39]

Chapter 6

Becoming 'El Che', 1956–59

'The inhabitants will draw favourable or unfavourable conclusions about the guerrilla band according to the manner in which any service or food or other necessity is solicited and the methods used to get what is wanted.'[1]

The two years, from December 1956 to January 1959, were a real turning-point in Che's life, during which he laid the groundwork for the global legend he became. According to Sinclair, the Cuban war and his experiences with the peasants 'turned him into an "agrarian revolutionary"', and gave him 'a set of unorthodox and non-Marxist ideas about guerrilla groups as the new "flag-bearers" of the revolution'. Though this view of Che's politics has been challenged, he certainly quickly gained a reputation as a legendary guerrilla commander. This was based on two aspects: his strong willpower in overcoming his asthma in a humid, subtropical climate; and his personal – at times, reckless – bravery. On one occasion, when his comrades felt it too dangerous to rescue a seriously-wounded comrade, Che 'leaped out of the bushes', and despite being 'well within firing range of the enemy soldiers ... quickly lift[ed] up his wounded comrade, put him over his shoulder and disappear[ed] into the woods'. He was also the first to volunteer for dangerous missions.[2]

During those two years, as well as becoming a highly respected guerrilla fighter – and one of the leading figures in the M26J – Che also met Aleida March, the young woman who would become his second wife. At the time of their meeting, in the Escambray Mountains – which she described as 'incredibly beautiful and the ideal setting for enchantment' – she was already a seasoned M26J activist in its urban underground network. According to her, Che later told her that, from the first time he saw her, 'he felt torn between his role as a strictly disciplined revolutionary and as an ordinary man with emotional and other needs'. It was sometime, however, before they acknowledged and expressed their feelings for each other. Nonetheless, March would remain his close life-companion until his untimely death in Bolivia in 1967.[3]

A disastrous start

The start of Castro's invasion was a disaster. As well as eighty-two men being crammed on a boat meant for just twenty, they quickly encountered a choppy Caribbean Sea, with most of them being violently seasick – while Che, who had no medication with him, suffered an asthma attack. Because of leaks and an engine fault, their trip took two days longer than planned. On 30 November – their planned arrival date – they heard on the ship's radio that País had, as arranged, launched armed uprisings in Santiago de Cuba and elsewhere, but that Batista's troops were suppressing them. Castro's force finally landed just before dawn on 2 December 1956 – on a swampy mudflat over a mile away from the shore, and over a mile south-east of where they should have been.

After two hours struggling through the swamp, they finally reached the beach – but then came under attack from sea and air. It seemed Che – along with the entire Rebel Army – was destined to meet his end within hours of landing in Cuba. The rebels split up into two smaller groups, and began moving inland for the Sierra Maestra, Cuba's highest mountain range. However, on reaching Alegría de Pío on 5 December, the exhausted and hungry rebels found Batista's troops were waiting for them. Their first battle saw many rebels abandon their equipment and flee from the ambush – others were mown down before they could run from the onslaught.

Che – forced to chose between saving his medicine pack or a box of bullets – chose the ammunition. Che later commented: 'This might have been the first time I was faced, literally, with the dilemma of choosing between my devotion to medicine and my duty as a revolutionary soldier.' While, in a letter to his mother, he wrote: 'Either I'm a doctor, or I'm a fighter.' More immediately, Che suffered a neck wound from a ricochet. In shock, and covered in blood, he thought he was mortally wounded, and calmly prepared to die. He was snapped out of it by Juan Almeida, who shouted at him to grab his rifle and run. Che got up, applied pressure to the neck wound – which proved only superficial – and followed the fleeing rebels into the surrounding jungle. Some of this he revealed in a letter, dated 28 January 1957, to Gadea, putting his survival down to 'my cat's lives'.[4]

Not dead

Batista issued a statement claiming total victory, and reporting that Che – along with the Castro brothers – was among those killed. Argentinian newspapers reported on the fate of the 'revolutionary young Argentinian doctor', with one announcing: 'Among the dead in this combat was Dr Ernesto Guevara de la Serna.' Naturally, Che's parents were greatly distressed. When his father came in clutching the paper, his mother cried: '"Ernesto?" In a second, her face became livid … She jumped up, [and] tore the paper out his hands.' After days of anxiety, Argentina's embassy in Havana informed them that Che was not among the rebels killed or captured.[5]

They passed the good news on to Gadea, who was still in Mexico, but about to leave with Hildita for Peru. Nonetheless, some uncertainty remained until 31 December, when his mother received a handwritten note from Che – using his family nickname, 'Teté' – saying he was well: 'Dear *viejos*, I'm perfectly fine. I've only spent two and I still have seven [cat lives] left … I'm still doing the same job; news is and will continue to be sporadic … A big hug to all.' Then, just before midnight, a letter was pushed under their door; inside was a card with a red rose and the words 'Happy New Year. TT is perfectly well.' The Guevaras were thus able to really enjoy the New Year's Eve celebrations. There would be other 'premature' announcements of his death – but, whenever possible, Che sent messages to reassure them he was still alive.[6]

Gadea had received the news of Che's death at work, when a co-worker handed her a newspaper: 'I could not go on reading … It was one thing to be in favour of the expedition, and another to face the pain of loss. Now it was time for the pain.' When she began to make plans to return to Peru, she found that the announcement of Che's death meant the Mexican authorities initially refused to recognise the validity of the note he'd given her before leaving for Cuba, giving his paternal permission for Gadea to leave with their daughter. Eventually, the pair left for Lima on 17 December. Her parents were pleased to see their granddaughter – now aged 10 months – and her father was proud to have a son-in-law involved in such a revolutionary movement. On 6 January 1957, she visited Che's parents in Buenos Aires – where she quickly discovered that Che was clearly the family favourite. There, Gadea received a letter from Che, dated 28 January 1957 – addressing her as 'My dear old lady', and asking how she and Hildita – 'love's petal most profound' – were. He also asked her to send photos of herself and Hildita, ending with 'A big *abrazo* for you.' Although she sent the photos, it appears Che never received them.[7]

The 'Armed Struggle' begins

Back in Cuba, Castro's Rebel Army had been decimated – only around fifteen out of the original eighty-two rebels made it to the mountains. Among those killed was López, the Cuban who'd so impressed Che in Guatemala. For more than two weeks, Che and Almeida – the unofficial leaders of their group – and those with them, were under constant threat of new attacks, and had little water or food. Although many peasants helped them with directions, and even food and shelter, the rebels also risked betrayals from others.

Consequently, they hid in caves until nightfall, before continuing their journey. They were often forced to eat raw crabs and drink rainwater – sometimes they went days without eating. They often went in circles – mostly avoiding combat, but also coming under attack from the air. Finally, on 21 December, Che and the small band of rebels – having hid their weapons, and swapped their uniforms for peasant clothing, met up with the Castro brothers, and the rest of the survivors. Many of them – Che included – had abandoned most of their weapons along the way, leaving the entire group with only nine weapons. They were severely criticised – and Che suffered an asthma attack; several years later, he recalled Castro's 'bitter reproach' for abandoning their weapons.

Once in the mountains, Castro established links with the urban M26J revolutionaries, who soon began sending more weapons and volunteers to join the surviving rebels in the Sierra Maestra. Among the new recruits was Dariel 'Benigno' Alarcón – one of the few who would manage to survive Che's fatal guerrilla campaign in Bolivia in 1967. Castro had initially taken Che's pistol off him – giving him instead what Che felt was a 'bad rifle'. A few days later, however, Che was given a brand new rifle with telescopic sights, which Che described as 'a jewel'. Che was also pleased to be made part of Castro's five-man '*estado mayor*' (general staff).[8]

Though now numbering thirty-two, they were still short of weapons and ammunition. After days of inaction – which Che found frustrating – it was decided to attack the coastal military barracks at La Plata. So, in early January 1957, they began an arduous journey to get into position – though Che was frustrated when Castro decided not to attack a smaller garrison on the way. The Battle of La Plata – their first real battle – began on 16 January 1957, with Che in the group that attacked in the centre. It was a success, with the rebels gaining weapons and ammunition, along with food and clothing – without suffering any casualties.

After this victory, they fought other engagements. But the harsh conditions in the mountains meant Che was kept busy as their doctor, as many rebels were soon suffering from swamp fever and diarrhoea – while Che himself continued to experience frequent asthma attacks.

On 22 January, during this early period of Cuba's Revolutionary War, Che recorded the first time he killed an enemy soldier. His account of this significant moment, though, is surprisingly very matter-of-fact: 'The man had been struck full in the chest, the bullet probably piercing his heart, and his death had been instantaneous; he already showed the first signs of rigor mortis.' It was also during this early period that Che quickly became known for his bravery, and his willingness to take on the most dangerous missions. On 30 January, the guerrillas were forced to relocate, when their camp was bombed – with Che being the only one to stay long enough to usher stragglers to safety and to pick up weapons abandoned in the initial panic.[9]

Bloodthirsty killer?

Contrary to later claims that he was a bloodthirsty killer, Che seems to have had 'the greatest respect for life, opposing summary executions and pointless combat'. After the battle, he gave medical treatment to wounded enemy prisoners, who were then released. This was something he would do throughout Cuba's Revolutionary War – and something he stressed later in his book *Guerrilla Warfare*: 'Survivors ought to be set free. The wounded should be cared for with all possible resources at the time of action.' He believed their humane treatment of captured enemy soldiers helped them win the war: 'Not only did they kill our wounded, they abandoned their own. Over time this difference had an effect on the enemy and it was a factor in our victory.' He also wrote of the significance of that first battle: 'The effect was electrifying and travelled far beyond that rugged region. It was like a call to attention, proving that the Rebel Army did in fact exist and was disposed to fight.'[10]

However, he also began to acquire a reputation for hardness and ruthlessness when it came to discipline – a reputation which dogged him for years. He was severe on Batista's soldiers sent out dressed as peasants, in order to discover where the guerrillas were. Once, when three had been caught, he called for their execution – but Castro decided to send them back to their barracks with a warning.

He also often demanded death for spies and traitors, and approved Castro's decision, at the end of January 1957, that desertion would be a capital offence. The first such death sentence that Che carried out was of a peasant who'd acted as a guide, but had then betrayed them to the army. In late February 1957, Che and Castro began to be suspicious – then documents were found proving his guilt. Yet when Castro pronounced the death penalty, no Cuban was prepared to carry it out. To end this dilemma, Che stepped forward and shot him in the head. Che later described most of the incident in an article 'Death of a Traitor'. Although the article doesn't say who pulled the trigger, his private campaign diary shows it was him – he recorded the death, in a so-far unpublished section, in a very clinical way: 'I ended the problem giving him a shot with a .32 [-calibre] pistol in the right side of the brain, with exit orifice in the right temporal [lobe].' Yet the rebels, as promised, looked after his children, telling them that their father, though a traitor to the revolution, was brave and didn't ask for clemency.[11]

Further campaigns

On 25 February, the guerrillas suffered a surprise attack, forcing them deeper into the hills. Che then experienced what he later described as '10 of the most bitter days of the struggle'. During the retreat, he suffered one of his worst asthma attacks – he was too weak to continue. While waiting for medical supplies, Che and another guerrilla were forced to seek shelter for two days. They then moved slowly to rejoin the others – shown graphically in Part One of the 2008 film *Che*. Che's own account describes him 'walking, supporting myself from tree to tree or on the butt of my rifle for support, accompanied by a frightened *compañero* who ... became nervous each time my asthma made me cough in some dangerous spot'.[12]

Che eventually caught up with the others on 11 March 1957. On 17 March – having been promoted to captain – he guided a group of over fifty new recruits to join Castro's army. However, as Che had failed to maintain sufficient discipline over the recruits' leader, Castro did not give him a leadership role when he divided the rebels into three expanded platoons. Instead, Che remained as the general-staff doctor. When Raúl suggested making Che – an open Marxist – political commissar as well, Castro refused. Nonetheless, Che remained one of Castro's top eight men, and was involved in making plans for their next operations.

By April, Castro's Rebel Army numbered over seventy combatants; and their limited actions slowly began to attract support of local peasants – along with more recruits from the M26J's city supporters, and some members of other political groups. These latter included young recruits attracted by the 'romance' of adventure. Che was initially dismissive – though one of these teenagers, Roberto Rodríguez, went on to become the heroic 'Vaquerito' ('Little Cowboy') who would head Che's 'Suicide Squad'.

During quiet periods, Che gave medical consultations to the peasants; though he could do little for most of their problems, which were essentially down to poverty, malnutrition and over-work. This deepened his commitment to a thorough-going revolution to remove the root-causes of their ill-health. Such actions served to widen the base of support among the peasants, increasingly vital as their numbers grew. Despite his continuing medical work, and his recurrent asthma attacks, by May 1957 Che had been made a full-time combatant. Following delivery of new weapons, Che was given charge of one of three Madsen machine guns: 'In this way, I began as a full-time combatant, for until then I had been as the troop's doctor, only participating in occasional combat. I had entered a new stage.'[13]

On 28 May 1957, the rebels attacked the El Uvero army barracks – their largest battle so far. Although Che tended to play down his role in the Battle of Uvero, he showed exceptional bravery and leadership. At one point, after shooting a soldier, he crawled forward under a hail of bullets to capture his weapon. In addition, Che continued to show real concern for wounded enemy soldiers: 'So once again I had to swap my rifle for a doctor's coat, which really involved little more than a wash of my hands.' Che stayed with the injured men for almost three weeks, tending to their wounds. Che saw this battle as a key one for the Rebel Army: 'For us this victory also marked our coming of age' – the Rebel Army's morale 'grew tremendously, [and] our decisiveness and our hopes for triumph also grew. And although the months that followed were difficult, we already possessed the secret of victory.' According to him, after that battle, 'the relationship of forces in the Sierra Maestra began to shift greatly' in favour of the rebels.[14]

On 17 July, Castro – pleased with how Che had brought back the wounded, and had also attracted new recruits – put him in charge of seventy-five guerrillas. By then, the Rebel Army numbered around 200, had a more-plentiful supply of weapons, and a much-extended 'liberated' area. Che continued to enforce a strict discipline: usually insisting on the death penalty for deserters – especially those who joined forces with outlaws and, claiming to be part of Castro's Rebel Army, began to rob, rape and kill peasants. One such deserter was the man who'd earlier helped Che when he was suffering so badly from asthma in February. After deserting, he'd passed himself off as Che and had begun raping young peasant girls.

Political differences

During this first year of combat, Che's political differences with many M26J leaders began to emerge more clearly. Before too long, the M26J became divided between the 'Sierra' ('Mountain') guerrilla fighters and the 'Llano' ('Plain') urban network. On 17 February, Castro had been interviewed by Herbert Matthews of the *New York Times*. Che had been absent at the time – possibly deliberately so, given his open commitment to communism, and his well-established opposition to Yankee imperialism. When the interview was published at the end of February 1957, Che was unhappy that Castro had said he'd no ill-will towards the US, and that he wasn't a communist.

Che was present, however, when Castro met with the urban leaders of the M26J's National Directorate (ND). These included Frank País, Celia Sánchez (who soon became Castro's confidante and lover), and Vílma Espín (who later became Raúl's wife). Castro insisted that the Rebel Army was the main part of the movement, and should thus decide overall strategy. Che, who wasn't on the ND, took little part in the discussions. Instead, he observed the leaders, concluding that most were not sufficiently revolutionary – 'I discovered the evident anticommunist inclinations of most of them.' He even suspected them of attempting 'to sabotage this column, and more directly, myself', by keeping him short of supplies. He was, however, impressed by País – describing him as having 'the look of a man totally dedicated and faithful to the cause'. He was also favourably impressed by Sánchez and Espín.[15]

Che was, however, encouraged by Castro's 'Appeal to the Cuban People', written following that meeting. It urged increased resistance and sabotage; and called for a nationwide revolutionary general strike. Che saw this as 'really revolutionary'. Che was then appointed by Castro as the main liaison between the underground urban network and the Rebel Army in the mountains.[16]

His suspicions of the Llano – many of whom were openly anti-communist, and saw him as a 'radical Marxist' – were deepened later in the year by the Miami Pact, which Llano leaders had concluded with some other opposition groups on 1 November 1957. This had been done without Castro's consent, and had excluded the Cuban Communist Party – known as the Partido Socialista Popular (PSP). The Pact had either watered down or even dropped the most revolutionary parts of Castro's original programme – and even looked to the US for support. Both Che and Raúl (also under attack from the Llano for his Marxism) were furious. Initially, however, Che kept quiet, waiting for Castro's response. But on 9 December, he forcibly expressed his opposition to the Llano leadership in a letter to Castro. He even threatened to resign if these moves were not repudiated as a betrayal of the Cuban Revolution: 'in light of this situation, there are only two solutions: [either you allow me to] act severely to prevent actions of this sort or I shall retire on grounds of physical incapacity or whatever seems best to you'. Later, in 1965, Che acknowledged his doubts at that time: 'My only serious failing was not having had more confidence in you [Castro] from the first moments in the Sierra Maestra.'[17]

Castro eventually decided to insist that the Rebel Army should determine the nature of the revolution – sending Che his response on 13 December. Two days later, Che wrote to Castro, saying his response had filled him 'with tranquillity and happiness … You know well that I have not the slightest confidence in the National Directorate – neither as leaders or as revolutionaries.' Castro then issued a statement, condemning the Miami Pact. Later, in early January 1958, Che ran off copies of Castro's letter; while, on 2 February, the magazine *Bohemia* printed Castro's statement in a special 500,000 edition. Che then wrote to Castro about his 'historic' declaration: 'Lenin already said it, the policy of principle is the best policy … You are now on the great path as one of the two or three [leaders] of America who will get to power by a multitudinous armed struggle.'[18]

Castro then sought to establish closer connections with the PSP – the best-organised political group in Cuba. This was made possible after the PSP – which had initially opposed Castro's armed rebellion – agreed to support his Rebel Army. The PSP had seen Che – with his open reputation as a communist – as a key person in their desire for closer relations with the Rebel Army. As early as the summer of 1957, they'd sent Pablo Ribalta, a young black Cuban, to join Che's column. Years later, Ribalta became Cuba's ambassador in Tanzania, and assisted Che when he was fighting in the Congo. It seems Che had specifically asked for someone to help in the political education of his fighters – many of whom, like the M26J leaders, were either anti-communists or politically unaware. When Ribalta arrived at Che's camp, he set up a political school, and persuaded some local communists to join the guerrillas. Initially, though, his PSP affiliation was kept secret. Over the following months, Che was increasingly determined to get his fighters acquainted with the main socialist texts and ideas. However, political differences would resurface in the following year.

El Comandante Che

As regards military matters, on 22 July 1957, Che had been promoted to '*comandante*' (major) – the highest rank in the Rebel Army – because of his performance during the Battle of El Uvero. At that time, only Castro himself held that rank. In making the promotion, Castro had described Che as: 'the most outstanding soldier in that battle, carrying out for the first time one of those singular feats that characterized him in all military action'. Che had then been put in charge of the Rebel Army's second column – which later became known as 'Column No. 4'. This promotion – and receiving a red star – made Che feel 'the proudest man in the world that day. The symbol of my promotion, a small star, was given to me by Celia [Sánchez].' With the promotion, also came a gift of a new wristwatch.[19]

In his new role, Che led several more battles that enhanced his reputation as a successful guerrilla leader. He continued to insist on high standards of conduct and total dedication to the cause: most deserters were treated severely. Yet most of those in his troop accepted this, as he never asked more of them than he did of himself. Che had long since left behind the concept of 'I' in his revolutionary struggles, and he tried hard to impart his outlook to his men. When some failed to live up to these standards, discipline was firm. To drive home the need for strict discipline, Che led his men to a hill where two deserters had been executed, explaining 'why desertion was punishable by death, and why anyone who betrayed the revolution must be condemned'. As always, though, he also insisted on treating the local peasants with respect, in order to retain and increase support. As he argued: 'fair treatment toward the peasantry – respecting their property, paying for what we consumed, tending their sick, helping those most in need – was the total opposite of the government's bestial policy.'[20]

Che's promotion to *comandante* meant he was now involved more directly in the leadership of the M26J. He continued to advocate a more politically radical position – often putting himself at odds with some in the leadership, including Castro himself. One example was his reaction to the 'Manifesto of Sierra Maestra', which Castro had signed with the more reformist urban leaders on 12 July 1957. Che saw it as a watering down of the more revolutionary demands the Movement should have. He was partly reconciled to acceptance because the pact helped guarantee that resources would continue to flow to the rebels. But he also believed that their original manifesto was what they were nonetheless really fighting for, and would be implemented once they had defeated Batista. Che was not the only rebel to take this more revolutionary position – Raúl, for instance, was another. Typically, though, Che was the most open and outspoken of the critics.

On 31 July, Che led his column in an attack on a small army post in the town of Bueycito. Although they had the element of surprise and were successful, one of their men was killed and three were wounded. Che himself had narrowly escaped death when, confronted by an enemy soldier, his submachine gun failed to fire; by the time he'd run for cover and repaired his weapon, the garrison had surrendered. Afterwards, on entering a nearby village in army trucks they'd seized, they were cheered by the inhabitants.

When Che returned to the base in the Sierra Maestra, he learnt that, on 30 July, País had been murdered by Batista's police. This was a real setback for the M26J, as he'd been their main urban contact. Che called him 'one of the purest and most glorious lives of the Cuban revolution', acknowledging that 'we lost one of our most valiant combatants'. In a letter to Castro – and distrusting the Llano – he suggested País should be replaced by 'Raúl, [or] Almeida,... I insist in the issue because I know the moral and intellectual character of the would-be leaders who will try to replace Frank.' However, Che – like the others – was encouraged by the protests that broke out in Cuba's cities in the days following País's murder, evidence that revolutionary ideas were spreading beyond the mountains of the Sierra Maestra: 'new forces were joining the struggle and the fighting spirit of the people was growing'.[21]

Around this time, some of the urban M26J leadership began to criticise Castro's control. In particular, this emerged over the formation of a second rebel army, and which other rebel groups the M26J Movement should align with. They concluded that an alliance with the PSP was impossible because of wide ideological differences, but that they could work with the DR. Once again, Che proved the most revolutionary – and the most inflexible – of the rebel leaders, even refusing to deal with the new urban leader who – over Castro's preferred candidate – had replaced País. Over the following months, Che would have several clashes with the new leader, who quickly saw Che as the one to rein in.

Revolution within the revolution

In August 1957, Che's column moved into El Hombrito, a small valley near the summit of the Sierra Maestra – and began calling it the 'free territory of Cuba'. Initially, as his group included many new recruits, the emphasis was on training. But, on 29 August, Che learned that around 150 soldiers were heading their way. He immediately planned an ambush. The plan went wrong, however, when Che opened fire too early. Nonetheless, despite the soldiers being much better armed than the guerrillas, Che's group eventually forced the soldiers to withdraw – although one of the rebels was killed and only one weapon captured. Che later wrote that attacking the vanguard section was the best way to ambush a much larger group of soldiers: 'Little by little, this tactic crystallized and finally it became so systematic that the enemy stopped entering the Sierra Maestra, and, scandalously, soldiers even refused to march in the forward guard.'[22]

To deal with continuing desertions, Che established a new disciplinary committee. Most accepted his authority – even those unhappy about the new committee: 'Everyone treats [Che] with great respect … When he gives an order you can see he really commands respect.' Yet he also continued to be compassionate to wounded soldiers. After one successful ambush, he severely reprimanded a rebel who'd killed a wounded soldier without giving him a chance to surrender, leading another wounded soldier to cry out, every time a rebel passed near him: 'Don't kill me! Don't kill me! Che says not to kill prisoners!'[23]

Once established in El Hombrito – as well as occasionally engaging in battles, and punishing bandits who were terrorising the local peasantry – Che turned his camp into a model of resistance and revolution. By October 1957, he'd formed a rebel state within a state. A dam was constructed to provide hydroelectric power. In addition, he set up a basic hospital, a bakery, a farm – and even their own armoury, which made landmines, rifle-grenades and mortars. He also used his time to overcome the illiteracy of many of his soldiers – literacy being one of the things he saw as important for the revolution to achieve. Politically important was the foundation of a newspaper – *El Cubano Libre* (*The Free Cuban*). The first edition came out on 4 November 1957, and the paper kept the Cuban people informed about the progress and achievements of the unfolding revolution. He often signed his articles as 'The Sniper' or 'The Irregular'.

Although most of the attacks and ambushes led by Che were successful, he also had some failures. Two ambushes, in late November and early December, went wrong; in the latter, Che was wounded: 'Suddenly, I felt a disagreeable sensation, a little like a burn or the tingling of numbness, a sign that I had just been shot in my left foot.' Che, and a more seriously wounded rebel, crawled to rejoin the rest of his column. Although he tried walking, Che was eventually forced to ride a horse; a doctor later removed the bullet. However, in early December, their camp was destroyed by Batista's retreating forces: 'A trail of burned-out huts … was all that remained of El Hombrito.'[24]

Nonetheless, as the year came to an end, Che began establishing a similar base at La Mesa. That camp soon had facilities similar to those in El Hombrito. The biggest difference was the establishment of 'Radio Rebelde' – used by Che to spread information about the policies that would be needed after the defeat of Batista, and to spread socialist ideas. Broadcasts – from 'the free territory of Cuba' – which began in February 1958, proved useful in combatting Batista's propaganda; giving news of successful guerrilla actions; and giving details of the various declarations made by the 26 July Movement. It also sent coded messages to the various guerrilla columns operating in different parts of Cuba. From around June 1958, Che also began to use Radio Rebelde to send occasional messages to his parents. His mother – by then 'very lonely, very sad, and very worried about him' – sent him a long letter: 'Teté my darling, I was deeply moved to hear your voice on the phone after so long. I didn't recognize it. You seemed like another person.'[25]

Che also established a school which, as well as teaching peasants and rebels to read and write, also saw him give lessons on politics and guerrilla warfare – along with more general lessons covering history, literature, philosophy and culture. This time, captured enemy soldiers were allowed to attend lessons. One was persuaded to join the rebels and, despite his initial fears about Che, ended up as an instructor – discovering that Che's 'cruel' reputation was untrue.

Consolidation and encirclement

The beginning of 1958 saw the rebels move down from the Sierra Maestra, to begin operations against outlying garrisons, plantations, towns and cities. In addition, the urban movement also stepped up its activities.

On 16 February 1958, the Rebel Army attacked the garrison at Pino del Agua once again. Initially, the attack began well; but then the soldiers began to fight back effectively. Although Che wanted to launch another attack, Castro ordered him – given his reputation for reckless risk-taking – to keep safe and not take part in the attack. As a result, Che reluctantly withdrew his column, and the rebels went back into the hills. Government despatches and some newspapers highlighted the involvement in this attack of 'the well-known Argentine Communist Che Guevara', who they claimed had been wounded. Over the coming months, there were other reports of his death – each was a 'time of anguish' for Gadea. On 27 February, Castro promoted Raúl, Camilo Cienfuegos and Juan Almeida as *comandantes* of their own columns – and rebel attacks increased.[26]

Several reporters visited Che's camp – impressed by the order and discipline, many came away as admirers and even open supporters. One such visitor, in the spring of 1958, was the Argentinian Jorge Masetti. On seeing Che ride into camp on a mule, and loaded with weapons, he used Radio Rebelde to report: 'The famous Che Guevara seemed a typical young Argentinian man from the middle classes.' Nonetheless, he was impressed by Che's response when asked why he was fighting in Cuba and not Argentina: 'I consider my fatherland to be not only Argentina, but all of America.' Unfortunately, when he sent recordings of this exclusive interview with Che, he found they'd never arrived in Argentina. After a second spell with the rebels, he eventually broadcast them in four episodes – 'It was the first time that Argentina had heard Che's voice and obtained direct testimony of the Cuban revolution.' When Masetti returned to Buenos Aires, he brought tapes for Che's parents that Che had recorded for them.[28]

In the third week of May 1958, Batista's army launched an 'encirclement and annihilation' offensive against the Rebel Army. Over 10,000 government troops were involved – while the Rebel Army only numbered 320 guerrillas. Che was initially charged with holding the western section of the Rebel Army's territory. Che's responsibilities included defending his area, and working out safe supply and withdrawal routes: 'This small territory had to be defended, with not much more than 200 functioning rifles.'[28]

Yet, in the midst of this fierce fighting, Che also pushed forward with agrarian reforms in the area he controlled. Then, much to his disappointment, he was ordered by Castro to take charge of the training school for the new recruits now flocking to Castro's Rebel Army. Che put them through a rigorous programme – as well as the physical and military aspects, there was also political education, to ensure they were fully committed to the ideals of the Movement. Che was further disappointed when Castro decided to move Radio Rebelde and *El Cubano Libre* to his own base. His disappointment and 'low spirits' about these decisions led Cienfuegos to write to him, saying: 'Che, my soul brother, I see Fidel has put you in charge of the Military School … You've played a very principal role in this showdown … Cuba needs you even more when the war ends, so [Castro] does a good thing in looking after you.'[29]

On 15 May, however, fearing defeat, Castro ordered Che back to HQ. On 22 May, Castro met with PSP representatives, to discuss a possible united front of revolutionary forces – but this was put on hold until Batista's offensive had been beaten back. By now, Che was in effect Castro's chief of staff and main confidant. On 25 May, Batista's offensive intensified, and Che rushed back to his area. For the next three months, Che was constantly moving to shore up his various fronts against the overwhelming forces the Rebel Army now faced. Che's diary shows just how desperate things were, with several of the guerrilla fronts being pushed back by superior numbers, and signs of growing defeatism and consequent desertions.

On 26 June 1958, he met with Castro again – by then, their situation looked serious. Two days later, Batista's army launched another major offensive – though it turned out to be the last one. As the soldiers advanced along a single road into the mountains, Che's units ambushed the vanguard battalion, destroying or disabling several armoured cars. When the troops came under sniper fire, they began to retreat, which soon turned into a rout. The army suffered eighty-six casualties, while Che's rebels had only three – and were also able to capture a large quantity of weapons and ammunition.

However, in an engagement on 3 July, things went badly, and Che had to organise a hasty retreat. In a self-critical diary entry, after noting that 'The position was bad and [the army] were encircling us, but we put up little resistance', he criticised himself for feeling something he 'had never felt before: the need to live. That had better be corrected in the next opportunity.' As Anderson notes: 'It is hard to imagine many other men in the same situation making this sort of critical self-judgment.' Che lost some close friends in the fighting; and, although the rebel forces managed to hold their positions, a sort of stalemate developed. Then, from 20 July, Che and the rest of the Rebel Army went on the offensive and, in early August, the last army units began to withdraw from the Sierra Maestra.[29]

The last major battle took place when enemy troops attempted to surround Castro's column. Castro called on Che for help – Che quickly saw he'd have to stop a force of some 1,500 special reinforcements from joining in the fighting. He arranged an ambush which successfully blocked the reinforcements, inflicted serious casualties on them, and took around fifty prisoners. As a result, he prevented Castro's possible death or capture. According to a US Marine Corps major, Che showed real tactical brilliance. By the end of Batista's offensive, the Rebel Army had lost fifty fighters – but Batista's estimated losses were over 1,000. Although the rebels had initially been forced to give up much territory, they'd not been defeated. Typically, Che was very optimistic: 'Batista's army came out of that last offensive in the Sierra Maestra with its spine broken, but it had not yet been defeated.'[30]

Sierra vs. Llano

Meanwhile, the political differences which had emerged at the end of 1957 continued into 1958. Several urban M26J members remained reluctant to prioritise the Rebel Army for supplies of weapons, medicine and food. Thus tensions once again developed between the Sierra and Llano sections of the movement. Once again, Che was the most outspoken critic of these urban leaders. Though he tended to underestimate the problems faced by the urban members, who had to deal with a constant reign of terror and intimidation, and regular assassinations by Batista's death squads. According to Pacio Ignacio Tabio II, 'Che's view tended to underestimate the role [of] the struggle in the cities … he saw the guerrilla war as an autonomous process, rather than the vanguard of the widespread dissent that it fed, and fed on.'[31]

Matters came to a head in April 1958, when the M26J, and other rebel groups, called a Cuba-wide general strike. The strike began on 9 April but failed badly. Castro blamed the failure on the Llano leaders, who – against his wishes – had excluded the PSP, which had repeatedly offered its willingness to be involved. So he took further steps to secure his overall control of the M26J's National Directorate.

On 3 May, though he was not a member of the ND, Che played a leading role in a meeting during which he blamed the latter for 'sectarianism' in blocking PSP involvement in the strike, and called for the top leaders to resign. According to Che, 'the division between the Sierra and the Llano was real'. After a long and heated debate, Castro put Che's proposal to a vote – this passed, ensuring that the '*Sierra* line' of 'direct armed struggle' would be followed. The ND was restructured, three of its leaders were demoted, and it was moved to the Sierra. Castro became 'General Secretary', and the Sierra Maestra became the Movement's command centre – with control over foreign negotiations, weapons and the Rebel Army. The urban centres now became outposts of the Rebel Army. Che was also pleased when, as the PSP became increasingly public in their support of the rebels, more communists joined the rebels, with many of them ending up in Che's or Raúl's columns. These successes led the leaders of eight anti-Batista political parties and groups to sign a Declaration in Caracas on 20 July, in support of the M26J's Rebel Army. This 'Unity Manifesto of the Sierra Maestra' was then broadcast over Radio Rebelde. Che, though, was disappointed the PSP were not invited to sign: 'The unity seems to be going well on the outside but in the announcement the Partido Socialista is not included, which seems strange to me.'[32]

Nonetheless, much to Che's approval, moves for a merger between the M26J and the PSP were firming up. Following a visit to Castro's HQ by Carlos Rafael

Rodríguez, it was agreed the PSP could send a permanent representative to the Sierra Maestra. Che recorded that 'Carlos Rafael left for the free zone. His impression is positive despite all the internal and external intrigues.' Rodríguez had already met with Raúl (who'd been a member of the PSP's Socialist Youth, but had been expelled for his part in the Moncada attack), and had agreed to carry out agrarian reforms in Raúl's area, and to set up a training school for guerrillas, which would be staffed by Communists. Three weeks after Rodriguez left, Luis Más Martín arrived; in September, Rodriguez returned and stayed with the Rebel Army until the end of the war.[33]

Three Prongs

In mid-August 1958, Castro decided on a three-pronged offensive, to take the fight from the eastern part of Cuba into the central and western zones. The key was to take the cities of the central area, thus cutting Havana off from the eastern half of the island. Castro gave Che instructions to take two columns from the Sierra Maestra to the plains of Camaguey and then onto Las Villas. Che and Cienfuegos – by then one of Che's closet friends – began leading their men, by different routes, to the Escambray Mountains in the Las Villas province of central Cuba. Cienfuegos was to go to the northern part of the province, and then move from there to Pinar del Rio in the west. Che, with almost 150 fighters, was to take the southern part of the centre – and to convince the various small independent guerrilla groups operating there to join forces with his column. He also had to prevent Batista's forces from getting to the east, where the Castro brothers were attacking Batista's troops. Che's group left on 31 August.

The six-week journey, on foot and horse, across difficult terrain – during Cuba's rainy season – was hard. A hurricane in early September made crossing rivers extra difficult. Che described their 'truly horrible' experiences thus: 'These were days of tiring marches through desolate expanses of only water and mud. We were hungry, thirsty, and could hardly advance because our legs felt like lead and the weapons were tremendously heavy.' During that journey – over 350 miles – there were frequent clashes with Batista's troops. Mostly, though, they tried to avoid any serious combat before they'd reached their destination. During the journey, Che broke an arm. But, as he later wrote: 'Despite the difficulties we were never without the encouragement of the peasants.' On 16 October – thanks to Che's military skills and leadership – they escaped an encirclement and at last entered Escambray proper.[34]

The number of people now wanting to join the rebels grew significantly. Che quickly gave the PSP in the area a key role in the struggle – something the other guerrilla groups (including a local M26J group) had been denying them. Che persuaded the five guerrilla groups in the area to join his column in attacking Batista's forces. This wasn't always easy; Che said: 'After laborious talks I had with their respective leaders, we reached a series of agreements and it was possible to go on to form a more or less common front.' On 26 October, they attacked the garrison at Güiní de Miranda. When the guerrilla firing the bazooka missed three times, Che grabbed it in exasperation, hitting the barracks with his first shot. The fourteen soldiers surrendered – but two rebels were killed and seven were wounded. Meanwhile, the ongoing tensions between Che and those Llano anti-communists in the M26J continued.[35]

The secretary of the local PSP Young Socialists was impressed with Che's leadership of these different groups: 'He measured his men for their fighting spirit but he knew how to distinguish perfectly between those of left or right.' Among the new recruits were several young fighters attracted by Che's adventurist spirit – many later became his bodyguards after 1959. This was despite his strict discipline – though each punishment came 'with an explanation, a sermon about the importance of self-sacrifice, personal example, and social conscience. [Che] wanted the men to know why they were being punished, and how they could redeem themselves.' As in the Sierra Maestra, he won their respect and devotion because he lived as they all did, refusing any extra luxuries, and taking the same risks as they did. Anderson thinks, though, that his 'austere revolutionary image' cost him personally – seeing his fondness for the mules he rode, and his adoption of pets, as 'signs that he craved tenderness and solace to ease the harsh life he adopted.'[37]

Increasingly, disenchanted members of Batista's army began to desert and join the rebels. As a result, Che was able to inflict much disruption in Central Cuba – blocking transportation routes, and destroying communication lines in the province. By then Che had almost 200 fighters, and established his base at Caballete de Casas. By mid-November, he'd established a new newspaper, *El Miliciano* (*The Militiaman*).

Although tensions remained between the various rebel groups, Che's successful attacks soon led him to be pre-eminent, with sections wanting to join him. He was able to persuade the DR to unite with his group – although they still refused to work with the PSP. On 3 December 1958, Che signed the Pedrero Pact with the latter, but disagreements within the M26J continued. Discussions, in late November 1958, failed to resolve the underlying tensions: 'They accused me of being a Communist and I accused them of being imperialists … When the argument ended we were more apart than when we began.'[37]

Romances old and new

During 1958, Che's personal life also developed. On 15 February, Gadea had written to ask if she could come to join him in the mountains – now that Hildita was old enough to be left with family. After almost five months, she received a reply, saying she 'couldn't come yet; the fight was at a dangerous stage, and an offensive would begin in which he himself wouldn't remain in any one place'. By then, Che and Zoila Rodríguez – an 18 year-old *mulata* peasant and single mother – had become lovers. According to one of Che's guerrillas, Che 'liked her a lot' – noting that although a 'lot of women went crazy over him ... he was always very strict and respectful in that sense ... but he liked that girl. They hooked up and were together for a time'. Che had first visited her home to ask her father – a rebel supporter – to shoe his mule. Che made a big impression on her: 'as a woman I liked him very much, above all his stare, he had such beautiful eyes, a smile so calm that it would move any heart, it could move any woman'. After carrying out various errands for the rebels, Che finally asked her to move to his camp. As well as helping out in the kitchen, she worked in the hospital, giving advice about which plants could be used for medicinal purposes. In late August, as Che prepared to leave for the Escambray Mountains, Rodríguez asked to accompany him. But Che refused to take her, so he and his young lover parted. Though, as she recalled: 'He left me in charge of his mule Armando.'[38]

In late November 1958, he met Aleida March for the first time. She was attractive, and eight years younger than him – but was not a communist. Though she eventually became his second wife, his published *Reminiscences* makes no reference to her. She'd joined the M26J while at university, and had often brought weapons and messages to the rebels in the Escambray Mountains before Che's arrival. In the failed general strike in April 1958, she'd been an armed combatant in Las Villas. After Che's arrival in Escambray, she became the principal courier between the local Llano and Che's guerrillas.

In late October 1958, March was instructed by the provincial leadership to take money to Che's forces, and, as the authorities were now looking for her, to stay with the guerrillas. As she said: 'it was clear my days in the underground struggle were numbered'. Wanted posters for Che (described as a 'communist') had been posted around Santa Clara, but when she first saw him, she 'realized the photo on those posters looked nothing like him'. Her first impression of him was not very romantic – she thought he looked old, dirty and skinny.[39]

The money was strapped to her body to conceal it – she got Che to remove the money from her waist: 'The adhesive tape was still giving me terrible pain, and I asked him for help to remove it.' In a letter Che sent her in 1965 – when he was fighting in the Congo – he told her that, when he saw the marks left by the adhesive tape around her waist, he 'felt an internal struggle between the (almost) irreproachable revolutionary and the other – the real one – overcome by shyness, while pretending to be the untouchable revolutionary.'[40]

Che, however, was initially reluctant to allow her to act as a combatant in his Rebel Army column. Instead, he suggested she be the base camp nurse. She firmly rejected that, pointing out that she'd taken many risks for the movement as an underground militant, and that: 'I thought my two years of clandestine work gave me the right to be incorporated into the guerrilla unit.' Che later told her that he was reluctant to let her join the guerrilla unit because he thought that she'd 'been sent by the leadership of the movement in Las Villas (largely made up of right-wing people) to monitor him because of his reputation as a communist'. Despite several guerrilla fighters supporting her request, Che still refused to give her a combatant role.[41]

Che's final push

Castro decided this was now the time to launch a final offensive to overthrow the dictatorship – seeing the crucial struggle would be in the central province where Che and Cienfuegos were. In late November, Batista's army began an offensive against Che's positions; but, by 4 December, the offensive had been shattered. Batista's forces became increasingly demoralised, with many choosing to surrender. Before their release, they sometimes took part in political discussions and lectures about the goals of the revolution.

Che and Cienfuegos then decided to go on the attack, before Cienfuegos returned to his area. During December, their columns captured most of the towns, closed the main roads, and blocked the railway lines across Las Villas. These actions cut Cuba in half, separating Santa Clara and Havana from the east of the country. On 18 December 1958, after capturing the town of Fomento, Che established a provisional M26J government there. His main target now was Santa Clara – his successful capture of it would consolidate his reputation as an effective guerrilla commander.

It was during the fighting as they headed for Santa Clara that Che and March came closer together. As March was sitting in a street in El Pedrero, in the early hours of the morning, 'Che passed by in a jeep and invited me to come along with him "to shoot a few rounds". Without a second thought, I accepted and jumped into his jeep. And that was it. In a way, I never again got out of that jeep.' From then on, she became his closest companion. Though there were several differences, she – like Che – was forthright in expressing her views, often to the point of tactlessness.[42]

During the last two weeks of December, as Che's column fought its way across the province to Santa Clara, her admiration 'transcended even the bounds of my growing romantic attachment to him'. As they set up HQ on the outskirts of Cabaiguán, Che recited a poem to her: 'This was one of the most beautiful ways he knew to express himself.' As the days passed, 'The more time we spent together, I could feel the sparks between us.' After he broke his right elbow on 23 December, as they captured that town, she gave him her black scarf as a sling: 'Over the years, that scarf came to symbolize so much for us.' Shortly after, he made her his assistant – although hardly ever engaged in combat, she was constantly at his side. She came increasingly to discuss aspects of the campaign with him. In a revealing reference to one of Che's favourite romance tales, she wrote of this period: 'He may not have had a companion with Sancho Panza's wisdom and sagacity but he had one who was loyal and constant.'[43]

By 27 December, they'd captured the last garrison before Santa Clara itself. Given what they'd been through, Che's fighters were euphoric and, to keep discipline as they entered the newly liberated towns, Che drew up rules of behaviour – including not frequenting bars and brothels. It was at the start of the offensive to take Santa Clara, as they set up HQ in the Central University that Che finally gave March a weapon: 'an M-1 rifle, saying that I had earned it. This was my first important achievement as a combatant … I felt very satisfied and extremely proud.' During the evening of 28 December, Che spoke to March about 'his personal life': 'He told me about his marriage to Hilda Gadea … and his daughter, Hildita … at the time Che appeared to be very much alone … It also brought me closer to the man.'[44]

The Battle of Santa Clara

Che's victories saw more civilians offering support and assistance. As a result, in just a few weeks, Che – now commanding around 350 guerrillas – controlled over 3,000 square miles of territory in the central zone – and prevented Batista sending troops against the Castro brothers. Che was now poised to fight what would become the greatest – and most crucial – battle of Cuba's entire Revolutionary War: the Battle of Santa Clara. Santa Clara was a large city, with a population of around 150,000, and was the capital of the Las Villas province. It was defended by over 3,000 soldiers, with superior weaponry and air support. Batista, aware of its importance, sent an armoured train with weapons and ammunition.

Che's main concern for the approaching battle – which he realised would be the decisive one – was the armoured train which could be used to evacuate the soldiers so they could regroup. Che was also worried about the army units which occupied a hill called El Cápiro, overlooking the city. His troops – which mostly only had light weapons, and were low on ammunition – were also worn out, having fought constantly for most of the last two weeks.

On the night of 27 December, Che established an initial command post on the university campus on the edge of the city. Later, after advancing, it was relocated to the city centre. On 28 December, he ordered his fighters to capture strategic points in the city. During this time, March was constantly at his side, often dodging bullets as they ran from building to building. As she knew Santa Clara's streets so well, she was able to guide him and his troops as they attacked one position after another. Her local connections meant she was also able to help gain support from the city's inhabitants. Later, they both recalled how each had been worried the other would be wounded, killed or captured.

At dawn on 29 December, Che's guerrillas moved into the city and the battle began in earnest. This time they were accompanied by civilians who sympathised with them and aided them in various ways.

Che then made the decision that greatly contributed to his legend as an exemplary guerrilla leader. He ordered and oversaw the removal of sections of the railway track leading into the city, using a bulldozer from the university's School of Agronomy. It led to an amusing misunderstanding between Che and March. As his assistant, she took notes, and when he'd said 'Caterpillar' in English, she (who'd never heard the term before) wrote it down in Spanish, rendering it mistakenly as '*catres, palas y pilas*' ('beds, shovels and batteries'). He later told their children, with the result that they often teased her by chanting 'Beds, shovels and batteries!'[45]

He then ordered his elite volunteer 'Suicide Squad' – named and led by the 18-year-old 'Little Cowboy' – to capture El Cápiro. This they did, and then began attacking the train. As they attacked, they came under fire from tanks and planes: 'Our men were fighting against troops supported by armored units and were forcing them to flee, although many paid for their boldness with their lives.' But the rebels carried on, and soon the battle began to go in their favour.[46]

As the rebels slowly advanced through the city, most of the army's commanding officers scrambled into the train for safety – completely unaware that the track had been ripped up. As the train advanced, it came off the tracks – and came under attack from Molotov cocktails and a hail of bullets. Che described it thus: 'our Molotov cocktails forced the men out of the armored train … Assaulted by men who from nearby positions and adjoining carriages threw bottles of burning gasoline, the train became a veritable oven for the soldiers.' At some risk, Che personally negotiated the surrender, by meeting unarmed with the commander. This successful operation gave the rebels a huge haul of weapons and equipment, much of which was quickly despatched to the rebel armies fighting in other parts of Santa Clara.[47]

Once again, there were news reports that Che had been killed, quickly denied by Radio Rebelde. Meanwhile, Santa Clara's citizens began erecting barricades of cars and buses, to slow the movement of the army's remaining armoured cars and tanks. Even the terrific bombing and strafing ordered by Batista failed to stop the guerrilla's advance. In the fighting to take the police station – defended by a large number of police and four tanks – the 'Little Cowboy' was killed. Between 31 December and 1 January, March was with Che in a captured tank, as they attacked the Gran Hotel (now the Santa Clara Libre Hotel) 'where the snipers on the 10th floor had kept up fire almost until the end of combat – surrendered to our forces'.[48]

By New Year's Day, Che's forces had secured almost total control of Santa Clara – apart from around 1,000 soldiers inside the Leoncio Vidal Army Garrison, commanded by Casillas. Che mobilised most of his fighters against it. However, when news reached Casillas that Batista had made a hasty escape from Cuba early on New Year's Day 1959, he slipped away. The acting commander contacted Che to negotiate an indefinite truce. Che, however, consulted Castro, who insisted on unconditional surrender. When Che informed the commander, he returned to the garrison, to discuss it with his men – but they'd already begun deserting their positions, throwing down their weapons and walking towards the rebels' positions to fraternise with Che's guerrillas. Once disarmed, Che allowed them to leave for Havana – and the Battle of Santa Clara was over.

Casillas, however, was captured – disguised wearing M26J arm band. When told he'd be taken to Che, he 'changed color and asked me if I couldn't take him to another jefe'. Officially, he was later shot trying to escape, but Anderson thinks that, given Che's reputation for strictly applying revolutionary justice, he was tried and executed. Twelve other local notorious Batista henchmen were also apprehended. Che took evidence from Santa Clara's citizens, about the torture and murders they'd committed. He then signed their death warrants, defending the decision thus: 'I did no more and no less than the situation demanded – i.e., the death sentence for those twelve murderers, because they had committed crimes against the people, not against us.'[49]

Havana calling

On the morning of 2 January, Che and Cienfuegos were ordered by Castro to advance towards Havana. Cienfuegos left first, as Che still had mopping-up duties and trials to attend to, as well as appointing Calixto Morales as the military governor of Las Villas. Finally, on the afternoon of 2 January, Che and his column left for the capital in a convoy of trucks and jeeps – with March visiting her parents before leaving. It was on the way there, when they were on their own in the jeep during a refuelling stop, that Che made his first declaration of love for March. He told her that he'd first realised he loved her when they were running in front of the tank in Santa Clara. March's initial response was somewhat muted: 'I was exhausted and half asleep, so I was hardly listening to what he was saying, I didn't even take it very seriously, as I still saw him as much older than I was.' She wasn't even sure she'd heard him correctly, writing later: 'I think Che didn't exactly choose the best moment to declare his love … But the ice had certainly been broken.'[50]

Early on the morning of 3 January, Che, Cienfugos and their guerrillas entered Havana. The Castro brothers, having captured the famous Moncada Barracks, where the M26J had begun, then headed for Havana. When Castro arrived, he rode triumphantly into the city, with the two leading Marxists in his Rebel Army – his brother Raúl, and Che – seated either side of him.

For Che, it was a remarkable achievement. In less than three years, he'd gone from being an unknown and rather romantic youthful wanderer and adventurer to being one of the best-known, most popular, and most important, guerrilla fighters in Cuba. At the beginning, he had begun to think deeply and seriously about his political philosophy. Now he was one of the most powerful – and most revolutionary – members in Castro's new provisional government. He'd achieved this position through his commitment to personal sacrifice, his transparent lack of personal ambition, and his refusal to compromise his political ideals. From the beginning of the guerrilla war, he'd lived according to his motto of '*todo o nada*' (all or nothing) – and by his rigorous refusal ever to allow himself any privileges or indulgences, and never demanding more of his fellow-fighters than he was prepared to do himself. He would stick to these principles of behaviour as a government minister in the years that followed.

Che's summary of the situation at the start of 1959 was clear: 'We won the war, the revolution begins now.' The next five years would see him transformed from the legendary guerrilla fighter into a revolutionary minister and roving ambassador for the Cuban Revolution. Those years would also see him reunited with his parents, and establishing a new family with March.[51]

However, his ideas about politics and economics soon began to diverge from the direction that Cuba – under increasing pressure from the US – took after 1959, as it developed ties with the Soviet Union. Increasingly, Che became determined to return to guerrilla warfare, to battle against Yankee imperialism. Within eight years, that romantic revolutionary cause had led to his murder in Bolivia.

1928–43

Che, aged 3, photographed by his father, 1931. (*Wikimedia Commons*)

Che, aged 8, with father, mother and siblings, 1936. (*Wikimedia Commons*)

The Guevara family, c.1944, L>R: Che, Celia (mother), Celia (sister), Roberto, Juan Martín, father, Ana Maria. (*Wikimedia Commons*)

Che (far R), with his Rugby Club teammates, Atalaya, c.1947. He earned the nickname, 'Fuser', for his fearless tackling. (*Wikimedia Commons*)

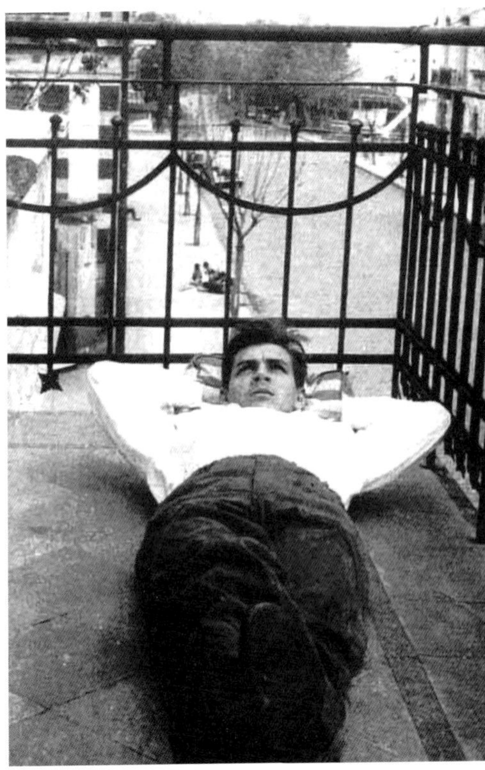

Che, aged 20, on the balcony of his family's house on Calle Araoz, Buenos Aires, 1949. (*Wikimedia Commons*)

MINISTERIO DE SALUD PUBLICA DE LA NACION
MATRICULA PROFESIONAL DE ENFERMERO
No 13.424
Fecha 22 dic.1950
Apellido y Nombre
GUEVARA
Ernesto
Clase 1928 Distr. 43
M. I. No 6.460.503
Céd. I. No 3.524.272
de Capital Federal
FIRMA DEL INTERESADO

Che's official document, as a professional nurse, December 1950. (*Wikimedia Commons*)

Che, aged 22, setting off on his solo trip on a motorised bicycle through northern Argentina, 1950. (*Wikimedia Commons*)

1951–53

Che, with 'La Ponderosa II', used on his famous 'Motorcycles Diaries' trip, 1952. (*Wikimedia Commons*)

Che, with Alberto Granado, on their 'Mambo-Tango' raft, Amazon R., June 1952. (*Wikimedia Commons*)

1954–56

Che, with Hilda Gadea, at the Maya site of Chichén Itzá in Yucatán, during their delayed honeymoon,1955. (*Wikimedia Commons*)

1956–59

Che, on mule in Las Villas, Cuba, 1958. (*Wikimedia Commons*)

Che, with Raúl Castro, in their Sierra de Cristal Mountain stronghold, south of Havana, 1958. (*Wikimedia Commons*)

Che, after the famous 'Battle of Santa Clara', December 1958. (*Wikimedia Commons*)

Che, next to Cuban President Manuel Urrutia, with Camilo Cienfuegos on the R., 1959. Around Che's neck is the black gauze scarf March gave him after he'd broken his arm. (*Wikimedia Commons*)

Che and his daughter, Hildita, with Camilo Cienfuegos, 1959. (*Wikimedia Commons*)

Che, 2 June 1959. (*Wikimedia Commons*)

Che, with Aleida March on his L. arm, walking in Havana, 1960. (*Wikimedia Commons*)

Che, talking with Simone de Beauvoir and Jean-Paul Sartre, 1960. (*Wikimedia Commons*)

Che, with Ricardo Masetti, c.1960.
(*Wikimedia Commons*)

Che, with Fidel Castro, c.1961.
(*Wikimedia Commons*)

Che, with Aleida March, Havana, 1961. (*Wikimedia Commons*)

Che, reading the newspaper, La Nación, in Puntra del Este, Uruguay, August 1961. (*Wikimedia Commons*)

Che, with Castro, meeting Ben Bella of Algeria, Havana, 20 October 1962. (*Wikimedia Commons*)

Che and Aleida March, with children, 1963. L>R: Aleida March, Camilo, Hildita, Celia (on his lap), Aleida. (*Wikimedia Commons*)

Che, meeting Zou Enlai, in February 1965, during his second visit to China. (*Wikimedia Commons*)

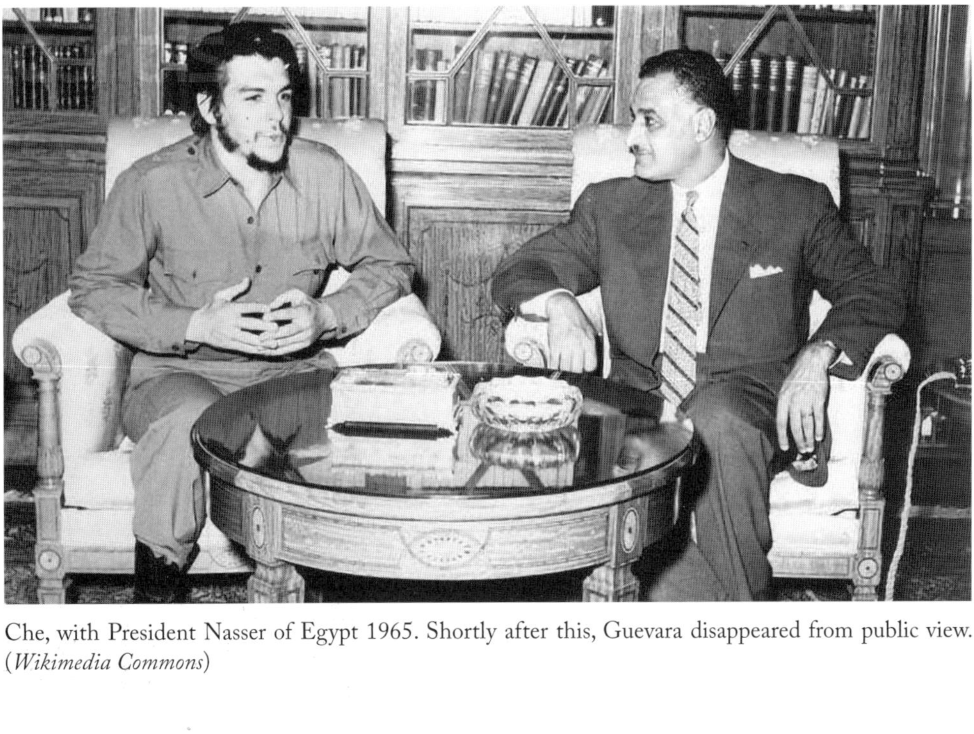

Che, with President Nasser of Egypt 1965. Shortly after this, Guevara disappeared from public view. (*Wikimedia Commons*)

Che in Moscow, 1965. (*Wikimedia Commons*)

Che, being met at Havana's airport, after his extended international tour. L>R: Fidel Castro, Aleida March, Carlos Rafael Rodriguez, and Cuban President Osvaldo Dorticos, March 1965 – 2 weeks after his controversial speech in Algiers. (*Wikimedia Commons*)

Che, in the Congo, 1965.
(*Wikimedia Commons*)

Aleida March, visiting Che in Tanzania, 1966, after the failed Congo mission. (*Wikimedia Commons*)

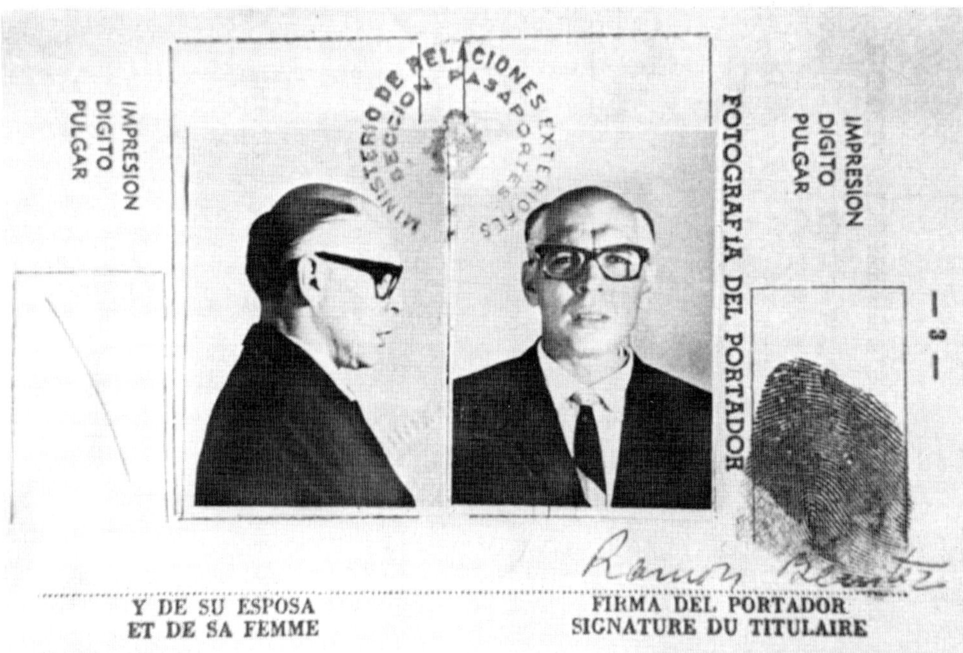

One of Che's false passports, as Ramón Benitez, 19 July 1966 – adopted in Prague after he'd left the Congo, before his secret return to Cuba. (*Wikimedia Commons*)

Che, disguised as 'Adolfo Mena González', the other alias he adopted for Bolivia, 1966. (*Wikimedia Commons*)

Che, in Bolivia, 1967. (*Wikimedia Commons*)

Che, on a mule, in Bolivia – taken by one of his guerrilla fighters, 1967. By August, he was often too ill to walk. (*Wikimedia Commons*)

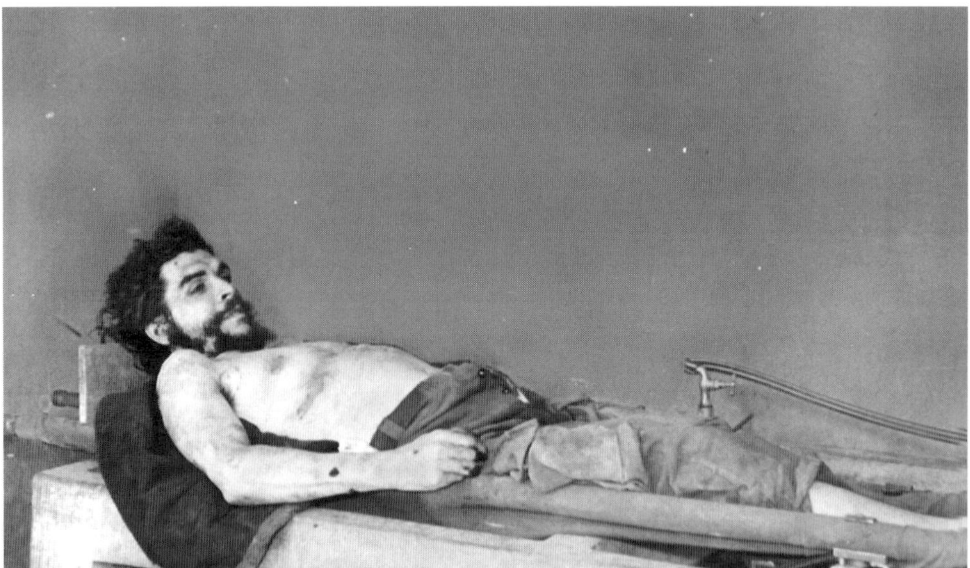

Che's body, put on display in Vallegrande, Bolivia, after he had been summarily executed, October 1967 (taken by CIA operative Gustavo Villoldo). (*Wikimedia Commons*)

Chapter 7

The Revolutionary Minister, 1959–63

> 'We are simply adjusting ourselves to the predictions of the scientific Marx as we travel this road of rebellion … That is to say … The laws of Marxism are present in the events of the Cuban Revolution…'[1]

The start of 1959 saw Che pulled in two directions. For some time, he'd seen himself as a Latin American – even an international – revolutionary. With Cuba's Revolutionary War over, it was thus by no means certain he'd stay in Cuba. Even though Che was second only to Raúl in closeness to Castro – and was granted Cuban citizenship in February by the new revolutionary government – he'd never promised to stay longer than he was needed. He made this clear to one of his officers on 3 January 1959, as they were approaching Havana: 'My mission, my commitment to Fidel ends here, with our entry into Havana.' Later, in 1961, soon after becoming Minister of Industries, Che told his secretary that he'd 'stick this out for five years', before taking off to fight a new guerrilla war.[2]

In fact, Che stayed for six years, as he also wanted to transform Cuba according to his socialist vision. After 1959, he was at the heart of debates concerning Cuba's economic and political direction – whether as head of the Department of Industrialisation, President of Cuba's National Bank, or Minister of Industries. Arguably, it was in those roles that Che made his most significant contributions to revolutionary politics. In June 1959, in an article for a Brazilian magazine, he described his – and Cuba's – role thus: 'we are now the hope of the unredeemed Americas. All eyes – those of the great oppressors and those of the hopeful – are firmly on us.' According to Yaffe, Che radicalised the Cuban revolution, and 'was central in driving the structural changes which transformed Cuba from its underdeveloped semi-colonial status to political and economic independence and integration into the socialist bloc between 1959 and 1961.' Yet most of this remains largely unknown – even to many of those who admire him.[3]

Reunions and separations

Soon after the victory of the Cuban Revolution, Che was reunited with his family. On 18 January 1959, his parents and two of his siblings arrived in Cuba, and were met at the airport by Che and March. This was the first time Che and his family had seen each other for six years; and they stayed until mid-February. According to March, it was 'a very emotional time' and 'from the moment he saw his parents Che exuded happiness'. His parents wanted to know who March was, and Che told them she was the woman he intended to marry. When his father asked him about his future plans, he said he was done with medicine: 'Now I'm a fighter who is working in the consolidation of a government. What will become of me? I don't even know in which land I will leave my bones.'[4]

Soon after, Gadea and their daughter Hildita, also arrived – and were met at the airport by Che's parents. But Che and Gadea met soon after, and she was in for a shock: 'With the candor that always characterized him, [Che] told me forthrightly that he had another woman, whom he had met in the campaign of Santa Clara. My pain was deep, but, following our convictions, we agreed on a divorce.' According to her, when Che realised just how hurt she was, he said: 'Better I had died in combat.' Because she saw the Cuban Revolution as important, she said she was 'happy that he hadn't died in combat'. At Che's suggestion, they agreed to remain 'friends, and comrades'. Despite the changed circumstances, Gadea stayed on in Cuba, and Che was able to develop his relationship with Hildita, who often spent days playing in his office, while he worked on government business.[5]

According to March, around 12 January, Che had asked her to read a letter he was sending to Gadea, asking for a divorce so he could marry 'a Cuban woman he had met during the struggle'. When she asked 'who was the young woman he intended to marry. He looked at me with surprise and said it was me.' March states that they'd not discussed it before – and didn't become lovers until after the victory of the Cuban Revolution, when 'on a memorable January night, barefoot and silent, Che came into my room … and we consummated an already strong relationship'. The divorce was granted at the end of May 1959, and Che and March were married on 2 June. It was a quiet affair, though Raúl and Cienfuegos were among those present. Before the marriage, the situation had been awkward, as Gadea and March didn't get on, yet both wanted to help Che in his new tasks.[6]

'Butcher of La Cabaña'?

Although Che would soon play an important part in Cuba's economic development, his first roles in 1959 were in other areas. To begin with, in January 1959, he was placed in charge of the La Cabaña fortress. This led to speculation that Che was being side-lined by Castro because of his politics. Given that Che was rarely willing to remain silent about his beliefs, it's possible

Castro did want him out of the limelight in the early days of the revolution. Castro was keen to avoid accusations that the revolution was communist, and had insisted that the PSP not be part of the victory march into Havana. This perhaps explain why – untypically – Che downplayed his communist beliefs when interviewed by the press that month: 'To label "Communists" all those who refuse to bow down is an old dictator's trick.'[7]

Che was tasked with rounding up Batista's most notorious henchmen who, before 1959, had committed extreme torture and murder. In addition, he was also asked to purge Cuba's professional army – something he thought Árbenz should have done in Guatemala. These tasks proved controversial although, from the beginning, Che insisted that people shouldn't take their own vengeance against such individuals – warning that anyone who did so would face trial themselves. To determine guilt and punishments, special revolutionary tribunals were established – with several of these public trials taking place in La Cabaña. As March acknowledged: 'These tribunals have always been controversial, and the facts about them have often been greatly distorted by our enemies.'[8]

These trials were overseen by a commission, headed by a captain who, before joining the Rebel Army, had been a lawyer. Although Che didn't take part in the trials or the executions, Batista's supporters – and the US government and media outlets – claimed he was carrying out a 'red terror'. They dubbed him 'The Butcher of La Cabaña', and even accused him of torturing prisoners – behaviour which would have been in stark contrast to his well-documented compassionate treatment of enemy captives. It's estimated there were around fifty-five executions at La Cabaña in the first three months; across Cuba as a whole, estimates suggest around 500 were executed in all. Che's role, as commander of the fortress, was to deal with some of the appeals, often interviewing family members pleading for clemency – and, at times, deciding in their favour. March later recorded how the process, though 'just', was 'painful and distasteful' to him.[9]

Castro's response to the criticisms was to compare the trials to the Nuremberg Trials at the end of the Second World War, and to ask why the US hadn't criticised Batista's crimes. Cuba's media – such as the newspaper *Revolución* – published eyewitness accounts of the barbaric methods used by Batista's police, and reported the discovery of secret graves of the mutilated bodies of young opponents who'd been tortured, raped and then executed by Batista's henchmen. According to a private national survey carried out at the time, these executions of murderers and torturers – by firing squad – were seen as a legitimate form of popular justice: 'over 90 per cent of the respondents supported the trials and executions'.[10]

As head of La Cabaña, Che also undertook other roles – working intensely, as ever. This was despite being in poor health by then, the result of twenty-five months of hard struggle in the mountains, involving hunger, lack of sleep and many asthma attacks. According to Gadea, after moving to the Escambray Mountains for the final phases of the struggle, Che had developed a 'minor tubercular condition in one lung'. Nonetheless, Che quickly turned La Cabaña into a training school for the men under his command, with a programme that included literacy classes, cultural events, and political education. He also began a magazine called *Cabaña Libre,* as well as setting up some small factories. In late January 1959, he became head of the army's Department of Training, and set up a Military-Cultural Academy. Che saw giving political and cultural education, before soldiers returned to their local areas, as helping to secure the revolution. In addition, he played an important role in discussions between the PSP and DR – in July 1961, these merged to form the Integrated Revolutionary Organisations (ORI). A year later, the ORI became the United Party of the Socialist Revolution (PURS) – with Che as one of its six-member Secretariat. At first, Che saw PSP members as more reliable, and so often appointed them as administrators. But this began to change because of what he increasingly saw as their 'orthodox' communism and sectarianism.[11]

The Revolution begins now

In the Escambray, Che had begun establishing a group around him who were sympathetic to socialism; and it seems he'd agreed with Castro that his role after victory would be economics – which he'd been studying since his time in Mexico. In January 1959, Castro and the M26J had formed a coalition government with some of Batista's other opponents, with Manuel Urrutia – an anti-communist liberal – becoming the new president. However, at the same time, Castro also set up the Office of the Revolutionary Plans and Coordination (OPRC). From the beginning, Che was part of this unofficial 'shadow government', which was composed of Castro's closest advisers. A situation of dual power between the ORPC and the government soon developed – before long, Che became increasingly influential on political and economic developments.

By the end of January, Che began to make his political agenda more public. At a PSP-sponsored event, he delivered a speech – 'Social Projections of the Rebel Army' – calling for revolutionary agrarian reforms; the creation of a strong domestic economy via rapid industrialisation; and the ending of Cuba's economic dependence on the US. This led him, in February, to outline once again his hopes for the future: 'Today, we are set on going to the big landholdings, even on attacking and destroying them ... The rebel army is ready to carry the agrarian reform to its final conclusion.'[12]

Particularly significant for his future course, he'd also argued in his January speech that Cuba was now the example that other Latin American countries should follow, seeing the Cuban Revolution as the beginning of the liberation of the continent: 'There is another [lesson] for our brothers of America … and that is to make agrarian revolutions, to fight in the fields, in the mountains, and from there to the cities.' According to March, 'steps were being made to establish Cuba's collaboration with liberation movements and other progressive struggles' from as early as February 1959.[13]

However, following another asthma attack, Che, was struck down by pulmonary emphysema in February. So, on Castro's insistence, in early March he moved to Tarará – a town by the sea but close to Havana – to recover. But his strict principles meant he was deeply unhappy about the house he was allocated: a luxurious house, previously owned by an important Batista supporter. After a letter, published in a magazine, had criticised him for staying in such a house, Che sent an open letter to *Revolución*:

> I must clarify to the readers … that I did not contract my sickness in gambling dens or staying up all night in cabarets, but working more than my body could withstand for the revolution … I chose the simplest [house], but at any rate it is still an insult to popular sentiments.

Che, who'd become addicted to Cuban cigars in the mountains, was annoyed when his doctors restricted him to one cigar a day. He got round it by having specially made cigars that were 1½ft long! When an assistant came in and caught him smoking, he chuckled and said: 'Don't worry about the doctors. I'm obeying their orders – just one cigar a day, no more, no less.'[14]

His recuperation in Tarará took two months – yet despite being ill, he continued to work. He used his bedroom as an office, and was sometimes visited by relatives of those facing execution. More importantly, his home became an unofficial 'shadow' government, where future plans were discussed and formulated – with Castro visiting most days. In particular, there were discussions about agrarian reform. In May 1959, the National Institute of Agrarian Reform (INRA) was set up. This absorbed the OPRC, and quickly became the de facto government. According to March, it was Che who was given the task of drafting the Agrarian Reform Law. This allowed the government to take over large estates and give them to landless peasants to work – though in collectives rather than as private holdings. These agrarian reforms angered both the US and Cuba's big landowners – and Urrutia resigned as president, being replaced by the moderate Osvaldo Dorticos. Increasingly, moderate ministers began to resign, to be replaced by more radical people. Che and his group of advisers –

left-wing members of the M26J and the Rebel Army, and representatives of the PSP – continued to work out plans for social, economic and political reforms, which Castro later accepted or remodelled.

At the same time, Che had several regular meetings with Carlos Rafael Rodriguez, a PSP leader – staying up 'practically the entire night discussing revolutionary theory and practice'. Later on, Che and Rodriguez were 'key participants' when 'political economy and the transition to a post-capitalist society' were discussed. Discussions were also held about merging the PSP and the M26J. Once recovered, Che moved from Tarará to a more modest house in Santiago de las Vegas, on the outskirts of Havana. Secret discussions then took place between Che, Raúl and members of the PSP on how to overcome anti-communist feelings in the Movement and wider Cuban society. March, who was still anti-communist herself, told Che she didn't trust Anibal Escalante, the Secretary of the PSP, and some of the other members. To her, 'It seemed like a conspiracy within another larger conspiracy.' Over the coming months, however, she began to read Soviet literature, and her 'political views slowly began to "redden" under Che's influence – he always had great powers of persuasion … He tried to convince me about communism, patiently clearing up my misconceptions, without me feeling that he was forcing his views on me.'[15]

A revolutionary ambassador

Che's next role was as a 'roving ambassador'. On 12 June 1959, Che was sent by Castro on what turned out to be a three-month diplomatic 'goodwill' mission to establish friendly relations with Yugoslavia, and several other states in the Middle East and Asia. He was also tasked with negotiating trade deals to find new markets for Cuba's exports – and thus reduce Cuba's reliance on the USA. At the time, Che's supporters wondered if he were being 'constructively demoted' because of his openly-expressed communist views. In fact, the trip came about when, in May, Che had suggested to Castro the importance of having good relations with other UN countries, given the increasing hostility of the US. Both Che and Castro also thought Non-Aligned reforming leaders – such as Tito, Nasser, Ben Bella, Nehru and Mao Zedong – would have valuable advice to offer their new revolutionary regime.

March – who, as his personal secretary, had accompanied him on most of his government trips around Cuba – did not go with him. Che's strict morality led him to say that it would look like a privilege, unfair on those who weren't able to bring their partners. She described this as 'a difficult time' for her – with Che getting angry with her when she became upset, after he'd refused to agree with Castro that she could go. Later, Castro again suggested Che let her join him, but he still refused. Instead, he sent her several postcards and letters. Towards the end of the trip, while in Morocco, he wrote:

> Aleiducha
>
> From the last leg of the journey I send you a faithful marital hug. I had hoped to remain faithful, even with my thoughts. But the local Moorish women here are truly stunning…
> Kisses
> 'Che'

Yet there is no evidence that he was other than totally faithful to her – before and after their marriage.[16]

In all, Che visited fourteen countries on that trip – including Japan, which was a big sugar importer. He also had meetings with Soviet representatives about increasing their purchase of Cuba's sugar. Che was greeted warmly both by crowds and by heads of state, and was able to successfully negotiate important deals, making his trip a big success. Castro's confidence in Che's ability to carry out such diplomatic missions meant he was sent on several more after 1959, becoming Cuba's foreign relations minister in all but name. In October 1960, Che went to China, negotiating Cuba's first trade deal with a 'socialist camp' country. According to March, Che's China trip had initiated thoughts about the different ways to achieve socialism: 'He was very enthusiastic about what he had seen in China. He admired the way they worked and how they were meeting the challenge of development.' March says Che's enthusiasm for the Chinese approach earned him 'the reputation of being a Maoist and pro-China.' However, as she says: although he 'was critical of what he saw in the Soviet Union, especially the privileges some leaders enjoyed. Nevertheless, he recognized the spirit of the people and of their revolution.'[17]

On his various trips, Che played an important role in establishing relations with other 'Third World' and ex-colonial states. He also played a crucial role in the secret negotiations that took place between Cuba and the Soviet Union. Initially, these were concerned with economic aid and trade – but eventually led to the decision to allow the USSR to place nuclear missiles on the island. Part of his duties on those trips was to attend government or embassy receptions. Typically, he didn't wear smart clothes. March was confused when a friend remarked to her that Che was looking elegant at one such reception, because his boots were scuffed and his uniform was creased. It was explained thus: 'Look, he has not one, not two, but three pens in his pocket!'[18]

Though Che – the archetypal wanderer – was 'back on the road', the reality was that he saw very little of the countries he'd long wanted to visit. Instead of travelling by motorbike or foot, he was transported by planes and official cars. In a letter to his mother, he wrote how frustrating it was that his 'dream of visiting all these countries has come true in a way as to thwart all my happiness'. Unable to enjoy 'untainted pleasures like dreaming in the shade of a pyramid or over the tomb of Tutankhamun', he had to attend endless meetings. However, during his first trip, he came to realise what his purpose in life was: 'now I have a sense of my historical duty ... I feel that I have a capacity to give something to others and an entirely fatalistic sense of my mission, which makes me quite fearless.' He ended the letter on a wistful note: 'I don't know why I'm writing all this: maybe I just miss Aleida.' On subsequent trips, he was usually accompanied by March, when she wasn't heavily pregnant.[19]

In the summer of 1961, Che made another trip to the Soviet Union – which would prove to have significance after his murder. In September, on the way back to Havana, his plane was forced to stop over in Shannon Airport in the Republic of Ireland for two days because of fog. On the second day, Che and two companions (all in military raincoats) left Shannon Airport and went to the Marine Hotel in Kilkee. Working in the bar was Jim Fitzpatrick, who had three heroes at that time: Che, Castro and Cienfuegos. He couldn't believe that one of them had just walked into his bar: 'I recognised him immediately. I was only about 16; I wasn't expecting to speak with Che Guevara.' Che went to order drinks – and, while waiting for their Powers whiskeys, mentioned his Irish roots: 'he told me his ancestors were from Cork'. In 1968, Fitzpatrick – by then an illustrator – was asked to produce an image for a commemorative exhibition to mark Che's murder the year before. It was he who turned Korda's photo into the famous red-and-black poster that soon began to appear globally.[20]

Department of Industrialisation

Shortly after returning from his first trip abroad, Che was given what would prove to be the first of his economic roles when, in October 1959, he was put in charge of the new Department of Industrialisation, a key role within INRA. For the next five years, Che increasingly focused on how industrial organisation, economic management, and political principles could allow an underdeveloped economy make the transition to socialism.

During 1959–61, Che's management contributed to a big increase in Cuba's economic development, along with a huge improvement in meeting the basic needs – including and healthcare – of the vast majority of Cuba's people. Che worked on this enthusiastically – in part, because it would improve the skills people needed to industrialise. However, the expenditure on all this caused certain economic problems after 1961. Che's critics often blamed these on his ideas and mismanagement. Such criticism, though, often fails to take into consideration the impact of Cuba's 'structural underdevelopment' before 1959. Cuba had become locked 'into a structure of underdeveloped, mono-crop dependency', with US monopolies dominating its economy. Another hugely significant problem – which exerted an increasingly negative impact on Cuba's economy – was the 'devastating impact of the US blockade' which began in October 1960. Both these factors 'significantly reduced the choices open to the Cuban government'. In addition, there were constant military attacks on Cuban economic targets – mostly sponsored by the US.[21]

As head of the new department, Che felt the first important step towards ending Cuba's neo-colonial economy was to increase agricultural output, in order to finance industrialisation and diversification of the economy. March acted as his assistant – she'd initially refused, but changed her mind when he told her 'with an ironic grin, he had been assigned a pretty secretary'. On her first day, she saw he had indeed been assigned an attractive secretary: the wife of Nuñez Jiménez, the Director of the INRA. Without informing Che, March asked her to leave, saying Che only needed one secretary. She only told him about this in 1966, when she'd joined him in Tanzania after his failed Congo campaign. As she said: 'By that time, I was no longer as jealous as I had been!'[22]

Che's new role also meant he was responsible for the various industries the new government nationalised: including oil, nickel, sugar-refining and tobacco. He then began drawing up plans for industrialisation, to make Cuba self-sufficient as quickly as possible – to reduce foreign exchange expenditure on imported goods. This was especially important, as the US increasingly refused to share vital technology. In regular visits around Cuba to promote his plans – often accompanied by March – he met many workers. According to her, Che was particularly moved by the plight of the nickel miners – and became determined to ensure they had adequate food and housing. He insisted that 'measures were taken to humanize their work, and the miners gained a sense of dignity … For the first time in their lives they were treated like human beings.' On a personal level, she knew 'how happy he was in those days, in the few moments in which he could escape into our private world'.[23]

In addition to these responsibilities, Che also took part in voluntary labour at weekends, Sunday mornings, and some evenings. March said:

> To this day, many people are astounded about how he managed to do so much voluntary work, given all the other responsibilities he had … On Sundays, after voluntary work and an arduous week at the ministry, Che

> would come home ready to enjoy the company of his children ... We would then have lunch ... Che would occasionally enjoy a glass of wine mixed with water – an Argentine custom he never lost; this was one of the few pleasures he enjoyed.[24]

Che saw education as vital for the success of his economic plans. He made speeches and participated in debates in Cuba's three main universities, urging students to get involved with the revolution: 'Why can't the university march ... on the same road as the revolutionary government and in step with it?' In order to achieve Cuba's industrialisation – and thus its independence – Cuba would need students qualified in useful subjects. He thus urged students to study subjects that would benefit society as a whole, rather than simply choosing subjects out of personal interest. He used his own life as a model – pointing out he'd moved from engineering to medicine, then on to military strategy, and now to economics. To underline his point, he enrolled on a number of advanced mathematics courses in order to be better able to carry out his economic responsibilities.[25]

Che the banker

On 29 November 1959, Che was appointed President of the National Bank of Cuba – thus putting him in charge of the country's finances. According to legend, Che got the job because of a misunderstanding. Castro asked which of his closest ministers was an economist – Che raised his hand, thinking he'd said 'communist' instead! On hearing the news of his new appointment, Che's father allegedly exclaimed: 'My son Ernesto handling funds for the Republic of Cuba? Fidel's crazy. Every time a Guevara starts a business, it goes bust.' Whatever the truth, Che later said he'd been appointed for revolutionary reasons: 'economic programs and the drive toward rapid advancement of the revolution was being strangled ... [I] knew nothing about banking but operated according to the revolutionary government's guidelines.' Later, he admitted he'd never really liked his banking role, preferring his industrial work at INRA.[26]

Typically, as soon as he'd been appointed, Che – who was unfamiliar with banking and finance – immediately began studying to make up for his lack of knowledge. One problem was that just before he fled from Cuba, Batista had transferred $424 million of Cuba's money to US banks. When Che asked for a loan, this was blocked by the US. As head of the bank, Che pushed for economic independence. Almost immediately, he took steps to control Cuba's foreign currency reserves and transactions, and import licences, by breaking ties with the International Monetary Fund, and nationalising various private banks. Later, most foreign banks were nationalised. He also withdrew all Cuba's gold deposits from the US; ended special guarantees to foreign corporations; and announced that Cuba would instead seek close trade and financial ties with the 'socialist' bloc of countries headed by the Soviet Union. As well as unsettling banking executives by his lack of formality and frequently having 'longhaired people with guns' in his office (mainly his bodyguards from the guerrilla campaign), his signature on Cuba's new banknotes upset their sense of protocol, as he just signed it 'Che'! Che admitted: 'I'm still more of a guerrilla than a bank chairman.'[27]

Minister of Industries

In February 1961, Che was given his final economic role – as Minister of Industries (MININD). This put him in charge of all the companies which had been taken into social ownership in August 1960 – which meant almost all the Cuban economy was now under his direction. He was impatient to forge ahead with industrialisation, but Cuba's under-developed economy presented many problems. His immediate aim was to end the 'sugar monoculture as the way to break out of Cuba's neo-colonial status and underdevelopment'. As March notes, 'This was a gigantic challenge that only someone like Che could have undertaken, given his willingness to work, his sense of responsibility, his creative spirit, as well as his ability to study and reflect on what he was doing.'[28]

An indication of Che's industrial priorities were evident in a televised speech he'd made on his return from a trip to the Soviet Union: '[the socialist countries abroad] … are countries where every last cent has to be used in production for development'. In the coming months, he again stressed the need to link industrial development to education and the goal of socialism: 'In the new stages of the revolutionary struggle, there will be no privileged officials or plantation owners. The only privileged people in Cuba will be the children.' He increasingly saw the next generation as crucial, and made many efforts to gain their support. However, when the US imposed, and then extended, an economic blockade against Cuba – cutting off over 75 per cent of Cuba's foreign trade – shortages of various items soon appeared, including meat, milk and shoes. As a result, rationing had to be introduced. Typically, Che was absolutely insistent that his own growing family didn't have items that ordinary Cubans didn't have.[29]

As part of his responsibilities, he made regular visits to the provinces 'to check on the advances in the industrial sectors of the country'. March accompanied him, making notes of his discussions with workers: 'He always wanted to get as close as possible to the workers, in order to get a real sense of their needs as well as being able to contribute to finding solutions to problems.' She said they enjoyed those trips:

> being able to share an intimacy that we could not have had under other circumstances. Eventually I was able to come to terms with my feelings of jealousy. I came to understand that Che took his work very seriously and did not allow minor distractions to get in the way.[30]

Che was, from the beginning, refreshingly open about how the Cuban Revolution had already made mistakes, and would probably do so in the future. As always, he was his own harshest critic: 'The main cause of our errors was our lack of a sense of reality at a given moment.' This was something Castro was reluctant to admit – and it led to one of the few instances in which their different viewpoints became public. Yet, Che – who'd conquered his asthma and who believed Cuba's example would inspire other revolutions – remained convinced that a change in direction and approach; a good dose of revolutionary passion; and the spread of revolution elsewhere, would help Cuba overcome these problems: 'Quietly and full of wrath, the working people will go forward until some day, some place, some spark will ignite and a new revolutionary flame will be lit in the Americas.'[31]

On 12 February 1961 – shortly after a trip to the Soviet Union – he admitted in an article: 'Revolutions ... are made of passion, of man's fight for social vindication, and are never perfect. Neither was ours. It committed errors and some of these were paid for dearly.' For him, the main problems facing Cuba and its people were: lack of awareness, lack of organisation, outdated machinery, and lack of technical knowledge. But he was confident that Cuba's people would overcome them – provided they realised that the country was involved in a sharp struggle against the forces of imperialism and capitalism. He also made the point that certain luxuries were less important than basic supplies. Although he was a centraliser, he was also always concerned about party bureaucracy, which March says 'he saw as the greatest danger of other socialist systems ... In his writings, he constantly warned of the serious problems created when the party ... substituted itself for the administrative apparatus.'[32]

In particular, he began to blame himself and his department for not having included workers in the early planning process: 'We can see clearly now that the people had nothing to do with drawing up the plan, and a plan with no worker participation runs a serious risk of failure.' He increasingly tried to move away from the influence and advice of Soviet planners – believing that shortages of raw materials and spare parts would have been seen much earlier if there'd be proper worker participation. He was clearly learning on the job and refining his views and ideas. As time passed, this attitude brought him into increasing conflict with those – including Castro and the PSP – who came to favour the Soviet approach as Cuba began to rely more on more of aid from the Soviet bloc. Che's attitude – as ever – was to believe that these problems (which now included dwindling foreign currency reserves because of loss of trade) could be largely overcome by enthusiasm for and dedication to the revolution.[33]

Yet, as the economic situation in Cuba continued to decline, Che was forced to accept that his push for rapid industrialisation was coming unstuck. His industrialisation plans needed the income from sugar sales. Although almost 7 million tons of sugar was produced in 1961, drought – and, in part, government policies – saw this then decline. There was also the increasingly negative impact of the USA's economic blockade. Che, however, was largely undaunted – he would soon announce a plan to double living standards, by getting Cuba to produce at least the basic goods which were normally imported.[34]

Pen and sword

Rather like Trotsky, Che wielded the pen as well as the sword in the fight for revolution. In addition to all his government tasks – after having wielded the 'sword' for over two years in Cuba's mountains – Che devoted considerable time to journalism, and writing in general. Writing was a particular passion, and he often wrote for the independent news agency *Prensa Latina* (Latin Press), which he'd persuaded Masetti to set up. Originally, he'd suggested March for this role but she'd declined, feeling she was 'not ready'. He also wrote for the Rebel Army's official magazine, *Verde Olivo* (Olive Green) – the colour of the Rebel Army's uniform, and the fatigues he invariably wore. His articles there soon led to the magazine earning the nickname 'Olive Red'. As well as writing, he often attended its staff meetings, and helped in other ways. Che continued to be responsible for overseeing the training of the army – out of that, came his first book, *Guerrilla Warfare*.

Che's typical workload was as follows: get up 'at around between 9 in the morning and drank a large cup of black coffee; in the evening, he often played chess, loved eating flan (his favourite dessert) – and taking baths to relax.' He would then work into the early hours of the morning. During this period, he wrote one of the classic works on revolutionary guerrilla warfare: *Guerrilla Warfare*, which covered the Rebel Army's practical experiences in the mountains, dealing with weapons, tactics and strategy, as well as stressing the importance of good relations with the people and the need, in Third World countries, to begin in rural areas. He also used his diaries to write his second book, *Reminiscences of the Cuban Revolutionary War* – though most of the chapters had already been published in the army's magazine. When it was published in Cuba, it proved immensely popular – typically, though, Che refused to profit from its sales. Instead, he put his royalties into revolutionary projects for the Cuban people. In addition, he wrote several other books and articles on various subjects.[35]

He also devoted time to giving interviews to the many intellectuals, Third World leaders and political sympathisers of the Cuban Revolution, who began to arrive in Cuba after 1959. For Che, this must have seemed similar to his time in Guatemala, when he – and many others – had ended up there to see Árbenz's revolution at first-hand, when it was increasingly under siege from a hostile and aggressive US. Except this time Che was no longer an observer, but an active revolutionary.

Two of the most famous people who came to Cuba – and who were keen to meet Che – were the French philosophers and writers Jean-Paul Sartre and Simone de Beauvoir, who stayed for one month. Although Che wasn't an existentialist himself, Sartre had been one of the philosophers he'd read and studied when young. Having discussions with them would have pleased Che. In addition, there was also 'an army of attractive women who flocked to Havana on various pretexts to talk to the handsome revolutionary'. According to March, her role in controlling the number of national and international visitors who wanted an audience with him, gained her 'the rather unjust reputation of being jealous and possessive'. Che's young brother, Juan Martín, described her as 'terribly jealous and possessive, especially of those who had been close to her husband before her,' but recognised that her 'jealousy was probably justified. Che was very popular with women.' Later, in 1966, she admitted she had been jealous.[36]

'Mrs Guevara'

In the early years of the Cuban Revolution, male chauvinism was a problem, holding back the full involvement of women. Che, however, encouraged March – as well as women in general – to take on political roles. In November 1959, she'd been part of a large delegation of Cuban women that attended the Latin American Congress of Women in Chile; her role was to manage the funds. While there, she met Salvador Allende in 1960, and appeared on the front page of one paper described as 'Mrs. Guevara'. When, in 1960, the Federation of Cuban Women was founded, headed by Vilma Espín (Raúl's wife), March acted as its national treasurer; and, at its first congress in 1962, became its General Secretary, staying on its national executive until the end of 1964, when their son Ernesto was born.

March also helped with the literacy campaign, teaching a family in one of the poorer sections of Havana. She recognised the problems of 'persistent male chauvinism that often blocked the incorporation of women into activities outside the home' – but noted that: 'Che backed me up in everything I did, both on a personal level and in family matters.' One aspect of the FMC's work was, as the US stepped up its actions against Cuba, was to get women into the National

Revolutionary Militia. While Che was on a trip to the USSR in 1961, March – pregnant with Camilo – went with the FMC to China. She, however, didn't have the same positive reaction to China as had Che, focusing on the deprivation. In November 1961 she went to the Soviet Union, where she saw 'another level of socialist development'. March herself 'had to juggle housework, work and four children' – made easier by the provision of day care, care in primary schools and scholarships and educational programmes the government began to bring in.[37]

Family matters

Che and March's family grew during his time in government. On 24 November 1960, while he was out of the country, March gave birth to their first child: a daughter, named Aleida. In May 1962, Camilo (named after Cienfuegos) was born, with March noting: 'Che's greatest dream was fulfilled, his male ego finally boosted, with the birth of a son, Camilo.' They then rented a larger house, to accommodate their growing family – March, who wanted a home separate from the garrison, chose it, with:

> Che agreeing rather reluctantly … We lived like the rest of the population, eating whatever food was available with the ration booklet that everyone had … We generally lived according to the spirit of the revolution and Che's austere lifestyle … I never worried too much about what we lacked. I knew we lived like every other Cuban who knew that sacrifices had to be made … Che never bothered much about material things, and that is how we lived.

Che had an office in their house on the second floor, where he often worked – it was where he kept his most treasured books, most of them marked with his notes or comments. 'This small room was his refuge', and where he had private meetings with comrades from all over Latin America 'to discuss common dreams for the redemption of our continent'.

Their last two children would be born there – Celia (named after Che's mother) on 14 June 1963 (Che's 35th birthday); and, finally, Ernesto, on 24 February 1965, born while Che was in Algeria on what would be his last trip as a representative of the Cuban government. From there, he sent his son a telegram, 'affectionately addressing the baby as "Tete", the pet name his family had given him when he was a little boy'. These additions would result in a move to an even larger rented house.[38]

'Tentacles of the Yankee Octopus'

Historically, the US had long seen – and treated – Cuba as a part of its 'own backyard'. But, by 1959, the Cold War was ten years old, making the US see 'communism' as an additional reason for interfering against the Cuban Revolution. Many of the problems Che's economic plans encountered were the result of, and were made worse by, the USA's increasingly hostile actions. This would prove to be a significant factor in his decision to return to guerrilla warfare – as a way to loosen the grip of the 'tentacles of the Yankee octopus'.

Despite various reforms after 1959, the US remained in control of huge parts of Cuba's economy. This was especially so as regards key industries such as oil, chemicals and minerals. During 1960, tensions between Cuba's new revolutionary government and the US increased – initially over the amount of compensation for US-owned land which had been nationalised in the first phase of agrarian reform. When the US refused to sell weapons to Cuba's new government, Castro had sought other suppliers. On 4 March 1960, *La Coubre* – a French ship carrying small-arms weapons and grenades from Belgium – exploded in Havana harbour, killing almost 100 people, and injuring hundreds more. Che, who was in an INRA meeting, rushed to the harbour to help treat the victims. At a memorial service for the victims the following day, Castro blamed the US – though the US denied any responsibility. It was at that memorial meeting that Alberto Korda took the famous photograph – in which Che's face expressed quiet but determined anger – which would soon be turned into the poster that became the familiar image of rebellion across the world.[39]

As a result, in May 1960 Cuba established full diplomatic relations with the USSR – and discussions began for Cuba to receive weapons from the Soviet Union to defend itself against US aggression. In the summer of 1960, the US – Cuba's largest customer – had reduced the amount of Cuban sugar that could be imported, and had then refused to export oil. Cuba announced a trade deal with the USSR, which agreed to purchase the sugar quota being blocked by the US. Payment would be in the form of oil and other goods and products. However, when the first shipments of Soviet oil began to arrive, the US government advised the US-owned oil refineries to refuse to process it. Cuba's response was to nationalise the oil refineries. By late August, Cuba had nationalised all remaining sugar plantations, as well as utility companies (most of which were also US-owned).

In September 1960, Committees for the Defence of the Revolution (CDRs) were established across the country, essentially turning ordinary citizens into armed popular militias to defend against any US-sponsored invasion. As far as Che was concerned, given the USA's hostility, Cuba also needed closer ties with the USSR. Later though – despite receiving loans and credits from the USSR – Che became increasingly concerned about the USSR's economic methods and system. Then, in October 1960, the US imposed a partial trade embargo on Cuba – this, known as 'El Bloqueo' in Cuba, eventually became total in February 1962.

The Bay of Pigs

As well as its economic measures, the US severed diplomatic relations with Cuba on 3 January 1961, while the CIA began aiding 'unidentified' bombing raids from US territory and various Central American states, and working with a group of pro-Batista Cuban exiles in Miami to launch a counter-revolutionary invasion. These tensions eventually led to the Bay of Pigs incident, in which Che played only a minor role. Che had expressed the hope that Kennedy would prove less aggressive than Eisenhower, and that he would not 'allow himself to be so influenced by monopolies'. However, Kennedy was as determined as his predecessor to 'solve the problem' of Cuba – and supported plans to overthrow Cuba's new revolutionary government. In late January 1961, Cuba's western province of Pinar del Río was placed on red alert; and Che, responsible for its defence, visited the region. As part of its defence, Che encouraged the formation of armed civilian militias – these received political education as well as military training.[40]

On 15 April 1961, US B-26 bombers – piloted by Cuban exiles – bombed the small Cuban air force base in Santiago, causing massive destruction. One immediate result was that on 16 April, at the funeral of those killed in the attack, Castro at last announced that the Cuban Revolution was now going to be a socialist one – much to Che's satisfaction. Che once again went to Pinar del Rio, in order to take charge of Cuba's troops there. On arrival, he warned the soldiers that a full-scale US invasion was likely. Che felt confident that Cuba's army would be successful in defeating the expected invasion. The test came on 17 April, when 1,500 exiles – supplied with US weapons – landed on Playa Giron (Bay of Pigs) – but on the south coast of Cuba. This 'Liberation Army' expected to find support among Cuba's citizens, but the vast bulk of Cuba's population did not support these 'Yankee' invaders, and Cuba's army and its armed militias quickly outmanoeuvred them. Around 160 Cubans were killed in the fighting, with the exiles losing over 100 men. In the end, around 1,200 of these would-be invaders were captured. They were eventually released, in return for over $50 million in food and medicine from the US.

Although Che did not take part in the fighting, he was nonetheless wounded – he accidentally dropped his pistol, which went off, with a bullet wounding him in a cheek and exiting from behind an ear, necessitating a day in hospital. Castro informed March who visited him – having dropped Adelieta (Aliucha) off with Celia Sanchez. Che was recovering from the operation when she arrived; he was very lucky – the bullet came within an inch of entering his skull.

Later, Che put their victory down to Cuba's people's sense of social justice and popular support, saying:

> You can't expect that a man who was given a thousand acres by his father and just shows up here to get his thousand acres back won't be killed by a countryman who is used to having nothing and now has a terrible urge to kill the guy because he wants to take his land away.[41]

Alliance for Progress?

Yet, despite the USA's economic and military aggression, Che's response was mixed when, in August 1961, the US announced details of its 'Alliance for Progress' (AfP), at a meeting of the OAS in Uruguay. He commented that 'the Alliance for Progress is not for Cuba but against her', and went on to draw a clear distinction between US and Soviet aid, in an attempt to convince other countries that Soviet aid was better, and pointing out that the US did not give funds to enable under-developed countries to become 'industrial-agricultural countries, at one and the same time'. Nonetheless, Che also made it clear that Cuba gave the AfP critical support: 'if and insofar as it means a real improvement for Latin America in the standard of living of all its two hundred million inhabitants'. He even met with the US representative and seemed willing to open a dialogue with the US, but the US was not interested. Later that month, Che wrote an article for his department's journal:

> what worries [the US] is the sudden appearance of popular powers and the possibility that these powers might acquire such strength that they can afford, as in the case of Cuba, to challenge US orders and implement an economic and social policy which the US would no longer be able to control.[42]

While at that OAS meeting in Punta del Este, Uruguay, Che (who had informed them he'd be there) met up with his whole family who'd travelled up from Argentina, and a 'very emotional and intense' reunion took place. Among those present was his adoring aunt Beatriz, who wanted him back in Buenos Aires. Despite being Cuba's representative at the conference, Che took all his meals with his family, sitting between his mother and his aunt, with 'a protective arm around each of their shoulders'. According to his brother, they all felt this might be the last time they saw him. As it turned out, it was – apart from his mother, who visited him in Cuba a few months later.[43]

In October 1961, Che went on a mission to see 'actually existing socialism' for himself. In what turned into a two-month trip, he travelled all over the Soviet bloc, as well as China and North Korea. While away, he concluded various satisfactory economic deals and loans – including for Czechoslovakia to build a car factory in Cuba. His agreements with China spurred the Soviet Union to up its commitment to buy Cuba's sugar. While in the USSR, he met up again with Nikolai Leonov, who was his interpreter – and they spent much time together. According to Leonov, Che told him that whether or not the Cuban revolution succeeded, he would 'go out with a machine gun in my hand ... I'll keep fighting to the end'. However, he was disappointed the USSR didn't agree to help build a steel factory in Cuba. He also was disappointed in that the number of official functions and meetings meant he had little opportunity to chat with ordinary Soviet citizens.[44]

A more positive experience took place during the annual celebrations for the anniversary of the 1917 November Revolution, when he stood in a place of honour next to Khrushchev, directly above Lenin's tomb – a man he had come to admire so much. While, in East Berlin, he met Tamara Bunke, a young German-Argentine woman and an informal Stasi informant, who acted as an interpreter. She was a communist, and was keen to help spread revolution. She would eventually – under the *nom de guerre* of 'Tania' – help Che in his ill-fated mission in Bolivia.

The Cuban Missile Crisis

The next military conflict involving Che was the Cuban Missile Crisis. After the Bay of Pigs invasion failed, Kennedy extended the economic blockade and approved CIA plans to ruin the Cuban economy via acts of sabotage, in what was called 'Operation Mongoose'. In January 1962, the US persuaded the OAS to suspend Cuban membership, and ban any arms' sales to Cuba. In addition, it stepped up its training of exiles to carry out sabotage in Cuba. Between February and October 1962 alone, it's estimated the US carried out 716 acts of terrorism on Cuban soil. Predictably, Che became more hostile to the AfP, calling it '"an imperialistic attempt to halt revolutionary impulses' and hinted that revolution across the continent was on the agenda: 'Latin America today is a volcano. It is not in eruption, but is moved by the immense subterranean rumbling that heralds [the revolution's] approach."'[45]

In this tense situation, the USSR offered to secretly place some intermediate/short-range nuclear weapons on Cuba, and to send some 40,000 Soviet troops to help it repel any new US-sponsored invasion. Castro discussed the offer with Che. Che argued that 'Anything that can stop the Americans is worthwhile.' Castro then accepted the offer, seeing it as way of persuading the US not to invade, and to leave its base at Guantanamo Bay. In late August, Che went to Moscow – ostensibly to discuss industrial matters – to successfully get the agreement amended to state that any attack on Cuba would be seen as an attack on the Soviet Union itself. Although the USSR agreed, it refused to make it public as Che had wanted. Che returned to Cuba, trusting that the USSR would honour all parts of the agreement.[46]

However, by the time Che had returned from the Soviet Union, US U-2 spy planes had photographed what seemed to be missile sites. On 16 October, the US – though having its own nuclear weapons stationed in Turkey, on the Soviet Union's south-east border – warned the USSR not to deliver any nuclear missiles to Cuba, and imposed a 'quarantine' to intercept Soviet ships on their way to Cuba.[47]

On 23 October, as tensions mounted, Che was once again sent to Pinar del Rio, where he established his HQ and began to build up ammunition supplies, while also delivering his usual morale-boosting speeches to the Cuban people, warning them that another US invasion was imminent. As discussions took place between the US and the USSR, low-flying US surveillance aircraft were fired on, and on 27 October, the Cubans shot down a U-2 spy plane, killing its pilot.

Castro, convinced a US invasion was imminent, called on the USSR to be ready to fire the missiles in such an event. However, without consulting Cuba, Khrushchev agreed a deal with the US which included removing the missiles in return for a US pledge not to invade the island. Both Che and Castro were furious, with Che commenting: 'when without consulting [the Cuban people], a pact is made to withdraw the missiles, they do not breathe a sigh of relief or give thanks for the truce. Instead they arise to give voice to their willingness to fight ... to fight alone, if they must.'[48]

An unorthodox communist

Despite these military distractions, Che continued his hard work to boost the Cuban economy. Encouraged by the fact that production had actually increased during the Cuban Missile Crisis, he pushed for better wages for workers, and for more technical training. In February 1963, he personally helped test a new sugarcane cutting machine, convinced that mechanisation of this vital crop would help industrialise Cuba. He spent many hours in demanding physical work in the fields, working harder than the others, and helping to repair the machinery. Despite an improvement in production, however, the final sugar harvest fell below what had been planned – and hoped – for.

Increasingly, however, he became concerned that the quality of goods coming from the Soviet bloc was often below-standard, leading him to wonder if the 'Soviet way' was not the way forward. In particular, he worried about using 'capitalist' methods – i.e. individual incentives – to increase productivity. He also began criticising the level of bureaucracy: 'We carbon-copied the experience of brother countries and that was a mistake ... [that] made a dangerous contribution to one of the phenomena that must be fought most in a socialist revolution, that of bureaucracy.' One way he did this was by continuing to do voluntary labour, and to pay regular visits to factories, during which he spent much time talking to the ordinary workers. And, when accompanied by photographers and journalists he insisted they do some physical labour while they were there. But he was disappointed to note that production meetings between workers and management were often poorly attended, commenting that: 'Where does the responsibility for workers' lack of participation and their apathy lie? Simply in that they see the meetings as an obligation to someone, not as a place to sort things out.' Increasingly, he stressed the importance of moral incentives over material ones – and tried to strengthen the connections between workers and their revolutionary government. According to March: 'He was establishing his Budgetary Finance System as an economic management system very different from how the economies in other socialist countries were run. Che rejected Marxism as a dogma, imbuing it with his own highly creative spirit.'[49]

In many ways, Che was a model revolutionary – convinced of the rightness of the cause, he was dedicated to all his duties, putting in long hours. Many close observers saw him as the most intelligent and persuasive of Castro's government. In fact, many people outside Cuba came to a similar conclusion. On 8 August 1960, Che's image appeared on the front cover of *Time* magazine, with an article identifying him as the 'brain' of the Cuban Revolution – with Castro as its 'heart', and Raúl as its 'fist'.[50]

He also continued to be strict about behaviour – he maintained his earlier personal austerity, and did not indulge himself or his family members with any luxuries – always turning down gifts, sometimes in a gruff way. He thus continued to display the individual sacrifice, honesty, loyalty and dedication that had marked his years as a guerrilla fighter. Although he expected much from those who worked under him, he expected even more from himself – often devoting large amounts of free time by doing voluntary physical labour. However, Che continued with an attitude that had earned him the nickname of 'Chanco'. Despite being one of the top three Cuban leaders, he 'always wore his uniform shirt out of his pants and open at the throat and his boots were never laced to the top'. Also, when he visited factories, he always visited and talked to the workers on the shop floor, before meeting with management.[51]

New battlefronts

As well as undertaking so many different government roles after 1959, Che also formulated his ideas about what became known as the 'New Man' concept. Essentially, he was attempting to create a new revolutionary philosophy and ethics. It was this which led him to question aspects of Soviet economic methods. He expounded his views in speeches, articles and at universities, arguing that citizens should put the development of the revolution before their own personal advancement. Never one to ask people to do what he himself was not prepared to do, he set a personal example. However, his – arguably romantic – view of citizenship: that people would be motivated more by the desire to help everyone have a better life, rather than by self-interest, was shared by very few. As Cuba relied more and more on Soviet aid, Che increasingly became a lone voice.

Although Che made common cause with communists across the world, he did so mainly because they were also opposed to imperialism. But it soon became clear he was no 'orthodox' communist. Che increasingly had a problem with the conventional 'Marxist' view supported by the Soviet Union that objective factors had to exist *before* any country could begin moving to socialism. He saw this as to do with their attempt to achieve 'peaceful coexistence' with Yankee imperialism during the Cold War. If anything, as the dispute between Moscow and Beijing developed during the 1960s, he tended to side with Communist China which, at that time, had a more combative approach to foreign relations.

Such views – often openly expressed – began to cause tensions between the Soviet Union and Castro's Cuba. His views also led to tensions with Cuba's communists, which continued up to 1965, when Che left Cuba. Cuba's – and the Soviet Union's – communists saw him as a hopeless romantic dreamer and adventurer, and they criticised his unconventional approach to industrial development, and his outspoken criticism of Soviet foreign policy. Often, when laid up with asthma, he would come up with startling plans and projects. One of these was to foment revolution across Latin America, including to lead a revolution in Argentina himself. Harris concludes that he 'was a dreamer, an adventurer, and an unrelenting rebel against the established order of things'.[52]

Certainly, after just a few years as a minister – something he'd said earlier would kill him – he began to feel frustrated by routine bureaucracy. According to his brother, he became increasingly weighed down by 'the routine, the bureaucracy, and the stifling atmosphere in which he was supposed to be getting the revolution underway'. To his closest friends, he talked of giving it all up, to return to waging revolutionary armed struggle against Yankee imperialism – in Latin America and beyond. For Che, there were two reasons for 'exporting revolution': for its own sake, and as a way to end Cuba's isolation. Believing revolutionaries were 'part of an army fighting in every part of the world', he increasingly thought of leaving Cuba for 'new battlefronts'. March suspected that, towards the end of his time as a minister, he 'was probably already planning for his departure' and his return to guerrilla warfare.[53]

Before leaving Cuba however, Che took an active part in a crucial debate over economics and the way forward for the Cuban Revolution. This 'Great Debate' lasted from May 1963 until the end of 1964 – and its outcome almost certainly played a significant part in his decision, in 1965, to resign from his posts and instead return to guerrilla warfare and international revolution.

Chapter 8

The Great Debate, 1963–64

'To build communism, a new man must be created simultaneously with the material base.'[1]

This chapter examines the 'Great Debate' – sometimes known as the 'Great Economic Debate' – which took place between May 1963 and December 1964. It was initiated by Che, and was a prolonged discussion about what economic methods Cuba should follow. Despite most of those taking part in this debate being ministers and administrators, many of the articles also reached a wider public. This was without precedence in a country belonging to the 'socialist bloc'. There was however, as noted by Farber, no *direct* involvement of the Cuban people themselves, thereby limiting the debate mainly to 'the upper echelons of the government and the political class'.[2]

For many, Che is someone who loved the romance of travelling, yearned for adventure, and was a noted practitioner of guerrilla warfare. Thus it may come as a surprise to discover that Che can be seen as 'an intellectual who studied Karl Marx's *Capital* with scientific rigour'; and that his 'most significant contribution' to revolutionary change lay in his economic ideas and practices while a minister in the Cuban government. According to Mandel, Che was an important economic theoretician 'in the tradition of Marx, Lenin and Trotsky'.[3]

The Great Debate arose from problems the Cuban Revolution began experiencing in building a socialist society in what was an underdeveloped economy. While the main focus was on economic questions, there was also a philosophical element – for Che, these two aspects were closely connected. In an interview he gave to *L'Express* on 25 July 1963, he made this connection clear: 'We fight against poverty but also against alienation … If Communism were to bypass consciousness … then the spirit of the revolution would die.'

That Che's wider philosophical and political ideas about socialism underpinned his economic ideas was recognised by Castro in a speech he delivered in October 1967, shortly after Che's murder in Bolivia: 'when we remember Che, we do not think fundamentally of his military virtues. No! … it is in … *the field of ideas* … that…we feel the tremendous loss that his death means to the revolutionary movement.'[4]

Che's economic ideas have been described as both a realistic assessment of Cuba's economic situation in the early 1960s, and an original contribution to Marxist theory. As well as Cuban ministers, economic planners and party leaders – including Che himself – European economists and Marxist activists, who supported the aims of the Cuban Revolution, also took part. These included the French Marxist economist, Charles Bettelheim, and the Belgian Marxist economist, Ernest Mandel. Yet, despite fundamental differences between the two sides, the debate itself was conducted, openly and publicly, in 'an atmosphere of dignity and mutual respect'. In *some* areas, Che's ideas prevailed – and thus the outcome of this Great Debate were not necessarily the *main* reason why, shortly afterwards, he resigned all his ministerial posts to resume guerrilla warfare.[5]

The Trotskyist Connection

Che's criticisms of Soviet economics were seen by 'orthodox' communists as 'Trotskyist heresy'. While in the USSR in 1964, Che invited some Moscow students to the Cuban embassy for discussions. He strongly criticised aspects of the Soviet economic model – and was surprised at how receptive his audience was: 'I had never before found an audience that was more attentive or more concerned, or that grasped my arguments more quickly.' Nonetheless, some students did accuse him of Trotskyism. Although Che said he wasn't a Trotskyist, his reply was interesting: 'I think that either we possess the capacity to demolish a contrary opinion by means of arguments or we should allow it to be expressed.' While just before leaving Cuba in 1965, he replied to charges against him made by several Soviets that his positions were 'Trotskyist' by saying: 'It is not possible to destroy opinions by force, because that blocks any free development of intelligence.'[6]

What made the Great Debate particularly unusual for a Soviet-camp country was that, in early 1964, Che invited Mandel – a leading member of the Trotskyist Fourth International – to take part in that debate. Mandel admired Che's courage in inviting him to Cuba for a debate that the Soviets and 'orthodox' communists had to accept, however grudgingly. *Revolución*, Cuba's 'largest and most influential daily paper', printed an interview with him, and he was also asked to deliver a speech at Havana University. According to Mandel, he was 'literally kidnapped' by Che's Ministry – and the Finance Ministry – to write a long article on the problem of 'value' in the economy of a transitional society. Che also had a four-hour meeting with Mandel – conducted in French.[7]

Shortly after his *Marxist Economic Theory* had been published in 1962, Mandel had sent copies to Che and Castro. Che read it 'enthusiastically and had large parts of it translated' from French into Spanish. In October 1963, Mandel was informed by the Cuban Trotskyist, Nelson Zayas Pazos – who worked in the Foreign Ministry – about the debate taking place between Che and his circle, who were arguing for centralising finances and strengthening moral incentives; and the 'orthodox' communists, who wanted financial independence for industries, and emphasised material incentives for increasing productivity. Zayas encouraged Mandel to get involved in the debate – which he did, by sending an article which supported Che's views; and arguing that if material incentives were to be used, they should mainly be collective rather than individual. He also argued their use needed to be limited, in order to avoid selfishness. By then, Mandel was also in touch with Gadea, Che's former wife, who was sympathetic to Trotskyist ideas. Through her and Zayas, documents of the Trotskyist Fourth International were regularly forwarded to Che.[8]

Transition to socialism

The Great Debate was centered on the transition from capitalism to socialism, and from socialism to communism – especially in an underdeveloped economy like Cuba's. Part of the problem for Marxists is that Marx himself, although providing valuable insights into the workings of capitalism, 'refused to dream up any "model" of socialism'. Thus, later Marxists have had to theorise about the transition to socialism – an undertaking made more difficult because Stalinism had in many ways distorted Marxist concepts. As Mandel pointed out: 'the theoretical framework required to analyse societies moving from capitalism to socialism does not yet fully exist'.[9]

When it came to a victorious socialist revolution occurring in capitalism's periphery, Che – like Mandel – saw the need for aid: either from revolutions in developed capitalist countries, or from the Soviet bloc. One of Che's criticisms of the Soviet Union after 1959 was that much of the aid provided to Cuba used the prices of the international capitalist market. Che also believed using capitalist techniques in post-capitalist societies – such as material incentives – would impede the transition to socialism. Despite some claims to the contrary, although Che advocated moral incentives, he accepted that material incentives – even though they could cause problems – were also needed. Hence both Che and Mandel 'emphasised those incentives which could stimulate collective behaviour, improvements in the conditions of work, education and responsibility'.[10]

Che was also concerned about bureaucracy – seen as a particular problem in underdeveloped countries attempting the transition to socialism. Yet Che was convinced that this 'did not mean it was impossible to resist bureaucratic degeneration, or that market relations would "necessarily" predominate'. Both Che and Mandel made 'a fundamental distinction between the existence of "market categories"... and the domination of the law of value'. Hence, unlike his opponents, Che didn't see the former necessitating the latter. Where Che and Mandel differed, at least in 1963, was over how to combat bureaucratisation. Mandel argued for democratic and centralised self-management by workers at the workplace, but under the control of a central authority directly chosen by workers' councils. However, although Che supported management of enterprises by trade unions, he only did so on the proviso that they were truly representative and not controlled by Cuba's 'orthodox' communists who, he pointed out, were not that popular in Cuba. On this issue, Mandel warned him against 'throwing the baby out with the bath water', arguing that 'Self-management by workers was entirely compatible with a central plan democratically decided' by the workers.[11]

Che considered it vital to have aspects of the socialist future in the immediate post-capitalist society – otherwise, there would be no socialist future. Ultimately, the main difference between Che (and Mandel) on the one hand, and Bettelheim on the other, was that the former were adamant that during the transition to socialism, while certain 'market mechanisms' would need to be used, the *crucial* aspect was that the market should not determine priorities – and that these 'market mechanisms' should be 'severely restricted and progressively eliminated'. Thus, both Che and Mandel were 'very hostile to ... any notion of enterprise self-financing'. In many respects, Che had adopted economic positions on the state budget and central planning that were fundamentally those expressed by both Mandel and Trotsky.[12]

According to Löwy, Che's ideas on philosophy, humanism, ethics, economics, politics and guerrilla warfare form a coherent whole which seem 'to transcend Stalinism and reformism, and to go back to the living sources of revolutionary communism'. However, although Che was against bureaucracy, he hadn't formulated a fully worked-out idea about socialist democracy by the time his life was cut short. Whether he would have done so, had he not been murdered, remains speculative – although Mandel certainly believed Che was heading in the direction of real socialist democracy. Additionally, Che believed a socialist economy had to have a humanistic perspective based on communist ethics.[13]

Che's transition

Shortly after becoming Minister of Industries, Che sponsored a seminar on Marx's *Capital* for leading members of his department. Although critical of some aspects of the Soviet model, Che hadn't at first believed these would necessarily prevent the transition to socialism. However, in 1963, Che began criticising the Soviet Union's economic model. For him, decentralised financial management of state-owned industries (known as the Auto-Financing System – AFS), and the use of material incentives for workers, were 'basically capitalist methods of organization, management, and investment'. By December 1964 – as a result of his ever-deepening study of Marxism – he attacked the Soviet Union for using the law of value (strict profitability), and instead argued for a central Budgetary Finance System (BFS). He concluded that Soviet methods failed to recognise the need to change people's attitudes and values. Those methods, he now felt, would merely reproduce capitalist social relations and consciousness, and, as a result, 'a crisis will come'.[14]

Che's ideas on economic issues – like his views on foreign policy – were closer to those of the Chinese Communist leadership, which accused the Soviet Union of 'revisionism' of, and a 'rightist deviation' from, Marxism. Che believed relying on capitalist methods would prevent the formation of the new socialist consciousness needed for the transition to communism. It was this outlook that saw him pitted against the dominant economic views of 'orthodox' communists. Overall, his ever-developing Marxist analysis made him increasingly aware of the problems surrounding the political economy of socialist transition, and even enabled him to see signs that risked the return of capitalism in the Soviet Union and the socialist bloc. Although he didn't believe that capitalism existed in the Soviet Union, he did argue that 'they have forgotten that Marx existed'. By 1965, as he left for the Congo, he had concluded – correctly – that 'without a dramatic policy change, capitalism would return to the Soviet Union'.[15]

The main arguments in Cuba's Great Debate surrounded the law of value and planning; the relationship between productive forces and production relations; and whether the nature of socially owned means of production should be based on commodity (or 'market') principles or on non-commodity ones. Twenty or so articles were produced during this period, with Che writing six of them. His main opponents were Carlos Rafael Rodríguez (president of INRA) and Alberto Mora (Minister of Foreign Trade) – both followed AFS. Yet, when Mora was removed from his post, Che asked him to join his Ministry as an adviser. Although disagreeing with Mora's arguments, in typical openness, Che charged him with a project intended to define a model socialist enterprise – saying 'one of them would be proved wrong but that the discussion would contribute to enrich and deepen an important polemic'. Some of Che's colleagues found this difficult to understand: Che's response was: 'Alberto just has a different opinion, but this work could help him test if he was right or not.'[16]

Although Che recognised that – given the US blockade and its aggression – Cuba needed economic help from the Soviet Union, he argued its capitalist concepts and formulas should be completely abandoned, and replaced with socialist motivation and the development of 'new' humans. Che felt Soviet advisers were pushing wrong policies on Cuba: keeping it reliant on sugar production; urging material incentives; and advising Cuba's nationalised industries to adopt financial self-management. For Che, these would prevent Cuba from having a more balanced economy that, through industrialisation, could become self-sufficient. In 1961, the Soviet Union sent Professor Anastasio Mansilla to Cuba, to develop a 'correct' Marxist education. Members of Cuba's Council of Ministers then began studying Marx's *Capital* with him. Che often challenged his interpretations – at one all-night session, unable to settle a heated debate, Mansilla threw up his hands and 'exclaimed that Guevara was right'.[17]

Che's economics

As Minister of Industries, Che applied a centralised BFS for the economic management of Cuban industries, and adopted policies which included emphasising moral incentives over material ones as a way of increasing production. But by 1963, national output and worker productivity began to stagnate and then decline – mainly because of the US economic blockade, but partly as a result of internal problems and mistakes. Some Cuban planners – and especially members of the communist PSP – blamed Che's policies, and argued that the Soviet model should be adopted for industry. They were backed up by the increasing number of Soviet experts and advisers arriving in Cuba, and by Cuban students returning from studies in Soviet bloc countries.

Opposition to Che's policies was particularly entrenched in INRA's Agricultural Department and in the Ministry of Foreign Trade, staffed mainly by pro-Moscow officials who saw 'orthodox' communist approaches to economic planning and management system as being most appropriate for Cuba. While several economists have criticised Che's economic approach as being idealistic and unrealistic, others – like Yaffe – have agreed with Mandel that Che, as well as playing 'a vital role in industrial organisation and economic development in Cuba', also 'made an indispensable contribution to socialist political economy'.[18]

After becoming Minister of Industries, Che had begun opposing the growing influence of Cuba's pro-Moscow communists, and what he saw as signs of increasing bureaucratism in the state. Essentially, Che had four main positions regarding the construction of socialism: planning as opposed to favouring the application of the law of value; for a central budget rather than financial independence of industries; for moral as opposed to material incentives; and the importance of socialist consciousness. As well as having significance for the development of the Cuban Revolution, this debate would have real importance for Che – arguably setting him on the road that would lead to his death less than three years later.

The Law of Value

According to Silverman, 'the Great Debate began with a controversy over whether the law of value operated in the Cuban economy'. Yaffe sees this as crucial because 'the law of value in "transition economies" is at the heart of the question about the feasibility of constructing socialism'. In particular, Che contrasted what classical Marxism said about the law of value being central to capitalism, to what Soviet economic manuals said about the need to use the law of value in the transition to socialism. Che argued that 'undermining the law of value is essential to resolving the conflict between man and nature which Marx wrote about'.[19]

By the end of 1962, Che's views on this topic were fully developed – and even included the argument that the law of value should not apply to trade between socialist countries – especially underdeveloped ones like Cuba. The Soviet Union and the Soviet bloc countries, however, believed it was necessary to use the law of value, even under socialism, in order to speed up the development of productive forces, *before* dealing with developing the socialist consciousness necessary for the transition to communism. Che, on the other hand, 'warned that depending on the law of value to foster development would undermine collective consciousness, obstructing the construction of socialism and communism'. He wanted to find alternative methods to develop both production under a national plan *and* socialist consciousness.[20]

Crucial to the debate on the law of value was Che's view that the products transferred between state-owned enterprises were not commodities because there was no change in ownership: 'We consider all such establishments to be part of the single large enterprise that is the State.' He also pointed out that Marx had defined 'commodity' in this way: 'In order to be a commodity, the product has to pass into the hands of a second party.' Mandel agreed with Che on this, pointing out that operating the law of value under AFS would allow enterprises to purchase cheaper foreign products and thus hinder development. Che's view was that the construction of socialism necessitated undermining and then abolishing the law of value.[21]

In February 1964, Che conducted the first review of BFS, concluding 'We deny the possibility of consciously using the law of value.' He also argued against the idea of the National Bank of Cuba (NBC) being the key regulator of all economic activity, rather than the state and its national plan. For him, 'the socialist state is the owner of the bank and its revenue, the factories it provides funds for, and the goods they produce'. In place of AFS using the capitalist profit motive to increase labour productivity, Che argued that BFS would do this by education to raise skills, technological and administrative improvements, and emphasis on moral as opposed to material incentives. In fact, under Che,

MININD had begun running pilot schemes in several factories to see if collective social incentives (better housing, more health and educational services) were effective. He also argued that enterprise efficiencies should remove 'the blind motive of profit, the operation of the law of value … placing them within a different framework – socialism'.[22]

Marx had seen socialism as working people – as a free association of producers – carrying out production according to a freely drawn-up and conscious plan. Thus, under socialism – a 'cooperative society based on common ownership of the means of production' – producers would not exchange their products, nor would the labour embodied in those products be accorded value, because 'in contrast to capitalist society, individual pieces of labour are no longer merely indirectly, but directly, a component part of the total labour'. But, under Stalin, the law of value had been elevated into an 'objective' law that couldn't be abolished and thus would have to operate under socialism. According to Löwy, Stalin – despite socialist planning – saw 'the survival of the law of value (and of commodity categories) under socialism … as an excellent training school for managing directors of enterprises!' After Stalin's death in 1953, the idea that the value of goods was decided by supply and demand had become the official Soviet position – and was followed by 'orthodox' communists like Mora.[23]

Even before the Great Debate, Che had followed a very different approach in Cuba's economy. In June 1963, only one month into the debate, his ideas were criticised by Mora in an article. Mora argued that the law of value didn't disappear in a socialist economy, and was related to limited resources and rising human needs. He thus saw the law of value as a crucial element in economic planning; and, in a comment clearly directly against Che, argued that even within the state-owned industries, the law of value still functioned. He also argued – again against Che – that the state-owned sector did not at all constitute 'one single large enterprise [as is thought by] some comrades'. Che's response came in an article published on 3 October 1963. However, before dealing with what were complex technical issues, Che was determined to make it clear who the 'some comrades' were: '"Some comrades" have neither first nor last names … they are the Minister of Industry who writes this article … not to mention others … supporting the budgetary financing system.'[24]

Che argued that Mora's definition of value 'does not correspond to the ideas of Marx', as Marx hadn't seen value as a relation between needs and resources; and that under the centralised BFS he'd developed for Cuba's state-owned industries, the movement of one product to another workshop, or from one enterprise to another, did not constitute 'an act of exchange or a commodity', because the state owned those enterprises. However, the strongest criticism of Che's ideas came from Bettelheim in January 1964. He, too, saw the law of value as an 'objective' law in economies in transition from capitalism to socialism. He further argued that Cuba should follow Soviet economic methods – and specifically rejected the argument put forward by both Che and Mandel, who argued that such views contradicted Marx.[25]

Che's response came in two articles in 1964: 'On the Budgetary System of Finance' (February), and 'The Meaning of Socialist Planning' (June). In them, he rebutted Bettelheim's views on law of value, and further developed his own ideas about planning. Che saw Bettleheim as arguing that, because the law of value existed in the USSR, it proved it was 'necessary'. Che argued that, instead of developing the law of value and commodity relations, a socialist government should 'liquidate as vigorously as possible the old categories' associated with capitalism. Che's views on this were clearly opposed to the official Soviet *Manual of Political Economy*, which spoke of the need to *develop* the law of value in the transition to communism. Instead, Che argued that the law of value – a blind and invisible law shaping the lives of individuals – was opposed to socialist planning. For him, economic planning was the 'way of life in a socialist society', in which human consciousness 'achieves at last a synthesis and directs the economy towards its goal: the complete liberation of man within the framework of a communist society'. Such beliefs were consistent with his philosophical views on the need for a *conscious* transition to communism.[26]

Che saw the capitalist law of value – guided by profit – as radically distinct from socialist planning, which focused on use values and the satisfaction of basic human needs. Typically, despite Cuba being increasingly reliant on Soviet aid for its survival, Che openly criticised Soviet planning methods which he believed were wasting 'the possibilities of development [that] the new production relationships offer for orienting the evolution of man in the direction of "the kingdom of liberty"'. For Che, although aspects of the law of value and commodity categories may well continue in some form during the transition, there was a fundamental contradiction between the law of value and socialist planning, which had to be resolved by progressively abolishing all aspects associated with capitalism.[27]

Central Planning

Che, as Minister of Industries, was determined to industrialise Cuba in order to reduce its dependency on foreign imports. Prior to the Cuban Revolution, even the World Bank had said this was vital for Cuba's development. He saw central planning as crucial to this: 'We can therefore state that centralized planning is characteristic of the socialist society, its definition.' According to Yaffe, Che's BFS – opposed to communist 'orthodoxy' – was based on his understanding of socialism as a transitional stage between capitalism and communism, and was 'an economic management system unique to socialism'.[28]

In Yugoslavia, in 1959, Che had seen for the first time a Self-Financing System of economic planning. His feelings had been mixed. At first, he'd liked the freedom of discussion, and said Yugoslavia had a 'Marxist economy'. He was also impressed by its self-management system, in which workers participated in the management of enterprises – and tried to introduce that in Cuba. Farber, though, has argued that this 'was explicitly rejected by Che Guevara'. In the end, however, Che decided Yugoslavia was 'managerial capitalism with a socialist distribution of the profit', and warned that it 'seemed dangerous', and could end up distorting 'what the socialist spirit should presumably be'. By 1960, as well as having misgivings about the Yugoslav model, he'd been listening to Marxists such as Paul Sweezy and Paul Baran, who'd come to Cuba and had expressed their criticisms of Soviet economics. Che soon came to see the 'orthodox' communist preference for AFS for enterprises after the revolution as wrong-headed and dangerous.[29]

Instead, as Minister of Industries, Che used a centralised budgetary system of finance and planning for all the industries which had been taken into social ownership. Che said it was 'the practical experience of the first days of managing the industries' that led him to adopt such a system. In October 1963, during the Great Debate, Rodríguez criticised Che's methods as 'bureaucratic centralisation' that harmed industry and would ruin agriculture. The main contribution on this issue, however, came from Bettelheim who argued that Che's approach was wrong because, in an underdeveloped economy during the transition to socialism, it was impossible to completely know social wants – therefore commodity categories and freedom of enterprises were necessary features.[30]

Although, in his 'The Significance of Socialist Planning', Che argued against Bettelheim's ideas, he did so fraternally, stating: 'Comrade Bettelheim's article (in spite of the fact that it takes issue with some of the ideas that we have expressed on various occasions) is of real importance, since it comes from a highly learned Marxist economist and theoretician.' For Che, the central issue was the relationship between productive forces and production (i.e. class) relations. The classical Marxist argument was that, especially in transitions from one form of class rule to another, these can sometimes become disconnected.[31]

Yet the 'orthodox' Marxist argument was that there was a strict conformity between productive forces and production relations. Therefore, a socialist revolution was impossible in a country with a low level of productive forces. This was still the official line of the Soviet Union's leadership in the 1960s – and, to an extent, of some Western Marxist economists such as Bettelheim. This was despite the fact that both Lenin and Trotsky had argued that some underdeveloped countries could prove to be weak links in the global capitalist system, and therefore be ripe for a revolution which could then begin to develop the economy using socialist methods. Which, of course, is precisely what had happened in Russia following the November Revolution in 1917.

Che saw denying the possibilities for the construction of socialism in less well-developed countries as a mechanistic view of Marxism. Thus he argued that Cuba, during 1959–62, had, just like Russia after 1917, been able to begin a socialist revolution – despite the backwardness and underdevelopment of its productive force. Referring to both Lenin and Marx, Che went on to argue that what applied to socialist revolution also applied to the socialist production relations it began to introduce, and accused Bettelheim of saying that 'the Cuban Revolution is an aberration'. Or, as Löwy put it: 'one cannot deny that the production relations in a society in transition to socialism are in advance of the productive forces without denying the very possibility of a socialist revolution in a backward country'. Essentially, Che argued for a dialectical approach that recognised that production relations do not reflect productive forces when: 'a new society appears to smash the old one ... when the new one ... is struggling to consolidate itself and destroy the old superstructure'.[32]

Under Che's BFS, though enterprises were able to withdraw funds in accordance with the plan, their income passed 'directly into the hands of the state'. In addition, business management was 'supervised directly by the central organs'. When President of the National Bank, Che had followed Marx regarding ending the financial autonomy of national banks. After he became Minister of Industries, Che criticised his successor, arguing that it 'would be absurd in a socialist economy' for the National Bank to finance 'itself out of its own resources'. To those who said his methods would lead to bureaucratism, he pointed out that centralisation would actually *reduce* bureaucracy, as it would remove duplications at the local level. However, he accepted there were problems regarding how his system operated in Cuba – as was to be expected in the early years of transition away from an underdeveloped capitalist economy. This was one of the reasons why Che placed so much emphasis on education and training. Once again, there were parallels between his views and Mandel's – including how involving as many workers as possible in the management of enterprises would help overcome this particular problem.[33]

For Che, centralised socialist planning – unlike the bureaucratic model followed in the USSR – had a much greater 'power of conscious decision', allowing the removal of the economic 'vestiges of capitalism' to begin from day one. This was in direct opposition to those like Bettleheim, who saw these as eventually disappearing, almost automatically, in some distant future. Mandel generally agreed with Che's position, and contrasted the self-financing of enterprises, which led to autonomy for managers, with central planning which enhanced self-management by local organisations of workers. In June 1964, Mandel – with help from Che – replied to the criticisms from the 'orthodox' Marxists who supported AFS in his article, 'Mercantile Categories in the Transition Period.' Like Che, Mandel saw there was a 'fundamental contradiction between the market and the plan'.[34]

However, Che's insistence on centralised planning did throw up some problems. Farber has criticised Che's insistence on 'a system of highly centralized planning' for being based on 'ill-founded assumptions'. Certainly, Che's Four-Year Plan, announced in 1961, was – as Farber has commented – 'unrealistic', with 'fantastical goals' that ignored 'economic limitations'. The Plan, which projected a doubling of living standards, is seen by Farber as an example of Che's voluntarism as regards socialist transformation. That there is some validity in this judgement is shown by the fact that in March 1962, Che admitted he'd designed 'an absurd plan, disconnected from reality, with absurd goals and imaginary resources'. One factor Che had underestimated was the ever-worsening impacts of the USA's economic blockade.[35]

Incentives

Many biographies of Che focus on his advocacy of moral rather than material incentives as the best way to increase production and, at the same time, aid the transition to socialism. In general, Bettelheim – and other supporters of AFS – were strong advocates of individual bonuses and other material incentives in order to boost productivity. Che, on the other hand, saw this approach as having moral and political implications – as well as economic ones – in post-capitalist societies. Che's ideas on the dialectical nature of changing economic circumstances and human consciousness aligned with those of Marx: 'circumstances are changed by men … [therefore] it is essential to educate the educator himself'.[36]

In opposition to Che, Bettelheim essentially put forward a strictly materialist argument, by suggesting that human consciousness will only change in accordance with the level of development of the productive forces. For Bettelheim, Che's attempts to influence human consciousness by moral incentives were mistaken, if not outright dangerous. According to Löwy, though, Che's thinking was 'much more subtle and dialectical' than Bettelheim's, and was based on his idea that socialism is built by using socialist methods. This is best illustrated in Che's 1965 article, 'Man and Socialism in Cuba':

'The process is twofold: On the one hand, society acts on the individual … while on the other hand, the individual undergoes a conscious phase of self-education … it is necessary to develop a consciousness in which values acquire new categories. Society as a whole must become a huge school.' Once again, Che's ideas were close to those put forward by Mandel who, in June 1967, wrote (in *Le grand débat économique*): 'There is constant interaction between the creation of the material infrastructure necessary for the flowering of the socialist consciousness and the development of this consciousness itself.'[37]

For Che, material incentives were hangovers from capitalism which tended to maintain the isolation and alienation of individuals, and hinder the development of humans as *social* beings. In addition, his travels to various 'socialist bloc' countries had shown him that it was managers and bureaucrats who tended to get the biggest material incentives. Although accepting some material incentives would still be necessary, he insisted these should not be the *main* way of achieving increased production. He also argued that, while they were being used, education should stress these needed to disappear as soon as possible; that most of those material incentives should come in the form of *social* benefits – such as hospitals and schools – rather than individual ones; and that they should be linked to skills acquired by education, to encourage people to study and raise their technical and cultural skill levels. For Che, as Cuba advanced to socialism, material incentives would die out, and be replaced by moral ones. As Löwy has pointed out, Che believed 'a genuine socialist society cannot be built' by using methods that undermine 'the development of collectivist consciousness'.[38]

Che thus rejected 'the wild idea of trying to realize socialism with ... the worn out weapons left by capitalism', arguing instead that '"To construct communism ... we must create a new man.' Che's advocacy of moral incentives and the importance of developing a socialist consciousness has been dismissed by many – including those on the left – as the ideas of an impractical idealist. Yet Che based his arguments on Marx. At the start of his paper, 'On the Budgetary Finance System', Che referred to Marx's 'Economic and Philosophical Manuscripts', and explicitly stated that, though it 'belongs to his youth [it] does not lessen its value as an expression' of Marx's philosophy. Significantly, Che stressed it was important not to forget 'the humanist nature ... of [Marx's] concerns' which, while developed by the young Marx, were nonetheless still 'representative of [his] thought'.[39]

A clear idea of how Che saw communism as creating new human relations and individual development is provided by the quotation he selected from that work: '(3) *Communism* is ... the complete restoration of man to himself as a social, i.e. human, being ... This communism, as ... fully developed humanism ... is the genuine resolution of the conflict between man and nature, and between man and man.' In an interview given by Che on 25 July 1963, he stressed the important link between incentives, morals and consciousness: 'A socialist economy without communist moral values does not interest me ... If communism neglects facts of consciousness, it can serve as a method of distribution but it will no longer express revolutionary moral values.' As he made clear in 'Man and Socialism in Cuba', the use of profitability and 'individual material interest as levers' would lead to 'a blind alley' and undermine 'the development of consciousness' needed for socialism.[40]

In 'Man and Socialism in Cuba', Che made it clear that he believed socialism needed to pursue increased production *and* developing consciousness at the *same* time, in order to create a 'New Man' – not wait for the first before starting on the latter. Because Che believed it was necessary to help humans develop fully as social and collective beings, he persisted in arguing for the primacy of moral incentives as conscious action by workers in the construction of socialism. This, he argued, would help people see work as a social duty, benefiting themselves and the rest of society – not as something forced on them just in order to survive. 'For Guevara, consciousness was the means to counter the worst aspects of capitalism inherited by socialism.'[41]

However, it's wrong to say Che dismissed material incentives – in fact, he recognised that the effects of imperialism and capitalism on Cuba 'meant there was an objective need to offer them [Cuban people] material incentives. But he opposed their use as the primary instrument of motivation.' Farber claims Che opposed material incentives – along with the production of any consumer goods or 'secondary comforts' – as a result of his 'bohemian asceticism' and 'principled anticonsumerism'. This is despite Farber later citing a speech in which Che stated that 'one of the premises of the construction of socialism [is] creating a sufficient quantity of consumer goods for the entire population'. Countering Farber's argument, Renzo Llorente argues that it isn't true that Che had no interest in increasing the quantity of consumer goods available to Cubans. In the course of one of his bimonthly meetings with colleagues from the Ministry of Industries, Che stated that the purpose of socialism 'is to satisfy people's needs, and their ever growing needs; if not, it is not worth being a socialist'.[42]

During his various trips to the Soviet Union and the 'socialist' bloc countries, Che saw that individual workers tried to go beyond their work quotas for purely private reasons, and not for the good of society. He saw this as not much different from capitalist society. Che didn't want to create in Cuba 'a second American society, even if everything belongs to the State'. As Löwy explained: 'It is in the light of his profound conception of socialism as a society that is qualitatively different from capitalist society, and not as statized imitation of bourgeois consumer society, that Che's rejection of the Soviet model for building socialism has to be understood.' Che argued that the form material incentives took was crucial to changing consciousness. Thus he also favoured the use of fraternal competition between teams of workers – via 'socialist emulation' – to foster solidarity, as well as increasing production.[43]

Voluntary labour

Che was a strong advocate of voluntary labour – and, typically, practised it himself on a very regular basis. He once visited a deep mineral mine to do a half-day of voluntary labour – even though asthmatics were not allowed down the mine because of the unhealthy conditions. Nonetheless, he managed to exceed the work norm – but then instructed the director *not* to increase the norm, as he said it would be impossible to maintain, for a full day, the rate at which he'd worked. For him, unpaid voluntary labour – initially carried out by the most conscious and committed workers – was a practical expression of the importance of moral incentives and its value as a way of developing a socialist consciousness. Che had expressed his ideas on voluntary labour in his October 1962 article 'On Being a Communist Youth', which praised those students who, during their holidays, helped with harvests and the literacy campaign: 'It is a labor of sacrifice … to spread our revolutionary message.'[44]

He saw voluntary labour – and 'socialist emulation' – as helping to prepare people for workers' self-management. During the guerrilla war against Batista, Che had got his troops to build medical centres and schools in the areas they controlled – establishing the idea of work as a social duty. During 1959–60, while head of the Department of Industrialisation and President of the NBC, he persuaded his *compañeros* to go with him to help build schools and nurseries in deprived areas, or to help with the sugar harvest.

In November 1964, Che launched his 'Plan of Integration' for MININD directors. This encouraged them to spend one month a year working in a role at least one level below their own; during this, they were expected to learn and teach. Managers and office workers were also encouraged to perform voluntary manual labour during part of their holidays. In addition, specialist work brigades were set up, formed from outstanding workers who volunteered. They went around the country, visiting workplaces relevant to their specialisms, and teaching their methods in areas of work where factories were having problems. From 1 January 1965, the 'Plan of Integration' was rolled out nationally.

Although Che saw voluntary labour as a social duty that brought social and collective benefits, and helped change consciousness, he insisted that workers shouldn't be pressurised into doing it: 'one of the things that I consider fundamental and important is that voluntary labour is not obligatory'. Instead, leaders and vanguard workers, by setting good examples, would create a 'moral compulsion' which would lead others to volunteer. He once reprimanded a comrade who got cross with a worker who said he was unavailable for work one weekend. She commented: 'Che told me this wasn't right; there were workers with personal problems who truly could not go.' For Che, who wanted work to be seen as a 'social pleasure', it was crucial that workers genuinely wanted to participate in voluntary labour. Although trade union leaders were initially reluctant, the Cuban Workers' Confederation (CTC) eventually supported it, and even took the initiative to form Red Brigades.[45]

Che's own considerable voluntary labour – despite his long hours as a minister – and his general approach to it, were similar Mao's ideas in China. This was thus another area in which Che's ideas tended to conflict with Soviet practices. Although Che's ideas on voluntary labour have been criticised as being very idealistic or utopian, he believed positive attitudes to it needed to be built up over time. Typically, he was open about sometimes finding his voluntary labour 'deadly boring'. However, for him, such 'free labour' was non-alienated labour, which needed to come from within, via the *conscious* participation of workers. This would create the moral attitudes needed for a truly communist society. Though 'orthodox' communists saw his aims as an example of 'voluntarism', Lenin himself had written, as early as 1919, about 'communist Saturdays', in which workers organised themselves, voluntarily, to do extra work. As Löwy points out, Lenin had seen this as the start of 'a revolution that is … more radical, and more decisive than the overthrow of the bourgeoisie, for it is a victory over … the habits left as a heritage to the worker and peasant by accursed capitalism'.[46]

Che's philosophy

In many ways, it is difficult to separate Che's Marxist philosophy from his economic ideas. His philosophical and political outlook was based on his views on revolutionary humanism and what socialism was all about. Central to his philosophy was the role of consciousness and ethics in building socialism. He'd become a Marxist much sooner than most of the other leaders of M26J, and between 1954 and 1963 he'd read, thought about – and made notes on – many of the classic Marxist texts. As with his economic ideas, Che made some original contributions to Marxist philosophy. These contributions were not dogmatic, and were developed in the context of differences that were emerging within the international communist movement in the 1960s. From the age of 17 he had kept notebooks listing the books he read, and writing down his thoughts about them. These notebooks illustrate 'The importance that he gave to philosophy, as a kind of central axis for the later development of his thoughts.' As he became more familiar with the early writings of Marx – who argued that capitalist social relations produced alienation and antagonism – he was determined to develop a collective attitude to productive work. This was reinforced by what he saw in Soviet bloc countries, where he felt the absence of appropriate political education 'were obstructing the transformation of consciousness'. Where the

Soviet Union left changing consciousness for later, Che believed 'it was vital that efforts to change consciousness be incorporated into socialist transition at the earliest stage'. This was because he believed 'communism would be reached much quicker by raising consciousness simultaneously with the productive forces'.[47]

In July 1962, as proof of how ways of thinking could be changed quite quickly during the transition to socialism, he told MININD directors: 'I also came from the bourgeois class, anticommunist and all that and I learnt a set of truths in the process of struggle ... this is a dialectical process in which everything is changing.' He then urged them to study Lenin's comments on the need to destroy the ideas associated with the old capitalist system: '*Compañeros*, I beg you ... [read] ... where he talks about the transition from the old society to the new society.[48]

Che saw Marxism as a science that must change and develop as history itself changed over time. Although well-versed in the Marxist classics, he didn't view Marx as infallible – on the contrary, he felt Marx had, at times, been mistaken. For instance, Che argued that Marx and Engels had misunderstood the true significance of Simon Bolívar for Latin America, commenting that Marx 'gave some race and nationality theories which are inadmissible today'.[49]

On several occasions, he criticised 'the scholasticism that has held back the development of Marxist philosophy' – at times arguing that such attitudes had 'hindered study of the period of the building of socialism'. Instead, he condemned all attempts to make Marxism some unchanging and unchangeable canon of 'truths' that simply had to be learned and repeated by the 'faithful'. As early as April 1962, he'd criticised the limitations imposed on Cuba by Stalinist dogmatism: 'There had appeared throughout the country ... dogmatism, sectarianism.' These were ideas that he repeated during the Great Debate in his articles 'On Party Militancy' (1963) and 'Man and Socialism in Cuba' (1965). It was this undogmatic Marxism – so different from what held sway in the Soviet bloc – that made him so attractive to rebellious youth in the 1960s and after.[50]

Che saw the writings of Marx – and of Lenin – as having established some crucial principles of revolutionary Marxist philosophy; bequeathed the important 'dialectical materialist' method; and provided some important and useful insights on how societies could carry out the transition from capitalism to socialism. However, for Che, because of the times and places they had written, they could not offer sufficient guidance on the problems of transition in mid-twentieth century Latin America. Löwy goes so far as to claim that, for Latin America, Che carried out 'the same task of revolutionary renovation with regard to the solidified "Marxism" of the official left that Lenin carried out with regard to the "Marxist" social democracy of the Second International'. Overall, there are four main aspects to Che's Marxist philosophy: ideas about socialist democracy;

his ideas about the 'subjective' factor in history; his concept of the 'New Man'; and his Marxist humanism.[51]

Socialist Democracy

Immediately after the Revolution, many skilled managers and workers had left Cuba; while many workers lacked the educational or skill-levels necessary for effective participation in planning and self-management. In addition, many workers – never having experienced democracy in their workplaces before 1959 – found it hard to accept that their views and input were needed. As a consequence, there remained an attitude – typical under capitalism – that saw management personnel as separate from shop-floor workers. Che was determined to break down this division between intellectual and manual labour. He thus urged his MININD directors to consult on a regular basis with workers, so they 'take up management work in the shortest time possible'. Nonetheless, writers such as Farber dispute whether Che genuinely sought ways of developing workers' participation in management – highlighting instead his administrative controls.[52]

Given the low level of education and technical skills, Che argued that, initially, centralisation was needed, until 'both the new consciousness and technical skills had been acquired by the working class'. His slogan was: 'centralise without obstructing initiative and decentralise without losing control'. To get workers ready for the self-management of the Cuban economy, Che set up various MININD policy initiatives, to operate alongside trade unions and political groups. To prevent bureaucratisation, Che insisted that senior managers and administrators had to have regular contact with workers: 'we need to go to the factories, to ... promote free, open discussions, without any form of coercion ... to collect all criticisms with honesty'.[53]

Initially, though, participation of Cuban workers in management was extremely limited. This was even true of how Che first ran his Ministry of Industries. Hence critics, such as Farber, claim that Che was, *in principle*, against the idea of workers' participation in economic planning. In 1960, he set up Advisory Technical Committees (ATCs) in nationalised industries, to encourage worker participation in management. As he saw these as having more of an 'educational' function, rather than leading to collective decision-making, Farber sees this as showing Che's opposition to genuine workers' management. But the situation was not as straightforward as Farber makes out – Che had said the ATCs were 'a laboratory experiment where the working class prepares itself for the great future tasks of the integral management of the country'. When they were abolished in 1962, Che stated that one reason was because 'Mass participation in the elections was poor. The elections were bureaucratic.' This was a dig at the Communists' control of the unions. Nonetheless, as Farber states, although Che favoured the participation of workers in the administration of enterprises, he didn't support 'anything resembling workers' control of production'. As noted earlier, Mandel criticised Che for holding such a position during the Great Debate, and attempted to convince him of 'the importance of building a socialist democracy'.[54]

Yet, in October 1961 – just eight months into his role as Minister of Industries – Che had called all those working in MININD to a meeting at which he admitted his own errors in this respect, as well as mistakes made by his Ministry. His deputy and closet colleague, Orlando Borrego, was at that meeting, and later reported that Che: 'submitted himself to such extensive self-criticism that we were all surprised'. Che had always subjected himself to self-criticism – but usually just in his diaries and notebooks. This time, he admitted that because of his heavy workload, he'd been running his Ministry along 'an executive method of organisation ... treating people as soldiers, commanding strict discipline and a lack of discussion'. What he now wanted to do was to make workers feel 'part of a great collective effort' to increase productivity and efficiency. To do that, according to Yaffe, Che saw workers' management as essential, and introduced several policies to prepare workers for 'increasingly decentralised and direct control over production ... Ultimately, these sought to give socialism the democratic, participatory character necessary to prepare society for transition to communism.'[55]

However, Che was not initially supportive of the independence of trade unions. Farber sees this as the result of what he calls Che's 'overall monolithic conception of socialism', which meant he was unable to 'conceive of the specific function that unions could fulfil in a socialist society'. Farber's assessment here is supported by what Che said in June 1961: 'the Cuban workers have to get used to living in a collectivist regime and therefore cannot strike'. By 1965, however, Che had already begun to alter his views, arguing that unions were necessary at the level of the local workplace to avoid abuses. Though, as expressed later in his *Critical Notes on Political Economy*, he still saw unions on a national level as unnecessary under socialism because there was no class exploitation.[56]

A more positive aspect of Che's views about socialist democracy is provided by his attitudes to the expression of different views. For instance, as Farber concedes, when Castro wanted anti-communist ministers to resign from the government, Che 'argued that ... they should continue in their posts'. In addition, as Principe points out, Che denounced the destruction by Cuban Stalinists of the plates for Trotsky's *The Permanent Revolution*; and also tried to get the Cuban Trotskyist leader Roberto Acosta Hechevarria released from prison, telling him: 'Acosta, you can't kill ideas with blows.' Generally though, critics tend to downplay Che's tolerance of dissent. For instance, Farber argues that: 'It is true that during Guevara's tenure as minister of industry in Cuba, he got along with, and even protected, the Trotskyists who worked under him … Guevara saw them as revolutionaries who differed from him on important matters, but allies nevertheless.' Yet Che also gave positions in his ministries to opponents who'd been dismissed. These included Enrique Oltuski – an old M26J adversary – when he'd been ousted as communications minister in 1961; and the poet Heberto Padilla (an old friend of Che's opponent Mora). Mora asked for a meeting with Che, who was an admirer of Padilla's poetry. When they arrived, Che was prostrate on the floor suffering yet another asthma attack. When Padilla began outlining his critical thoughts about what he'd seen in the Soviet Union, Che stopped him by saying he'd already seen for himself that it was a 'pigsty', and that China offered a better model. He then urged Mora to give Padilla a job in the Ministry of Foreign Trade, saying 'These are not good times for journalism.'[57]

The Subjective Factor

Marx had said that it wasn't enough for philosophers to interpret the world: the point was to change it. For Che, Marxism was above all a philosophy of revolutionary *action* – he thus explicitly rejected the view that revolution didn't need to be *made*, as it would come about, inevitably, from the ever-worsening contradictions of capitalism. Instead, Che – like Marx, Lenin and Trotsky – stressed the importance of humans in making history, including revolution. In 'On Party Militancy', he referenced Lenin, who'd come to the conclusion that 'the transition from one society to another was not a mechanical transition. Conditions could be speeded up to the maximum by what we might call catalysts.' Although Che pointed out that 'catalysts' was his term, not Lenin's, he argued that his term nonetheless contained Lenin's 'central idea'. Che thus argued – as had Marx and Trotsky in the concept of 'permanent revolution' – that 'intermediate stages could be skipped' *if* there existed 'a vanguard of the proletariat' with 'a clear idea of what direction to take'. This underpinned one of his most famous sayings: 'The duty of a revolutionary is to make revolution.' Later, it would form part of his belief that Marxists shouldn't 'await with folded arms' for all the requisite objective factors to be in place before acting – and thus of his idea that guerrilla warfare *could* act as a catalyst to speed up progress to a socialist revolution.[58]

Such views have led Che's critics, such as Farber, to accuse him of 'voluntarism – or even a 'hypervoluntarism' or an 'ultra-vanguardism', 'that expressed itself both in politics and economic policy'. According to Farber, this dated back to his experience of guerrilla warfare in the Sierra Maestra, and ignored the fact that 'In classical Marxism … historical change is the product of the interplay of objective and subjective factors that are in constant tension.' Löwy, however, rejects the idea of Che being guilty of 'idealist-voluntarist subjectivism'. In fact, while Che had said that the guerrilla war had 'hastened the course of events' in Cuba, he was also fully aware of the objective factors needed for a successful revolution. Nonetheless, he believed the conscious actions of a vanguard could push events towards revolution, if most circumstances were in place. This is precisely what Marx had meant in 'The Eighteenth Brumaire of Louis Bonaparte' when he wrote that, while taking into account 'the given and inherited circumstances' they face, 'Men make their own history.'[59]

Like Trotskyists and Maoists in the 1960s, Che and his followers tended to see the official 'orthodox' communist parties as having become reformist rather than revolutionary after the Second World War. Che was convinced that, at certain times, the right *subjective* revolutionary leadership could help bring about change – even if not all the objective factors were favourable. Che thus contradicted 'the defeatist attitude of revolutionaries or pseudo-revolutionaries who … sit down to wait until … all necessary objective and subjective conditions are given without working to accelerate them'. However, despite what some critics have claimed, Che didn't think that simply establishing a guerrilla group could bring about revolution on its own: 'It must always be kept in mind that there is a necessary minimum without which the establishment and consolidation of the first centre is not practicable.' The crucial point, though, as Yaffe has pointed out, was that Che was convinced that: 'consciousness, the subjective element, could become such a powerful force that it could materialise in objective reality [and] complete the prerequisites for revolution'.[60]

The 'New Man'

Che saw changing human consciousness and social relations as equally important as increasing production and productivity in the transition to socialism. For Che, a socialist consciousness meant 'a principled commitment to the social and economic justice aims of the Revolution' which transcended individual self-interest. To develop that socialist consciousness, and so overcome the capitalist values and culture which most Cuban people possessed in 1959, Che saw the creation of a socialist 'New Man' as crucial. Marx had actually commented on this aspect, stating that a new communist society would not develop 'on its own foundations, but on the contrary, just as it emerges from capitalist society … still stamped with the birth-marks of the old society from whose womb it has emerged'.[61]

Although some have seen Che's stated aim of trying to create a 'New Man' as yet another of his romantic, utopian dreams, his ideas were in fact based on a close and intensive study of Marx's *Capital*, and of other classical Marxist writings. His entire approach was geared towards creating a new consciousness and new social relationships among people, in order to facilitate the transition to socialism. In developing such a socialist consciousness, Che emphasised the importance of education and training. In March 1962, in 'Our Industrial Tasks', he stated: 'we must create a socialist conscience by enlisting the workers in all of the practical tasks of the building of socialism ... in the planning of the economy'. Later, in 'Man and Socialism in Cuba', Che made the connection clear: 'It is still necessary to accentuate [people's] conscious – individual and collective – participation in all the mechanisms of direction and production' in order to break 'the chains of alienation'. In that work, he also warned against the view that socialism can be achieved 'with the help of the blunted weapons left to us by capitalism'. For Che, achieving a truly communist society would require much more than changing the economic structure – also necessary would be changing human consciousness and values.[62]

This is why Che wrote so much about, and made so many efforts to create, this revolutionary 'New Man'. Far from being romantic idealism, Che's ambition in fact reflected what Marx himself had written about how, among free communist workers: 'the brotherhood of man is no empty phrase'. Che wanted the revolution to create communist humans who were the complete opposite of the isolated, alienated individuals created by capitalism. He thus strove to eradicate those aspects of capitalism which still existed *within* people after the 1959 Cuban Revolution: 'The flaws of the past are translated into the present in the individual consciousness, and constant efforts must be made to eradicate them.'[63]

One obvious approach was via ideological education to raise cultural levels and understanding. However, Che believed this must be an *active* process, in which workers would educate themselves: 'On the one hand society acts upon the individual by means of direct and indirect education, while on the other hand the individual undergoes a conscious phase of self-education.' That was why he put so much emphasis on *not* using capitalist economic methods in building socialism: 'That instrument [of mass mobilization] must be fundamentally of a moral character.' For Che, if that were done, then the 'new communist man' will 'thus achieve total awareness of his social being, which is equivalent to his full realization as a human being, having roken the chains of [capitalist] alienation'. This is what he saw as the fulfilment of Marx's idea of the universal 'brotherhood of man', and the transcendence of the capitalist division between private and public – or what Che saw as the 'I'.[64]

Che wanted to create a new person – selfless and idealistic, dedicated to the good of fellow humans and society – who would come to see work as a social duty and would thus achieve their 'full human condition', when producing without being compelled to sell themselves as commodities. Some, though – such as Farber – have criticised Che's conception of a 'New Man' as not seeing beyond the 'individual's sacrifice for the collective good', and failing to leave room for the individual 'self-fulfilment, expression, and freedom' that the early Marx wrote valued. Farber also criticised Che for neglecting issues such as increasing consumer goods, raising the standard of living of the Cuban population, and working people controlling their fate by making democratic decisions about social, economic, and political matters. Yet Che addressed those very topics at length elsewhere.[65]

Llorente, however, argues that Farber's criticisms of Che's views about creating the 'New Man' fail to acknowledge that Che believed overcoming capitalist alienation would allow workers to experience 'the happiness of fulfilling a duty [in working], of feeling [one]self important within the social mechanism'. Llorente also accuses Anderson of presenting a misleading view of Che's ideas by omitting relevant parts of what Che wrote – such as: 'we are ... zealous defenders of our individuality'. Such partial quoting of Che's writings is also evident in relation to Che's 'Man and Socialism in Cuba' – with Farber stating that 'it is impossible to tell what Che Guevara had in mind' when he referred to the 'first period in the transition to communism or in the construction of socialism'. Yet a close study of Che's works – including his *Critical Notes on Political Economy* – reveals that he was speaking of a transitional stage from capitalism to socialism in an underdeveloped country.[66]

Che, as a Marxist, rejected the idea of there being any unchangeable 'human nature'. In fact, he explicitly rejected 'Utopian' views of the innate 'goodness' of humans. Instead, he believed human beliefs, values and behaviours are largely the result of the kind of society in which they live, as 'determined by production relationships'. Thus, for Che, what was utopian was 'not envisaging the possibility of a "new man"' – and not recognising that the 'concrete experience of the Cuban Revolution' showed that the creation of a new human consciousness was 'an objective possibility'. As Löwy concludes: 'The theme of the new man as the ultimate aim, the polestar of the socialist revolution, is the touchstone, the central driving idea, of Che's revolutionary humanism, in the light of which the whole of his political thinking needs to be understood.' This concept of the 'New Man' 'is the thread that all his thoughts follow' – and can be seen in almost everything he wrote, both before and during the Great Debate.[67]

Humanism

In fact, contrary to those who criticise Che for ignoring the individual, Che's vision of socialism was an essentially humanistic one. He saw the Cuban

Revolution as both a Marxist and a humanist endeavour to build: 'a Marxist, socialist system ... in which man is placed at the center, and in which the individual, the human personality, with the importance it holds as an essential factor in the revolution, is taken into account.' Like Marx, he was 'interested not only in the historical development of modes of production, but also their impact on human beings'.[68]

One of the most important contributions Che made to the development of Marxist humanism – and to revolutionary politics in general – was to stress that 'Communism is a goal of humanity that is reached consciously.' This was his take on Marx's comment, in the 'Economic and Philosophical Manuscripts', that '[Communism] is the solution of the riddle of history and knows itself to be the solution'. This is what underpinned Che's view of the importance of socialist planning in the transition to socialism in Cuba – that 'Man is the conscious actor of history. Without this consciousness, which encompasses his awareness, as a social being, there can be no communism.' Crucially – in terms of rejecting accusations that Che thought leaders and vanguards alone could bring about these changes – Che was clear that the people as a whole must 'really become the creator and leader of their history, where their own happiness will be built by their own hands'. This was fully in tune with the classic revolutionary Marxist position that 'the emancipation of the working people will be the task of the working people themselves'. And it is certainly how Che viewed Cuba's early attempts to bring about a socialist transition: 'the masses now make history as a conscious aggregate of individuals who struggle for the same cause', and that the Cuban people were 'individuals who have achieved the awareness of what must be done, men who struggle to leave the domain of necessity and enter that of freedom'.[69]

Che's humanism explains his comment about love being the most important characteristic of a true revolutionary. During the Great Debate, Che became familiar with the early writings of the young Marx – in particular, the 'Economic and Philosophical Manuscripts'. From these, he accepted Marx's ideas about the liberation of humans, as social beings, being achieved by the transition to communism, which would eventually bring to an end the alienation resulting from the inhumanity of capitalism. From this, Che argued that Marx's *Capital* was not 'anti-humanist'. On the contrary, Che saw Marx's major work – which included explanations of how the transition from capitalism would end the situation in which humans were controlled by 'things', to one where humans rationally controlled 'things' – as showing a dialectical connection with humanism. In his 'On The Budgetary System of Finance', Che argued for the humanist nature of *Capital* which, he argued, had a: 'humanist character – humanist in the best sense of the word'.[70]

Like Trotsky before him, Che distinguished between Marxist humanism and 'bad' humanisms (such as bourgeois or Christian humanism) which, by claiming to be 'above class', actually tried to prevent the only way of truly liberating humanity: the proletarian revolution. Löwy thinks Che's humanism was almost certainly influenced by Aníbal Ponce (1898–1939), one of the pioneers of Marxism in Latin America – his book, *Humanismo burgués y humanism proletario* (1935) was reissued in Cuba in 1962. This argued that 'the "new man", the "complete man", the person who unites theory and practice, culture and labor, can be brought about only through the coming to power of the proletariat'. Che's Marxist humanism was thus very much a revolutionary humanism, and was expressed in his writings on the role of humans in the revolution.[71]

During the Great Debate, Bettelheim – as well as criticising Che's economic ideas – also largely rejected Che's focus on humanistic, ethical and moral aspects. Such criticisms ignore Che's view of a revolutionary as someone who has ideals and takes concrete actions to put those ideals in practice. Gadea, his first wife, had acquainted him with some of the works by the great Latin American Marxist, and founder of the Communist Party of Peru, José Carlos Mariátegui. In the early 1960s, some of his works were republished in Cuba. Significantly, in a chapter titled 'Ethics and Socialism', Mariátegui had argued that Marxism is not anti-ethical – and that a true socialist morality 'is formed in the class struggle, carried on in a heroic frame of mind, with passionate will power'. Che's revolutionary humanism was very much in that tradition.[72]

Che's ethical values and humanism were, ultimately, based on the love of humanity itself – hence his strong sense of internationalism. He believed an 'authentic revolutionary' should have a generous love of people, of humankind – and is precisely why he urged young communists 'always to feel as one's own the great problems of humanity', to be true internationalists, and to show practical solidarity with the world's exploited and oppressed. Farber, among others, has challenged this view of Che's 'love', describing it as 'an abstract love of the people ... without a concrete human object'.[73]

A more positive view of Che's 'love' is not negated by Che's *Message to the Tricontinental* of April 1967, in which he stated that 'hatred' was an essential part of the revolutionary struggle. As Löwy argues, Che's 'love of humanity' was not some kind of religiously inspired love that applied equally to exploiters and oppressors. Quite the reverse, Che argued that: 'Hatred ... a relentless hatred of the enemy' was necessary, because 'a people without hatred cannot vanquish a brutal enemy.' Farber thus believes it wrong 'to portray Guevara as a warm, affectionate, and loving revolutionary', seeing the views expressed in the 'Message' as incompatible with love, thereby rendering Che's worldview at best incoherent. However, Michael Principe argues that Che 'attempted to imagine and to live a new subjectivity, one where "if you are capable of trembling with indignation each time that an injustice is committed in the world, then we are comrades"'. Essentially, Che's revolutionary humanism gave new Marxist meanings to the concepts of humanity, justice, dignity and freedom – and the important place these had in the construction of a socialist future.[74]

Defeat in victory?

In 1967, Castro stated that there was no place for the law of value in Cuba's transition to socialism; and that the use of moral incentives was correct. Thus Che seemed to have largely triumphed in the public debate about socialist economic planning – leading Löwy to conclude that: 'Che's economic theses' had 'become to a very large extent the theses adopted by the Cuban government.' However, along with his economic arguments, Che had also raised issues which concerned 'how much freedom the proletariat would have to make its own decisions'. This equally-important philosophical-political debate, though – about the role of workers and political power – was *not* made public. According to Mandel, Che had been defeated in that one. Yet Stutje argues that, as Che was the most popular of the island's revolutionary leaders by the time he left Cuba in 1965: 'If the voice of the people had been heard, Che would have won the political as well as the economic round.' By then, Che had come to see socialist democracy as crucial, as revealed in the long letter he sent to Castro on 26 March 1965, after deciding to leave his government posts: 'How can worker participation be achieved? That is a question I have not been able to answer. It is my greatest failure.'[75]

Initially, there were signs that Che and the group around him were growing stronger than the 'orthodox' pro-Soviet communists in Cuba. According to Mandel, he'd been assured that workers' assemblies and workers' self-management would soon emerge. However, in the summer of 1964, certain personnel changes occurred that favoured 'orthodox' communists. For instance, Dorticós was appointed Minister of the Economy and Director of the State Planning Board. More significantly, Che's closet aide, Orlando Borrego, was placed in charge of the sugar industry – which was *not* under Che's control. Che, though, seemed reluctant to split the party by openly appealing to the Cuban people; while Mandel ignored suggestions that he should try to persuade Che to do so, fearing it would make it more difficult for Che in the struggle against pro-Soviet currents in Cuba. Nonetheless, it's possible that defeat on these wider political issues helped Che make his ultimately fatal decision to resign his ministerial posts, leave Cuba and return to guerrilla warfare.

Chapter 9

Failure in the Congo, 1965–66

> 'I carry to new battlefronts … the feeling of fulfilling the most sacred of duties: to fight against imperialism wherever it may be.'[1]

In April 1965, Che suddenly disappeared – triggering worldwide speculation about possible reasons. The reason was that he'd gone secretly to the Congo, to conduct guerrilla warfare. The above extract – from the 'Farewell Letter' he'd written to Castro before setting off – shows his commitment to international revolution and the struggle against imperialism. While some have seen Che's decision to fight elsewhere as resulting from 'romanticism or boredom', internationalism and anti-imperialism had, by then, become central to his moral and political outlook. According to Llorente, Che attempted to apply 'ethical considerations to international politics', while Sinclair argues that Che saw himself as 'a crusader of commitment, and that was the fundamental motive for his going'.[2]

For Che, national borders had long had 'little bearing on the degree of concern' people should 'show for the well-being of other people' – hence his willingness in 1959 to risk his life fighting in Cuba. Löwy argues that: 'For Che … proletarian internationalism was not only a moral imperative … [and a] … manifestation of humanist values, but also and above all a practical and real necessity in the revolutionary struggle against the common imperialist foe.' The final exposition of Che's internationalism can be found in his *Message to the Tricontinental* – written at some point in 1966, but not published until April 1967. In it, he explained how 'imperialism is a world system, the final stage of capitalism'; how 'it must be beaten in a great worldwide confrontation'; and how the head of that imperialist system 'is none other than the United States of North America'.[3]

Che believed 'the beginning of a revolutionary war' could contribute 'to the development of new conditions in the neighboring countries'. The tragedy as regards Che's mission in the Congo was that, even before he arrived, he was aware many of the leaders of African liberation struggles didn't share his outlook. This had become apparent at a meeting in Dar es Salaam in 1965: 'I tried to show them that we were talking not of a struggle within fixed frontiers, but of a war against the common enemy ... No one saw it like that.' Thus Che's internationalist aims seemed doomed to meet with failure in the Congo.[4]

New battlefronts, revolutionary networks

Che desired a united front among anti-colonial and anti-imperialist forces – and the socialist bloc countries – to stretch the forces of imperialism thinly, thus making revolutionary victories more possible. Hence his call to the Tricontinental to 'create two, three, many Vietnams' – to help take pressure off Vietnam, and off Cuba itself. As early as 1959, Che had been involved in setting up a 'Liberation Department' to assist overseas guerrilla movements; and had held private meetings in his ministerial office 'with *compañeros* from all over Latin America to discuss common dreams for the redemption of our continent', and 'to create a more just and equal world'. Significantly, 'he was prepared to "risk his own skin", as he put it.' Yet the results in countries such as Guatemala, Venezuela, and Nicaragua had proved disappointing. In March 1962, Che had been particularly saddened to learn that 'El Patojo' – a close companion since 1954 – had been killed fighting in a Marxist guerrilla campaign in Guatemala.[5]

In September 1963, his *Guerrilla Warfare: A Method* – an update on his *Guerrilla Warfare* – had made an explicit call for guerrilla warfare in Latin America. He argued that violence shouldn't be 'the monopoly of the exploiters', and criticised the refusal of regional communist party leaders to support armed struggle. In fact, from as early as 1962, he'd begun recruiting likely leaders from among Latin American students studying in Cuba, in order to establish a trans-continental network of revolutionaries. One of those was Ricardo Gadea, the younger brother of Che's first wife, who described Che as: 'the most charismatic, sensitive, and involved, as a Latin American'. Training took place in the Sierra Maestra – often overseen by Che himself. One other country Che took an interest in was Bolivia. In a meeting in Havana with Bolivian communists, Che allegedly pointed out how the Cuban Communist Party had opposed Castro's rebellion: 'If we'd listened to them, there wouldn't have been [a Cuban revolution].' Unfortunately, in view of what happened subsequently with his mission in Bolivia, Che later accused Mario Monje, the Bolivian Communist leader, of opposing guerrilla campaigns because he was afraid.[6]

Failure in Argentina

Following the victory of the Cuban Revolution, Che had spoken openly of his desire to help spread revolution across Latin America, and had increasingly spoken to friends of his 'desire to return to the revolutionary armed struggle'.

The 'new battlefront' that particularly appealed to him was his home country, Argentina. In 1987, Castro said Che had spoken of his desire to begin guerrilla warfare there as soon as the Cuban Revolution was secure. Instead, he'd served as a minister for six years; by 1965, however, he'd become increasingly restless – partly, perhaps, because he feared that if he waited too long, he'd be too old to return to the hardships of guerrilla warfare. Certainly, by then, Che was 'asthmatic, softened by years of administration', leading some historians to wonder whether he was physically-fit enough to be a guerrilla: 'His asthma attacks had continued while in Cuba, and the medicine he took, combined with the natural progression of age, had added considerably to his frame.'[7]

When a military dictatorship took control of Argentina in March 1962, Che had considered it time to establish a guerrilla group there. So he'd asked his friend Alberto Granado, along with Jorge Masetti, to recruit potential fighters. As numbers proved insufficient, several Cubans close to Che volunteered to join the group – and training had begun in Cuba. Che had decided the best starting point would be Argentina's northern jungle, near La Salta and the Bolivian border. In May 1963, the group arrived in Bolivia. Calling themselves the People's Guerrilla Army (Ejército Guerrillero del Pueblo – EGP), they were led by Masetti. In October, they'd moved into Argentina, and it seems Che had planned to join them, once the group had established a base. He'd ordered them to avoid military operations until they had fully explored the area, but from November 1963 they had been increasingly harassed by the army. Masetti had then become authoritarian, while the group had proved too small – and too divided – to make a real impact. By April 1964, most of the guerrillas had been killed or captured by the army, and it was thus all over.

Che had first learned of the unfolding disaster in Argentina in March 1964, while on his way back to Cuba after attending the UN Conference on Trade and Development in Geneva. A hint that Che was seriously intending to return to the fray himself is provided by what he'd said at that UN Conference: 'We clearly understand and frankly say that the only solution to humanity's problems at the moment is to completely suppress the exploitation of developing countries by developed capitalist countries.' It seems 'The failure of his Argentine forces only reinforced his desire to put himself back into the middle of the fray.'[8]

A caged lion

Che had arrived back in Cuba on 18 April 1964, clearly pained that people close to him had been fighting – and dying – while he remained a minister. In a conversation with Granado, shortly afterwards, Che said: 'here you see me, behind a desk, fucked, while my people die during a mission I've sent them on'. According to Luther, Che's 'wandering soul had been too long confined to the same area'. This state of mind is confirmed by a conversation he had with Mora and Padilla in July 1964. Mora – his opponent in the 'Great Debate' – had just been sacked, and was leaving Cuba to study political economy, and Padilla had decided to leave with him. However, before leaving, they'd gone to see Che. According to Padilla, Che walked up to Mora slowly, saying: 'I live like someone torn in two, twenty-four hours a day, completely torn in two, and I haven't got anybody to tell it to.' According to Anderson: 'As they spoke, Che was searching for a way back to the battlefield, even as he worked himself to the point of exhaustion on Cuba's industrial economy.' Further corroboration of Che's feelings at this time comes from the leftist Uruguayan writer, Eduardo Galeano, who met Che in August 1964: 'Che was not a desk-man. He was a creator of revolutions ... Somehow, that tension of a caged lion that his apparent calm betrayed had to explode.' By the end of summer 1964, Che had already decided to leave Cuba and return to the revolutionary battlefield.[9]

In November 1964, Che visited the Soviet Union once again – partly to see if it would, after all, support his idea of fomenting a continent-wide revolution in Latin America. He got a clear negative answer. On his return, Che stayed away from a Soviet-sponsored Conference of Latin American communist parties taking place in Havana. Those parties criticised Cuba's sponsorship of guerrilla forces in the region, and made it clear they supported the Soviet Union's 'peaceful coexistence' line. However, on 30 November, Che made a speech in Santiago attacking them for their opposition to armed struggle. Significantly, he'd also condemned the massacres carried out by Belgian paratroopers in the Congo, as showing the 'very nature of imperialism which bestializes man'. After that speech, Che and March met with Granado and his wife, over a pizza at the Fontana de Trevi restaurant – it was the last time the two friends would meet. Although Che had said nothing during that meal, a small group were already aware he'd decided to leave. Attempts to persuade him to stay a few more years, to prove his economic model was better for Cuba than the Soviet one, failed.[10]

'Colonialism is doomed'

A further indication of Che's growing determination to return to guerrilla warfare was provided by his speech at the UN's General Assembly in December 1964. His famous 'Colonialism is doomed' speech there – delivered on 11 December – became an international sensation. Despite having polished his boots, combed his hair and beard, and having had his olive-green uniform pressed, his appearance contrasted sharply with those of the other delegates. But his speech had been much more of a departure from the speeches normally delivered there. As well as being a 'harangue worthy of the most famous apostle of revolutionary socialism', it was very much his own view of things, rather than a reflection of official Cuban policy. He'd made a vociferous attack on the US as an imperialist and war-mongering world power, as shown by its actions in Vietnam, Laos and Cambodia. Significantly, he berated the US for its support of apartheid South Africa, and of neo-colonial leaders in Africa. In particular, he noted how imperialist countries had: 'murdered thousands of defenceless citizens of the Congo'. He'd then criticised racial inequalities and white violence in the US itself, stating: 'How can the country that murders its own children and discriminates between them daily because of the color of their skins … claim to be the guardian of liberty.'[11]

He'd made it clear that, although he was an Argentine and a Cuban, 'I feel I am a patriot in any Latin American country'. Che then declared his intention to support revolutions in Latin America: 'I would be prepared to give my life for the liberation of any country in Latin America, without asking or demanding anything from anyone or exploiting anyone.' He'd then announced his support for liberation wars – pointing out that Cuba was part of the 'nonaligned Third World': 'We have declared ourselves to be within the group of Nonaligned countries … because the Nonaligned countries, like ourselves, fight imperialism.' He'd made it clear that Cuba sympathised with all those peoples who struggled for their freedom: 'we morally support and stand in solidarity with peoples who struggle anywhere in the world to make a reality of the rights of full sovereignty proclaimed in the UN Charter'. Not content with attacking the US, he'd also made a strong attack on the Soviet Union's policy of 'peaceful coexistence', saying its apathy was a form of betrayal: 'As Marxists we have maintained that peaceful coexistence among nations does not encompass coexistence between the exploiters and the exploited, between the oppressors and the oppressed.'[12]

The following day, Che had appeared on the 'Face the Nation', CBS's Sunday news programme, where he'd made the point that, as regards the USA's two conditions for the restoration of normal relations (ending military links to USSR and abandonment of exporting revolution to Latin America): 'We place no conditions on the establishment of relations, but neither do we accept conditions.'

He also sent a public letter to Malcolm X, the famous African-American activist. Malcolm X had invited Che to speak at a rally planned for 13 December, but Che was unable to attend. Instead, Malcolm X read his letter out, saying how much he admired Che, describing him as 'one of the most revolutionary men in this country right now'.[13]

Where's Che?

Yet – despite the various hints about his intentions – it came as a real surprise when Che disappeared from public view in April 1965. There was much speculation, both within and outside Cuba, about possible explanations. These included a falling-out with Castro, or Che's frustration at the problems which had emerged during his Four-Year Plan. Luther, for one, argues that Che was ready for moving on because he was 'Disillusioned by Castro's compromising' and saw Cuba reverting back to reliance on sugar as 'a betrayal of his dreams of industrialization'. It is certainly true that, by early 1964, Che himself had accepted that his Four-Year Plan was meeting great difficulties – in large part, as a result of the US blockade. Che's desire to leave the burdens of ministerial office were increased by the almost 'constant conflict' he was in with the 'orthodox' communists 'right up to the time of his resignation from the cabinet in 1965'. Che particularly opposed their view that 'the proper conditions for a socialist revolution in Latin America and the rest of the Third World did not yet exist'. They, in turn, saw Che as exhibiting '"pathological" revolutionary adventurism'.[14]

However, when questioned about Che's disappearance on 30 April 1965, Castro merely replied that Che 'would always be where he could be of most use to the revolution'. Che – increasingly aware that the Soviet Union's policy of 'peaceful coexistence could hardly be obtained by igniting armed guerrilla conflicts wherever he could' – realised his desire to aid revolutionary movements in the USA's 'backyard' conflicted with Soviet interests. Although the Soviet Union saw Che as having the deepest understanding of Marxism among Cuba's political leadership – they now began to see him as 'the revolution's foremost revolutionary heretic, an enfant terrible with international aspirations'.[15]

Family implications

Che's plans to return to guerrilla warfare obviously had implications for March – and his decision to return to the battlefield has led some writers to speculate that Che and March's relationship wasn't a close one. Certainly, they were very different. Che was very much an intellectual and loved studying books, was austere (his *austeridad* was legendary) and did not appreciate luxuries. March, though, was more interested in films, social gatherings and the good things in life.

However, it seems they 'enjoyed each other's company, had a strong physical attraction for each other, and, by all accounts, were faithful. Both enjoyed an open, earthy repartee.' Once, on a visit to his mother-in-law in Santa Clara, she asked him if he wanted a bath: '"Not if Aleida's not in it," he quipped.' They also shared 'bluntness of speech' – if anything, she was 'less tactful and even more brutally honest than Che'. They were also both 'romantics at heart'. Although Che rarely showed this side in public, 'At night, in the privacy of their bedroom, he would recite poetry to Aleida. This thrilled her.' And, although women often surrounded him – and despite the macho culture of Cuba accepting that many men would have second or even third 'wives' – Che didn't respond to even obvious flirting. On one occasion, he actually reprimanded an attractive young woman for flirting with him.[16]

Africa calling

As early as 1963, Cuba had established close ties with Ben Bella's Algeria – and Che had mentioned African countries in his famous UN speech. By 1964 – apart from the Congo – there were rebel forces fighting right across the African continent, whether against Portuguese colonialism in Angola and Mozambique, or against the repressive apartheid regime in South Africa. Not surprisingly, Che thus began to see the chances for anti-imperialist guerrilla warfare in Africa as a real possibility, saying in 1964: 'Africa represents one of the most important battlegrounds, if not the most important.' And it seems Castro, while assuring Che that attempts would continue to build bases for his ultimate dream of armed struggle in Latin America, advised him to go to the Congo as useful preparation.[17]

On 17 December 1964, Che flew to Algeria, at the start of what became a three-month trip before returning to Cuba. Officially, he was acting as a roving ambassador; unofficially, he was making further preparations for returning to the fray. After Algiers, he visited several other African countries, before returning to Algiers in late January 1965. While there, he met leaders of liberation groups, toured guerrilla training camps, and spoke to journalists and students – in what Luther described as 'a glimmer of the "old" Che'. By the end of 1964, it had become clear that Latin American communist parties wouldn't support guerrilla warfare in their own continent. Consequently, both Che and Castro saw Africa as offering more immediate revolutionary opportunities. More specifically, Che had become certain that a rebellion in the Congo was likely. He'd been proved right in the summer of 1964, and had mentioned the possibility of his leading a Cuban-sponsored anti-imperialist armed struggle there to a group of visiting Africans.[18]

In February 1965 he flew to China; according to Richard Gott, one purpose of the trip was to discuss Chinese backing of the various Congolese rebel groups. On that trip, Che was accompanied by Osmany Cienfuegos (the older brother of Che's friend, Camilo) and Emilio Aragonés – both of whom would soon be heavily involved in Che's Congo mission, suggesting that plans were already being made. At the same time, Che's old PSP friend, Pablo Ribalta, had just been made Cuba's ambassador in Tanzania, which bordered the Congo.

On 24 February 1965, he returned to Algiers to speak (as a 'Cuban observer') at the Second Seminar on Economic Policy in Afro-Asian Nations, organised by the Organisation of Afro-Asian Solidarity. In what turned out to be his last public speech, he argued that, in the struggle against imperialism, there were 'no borders' – and that 'We cannot be indifferent to what happens anywhere in the world.' He accused the Soviet bloc countries of being 'accomplices of imperialist exploitation', and told them they had 'the moral duty to put an end to their tacit complicity with the exploiting countries of the West'. Even more to the point, he demanded that the socialist bloc should fund national liberation struggles in such countries as Vietnam and the Congo:

> Arms ... must be delivered to the peoples asking for them to use against the common enemy, with no charge and in the quantities needed and available ... The reply to the ominous attacks by United States imperialism against Vietnam or the Congo should be to supply those sister countries with all the defense equipment they need, and to offer them our full solidarity without any conditions whatsoever.

By criticising them publicly in this way, Che had effectively burnt his bridges. Che's speech marked a turning point, and was in effect the announcement of his decision to step down from his government posts in March 1965.[19]

After the meeting, however, he met Ben Bella and Nasser, revealing the difficulties he'd experienced as a minister: 'I used to talk a lot about social transformation and then I was given the task of supervising that transformation.' Nasser tried to talk Che out of his idea of leading a contingent of Cuban fighters to the Congo, warning him that the presence of a white foreigner would not go down well; he'd be like 'Tarzan, a white man among blacks, leading and protecting them'. Ben Bella, however, was more supportive, 'and allowed Che to establish a base in the hills overlooking Algiers'. Che – and representatives of other Latin American revolutionary groups, with the support of the Cuban government – then used it for training purposes. But this was made more difficult after Ben Bella was ousted by a military coup in June 1965.[20]

Before returning to Cuba, Che gave an interview to Josie Fanon, the widow of Franz Fanon, the author of the anti-colonialist *The Wretched of the Earth*, stating that Africa was one of: 'the more important fields of struggle against all forms of exploitation existing in the world – against imperialism, colonialism, and neo-colonialism'. He also visited Tanzania, which would soon play an important part in his Congo mission. However, a meeting with a large number of these leaders in Dar es Salaam, did not go well. Whereas most wanted their soldiers trained in Cuba, Che commented that: 'a revolutionary soldier [could only be formed] in warfare ... I therefore suggested that training should take place ... in the nearby Congo, where the struggle was ... against North American imperialism, in its neo-colonial form', and called for the unity of all the anti-imperialist movements. But many leaders were against the idea that their fighters might be killed while fighting in the Congo.[21]

Among those Che met were Laurent Kabila and Gaston Soumaliot, two of the Congolese rebel leaders. Che was particularly impressed by the leftist views of Kabila, saying he 'understood perfectly that the principal enemy was North American imperialism'. He was particularly pleased to discover that Kabila – unlike some African leaders – supported outside involvement of non-African countries in the Congolese rebellion, and agreed with Che that 'the problem of the Congo is a problem of the world'. As previously agreed with Castro, Che offered Kabila Cuban arms and military advisers. Given its central position and size, Che had come to see the Congo as an opportunity for establishing a *foco* that could train guerrillas who could then radiate outwards to all parts of the continent to bring about a pan-African revolution. But he also gained his first awareness of just how divided the Congolese leaders were, despite the existence of a National Liberation Council. Yet, despite some misgivings, Che decided to continue with the Congo mission. On his way back to Cuba on 13 March 1965, the plane was forced to stop over in Ireland for some repairs. During the two days there, news reached him that Congolese government troops, led by white mercenaries, had launched attacks that threatened to overrun the 'liberated territory' held by the rebels in eastern Congo.[22]

A political rift?

When he arrived back in Havana on 15 March, he was met at the airport by Castro and March (who'd just given birth to their last child, Ernesto). This turned out to be his last public appearance in Cuba. Also present to greet him were his daughter, Hildita (aged 8), Raúl and Dorticós. However, Dorticós and even Raúl (who'd been his close political ally for many years) were by now opposed to Che's criticisms of the Soviet Union. According to Anderson, their relationship had been cooling for some time, as Raúl had begun moving closer to the USSR.

Almost immediately following his return, there were nearly two full days of heated discussions in private, the full details of which have never been made public. Parts of it were, however, overheard: apparently Che said to Castro: 'All right, the only alternative left me is to leave here for wherever the hell, and please, if you can help me in any way in what I intend to do, do so immediately; and if not, tell me so I can see who can.' While one Soviet official reported that Che and Castro accused each other of departing from their official line on foreign relations.[23]

Certainly, during 1964, it appeared differences were emerging between Che and Castro. Castro had given interviews, hinting Cuba would stop funding revolutionary groups in the Americas, in return for reduced US sanctions. Che hadn't been pleased by this – and, on 24 July 1964, he'd given a speech in Santa Clara in which he said that imperialism should be fought 'whenever it appears', and made it clear he wasn't in favour of appeasing the US. Che's position had hardened in August 1964, when the US had escalated the Vietnam War by bombing North Vietnam. For Che, this was yet another crime by Yankee imperialism – and, on 15 August 1964, he made another speech in which he said that imperialist aggression anywhere would be met by people determined to fight for or defend their independence.[24]

On 13 March 1965, Castro himself mildly echoed what Che had said in Algiers, criticising both the USSR and China for giving insufficient aid to the Vietnamese in their struggle against US imperialism. Furthermore, Castro's public greeting of Che on his return from Algiers two days later, would suggest a deliberate 'seal of approval' for Che's speech – later confirmed when it was printed in the Cuban government's quarterly newspaper. In addition, at camps in Pinar del Rio Castro had been overseeing the selection and training of a force that Che would take with him to the Congo. As Reid-Henry states, Castro's comments and actions were not those of 'a man diametrically opposed to Che's position'.[25]

Farewells

By late March 1965, Che – having decided he was going – started to put out stories that he was going to cut sugarcane for a while. He then he began to withdraw from public view, only saying goodbye to a few who could be trusted to keep the secret. By then, Che was clearly 'committed to … fomenting revolution on a truly international scale … in countries under the control of oppressive regimes backed by US imperialism'.[26]

Che then began writing 'farewell' letters, and giving away 'personal belongings'. As well as leaving his government post, Che's decision also meant leaving his wife and five children. This was a difficult decision for him – but, as a dedicated revolutionary, Che 'was a man totally committed to carrying out his convictions', and putting the revolutionary cause before personal desires. Che was very close to his five children, and also wrote a farewell letter for them – to be read to them only in the event of his death, urging them to 'feel deeply any injustice committed against any person in any part of the world … Until always, little children. I still hope to see you again. A really big kiss and a hug from Papá'.[27]

He didn't see Gadea to tell her goodbye – instead, he phoned to say he was going to cut sugarcane. However, he saw Hildita, telling her that he'd come back later, and writing a letter for her – as Luther stated, Che 'had always made a sincere effort to be close to his firstborn, often taking her to work with him where she would play on the floor as he conducted his economy business'. Gadea, his first wife, confirmed this, mentioning Che's frequent visits to her; how Hildita often spent Sundays in Che's home with his other children; how on his trips he frequently sent her postcards or short letters; and stating how he 'tried his best to prevent our separation from affecting her'. Neither Hildita nor Gadea ever saw him again – although Hildita did receive a belated birthday card two months after her 9th. birthday. In it, he said he was 'a little far away' and that it would be 'a little while' before he'd be back; he asked her to look after her brothers and sisters, and said he was 'always thinking of her'. After Che had left for the Congo, none of his children would ever see him again, as their father. For their next – short – time together, he would be 'Uncle Ramon'.[28]

Che's romantic streak was reflected in the farewell letter he sent his parents, written just before leaving Cuba for the Congo. After referring to his favourite book, *Don Quixote*, he wrote:

> Many will call me an adventurer, and that I am; only one of a different kind – one of those who risks his skin to prove his beliefs.
>
> It could be that this may be the end … If it is so, I send you a last embrace. I have loved you very much, only I have not known how to express my love.

He also sent a postcard to his father, which gave a clue to where he was and what he was doing: 'Viejo: from the Saharan sun to your [Argentine] fogs. Ernesto renews himself and goes for the third [round]. A hug from your son.' In addition, he wrote personal dedications in some of his favourite books for his closest friends – but left them on a shelf to be discovered later – including one to Granado, along with a letter, writing: 'My rolling house has two legs once gain and my dreams will have no frontier – at least until the bullets speak.'[29]

His farewell letter to Castro and the Cuban people stated: 'I state once more that I free Cuba from any responsibility, except that which stems from its example. If my final hour finds me under other skies, my last thought will be of this people and especially for you.' He also gave what would be his final talk to his staff at the Ministry of Industries. According to Luther, Che 'was, at heart, a revolutionary and traveller, not a banker or minister of industry or diplomat. It was time to do as he had always done – hit the road in search of himself.'[30]

Leaving 'my only one'

Although Luther states that 'Che's second marriage, much like his first, was a lower priority than his politics and revolutionary passion: he and Aleida were far from close', it seems Che loved March very much. According to her book, their love was tender and 'romantic', with Che writing love letters and poems for her, and also making tape recordings for her and the children while away. On one of his last trips before leaving for the Congo, he sent a letter to March, saying: 'My darling, This might be my last letter for sometime … For the moment, I send you passionate kisses … A final one, passionate, with no rhetoric, from your Ramón.'[31]

In March 1965, he'd stopped over briefly in Paris and sent her a postcard (a portrait of Lucrecia Crivelli, by Leonardo de Vinci) from the Louvre:

> I was dreaming of holding your hand in the Louvre, and here you are … – a little chubby and serious, with a sad sort of smile … waiting for your lover who is far away (Is it who I'm thinking of, or another?).
>
> Kisses and a huge hug for everyone and a special one for you,
>
> From Marshall Thu Che

In another letter from this time, he wrote: 'I am more in love with you each day and my home beckons me – [and] the children … Sometimes, I think this is dangerous, diverting me from my duty. Moreover, you are so essential to me and I am only a habit for you.' In other letters, he often referred to her as '*mi única*' – my only one. When he finally left for the Congo, he left her his watch, 'which had a great sentimental value'. Although March 'tried repeatedly to convince him to take her with him – both on his mission to the Congo and to Bolivia', Che declined – but promised to send for her and their children when the revolution was in a more 'advanced stage'. Deep down, she'd always known that he would 'fight to the death if necessary against imperialism and for the establishment of socialism'.[32]

While he was in the Congo, although Che and March had assumed that communication would be difficult, it proved not to be the case. Consequently, letters were regularly exchanged – taken mostly by Cuban liaison cadres who travelled back and forth between the two countries, or Cuban fighters going to the Congo to join Che. For March, the letters she received from Che were among her 'most precious possessions', and, according to her, show that she 'wasn't the only one being tested by our separation', and also 'the enormous sacrifice it was for Che to leave us behind'. His first letter from the Congo read: 'To my only one in the world, (I've borrowed this phrase from old Hickmet), What miracles you have performed with my poor old shell ... I dream of the concave space in which you comfort me, your smell and your rough rural caresses ... A long kiss, like our kiss when we are reunited. I love you, Tatu.' When it came to her joining him in the Congo, he made it clear in an early letter that when she came, she needed to come as a combatant, not 'the little wife'. He also wrote that much of his life had involved 'having to hold back the love I feel for other considerations. That's why I might be regarded as a mechanical monster. Help me now Aleida, be strong ... When we married, you knew who I was.' Nonetheless, according to her, in other letters:

> He constantly expressed his pain at our separation, but asked me not to despair. He urged me to study French so that I could function more effectively if I went to the Congo. Although I tried to fill the void as best I could, I never really came to terms with life without Che.[33]

March did not receive the farewell letters for her and the children until October 1965, after Castro had made public Che's letter to him. Raúl's wife, Vilma Espín, came to their house with the letters. The letter for her was marked 'Only for you', and contained tape recordings he'd made of him 'reading some of the poems we had shared in our intimate moments'. He went on to say that, by leaving those tapes, 'he was leaving the best part of himself', and assured her she was 'part of his world forever'. As well as poems by Nicholás Guillén, there was also Neruda's '*Adios: Veinte poemas del amor*'. When she heard his voice reciting what she referred to as 'our poems', she 'cried uncontrollably, unable to stop. They were tears of joy, but at the same time I was conscious of a gigantic abyss opening inside me.' She came to see them as being 'truly the fruits of a great love, of our love'.[34]

Why the Congo?

His decision to go to the Congo wasn't a random one. After gaining independence from Belgium in May 1960, the leftist Patrice Lumumba had become the Congo's first democratically-elected Prime Minister. But a civil war had then broken out, with Katanga province breaking away under Moïse Tshombe's leadership. In December 1960, Lumumba had been overthrown by a US-sponsored coup, led by Mobutu. Then, in January 1961, Lumumba had been brutally murdered in Katanga with the direct involvement of CIA agents. It had been these – and other – US actions which had led Che, in his December 1964 speech at the UN, to castigate the UN for failing to stop Western imperialist countries from violently intervening in the Congo, stating that: 'All free men throughout the world must make ready to avenge the Congo crime.' There were also personal reasons for Che's anger – according to Luther, 'Che had looked upon Lumumba as a brother in revolution.' Not surprisingly, Che saw events in the Congo as 'yet another example of American imperialism at its worst and began to use the Congo in his writings and speeches'. March noted that although Che planned to stay in the Congo as long as necessary, 'He would then return to Latin America to fulfil his long-held dream of achieving the liberation of that continent.'[35]

Che clearly saw this mission as part of his long-standing commitment to 'the great contemporary issue of relentless struggle against Yankee imperialism'; and, as March comments: 'Che, together with the group he led, aimed to strengthen as much as possible the liberation movement in the Congo.' In particular, according to the Cuban ambassador in Tanzania, 'Che saw the Congo as a good site for a training base for liberation movements that would revolutionize all the African countries and in particular, bring down the infamous white supremacist regime in South Africa.' While Victor Dreke – Che's second-in-command in the Congo – explained that, though Che would have preferred to go to Argentina, the Congo mission had further motives: 'It enabled him to follow a double objective: to prepare a group for Latin America, and to create a third front [against imperialism], in Vietnam, Latin America, and Africa.'[36]

'Everywhere and nowhere'

After Che dropped out of public view, he began training with 100 mostly black Cuban fighters who'd fought in the Sierra Maestra, and had volunteered to fight in the Congo. He was keen to establish a Cuban-led military centre in the eastern Congo that would train revolutionaries from across Africa, before they returned to their own countries to begin guerrilla campaigns. Before leaving, a false report was released saying Che had gone to the Dominican Republic to take part in the civil war there, but had been killed shortly after arriving. In some ways, Che was beginning to be something of a popular hero, who was 'everywhere and nowhere'. According to Luther, the number of different rumours can be seen as marking 'his transition into a cultural icon' two years before his murder. Thus, 'Che was already cast in the public eye as a fighter, a warrior of his own making'. Other rumours were wilder, including that Che was 'suffering from a severe heart disease due to asthma'; that 'an irreparable break with Fidel [Castro] had forced him to take refuge in the Mexican embassy to avoid being executed or imprisoned; or that he 'had travelled to the USSR for surgery, and there been liquidated for his Trotskyist views'.[37]

Just before Che left for the Congo, March was surprised one Sunday morning when he didn't go for his usual voluntary work, but stayed at home instead, taking a series of family photographs. He then astounded her by saying he'd booked a beach house for them all at Bocaciega – this was 'something he had never done before'. That short break became a 'sad memory' for her, because 'When the children were in bed and we were alone, he told me he would be leaving soon. I felt as if the world was about to end.' Then, at dawn on 1 April, Che left his home disguised as Ramón Benítez, clean-shaven and wearing glasses, to join his fellow guerrillas at their camp – who didn't immediately recognise him. While the CIA spent time trying to confirm the rumours, Che and his group slipped quietly out of Cuba and entered the Congo in secret.[38]

Start of the mission

The poverty, suffering and oppression Che had encountered during his visits to various African countries before 1965 had once more touched a nerve regarding the 'plight of the common man'. In all, around 150 Cubans volunteered to go with Che – he and the small group with him arriving in Dar es Salaam on 19 April. The rest arrived in several batches over the following weeks. Not even the Cuban ambassador, Ribalta, recognised him. Officially, Dreke was the commander of the Cuban force – Che just the group's doctor. To avoid using names in communications, Che gave them code names, based on Swahili numbers: Dreke was 'Moja' (one), while Che was 'Tatu' (three). This soon caused confusion when it became apparent that 'Tatu' seemed to give more orders than 'Moja'. José Maria 'Papi' Martínez – an experienced guerrilla fighter – was 'Mbili' (two).[39]

Che – who hadn't even told Kabila, or any of the other rebel leaders, that he was coming – travelled to Kigoma, a village on the east shore of Lake Tanganyika. After a couple of days, they crossed the lake and Che, along with thirteen other Cubans, arrived in the Congo on 24 April 1965. The Congolese political commissar, Godefroi Chamalesco, was Che's main link to the rebels and their National Revolutionary Council, until the local leader, Kabila, arrived. However, early on, when Chamalesco, introduced the Cubans to the various field commanders for the first time, Che noted that he 'did not seem all that popular among the brigade leaders'. The reason being that he, like the other political leaders, very rarely visited the front line commanders. When Che finally revealed who he was, Chamaleso was shocked, worried that his presence might cause an international scandal.[40]

Within just a short while after arriving in the Congo, Che began to feel that the rebel movement he'd come to help was unlikely to win against the neo-colonial government. The rebels he'd come to support were divided; had weak or corrupt leaders; hadn't established support among the local population; and generally lacked discipline. Just four months after arriving in the Congo, Che's *Message to the Fighters* of 12 August 1965, shared this bitter conclusion with his Cuban troops: 'The leaders of the movement spend most of their time outside of the country ... indiscipline and a lack of self-sacrifice are the main characteristics of all the guerrillas. A war is not won with such troops, of course.'[41]

Che was left with several commanders who often disagreed. One particular problem was language: the troops (Tutsi from Rwanda, Ugandans, as well as the Congolese) spoke different languages and several of the junior commanders did not speak French. While Che – though taking a Swahili phrasebook with him – never mastered the language. In addition, many of the rebel fighters' religious beliefs involved reliance on *'dawa'* – a potion said to protect people from bullets. As Che noted: 'I was constantly afraid that this superstition would rebound against us, that we would be blamed for any military disaster involving many deaths.'[42]

Nonetheless, Che at first remained convinced that the Congo would be a good base from which to revolutionise Africa. Consequently, while he waited for Kabila to show, he drew up a training programme for the Congolese troops. But the local commanders said they needed approval from Leonard Mitoudidi, the military chief of staff of the National Liberation Council (NLC). Thus his plans were undermined almost from the start by delays and a reluctance to undertake serious military action. Additionally, many rebels had no real idea of how to handle weapons safely, while Rwandans and Congolese tended not to get along. Furthermore, many field commanders tended to exaggerate the number of fighters they had – which Che soon realised were just 'inventions'. Che also quickly discovered that drunkenness was a problem – often leading to disobedience, fights and inaction. Instead, he found much of his time was taken up with attending to troops infected with malaria or STIs, or to local peasants. All this inaction began to undermine the morale of the Cuban combatants.[43]

In order to improve morale while waiting for Kabila, Che began education classes in French, Swahili and general culture – much as he had done in the guerrilla war in Cuba. He also maintained his personal discipline, while continuing with his own intensive study programme. According to March:

> He increased the number of books he requested, broadening his reading list. It is extraordinary how, in the midst of all the problems and hardships he experienced in the Congo, and the growing sense of disaster, he continued to

study philosophy and other subjects he thought would help him understand better how the Third World could achieve socialism.

Che was clearly determined to make his Congo mission work, believing he could repeat earlier successes. As Luther notes: 'if more people had been like Che, there was probably nothing he could not have accomplished'.[44]

When Mitoudidi eventually arrived on 8 May, he informed him that Kabila wanted Che's identity kept secret, but agreed with Che that it would be safer to move the training camp to a mountainous area, away from the Lake shores. Che immediately began to establish a self-sufficient base – like the earlier ones in El Hombrito and Escambray in Cuba. As well as building huts and carrying on with classes, Che also began to train the Congolese troops to instil more order and discipline.

Death of a mother

Che had always shared a close relationship with his mother, who understood his wanderlust and love of adventure. However, as he was setting up camp in the Congo, she was in hospital in Buenos Aires, dying of cancer. Like most of the world, she was totally unaware of his whereabouts. His mother had asked family members to ask March where he was, having had a letter on 13 April from Che, saying he was cutting cane and then going to work in a factory, and concerned about rumours over his disappearance.

March spoke to Celia over the phone on 18 May, by which time Celia was in a near-coma. Although March tried several times to tell Che about his mother, he didn't learn of his mother's condition until another batch of Cuban fighters brought him news that his mother was in hospital with cancer. By then, though, she was already dead, having died on 19 May, surrounded by her family, including Che's father – but not her much-loved son. When Che eventually found out, he wrote: 'I had to spend a month in uncertainty … in the hope that there had been a mistake – until, finally, confirmation of my mother's death arrived.' He was further upset to realise that she'd never know what he'd written in his farewell letter to his parents. As it turned out, she had written Che a letter – without mentioning her illness – just before she died. In it, she wrote how his sudden disappearance had only deepened her concern, resulting in 'a sea of confusion, and even greater anxiety and alarm'. She even worried that the rumours of a falling-out with Castro might be true. She closed her letter saying she was just an 'old woman who hopes to see the whole world converted to socialism', and agreeing that: 'Yes, you'll always be a foreigner. That seems to be your permanent fate.' Che later sent March 'a sorrowful letter', in which 'he expressed the hope "she had not suffered physically and hopefully she hadn't time to think about me"'. Che wrote a moving short story, 'The Stone', in memory of his mother:

> In it, he poured out his sense of loss, feeling 'a physical need for my mother to be here so that I can rest my head in her bony lap. I need to hear her call me her "dear old fella" with such tenderness … There is no need to ask her for forgiveness. She understands everything.'

At her funeral, a framed photo of Che was placed on the coffin. The 'special bond that had always linked Celia and her firstborn son … had endured … right to the end'.[45]

Problems

In the Congo, however, the new environment meant various tropical diseases – including malaria – began to hit the Cuban troops, including Che himself: 'During the first month, no fewer than a dozen comrades paid for their apprenticeship in this hostile land with raging fevers whose after-effects were equally trying.' For almost a month, many were too ill to do anything – while those who did not succumb found the inaction monotonous. On 16 May, Osmany Cienfuegos arrived with seventeen more Cubans, bringing their number up to over sixty. When, on 22 May, Mitoudidi finally gave an order for the troops to attack Albertville, many of the troops were still ill. Che, however, felt that they should nonetheless show willingness to fight, despite the problems. Che persuaded Mitoudidi – seen by Che as a serious rebel leader – that they should first reconnoitre the target. While he waited for the scouting groups to return, Che soon realised that although some of the troops were well-armed, the overall situation at the various fronts remained poor. In particular, some commanders were getting drunk in front of their men, many of whom were lazy and not willing to carry out training – and some of whom intimidated the local peasants to get food: 'The basic feature of the People's Liberation Army was that it was a parasitic army.' These obvious problems did not go down well with many of the Cuban troops, who'd left their families to help these rebels.[46]

Not in control

Che's biggest problem was that he couldn't act without orders from Kabila, who remained frustratingly out of touch: 'Each morning we were given the same old tune: Kabila has not arrived today, but certainly tomorrow, or the day after tomorrow.' Then, to make matters worse, Mitoudidi drowned in a mysterious boating accident. Also frustrating was that although arms continued to arrive, these tended not to be used well. Finally, at the end of June, Kabila sent orders for the rebels to attack a military base and hydro-electric plant, in what would be the Cubans' first serious military action. As Che knew it was heavily guarded, he suggested smaller actions. He was overruled and ordered not to take part. Che thus reluctantly picked a combined force of around 200 Cuban and Rwandan fighters for the attack.[47]

The attack, which began on 29 June, was a disaster: once the shooting started, many simply fled in panic. During that encounter, four Cubans were killed – and the documents on them meant the CIA now knew that Cubans were involved, although they had no idea Che was present. Not surprisingly, this first encounter did nothing to improve the morale of the Cuban volunteers, who began openly to question 'the logic of fighting for people who would not fight for themselves'. In his diary, Che noted that it was often the officers who 'took the lead in running away', while 'each of our fighters had glumly witnessed assault troops melt away at the moment of combat and throw away the precious weapons in order to flee more quickly'.[48]

Not surprisingly, after this first fiasco, and the three months of waiting before it, many of the Cubans now began to speak of going back to Cuba. Che tried to encourage them to stay, convinced he could still turn the situation round. Finally, Kabila arrived, with Masengo, a new commander to replace Mitoudidi. Che was disheartened to hear Kabila was now hugely critical of Soumaliot, the political leader of the rebels. Then, after only five days, he left – the effect was to throw many of the Congolese troops back into inaction: 'Soldiers whose task it was to dig trenches said they were not to work today because the leader had gone away.'[49]

To make matters worse, the different rebel military leaders failed to reach agreement; relations between Rwandans and Congolese worsened; and more fighters deserted. The few attacks that were launched had limited results. However, as with the first actions, Che was still ordered not to fight himself. He became increasingly disheartened, beginning to see his original belief – that the Congolese Revolution would be successful in three to five years – as 'a very optimistic target ... unless something changed in the way the war was conducted. But that possibility seemed more remote with every day that passed.'[50]

As a result, he gave up on the idea of establishing a training camp for guerrillas from other African countries. The morale of the Cubans continued to decline, despite the arrival of his former bodyguard, Harry 'Pombo' Villegas, with some fresh troops from Cuba. Che's training role became increasingly difficult, as several rebel leaders now decided not to send their troops for training. Then, in September, Tanzania began to make things more difficult for the Congolese, while Tshombe's troops – aided by Belgian paratroopers and by mercenaries led by 'Mad Mike' Hoare – went on the offensive. Gradually, Tshombe's military campaign began reducing the territory controlled by the rebels.

In early October 1965, still determined to make a success of the mission, Che tried – unsuccessfully – to get Masengo to agree to recruiting local peasants for an independent column, so as not to have to rely on the existing rebel forces; and to set up an overall general staff 'that would direct operations on all fronts'. In a letter to Castro, dated 5 October, Che made it clear how bad the situation was, admitting he'd maintained 'a groundless optimism in the face of the actual situation', and stating that: 'I can assure you that were it not for me this fine dream would have collapsed with catastrophe all around', urging Castro not to believe any reports that painted a different picture, as they 'have nothing to do with reality'.[51]

Meanwhile, malaria and other tropical diseases continued to have an impact on the Cuban volunteers – including Che himself, who also experienced his usual asthma attacks. However, Masengo did agree to take Che on a short inspection trip to some of the nearest bases – but then was called to Kigoma, as a result of the power struggle within the NLC, but promising to return the following day. A week later, he still hadn't returned. Meanwhile, Castro continued to send batches of Cuban volunteers. – the fifth group arrived just after Che had left for the front, and included two more of Che's comrades-in-arms from the Sierra Maestra: Fernández 'Vinegar' Mell, who said the news in Cuba was that Che's mission was going well; and Emilio 'Tembo' Aragonés, the PURS Secretary. Castro had told them that Che seemed 'overly pessimistic' – but, not long after their arrival, they realised why Che was concerned: 'Underneath that calm demeanor he had, always writing, reading, and thinking, Che was a man of enormous activity. He was an erupting volcano who wanted to do things, and in the Congo, he wanted it to be like it was in the Sierra Maestra.'[52]

As soon as he had news of the latest arrivals, Che headed back, concerned that Castro was recalling him to Cuba. He came back more hopeful from his trip – largely because he'd had some positive meetings with local peasants, including giving them some healthcare and promising to send medical supplies. However, despite being encouraged by getting some of the Rwandans to stay and fight, he was disappointed that the local commanders still refused to send their men to him for training.

No way back?

On 3 October, Castro made Che's farewell letter public – partly to explain why Che was not included in the leadership of the newly-formed Cuban Communist

Party. Che's reaction to this was mixed – on the one hand, it was evidence of his seriousness to further revolution against imperialism, and he tried to use the announcement to rebuild morale among his troops. But it also meant that, having renounced his Cuban citizenship, he couldn't really return – and, as he noted later, many of his Cuban troops reacted negatively to that renunciation: 'my farewell letter to Fidel … meant that – just as they did many years ago, when I was starting out in the Sierra – the comrades saw me as a foreigner in contact with Cubans'. To make matters worse, in mid-October, several rebel leaders began negotiations with the government, while Che's Cuban volunteers became increasingly unhappy. Che was forced to admit that things were difficult: 'the Liberation Army was falling apart'. He thus felt he couldn't ask the Cubans 'to have confidence in victory' – even though he still believed that 'things could be sorted out'. By then, he was aware morale was continuing to decline: 'That romantic time when I could threaten to send to send someone back to Cuba was long past; if I did that now, I would be reduced to half the present numbers, with luck.'[53]

Then, to make matters worse, there was a renewed government offensive, with the rebel forces still reluctant to resist. As a result, his base camp was overrun by the enemy on 24 October. This was something Che blamed on himself, as he had not posted any sentries on the route that the enemy had unexpectedly taken. This caused Che to write: 'My own morale was terribly low; I felt I was to blame for the disaster because of my lack of foresight and my general feebleness.' While Che and the Cubans made an orderly retreat, the Congolese rebels just fled. On reaching a hilltop Che commented: 'I reflected bitterly that there were 13 of us, one more than Fidel had had at a certain moment, but that I was not the same leader.' While establishing a new base, a sixth Cuban died from wounds received in the attack – this affected Che (who'd tended his wound) deeply, seeing his body as 'a mute and virile accusation … [of] my stupidity and lack of foresight'. He then gave his men 'a soliloquy loaded with reproaches against myself. I recognized my mistakes …' Che promised to ameliorate his guilt 'by working harder and more enthusiastically than ever'.[54]

The end of the mission

In the event, he wouldn't have time to do so. On 30 October, as the enemy continued their offensive, Che was warned by Aragonés and Mell to leave his base and retreat to their base on Lake Tanganyika, as the rebel troops were putting up no resistance and Che risked being cut off. Although the other Cubans felt the dream of a Congolese revolution was over, Che – while acknowledging many setbacks – argued that November would see a turning point. But then

Tanzania – the most important rebel backer, and the one which had given most help to the Cuban mission in the Congo – finally decided to withdraw its support, and began blocking supplies. Che called it 'the coup de grâce for a moribund revolution'. On 4 November, Che received a telegram from Castro: offering to send more troops if he wanted to stay, but also saying he would help if Che decided it best to withdraw. But, above all else, Castro warned: 'avoid any annihilation'.[55]

Despite all the setbacks and problems, even at this stage Che was prepared to fight on with a small handpicked group: 'Cuba will not go back on its promises ... We would abandon the struggle only if ... the Congolese asked us to do so, but we shall fight for this not to happen.' In the end, the decision to leave was made by the rebel military leaders who decided to end the struggle. Che was angry – and asked for this in writing, as 'there was a thing called history'.[56]

On 18 November 1965, after seven months of frustration and struggle, Che began preparations for withdrawal from the Congo. What undoubtedly made it worse for him – and the other Cubans – was that this was kept secret from the Congolese rebels. Even then, Che still seems to have been undecided – contemplating remaining while the rest of the Cubans left: 'the thought of remaining in the Congo continued haunt me long into the night'. Luther wonders if this was because 'he thought he had nowhere else to go'. But, in the end, he decided to go with the rest of the Cubans. Launches turned up on the night of 20 November. The first boat took some Congolese troops to a neighbouring village, so they wouldn't know the Cubans were leaving the Congo. Che and the Cubans were the last to leave. When the rest of the rebels realised what was happening, they begged to go with them – this upset Che: 'I had to chase away men who kept imploring us to take them too; there was no element of grandeur in this retreat, no gesture of defiance.' With many of the Cubans clearly excited to be leaving, Che's mood was despondent: 'I felt more alone than I had done even in Cuba or on any of my wanderings around the globe.' No wonder Che's diary contains the bitter comment that: 'This is the history of a failure.'[57]

Immediately on arriving back in Tananzia, Che – described by the CIA as the 'roving incendiary' – began thinking of his next mission. Turning to three of his closest comrades – Pombo, Tuma and Papi – he said: 'Well, we carry on. Are you ready to continue?' When asked where the new place might be, Che answered: 'Wherever.' According to Pombo, Che 'could not return to Cuba without having achieved success ... he had to continue the struggle'.[58]

Self-criticism

Nine years before, Che had left on the *Granma* to play an important part in what proved to be a victorious revolution. Now it seemed he was being carried away from 'a defeated revolution to destinations unknown'. After withdrawing from the Congo – as secretly as he'd arrived – Che and the Cubans headed to Dar es Salaam. Although preparations were made for the Cubans to fly back to Cuba, Che chose to remain – despite Castro's pleas. Initially, Che wanted to go straight from Tanzania to a new destination. According to Dreke, Castro struggled to keep Che from going straight to Argentina.[59]

Once in Dar es Salaam, Che stayed in the Cuban embassy until February 1966. On 28 November, Che – despite being proud of his Cuban fighters – wrote to March, saying, he was 'returning, along the road of defeat, with an army of shadows'. Tellingly, he also stated that: 'the time has come for the last stage of my journey – the definitive one. Only a handful of select men will come with me.' However, he clearly felt the pull of home, and of March herself:

> You know I'm a combination of adventurer and bourgeois, with a terrible yearning to come home, while at the same time, anxious to realize my dreams. When I was in my bureaucratic cave, I dreamed of doing what I have begun to do … my need for you is virulent and physiological, and cannot always be calmed by Karl Marx or Vladimir Ilych … receive an embrace yourself – not the last one, but with all my love and the desperation as if it was our last embrace. A kiss.[60]

Although he'd said that the need for secrecy meant he couldn't see her for a long time, in December 1965 – at his request – Castro gave March permission to visit him. She arrived in Dar es Salaam in January 1966 and, for the next six weeks, they stayed in the small embassy flat. This would prove to be their longest time together as just a couple. During it, Che took 'romantic photographs of the two of them'; Aleida later described it as 'the closest thing she ever had to a honeymoon'. There – as well as recovering physically from his months in the Congo (his asthma and malaria had resulted in a significant weight-loss – according to his youngest brother, he'd 'lost twenty kilos') – he taught her French, and recorded stories for their children. Nonetheless, Che was encouraged by the first conference of the Organisation of Solidarity of Asian, African, and Latin American Peoples – the Tricontinental – which had taken place in Havana from 3–15 January 1966. This seemed to bode well for his dream of international solidarity and revolution.[61]

By the time March arrived, a deeply-disheartened Che had already written up his Congo diaries. While March was with him, he wrote his severe critique of the

USSR's *Manual of Political Economy*, and also began work on his 'Philosophical Notes' and his 'Economic Notes'. As well as making a general analysis of why the mission had failed, he'd subjected himself to his usual honest self-criticism. He was ruthless: 'I set off with more faith than ever in the guerrilla struggle, yet we failed. My responsibility is great; I shall not forget the defeat, nor its most precious lessons.' One mistake he identified was not informing the leaders of his intention to bring a group of fighters to the Congo: 'I was not unaware of the fact that a negative would place me in a difficult position, because now I couldn't go back, but I calculated that it would be difficult for them to refuse me.'[62]

In addition, he admitted he hadn't found a way of effectively communicating to the rebels the wider importance of the mission – most were nationalists rather than internationalists. Plus, he noted that his behaviour had been erratic: 'for much of the time my attitude might have been described as complacent, but sometimes I displayed very bitter and wounding outbursts, perhaps as a result of a trait of character.' Che's strength had always been that he maintained close contact with the ordinary people he fought for and with. Yet he noted that he'd often withdrawn into his own world (something he'd always seemed to do) to read and write – which made him seem apart from the rest. He also noted the poor attitude some of the Cubans had towards the Congolese, and that he'd failed to instil in the Cuban troops the same dedication and passion he felt for the Congolese people:

> At first I tried to apply moral coercion, but this failed. I tried to ensure that my men had the same view of the situation as myself, but I failed. They were not prepared to look optimistically at a future that had to be glimpsed through such a dark fog in the present times.[63]

He also singled out his failure to learn Swahili – although he was able to communicate with the leaders in French, his lack of Swahili limited his contacts with the ordinary rebels. Although Che was honest enough to admit that his Congo mission was a failure in the short term, in the long term it led to several successes. In April 1965, he'd promised Neto's liberation movement – fighting against Portugal's rule of Angola – that Cuba would assist. By May 1991, 450,000 Cuban combatants had helped Angola, Guinea-Bissau and Cape Verde, and Mozambique and Namibia, gain independence. They had also defeated South African armies and a US-backed insurgency, thus contributing to the collapse of apartheid South Africa – something acknowledged by Nelson Mandela: 'Hundreds of Cubans have given their lives … We vow never to forget this unparalleled example of selfless internationalism.'[64]

Destination Prague

Despite what had happened in the Congo, Che was determined to extend the struggle against US imperialism in Latin America – and was already putting together the key people who would accompany on his next mission. In early March 1966, Che – accompanied by Papi' – left Dar es Salaam for Prague, to make preparations. March, who was left behind, felt 'devastated', fearing she might not see Che again. She returned to Cuba, and gave the children the tapes Che had made for them. A few days later, she was informed that there was a notebook for her. In it, was a piece entitled 'Delivery', which reflected 'the sadness and certainty he felt at the prospect we would not see each other for a long time'. Addressed to 'My love', it went on to say:

> This will be a real farewell ... Now the flag is raised for my last race ... If one day you feel the force of an overbearing presence, don't turn around, don't break the spell, just keep on preparing my coffee, and let me experience you in that instant, for always.[65]

As it turned out, they did meet again. In April 1966, after repeated requests, March was allowed to travel to Prague, where they stayed in two different houses. Although she described Prague as 'an enchanting city', they didn't have much time to explore it together, because of the need to maintain secrecy. Nonetheless, 'It was enough for us to simply be together again.' The original plan was for her to stay until 2 June (their wedding anniversary), but this was brought forward because of fears of another US attack on Cuba. March, unhappy about having to return early, went out to buy him some cufflinks – something small that 'he would always be able to carry with him'. As the cufflinks were never returned to her after his death, March assumed they'd been taken as war trophies.[66]

Che initially thought of going to Peru, but then selected Bolivia, where the civilian government had been ousted by a military coup in November 1964, causing mass protests and a general strike in May 1965. Consequently, in April 1966, Papi was sent there to investigate – with Pombo and Tuma following him there later. Meanwhile, in July, after meeting up with 'Tania' Bunke – who would be one of those helping him in Bolivia – Che began planning for a secret return to Cuba, where he could prepare for what was to become his final mission. He'd drawn some important lessons from his Congo experiences; and had concluded: 'Some mistakes I will never make again, other perhaps I will – and there will be new ones that I shall commit.' The mistakes he made in Bolivia would have fatal consequences not only for him, but also for most of those who went with him.[67]

Chapter 10

The Fatal Mission, 1966–67

'Wherever death may surprise us, let it be welcome if our battle cry has reached even one receptive ear, if another hand reaches out to take up our arms.'[1]

On 21 July 1966, Che returned secretly to Cuba – as 'Ramón'. He was heavily disguised: he appeared naturally balding, as hair had been plucked out; he was clean-shaven; wore thick glasses; and had padding around his body. According to March, he looked 'corpulent and slightly hunched over', as if 'he was in his 60s'. Castro later revealed Che had felt awkward about returning to Cuba, after Castro had read out his 'Farewell' letter, and that it was he who'd persuaded Che to return. While Che was still in Prague, Castro had sent a letter – written 'with deep affection' – arguing that the best place to carry out guerrilla training would be in Cuba's isolated mountains. After his return, Che remained in hiding throughout – apart from meeting several times with March and a few trusted comrades. He went immediately to San Andrés de Caiguanabo, in Pinar del Río, to begin preparations for what would prove to be his final mission. Before leaving Prague, Che had penned a quick note to March, sending her 'A warm kiss, because it is very new and full of hope. Another big one for the children. Your Ramón.' Once Che had arrived in Pinar del Río, Celia Sánchez drove March there, so that she could be reunited with him; though she had to return the next day, as a prolonged absence 'would provoke rumors or questions'.[2]

Despite subsequent rumours, Che didn't go to Bolivia on Castro's orders. Although he didn't ask him to 'abandon or postpone' his plans, Castro worried that Che hadn't had 'enough time to devote [himself] entirely to this matter … to the greatest possible extent'. Although Castro seems to have 'shared Che's desire to see the revolution extended to Latin America', he tried to persuade Che to stay, believing conditions in Bolivia weren't right 'just yet for Che to lead the struggle'. However, he was well-aware of Che's stubbornness and impatience, recognising he had the 'unyielding character of a whole-hearted revolutionary'. Che, determined to resume the struggle against Yankee imperialism, argued that Cuba needed another ally in Latin America. As Che told Castro, he believed that could only be achieved by an experienced guerrilla leader starting a revolution in one of those countries: 'That leader is me. *You* can't start a revolution elsewhere because you must carry on as leader of this one. *I* can, and I will, damn it!'[3]

Why Bolivia?

Although he would have liked to bring revolution to his native Argentina, the failure of Masetti's mission initially ruled that country out. Che had also seen Peru as a possible centre – but that now had an elected reforming government, while several guerrilla groups had been suppressed there in the preceding years. For various reasons, Colombia, Venezuela and Brazil were also ruled out. Far from Castro seeing Bolivia as a useful 'suicide mission' that would allow him to 'invoke Che's [martyred] legacy without having to deal with Che's policies', it's clear 'Che was neither sent against his will nor coerced into the mission'.[4]

Che selected Bolivia largely because of its strategically central position in Latin America, having borders with Argentina, Chile, Peru, Paraguay and Brazil. Once an initial base had been securely established there, Che believed he could form a permanent training base that could act as a launch-pad for different guerrilla movements to branch out into surrounding countries. In addition, Che was given information by various individuals and groups that Bolivia seemed to have the best revolutionary potential. While in Bolivia in 1953, he'd witnessed many demonstrations by 'the armed *campesinos* and workers of the revolutionary militia' in support of a radical programme of nationalisations and land redistribution. As his youngest brother said, Che's intention to 'create a hotbed of insurgency in Bolivia' – and then to spread it to neighbouring countries – was not a rash decision. 'The whole of Latin America was in turmoil at the time', and rebellion was 'already latent' in Bolivia. In fact, Ali confirms that 'Che's choice of Bolivia as a possible insurrectionary site in the mid-1960s was not as light-minded as it seemed to the more orthodox sections of the Latin American and global left at the time.' While Che was being hunted down, the army massacred striking miners, triggering a crisis within the government and the army. This is why we have Che's *Bolivian Diary*, as the Bolivian Minister of the Interior later resigned and sent the diaries, and other documents, to Havana.[5]

Preparing for 'Mission Bolivia'

Castro had already begun selecting a band of guerrillas more skilled than many of Che's troops in the Congo had been. Many of them – like Dariel 'Benigno' Alarcón – were combatants who'd fought with Che before. Initially, they weren't told precisely what the mission was, or that Che would be with them. When he first arrived, none of them recognised him. However, he gradually let slip details which led several of them to realise that 'Comandante Che' was once more with them. March watched through a window as 'their faces reflected the euphoria they experienced, knowing that the troop would be led by their leader'. Che immediately stepped-up their training, to ensure they were ready for combat in harsh terrains.[6]

March and Che were able to make further 'clandestine encounters' – for her, the most important thing 'was to have him nearby, away from danger … beyond the reach of an enemy bullet'. Sometimes, she accompanied Che and the other combatants on training hikes, feeling 'as free as the wind, following Che as in the old days'. At times, she also cooked for the small group; after which, they often watched films – usually Westerns. Once, in August, she took their 3-year-old daughter Celia with her. Although Che enjoyed playing with her, and March took what she described as 'some beautiful photographs', Celia was unaware that 'Ramón' was her father.[7]

Armando Hart – the Organisation Secretary of the CCP – also visited the farm, giving Che an opportunity to exercise his intellect as well as his body, by discussing philosophy and Freud's psychological theories. Earlier, in December 1965, Che had suggested to Hart that his own study plan should be the basis for a guide to Marxism – but emphasising that Soviet manuals be excluded, as they had 'the drawback of not allowing you to think for yourself, because the party has already done it for you … In terms of methodology, it is as anti-Marxist as can be.'[8]

Farewell 'Uncle' Ramón

As summer turned to autumn, small groups of Cuban guerrillas began leaving for Bolivia, to prepare the ground for the arrival of the rest of the group – with Che confident he wouldn't encounter the same problems he'd experienced in the Congo. Although March tried to persuade him to stay for another year, to complete his political projects in Cuba, he was 'convinced that the pillars of the Cuban revolution were strong'. Instead, he believed there was 'much to be done' in Latin America, and 'he was eager to contribute to eliminating the evils that had prevailed there for centuries'. However, before he left for Bolivia at the end of October, he had an emotional reunion in a safe house in Havana with four of his children, most of whom he'd not seen since he'd left for the Congo, over eighteen months earlier. Hildita, his eldest child (then aged 10), was not present, as Che feared she'd see though his disguise and might let slip that 'Daddy was home'.[9]

Che was introduced to them as 'Uncle Ramón', a friend of their father. Over lunch, he told them that he'd been sent by their father to give them his love and 'little pieces of advice for each of them'. It was very difficult for both Che and March – especially as Che had to limit his parental affection to that appropriate for their father's friend – according to March, 'This was one of the hardest tests he ever had to undergo'. When Aleidita – aged 5, and the eldest present – hit her head, Che automatically went over to comfort her. According to March: 'He treated her so tenderly that, a little while later, she came up to me to tell me a secret: "Mummy, that man is in love with me!" Che heard her whisper to me. Neither of us could speak: we just became pale, overwhelmed by emotion.' According to Anderson, 'tears welled up' in Che's eyes. Especially hard was when they gave him kisses 'for him to take to their father'. It would prove to be the last time they saw Che alive.[10]

At a farewell banquet for the men, Castro gave Che advice and encouragement. At the end of the meal, they hugged each other in a last embrace – according Benigno, after Che left for the airport, Castro 'walked away from the men and sat by himself ... The men wondered if he was weeping.' Before flying out, Che sent March a poem that she treasured 'as one of the most cherished mementos Che left me.' The final verse read as follows:

> My only one in the world:
> I secretly extracted from Hickmet's poems this sole romantic verse,
> to leave you with the exact dimensions of my affection...
>
> Farewell, my only one,
> do not tremble before the hungry wolves
> nor in the cold steppes of absence;
> I take you with me in my heart
> and we will continue together until the road vanishes...

She cried on the way home, wondering: 'if we would experience yet another cycle of separation and reunion'. This time, though, she 'resisted Che's departure less', partly because she 'imagined a reunion would not be too far off'. Even if there might be 'five years of separation', she 'firmly believed [they] would be reunited again'. However, although March said Che's optimism 'never allowed [her] to contemplate the final outcome', it was their final separation.[11]

The Bolivian Communist Party

Like so many communist parties in the 1960s, the Bolivian Communist Party (BCP) was split along pro-Soviet and pro-Chinese lines. The latter group were much more open to guerrilla warfare; but even Marío Monje, the BCP's Secretary-General, and leader of its less-militant pro-Soviet wing, had apparently told Castro in January 1966 – during the Tricontinental Conference – that he was considering the possibility of establishing a guerrilla force in Bolivia. However, as suggested by Anderson and Harris, this may have been merely to prevent Cuba supporting the Maoist faction. In fact, Monje later denied having said this – instead claiming that Castro had merely asked him to assist a 'mutual friend' return to his country via Bolivia. After Che's murder, Castro accused Monje of going back on his word to help Che in Bolivia. Although Che seems to have been aware of this uncertainty, he nonetheless persisted with his plan to go to Bolivia – no doubt believing 'as he almost always did, that revolutionary zeal and fervor would carry him and his men through'.[12]

Several Bolivian communists claimed there was widespread discontent with the military-backed government and growing US economic and political influence in the country. They also confirmed what Cuba's intelligence service believed: that Bolivia's security and military forces appeared to be 'the most ineffective and badly organized in Latin America'. Several of these Bolivian communists had received training in Cuba – and had helped Masetti in his unsuccessful mission in Argentina. In March 1966, Che had sent José María 'Papi' Martínez to Bolivia to assess evidence of growing unrest in the militant mining areas. The Bolivian Communists Papi met apparently confirmed these assessments, and claimed Cuban support was all that was needed to help topple the government.[13]

Che eventually selected the isolated and sparsely-populated south-east of the country, where he calculated that his initial group would be able to safely establish itself until it was ready to undertake military operations: 'to survive; then to act', as he expressed it in his *Message to the Tricontinental.* Yet this area also seems to have been recommended by Monje – possibly as an attempt to force him into Argentina as quickly as possible, as he didn't want a revolutionary guerrilla movement to develop in Bolivia. As Luther comments: 'The area was no place to wage war and could easily turn into a trap.' Nonetheless, Che's revolutionary commitment, along with his impatience to begin, probably persuaded him to go along with that choice.[14]

Preparing the *foco*

By August 1966, while still training in Cuba, Che had selected the valley of the Ñancahuazú River as the base for establishing his small guerrilla nucleus. He reckoned six months' training would be necessary before undertaking military actions. Once ready, his group would then move north towards Bolivia's main cities and important lines of communication. Small groups would then strike simultaneously at several points, to force the army to spread troops across a wide area. These groups would then retreat to Ñancahuazú, to draw the inexperienced troops into ambush zones prepared earlier. Guerrilla victories would then encourage Bolivia's peasants and miners to either join or support his guerrilla army. Success would in turn help encourage similar developments in the countries bordering Bolivia. As such movements spread, the US would intervene and would be weakened, allowing Latin America to liberate itself from US imperialism and establish socialism.

As Che distrusted Monje, he delegated the most important aspects of the preliminary preparations for his *foco* to two brothers – Roberto 'Coco' and Guido 'Inti' Peredo. They'd joined the BCP's youth wing at a young age; and, in 1960, had helped prepare guerrilla *focos* in Argentina and Peru. They also had a taxi business based in La Paz – the perfect cover for clandestine activities. In August, they'd bought an abandoned ranch about fifty miles north of Camiri. Though it seems that by then, Che had begun to think a base further north might be better. According to Anderson, Che 'told his men to purchase land there, and to transfer the weapons they had stored in Santa Cruz'. But Che's team advised sticking with the ranch that had already been bought – 'At last, Che relented.'[15]

'Tania'

While Coco began readying the farm for the arrival of Che and the Cuban guerrillas, Inti returned to La Paz to make logistic preparations – all without the knowledge of Monje and the other Communist leaders. These activities included purchasing a warehouse in which to store weapons and ammunition, which began arriving from Cuba.

Key to the La Paz organisation was Tamara 'Tania' Bunke, whose role was to liaise between La Paz and the farm. Invited to Cuba by Che, she'd became part of a group of Argentines who met regularly at his house. She was an enthusiastic supporter of the Cuban Revolution, and KGB veteran Alexandr Alexiev believed Che had 'conquered her with his ideas; he was such a convincing and attractive personality'. She was certainly loyal to Che, but despite speculation about them having an affair, there's no evidence to suggest anything other than common revolutionary interests.[16]

In March 1964, Che had asked her to go to Bolivia, under a false identity, to gather information – though apparently not telling her that he intended to go to Bolivia himself. She'd posed as a professor of indigenous languages and cultures, which allowed her to travel across Bolivia. In early 1965, she'd obtained a job in the President's Information Office. This, and the contacts she'd made in cultural and diplomatic circles, enabled her to gather information which was used to forge credentials for Che and his guerrilla, allowing them to travel freely within Bolivia.

Message to the Tricontinental

Although not made public until 16 April 1967, the overall strategy behind Che's Bolivia mission was clearly set out in his message to the Second Conference of the Tricontinental. Written before he left Cuba for Bolivia, its title – *'Create Two, Three,… Many Vietnams'* – was based on his belief that the US was 'the great enemy of the human race'. It was also part of his concept of 'proletarian internationalism' and the need for 'international proletarian armies' to combat it:

> Let the flag under which we fight be the sacred cause of the liberation of humanity, so that to die under the colors of Vietnam, Guatemala, Laos, Guinea, Colombia, Bolivia, Brazil – to mention only the current scenes of armed struggle – will be equally glorious and desirable for a Latin American, an Asian, an African, and even a European.[17]

He believed new and successful guerrilla insurgencies in Latin America would force the US to deploy forces there – thereby weakening it, and taking pressure off Vietnam and Cambodia: 'Little by little … [the US] will find themselves obliged to send growing numbers of regular troops to secure the relative stability of a power whose national puppet army is disintegrating in the face of the guerrillas' struggles.' As he saw it, Latin American guerrilla groups should create coordinating committees 'to make the repressive tasks of the Yankee imperialists more difficult'.[18]

The Eagle lands

Che left Cuba in the early hours of 22 October 1966, arriving in Bolivia on 1 November, posing as Ramón Benitez, a Uruguayan businessman. He was accompanied by a close Cuban comrade, Alberto 'Pacho' Fernández. After meeting up with Pombo, Tuma and Papi, they contacted Tania. She gave Che credentials showing him to be 'Adolfo Mena Gonzalez', an economist and special envoy of the OAS. Che and Pacho then travelled to the Ñancahuazú farm, arriving during the night of 6 November. The next day, Che began his diary, and wrote to March.

He decided to establish a camp away from the farm, leaving just a few people behind. By 16 November, they'd dug a tunnel for storing tinned food and 'anything that might be compromising'. As the days passed, Che grew impatient that they'd not heard from La Paz about other guerrillas coming. From 20 November onwards, some began to arrive, initially bringing numbers up to twelve. Most of these – selected by Che himself – were veterans of Cuba's Revolutionary War, and/or his campaign in the Congo. There were also three dissident members of the BCP's youth wing, who'd been recruited by the Peredo brothers, and trained in Cuba. Inti had come with the new arrivals, meeting Che for the first time. His book, *My campaign with Che*, described the scene: 'When we arrived, his eyes sparkled with joy. The man most wanted by imperialism, the legendary guerrilla, the strategist and theorist of projects of international ambition' was there, seated on a tree trunk, 'in the heart of one of the most exploited and oppressed countries on the continent.' Che was then informed that Juan Pablo 'Chino' Chang – an old friend of Che's first wife – had arrived in Bolivia, with twenty Peruvians he wanted to bring straight away. Che thought this 'inadvisable because it would internationalize the struggle', before they were sure of Monje's attitude. Che agreed they could come – but only after combat had begun. On 29 November, they began work on the second camp, and also explored other possible camp sites.[19]

Communications with Cuba were irregular – mostly via visitors. In December 1966, March received what proved to be her last letter from Che. It was delivered by Chino – the 'unofficial route' which Che wrote was 'more intimate'. In the letter, which began with: 'To my only one', he revealed 'There are days when I feel so homesick, it takes a complete hold over me.' It ended with: 'Give a kiss to the little pieces of my flesh and blood ... For you, a kiss filled with sighs and sorrow from your poor, bald Husband.'[20]

During December, they – including Che – dug more storage caves, for food, weapons and the radio; established observation posts; and began cutting trails through the dense undergrowth. Also, because food was already running short, they began hunting. After moving to the second camp, Che and his fighters began exploring the area. As well as realising how difficult the terrain was, they discovered their maps were 'very bad', and began making better ones. On Christmas Eve, they held a party – but were back at work on Christmas Day.[21]

Abandoned

In addition to the Cubans, there were also nine Bolivian communists, mainly recruited by Coco. Che's diary shows he hoped to have at least twenty Bolivians in his group before beginning military action – seeing the presence of Bolivians as important for the success of his mission. However, his hopes were frustrated by Monje, who arrived on 31 December, along with Tania. Monje made it clear he'd only send volunteers if he were given total political and military command. He also insisted Che shouldn't contact Bolivia's pro-Mao communists.

Che's experience in Cuba had taught him that military leadership should rest with those actually fighting. While recognising that 'the non-combatant organization [of a] revolutionary guerrilla army' was important, he believed its role was 'auxiliary', and that it should be 'under the direct orders' of a military commander, since 'the armed fight is the crucial factor.' Che also felt Monje lacked a sufficiently-internationalist revolutionary outlook, and the military experience, to be a leader. Given his experiences in the Congo, where he'd been dependent on political leaders who were often absent from the areas of military operations, Che refused to relinquish control to Monje and the other BCP leaders, whom he considered 'weak and untrustworthy'. So Monje told the Bolivians in Che's group that if they didn't leave with him, they'd be expelled from the party. To his surprise, they all chose to stay. On 1 January 1967, Monje left for La Paz; he then wrote to Castro, withdrawing any official support for Che's mission.[22]

Che's small band – now numbering around twenty-five guerrillas – were clearly on their own. He explained the situation to everyone, and 'predicted difficult times ahead and days of moral anguish for the Bolivians'. Loyola Guzmán – a member of the BCP Youth, and judged by Che as 'very determined' – was put in charge of finances in La Paz. By 4 January, the radio cave was ready; but target practice had to be postponed because of heavy rain, which often created problems in crossing swollen rivers. Additionally, signs of difficult personal relations led Che to launch 'a little tirade … about the need for greater discipline'.[23]

Despite 'very inclement weather', Che, as ever, led by example – doing his turn at sentry duty. However, the heavy rain penetrated the cave where the radios were stored, and damaged them; while some of Che's books were partly destroyed. Although still able to receive messages, they were often unable to contact Havana or their urban network in La Paz. Rain continued to be a problem until 17 January, hindering work on improving trails and building defensive trenches. By then, they'd also had the first case of malaria. Then began several days of practising defence and offensive actions, and withdrawal techniques. Later, they discovered Monje was dissuading Bolivians who'd trained in Cuba from joining Che. In his monthly summary, Che judged this to be 'treacherous', concluding that 'The party has taken up arms against us'. On 26 January, Moisés Guevara arrived, and agreed to bring recruits. Che then decided on a '10–day march', to get the fighters fit, and to acclimatise them to the harsh conditions. As he noted: 'Now the real guerrilla phase begins and we will test the troops; time will tell what they can do and what the prospects for the Bolivian revolution are.'[24]

The '10–day march'

On 1 February, the training march began. This trek – meant to last just a few days – turned into an immensely tiring six-week expedition, in which they got lost, ran out of food, and encountered real problems because of a mixture of intense sunshine, heavy rainfall and swollen rivers.

Many of the guerrillas 'failed to maintain a good pace' because of the difficult terrain; heavy rain meant marching days ended early; and poor maps continued to cause confusions. Che noted that the paths by the river Ñacahuazú were 'so rough on our shoes that several *compañeros* are already almost barefoot'. Rafts had to be constructed in order to cross the swollen Río Grande; while, on 9 February, 'pandemonium broke out' when the rest of the group missed a marker indicating that Che's section had turned off the main path. As a result, 'groups went in all directions'.[25]

Their first night march 'served to show how much there is to learn'. When they stopped, Che noted he was 'completely exhausted' and had an upset stomach, having 'not eaten anything all day'. On 18 February – March's birthday – plans to cross a mountain range to reach the Rosita river were foiled by steep cliffs. This 'partial failure' was followed by another 'lost day' when, trying a different direction, they came across yet another impassable cliff.[26]

There then followed further days of 'slow, uneven progress'. By the end of the third week, everyone was exhausted, and some were feeling ill. This included Che, who noted on 23 February that it was a 'bad day' for him, as he 'was exhausted and moved through willpower alone' and 'felt faint'. Further problems arose because the 'topography is different from what is marked on the map'.[27]

Yet more 'bad days' meant they made very little progress: some got lost, and tempers became frayed – forcing Che to warn them that these hardship were 'an introduction to what was in store' and shouldn't lead to 'shameful incidents'. On 26 February, one of the exhausted fighters fell into the river and drowned in the strong current – with Che recording that the man had 'had a great determination to succeed', but that the rigours had proved 'beyond him'. The remaining days of the month proved equally exhausting, made worse by the fact that their last rations had been eaten. Che's monthly summary noted that: 'The men are still weak and not all of the Bolivians are able to hold up; the last few days of hunger have dampened their enthusiasm.' He also found fault with some of the Cubans, noting that: 'The next phase will be combat, and that will be decisive.'[28]

As the trek continued into March, hunger further slowed down progress. On 4 March, he recorded: 'Troop morale is low and our physical strength is deteriorating day by day: I am showing signs of edema in my legs.' On 7 March, four months since arriving at the farm, Che noted: 'The troops are discouraged with each passing day, seeing the end of our provisions but not of our journey.' They finally reached the Ñacahuazú river on 14 March; but Che once again recorded that: 'The men's morale is low', with swollen feet becoming 'an alarming problem'; while Che himself was 'extremely weak'. When crossing the swollen river, the raft overturned, and 'Carlos' – considered by Che to be one of the best Bolivian recruits – was swept away, along with a lot of ammunition. Progress remained slow until, on 20 March, they finally reached the base camp. During those last days, Che was concerned by a light airplane that was circling the area.[29]

Good news, bad news

Once back, Che was pleased to discover Coco had arrived with more Bolivian recruits. In addition, Moisés Guevara – an important union leader among the leftist tin miners – had brought eight unemployed miners. This brought the number of Bolivian guerrillas to around twenty. In addition, there were also three Peruvians, led by Chino – more Peruvians arrived later, to undergo training before returning to Peru to begin operations there.

However, Che wasn't pleased that Tania – his main contact with the urban network – had also arrived, apparently wishing to become a combatant. Tania's abandonment of her La Paz network put the group at a serious disadvantage. In addition, the jeep she'd left behind in Camiri had contained documents and photographs which were discovered by the authorities. Régis Debray – a French communist and journalist who was to act as a messenger and liaison between Che and Castro – had accompanied Tania. He had become Professor of Philosophy at the University of Havana, and before leaving for Bolivia in 1967, had published *Revolution within the Revolution?*, aiming to 'revolutionize revolutionary thought' concerning guerrilla warfare in Latin America. In addition, Ciro Bustos – an Argentinian journalist Che hoped would help establish a *foco* in Argentina – had also arrived.[30]

Che was particularly disturbed to learn that two new Bolivian recruits had deserted and been captured by the army. Troops had then moved into the area, and a soldier had been killed by one of Che's guerrillas. On 16 March, the army had raided the farm, and had captured another Bolivian recruit. As a result of the information obtained, the army had discovered the guerrillas' base camp and supplies. Not surprisingly, all this had unsettled everyone – as Che noted in his diary on 20 March: 'Everything gives the impression of utter chaos; no one knows what to do.'[31]

Premature combat

Thus the army already had the initiative. The captured guerrillas had also revealed that Cubans were in the group, with 'Fernando' as the leader. Though the army didn't suspect that 'Fernando' was Che, they relayed the information to Bolivia's intelligence services and the CIA. The latter immediately sent two agents to La Paz.

Contrary to Che's plans, fighting had broken out at least one month prematurely – before they'd established themselves, or were ready to begin military operations. They'd still not recruited enough additional fighters, while many were already exhausted and hungry. Nonetheless, Che was determined to stay and fight. However, as Harris states: 'All of Che's subsequent efforts were little more than valiant, but futile, attempts to put up a good fight in the face of overwhelming odds.' Although, over the next eight months, they carried out several successful 'hit and run' ambushes on army units, they were never able to launch major offensives or capture army bases, as had happened in Cuba. Thus some – such as Luther – conclude that 'Che's theories about creating revolution where none existed' had proved false. This, however, is a misreading of what Che had argued: that guerrilla warfare *could* act as a catalyst before waiting for *all* factors to be in place. As noted previously, some Bolivians had told him that several of those factors already existed.[32]

Che's group now comprised forty-four combatants, with most leadership roles filled by the more-experienced Cubans. Che's second-in-command – and head of the rearguard – was Juan 'Joaquín' Acuña. Joaquín was a close comrade from the Sierra Maestra days, and a member of the Central Committee of the CCP. The only Bolivians to hold posts of responsibility were the two Peredo brothers.

Che held discussions with Chino, Tania and the two journalists. He agreed to give Chino money to establish a *foco* in Peru; and then spoke with Debray and Bustos. Castro had been impressed by Debray; Mandel, too, had praised him, though criticising his views about 'spontaneous party formation'. Che, however, was less sure – and refused his request to join the guerrillas as a combatant. Instead, Che wanted him to take letters to Sartre and Bertrand Russell, to organise an international appeal. Bustos was told to return to Argentina, and send recruits for training.[33]

On 22 March, Che moved everyone to another camp where the vanguard were already waiting. He then ordered Coco and five others to set up an ambush site, and sent out patrols. They soon learned that a column of soldiers was marching towards their camp. Thus, on 23 March 1967 – just three days after their exhausting training march – Che's group had its first major contact with the Bolivian army. The ambush team caught a thirty-strong army unit in crossfire: seven soldiers were killed, some fled, while fifteen surrendered. Several badly needed weapons were also captured – along with papers showing another patrol was approaching from the opposite direction. Wounded soldiers were given medical treatment, and – after their uniforms had been taken – were freed the next day. All this surprised the soldiers, but Che was merely continuing the humane practices followed in the Sierra Maestra.

Outnumbered, surrounded

Having lost direct contact with the urban network, Che's group received no more recruits; while hopes of recruiting local peasants – as had happened in Cuba – came to nothing. Many peasants, fearing army reprisals, acted as informants. Over the ensuing months, as encounters with the army increasingly resulted in deaths and injuries, their numbers gradually diminished. Although this first encounter had been successful, the army now knew there were guerrillas in the area. This made it more difficult for the three visitors to leave the group. At the same time, tensions emerged between some of the Cuban and Bolivian fighters.

Nonetheless, on 25 March, they decided to call themselves the National Liberation Army of Bolivia (Ejército de Liberación Nacional – ELN). Che then issued *Communiqué No. 1: To the Bolivian People*, refuting government claims that fifteen guerrillas had been killed. It stated: 'Hostilities have begun', and appealed to those who felt 'the time has come to … rescue a country being sold off in great slabs to Yankee monopolies.' In his diary, he noted that the radio reported that 'Tania has been identified, which means we have lost two years of good and patient work.'[34]

On 28 March, they heard over the radio that 2,000 troops were now surrounding them. Che decided to establish a new camp, and split his forces into three groups: a vanguard headed by Manuel 'Miguel' Hernández; a centre group (containing the visitors) headed by Che; and a rearguard headed by Joaquín. However, the next day there was a clash in a ravine which Che had said shouldn't be entered: 'in recent days my orders have been repeatedly ignored.' Having had 'to hit the road before I expected', his monthly analysis concluded: 'The situation is not good, but now begins a new testing phase for the guerrilla force.'[35]

As they moved to a new camp, Che decided six needed to stay behind temporarily to guard the remaining supplies – noting that 'The three Cubans are staying under protest.' On 3 April, Che discussed departure options with the three visitors. They agreed to be dropped off at Gutiérrez; but the next day was 'almost a total disaster', when they discovered soldiers were in the area. Over the following days – sometimes of 'great tension' – they often saw large groups soldiers, but avoided combat. On 8 April, Che was informed the army had uncovered the bulk of their supplies – including most of his asthma medicines. They'd also discovered photographs taken by Tania of the guerrillas – including of Che. They continued carefully, 'removing all traces of our presence'.[36]

As Che had written in *Guerrilla Warfare: A Method* – and knew from experience – the most dangerous period for a guerrilla *foco* was building a secure base *before* the opposing military discovered their presence. Che also believed that if a guerrilla group couldn't successfully attack enemy forces during the early stage, it would have little chance of surviving. In *Revolution in the Revolution?*, Debray had written that once a guerrilla group was discovered, it mustn't allow itself to be contained within a specific zone. Yet this was now precisely Che's position: restricted to a small area they hadn't fully explored, and which provided few opportunities for hiding, or finding food. Nonetheless, Che and many of his men seemed to believe they could still make their mission a success. Harris believes the reason why Che remained optimistic, following their premature discovery, was because he remembered how Castro's forces had been reduced from eighty to only twelve after the start of their campaign. Yet, as Harris commented: 'Anyone else undoubtedly would have concluded under the circumstances there was no choice but to abandon the entire venture and escape while it was still possible to do so.'[37]

On 10 April, they ambushed another army unit – killing ten, wounding seven, and taking twenty-eight prisoner. Once again, the wounded were treated and, after their weapons, rations and boots had been taken, they were released. However, one of the Cubans was also killed; two days later, tensions between some of the Cuban and Bolivian recruits led Che to call everyone together to make 'a new call for unity as the only possible way to develop our army'. The next day, 13 April, they learned the US was sending military 'advisers', including the Special Forces' Green Berets, to Bolivia. Che wondered if the US would now be forced to intervene heavily in what would become a 'new Vietnam' for them. The ELN's *Second Communiqué*, dated 14 April, urged Bolivian troops in future to throw their weapons away, remain still, and never to 'go to the front of the column when marching near combat zones'. Instead, they should 'make the officers ... take those extremely dangerous positions'.[38]

With Tania and a guerrilla both running high temperatures, progress slowed. Che thus divided the fighters into separate two groups. Joaquín's group comprised fourteen – including Tania, some in poor health, and those Bolivians Che considered the least useful. In Che's group were the two remaining visitors. The plan was that once the visitors had been safely dropped off, the two groups would reunite within three days and move quickly to a more favourable area. In the end, they were unable to do so. According to Luther, that decision 'seems foolhardy' in retrospect, as Che's 'forces were already too small, and there was no way for them to communicate once they had separated'. Some have attributed this strategically unsound decision to Che's 'deteriorating health and morale'.[39]

On 19 April – despite having advised Debray and Bustos to wait, because troops were nearby – Che reluctantly let them leave. He gave Debray the *Second Communiqué*, along with an urgent coded request for Cuba to send a new radio and the next batch of fighters. In his *Summary* for April, he noted that his 'lack of energy to stop them' was a mistake. Che then began moving to join up with Joaquín. However, the military established where his group was, and began bombing the area. As he later recorded in his diary, Debray and Bustos (the latter having made made drawings of the guerrillas – including of Che) had been quickly picked up by the army. The government made much of the presence of foreign guerrillas; as a result, peasants were increasingly reluctant to help them.[40]

From then on, Che tried desperately to reunite with Joaquín, tracking backwards and forwards in the harsh terrain, with the army increasingly able to follow their movements. The remainder of April saw Che's group experiencing less successful encounters with the army. After one ambush, they were nearly surrounded by troops. Although managing to withdraw in time, one guerrilla got separated from the rest, and Che had to send two guerrillas to search for him – thus further reducing his 'already meagre troops'. Che noted that 'there was a lack of discipline and foresight', although 'morale is very high'. On 25 April, they were nearly surprised by around sixty troops; their ambush didn't go well, and they lost Eliseo 'Rolando' Reyes, another Sierra Maestra veteran – seen by Che as a leader of a second front. Che was close to him, describing him as 'the best man of the guerrilla force'. This clash forced Che to move away from where he was supposed to have met up with Joaquín. Although morale remained 'good' at the end of April, Che noted that 'we are totally cut off'. From then on, things began to deteriorate.[41]

During May, food became increasingly short; with Che commenting they had 'entered the era of the bird' – as they often had to supplement rations by hunting small birds. Their poor maps left them unsure of their exact location, so they decided to head back to their old camp. By 6 May, they were down to their 'next to last meal', but arrived at the camp the next day – the six-month anniversary of 'the official establishment of the guerrilla force' – and were able to retrieve food from one of the caves. Despite a more successful ambush on 8 May, they were soon short of food again, with Che recording: 'I felt faint'. The alternation of lack of food followed by gorging made most of them ill, forcing them to rest until they were again able to walk. On 16 May, Che succumbed to vomiting and diarrhoea – he lost consciousness for a time and had to be carried in a hammock. When he awoke, he 'was covered in shit like a newborn baby'.[42]

On 24 May, having marched by night to avoid soldiers, they reached the Ñacahuazú – and the camp they'd used on the first day of their hiking expedition in February. After three days of trying to obtain more food, Che's group – 'like curiously charitable brigands' – entered a town where they replenished their supplies from the local store – though, as always, paying for what they took. On reaching a settlement near the railway line running to the Argentine border, Che wistfully noted how 'It was so peaceful there, like another world.' He considered heading for the Río Grande, on 'a rather dangerous trip'. But, at the last moment, decided to head north instead. As Reid-Henry noted, 'He would never again be in a position to consider returning to his homeland.' Despite a couple of successful ambushes at the end of May, Che was increasingly concerned about the failure to meet up with Joaquín – and their failure to recruit a single peasant.[43]

Although his group was now down to twenty-five men, their third ELN *Communiqué*, issued in May, stated they 'will not stop short until final victory is achieved'. However, unknown to Che, the CIA were now aware he was in Bolivia. Initially, after his disappearance from Cuba in 1965, the US had assumed he was dead. But, on 11 May 1967, they sent a memo to the US president, revealing 'the first credible report that 'Che' Guevara is alive and operating in South America'. The CIA then dispatched more agents to the area – including Felix Rodríguez – to track Che down.[44]

Still trying

Although Che successfully prevented the army from trapping and wiping out his guerrillas until July, their situation – and morale – worsened over the next two months. Tellingly, on 3 June, Che let an army truck pass without attacking it: 'I did not have the heart to shoot them, and my brain did not react fast enough to figure out how to detain them.' Though they had a partially successful ambush on 10 June – Che recording that 'we have maintained our pattern of clashes resulting in casualties' – they tried to avoid army patrols. News of political confusion in La Paz encouraged him: 'Rarely has potential for a guerrilla catalyst been so clear.' On 14 June – his youngest daughter Celia's birthday, and his own – he commented that he was 'inevitably approaching the age when I need to consider my future as a guerrilla, but for now I am still "in one piece"'. It proved to be his last birthday.[45]

By 23 June, Che's asthma was becoming 'a serious problem', and he had 'very little medicine left'. It continued to worsen over the next few days, making sleeping increasingly difficult. News of an army massacre of striking miners (including women and children) seemed to show potential for revolution in Bolivia. Following another successful ambush, Che decided to remain where they were, hoping to take the soldiers' weapons when it was dark. However, they came under attack: Pombo was wounded in the leg, while Tuma received a fatal wound, reducing Che's group to twenty-four. Che recorded the impact of this death of 'an inseparable *compañero* of recent years ... whose absence I feel now almost as if he were my own son'. A few days after they'd buried Tuma, Che explained to his men what Tuma's death meant to him personally – and 'criticised the lack of self-discipline and the slowness of the march' which had contributed to the loss of Tuma.[46]

At the end of June, the army announced that Che was in Bolivia – he was pleased they claimed they were dealing with 'a perfectly trained guerrilla force' that included Vietcong commanders, and that he planned an 'insurrection in the mines'. This led him to comment that, politically, 'Things are turning out beautifully.' However, his 'Analysis of the month', despite noting that news of the guerrillas' victories were 'growing like wildfire, now we are invincible superhumans', commented on the failure to recruit a single peasant – in part down to the army using 'fear or by fooling them about our goals'. Che estimated they needed to recruit from 50 to 100 new fighters – and thought the mine massacre 'greatly improves our outlook'. More importantly, though, he noted that 'although the army does not know this ... the gradual loss of men ... constitutes a serious defeat'.[47]

The ELN's *Communique No. 4* was issued in June; countering the government's 'foreigner' propaganda, Che stated his long-held internationalist views: 'any citizen who accepts our minimum program, the liberation of Bolivia, is accepted into our revolutionary ranks ... That is how we interpret genuine revolutionary internationalism.' Their fifth – and final – *Communiqué* also came out in June. This referred to the mine massacre, stressed the need for armed revolt, and urged miners not to listen to the BCP – described as 'the false apostles of mass struggle'. Instead, Che argued that support for the guerrilla vanguard would catalyse things 'to the point where a revolutionary situation is created and state power can be overthrown'. The *Communiqué* ended by appealing to the miners 'to join workers of the underground'; but the hope expressed in its last three words – 'We await you.' – wasn't fulfilled.[48]

On the run

Heavy rain and cold marked the start of July, and cutting paths through the difficult terrain began to slow them down. On 1 July 1967, Bolivia's president claimed Che would be wiped out 'in a few days'. As they moved through the region, they noted that the army's repression was causing families to abandon their farms – making it difficult to obtain food supplies, as 'the people received us in terror. On 6 July, Che initiated what Harris described as 'the most daring action of the entire guerrilla operation'. They attacked the army post in Samaipata, and took the eleven soldiers prisoner – before later releasing them. They also raided the local pharmacy for asthma medicines, but failed to get those Che needed. This action – close to the main town of Santa Cruz – was 'a propaganda victory' for the ELN. It made national news, enhancing Che's legendary reputation – and led Argentina and Peru to close their borders with Bolivia, and to put their armies on alert. Sinclair believes that 'had Che been more aggressive at this moment ... the growing legend of the invincible guerrillas would have brought in recruits and might well have caused the downfall of Barrientos'. But Che's success meant the army stepped up its counter-insurgency campaign; from then on, Che's guerrillas were increasingly on the run. In addition, Che's asthma continued to worsen: on 8 July, he had to inject himself 'several times' – 'finally using an eyewash solution'.[49]

Having failed to get asthma medicines, Che decided to return to one of the supply caves established early on, to retrieve medicines stored there. They encountered difficult paths that often led nowhere – and increasingly often lost the trails cut by the *macheteros*. On 12 July, the radio reported that a clash between troops and Joaquín's group had resulted in the death of one guerrilla. For the next couple of weeks, Che's group managed to avoid army patrols – but were encouraged by news that 'the government is disintegrating rapidly. Such a pity we do not have 100 more men right now'. On 15 July, the radio broadcast that the government was launching 'Operation Cynthia' to 'wipe us out within a few hours'.[50]

Towards the end of July, in otherwise successful ambushes, Papi and another guerrilla were killed, and another wounded. As they withdrew, they left behind several knapsacks and medicines – and Che's copy of 'Debray's book, with my notes in it, and a book by Trotsky'. As Che – now reliant on ineffective sedatives to relieve his asthma – noted in his monthly analysis: 'Now we have 22 men, with three disabled (including me), which decreases our mobility.' In addition, there were now 'units that appear to be more combative'. On the positive side, he noted that 'the morale and combat experience of the guerrilla fighters is increasing with each battle', and that the political crisis hitting the Bolivian government was 'growing.' Nonetheless, they had still neither met up with Joaquín's group, nor obtained the asthma medicines Che now needed increasingly desperately.[51]

By August, Che – and many of the others – was sick and exhausted. His asthma was hitting him 'very hard' and he'd used his last anti-asthmatic injection, with only ten days' worth of tablets left. On 3 August, he tried 'an intravenous

Novocain injection, to no avail'. Yet whenever they camped, Che continued to write up his diary, read and make notes – his usual practice, even on military campaigns. On 7 August, his diary entry states: 'Today marks exactly nine months since I arrived and we established the guerrilla force. Of the initial six, two are dead, one has disappeared, two are wounded; and I am suffering from asthma with no idea how to overcome it.' Against his better judgement, he sent several men ahead to get the medicines he needed from one of their caves, telling his men that 'We are in a difficult situation', and that he was 'a complete wreck'. He thus gave them a choice: they could either continue the struggle and 'become revolutionaries, the highest form of the human species', or, if they didn't feel up to it, they 'should say so now and abandon the struggle'. All the Cubans, and some of the Bolivians, 'committed themselves to stay until the end'.[52]

Che then developed an abscess on a heel, making it impossible to walk. He continued by riding on one of their pack mules, although he subsequently developed a fever. However, on 10 August, he was pleased by a speech made by Castro at the first conference of the Organisation of Latin American Solidarity (OLAS). As well as hailing Che as an 'Honorary Citizen of Latin America', Castro made it clear that Cuba would continue to spread revolution. The Conference then endorsed a resolution saying 'guerrilla warfare was the fundamental path for the Latin American revolution'. This occurred while Ernest Mandel was in Cuba, where he'd been since June 1967 having been invited back by Castro. The main reason seems to have been that Castro wanted to make 'public corrections' of his comments in January 1966, when he'd referred to 'the stupidities' of Trotskyism. According to Reid-Henry, Castro even mentioned having just read Deutscher's trilogy of Trotsky, arguing that maybe Lenin should have agreed with Trotsky and done more to hasten revolution in the rest of Europe. Castro concluded, echoing Che's internationalist outlook, that 'Marx was right when he said there can be no real revolution until there is a world revolution ... Unfortunately, the imperialists seem to be the only true internationalists left.'[53]

On 14 August, news came that the army had discovered the cave with Che's medicine – leading him to comment: 'I am now condemned to suffer from asthma indefinitely.' The following day, the radio reported that two guerrillas from Joaquín's group – which was 'being pursued relentlessly' – had been captured and interrogated. On 19 August, two ill Bolivian recruits said they wished to leave; though agreeing Che postponed their departure, as they knew the route they were following which Che hoped would allow them to meet up with Joaquín. On 24 August, they came across soldiers on the opposite side of the river – but Che decided not to engage them. That day, they ate a condor vulture and even 'a rotten cat, all of it ending up inside us'.[54]

On 26 August, 'Everything went wrong' – although firing on some soldiers, they killed none and the soldiers escaped. In the confusion, some guerrillas began shooting in the direction of their comrades and Che 'lost control and roughed up' one of them. When they later saw around thirty soldiers, they avoided attacking; running low on water and food, they tried instead to withdraw to a safer area. On 28 August, Che sadly noted that they'd had to kill their mare: 'I had done everything to save her, but our hunger was becoming severe.' Many guerrillas now became really ill through lack of water. Not surprisingly, Che's summary for August was grim: 'Without doubt, this was the worst month we have had in this war ... We are at a low point in our morale and in our revolutionary legend.' One positive was that he noted that Inti and Coco 'are becoming more and more outstanding as revolutionary and military cadres'.[55]

The final stage

September began badly, with news that ten guerrillas, led by Joaquín, had been killed by the army at the end of August. Although initially dismissed by Che as a 'trick', it was true; though it wasn't until the end of the month that he finally accepted it. Ironically, the massacre took place just 'a day's march from where Che and his men were located'. Among those killed were Joaquín, Moisés Guevara and Tania. Although Paco and one other Bolivian escaped, they were soon captured, and interrogated by Felix Rodríguez and other CIA agents. One of the soldiers released by Che in August had told Rodríguez how many fighters Che had left, how slowly they were walking, and that Che was ill.[56]

On 3 September, while on a mission to purchase food, a section of his force ran into forty soldiers; although they managed to kill one, they were forced to withdraw without any food. As they continued trekking and crossing rivers, they came across more and more squads of soldiers. On 10 September – 'A bad day', with 'planes and helicopters' flying over the area – weapons, and Che's shoes, were lost while crossing a swollen river. The next day, he learned that the government had announced a $4,200 reward for his capture – alive or dead. Later, they heard that sixteen members of their urban underground network had been arrested, including Loyola Guzmán. They were now totally on their own – which naturally eroded morale.

Crossing rivers continued to be difficult, as were attempts to buy food from peasants: the number of soldiers now in the area meant that 'People here are quite afraid and try to avoid us'. Increasingly, many guerrillas were unable to carry their heavy loads; while Che recorded 'I had pains in my liver and was vomiting; the troops are exhausted from these unproductive hikes.' On 26 September, they headed for the village of La Higuera. When they discovered that the mayor had been warned that guerrillas were in the area, Che ordered the vanguard to leave for Jagüey. Thirty minutes later, shots were heard, and Che set up defensive positions in the village. Soon, three of the vanguard returned, reporting that three of them had been killed in an ambush – including Coco – while another was missing. As they withdrew from the village, the rearguard came under heavy fire, with Inti and two others becoming separated from the group. While Inti eventually caught up, the others were captured by the army. As Che noted the following day: 'Our losses have been very great this time; the deepest loss is that of Coco.'[57]

The army's new Ranger Regiment was now deployed to nearby Vallegrande. This unit – set up in April 1967 with US backing and weapons – had been trained in counter-insurgency by US Green Berets and CIA personnel. The decision to concentrate on this area was made by Rodríguez, following lengthy interrogation of one of the captured guerrillas. By 27 September, the first of these units was already in the vicinity of La Higuera. The guerrillas – now numbering just seventeen – were forced to move by night and to hide by day, in order to escape detection.

According to Anderson, Che 'was breaking every rule sacred to guerrilla warfare: moving in the open without precise intelligence about what lay ahead, without the support of the peasants, and knowing that the army was aware of his approach'. On 28 September, Che recorded: 'Day of anguish, and for a moment it seemed it would be our last.' He noted that 'the possibilities of escaping are remote if they discover us'. The next two days were also 'tense', and movement became increasingly difficult for the sixteen surviving guerrillas, several of whom were now wounded. His monthly Summary recorded that the recent losses had 'left us in a perilous position', while the army was 'demonstrating more effectiveness in action'. Che's immediate aim was thus 'to escape and seek more favorable areas; then to focus on contacts'. The problem was that they were now surrounded by troops trained in counter-insurgency; but, because of fatigue, hunger, illness and wounds, they were unable to move quickly through the difficult terrain.[58]

Anderson suspects that, during those last weeks, Che 'knew his time was running out'. Just before the end, he wrote a poem for March, intended as a 'last will and testament' – this was 'Against Wind and Tide':

> This poem (against wind and tide) will carry my signature.
> I give you six sonorous syllables,….
> the unerasable memory (always latent and deep) of the children
> who, one day, you and I conceived,
> and the piece of life that remains for me…..

By the end of September, even Che realised their situation was now desperate – in fact, he only had eight more days to live.[59]

End of Che's 'fatal mission'

Che's guerrillas were now on their last legs. The Rangers' Regiment – numbering some 1,800 troops – had thrown a tight circle around them, and local peasants were increasingly informing the army about their movements. At first, they spent the days on the crests of ridges, to avoid the increasing number of army patrols; and moving into hollows at the base of these ridges at night. On the evening of 3 October, Che learned that the two Bolivian guerrillas who'd been captured by the army in La Higuera, had given 'abundant information about Fernando [Che], his illness and everything else'.[60]

On 6 October, Che noted that they 'were now in a hole'. The following day – destined to be their last as combatants – Che and his men were hiding in the ravine known as Quebrada de Yuro, near La Higuera. His final entry began: 'The 11–month anniversary of our establishment as a guerrilla force passed in a bucolic mood, with no complications, until 12:30,' That night, they set off by moonlight, aware they were leaving tracks, stopping to rest at 2.00 am 'because it was futile to continue' as many struggled to cope with night walking. His very last comment was to dismiss radio reports that the guerrillas were in another area as: 'diversionary'.[61]

On Sunday, 8 October, several companies of the Rangers deployed in the area. Che and his group had stopped to rest in the ravine for the day, planning to continue escaping once night fell. However, around noon, some soldiers ran into the guerrillas – in the fighting which followed, two soldiers were killed and several others wounded. Reinforcements arrived and, although Che tried to confuse them by splitting his group into two, the circle around them gradually tightened. One group, led by Inti, made for one end of the ravine, managing to hide until nightfall, when they were able to escape. Although half of them were killed in encounters with the army over the next few weeks, the rest survived. Pombo, Benigno and Leonardo 'Urbano' Tamayo managed to return to Cuba; while Inti, and two other Bolivians, went into hiding. Later, Inti tried to continue what Che had started – in July 1968, he released a dispatch which said 'Guerrilla warfare in Bolivia is not dead! ... We are convinced that the dream of Bolívar and Che – that of uniting Latin America ... will be achieved through armed struggle.'[62]

Che, meanwhile, had tried to escape via the closest exit from the ravine – but the army was entrenched above, and Che and his group came under withering automatic fire. As the guerrillas rapidly retreated, units pursued them. In the fighting, a bullet knocked off Che's black beret, while two others tore into his left leg, causing him to fall to the ground. As the soldiers concentrated their fire on where Che had fallen, Simeón 'Willy' Cuba – one of the Bolivian miners (previously seen by Che as a potential deserter) – rushed to him, helping him move out of the line of fire. However, they then ran into a group of soldiers and were ordered to surrender. Che's reply was to support himself against a tree and fire his rifle. The Rangers returned fire, and one bullet hit the barrel of Che's carbine, rendering it useless and wounding him in the right forearm. With no bullets for his pistol, just before 4.00 pm, Che and Willy raised their hands and surrendered. Once taken prisoner, Che's captors discovered poetry books by Cuba's Nicolás Guillén and Chile's Pablo Neruda in his backpack. Neruda, who'd once met Che, had been flattered to learn that during Cuba's Revolutionary War, Che had read out extracts from his *Canto general* to his guerrillas. On learning that Che had this book with him when captured, he wrote: 'I keep on seeing in Che Guevara the pensive man who in his heroic battles always had a place, next to his weapons, for poetry.'[63]

Murder in the afternoon

For Che's final moments, we only have the often-contradictory testimony of his captors and murderers. Che and Willy were brought before Captain Prado, who immediately ordered his radio operator to inform divisional HQ in Vallegrande that they'd captured Che Guevara. Prado was ordered to bring them to La Higuera; as there was no transport, Che was carried on a blanket by four soldiers. They reached La Higuera shortly after dark, and the two prisoners were thrown into the two-roomed school: with Che – in pain, and bound hand and foot – in one room, and Willy in the other. Later, Aniceto 'Aniceto' Reinaga was brought in, and placed with Willy. That night, the bodies of four other guerrillas were brought to La Higuera: two of them were thrown into Che's room.

During the night, and into the following morning, Che – bleeding from his wounds and experiencing difficulty breathing – was interrogated by several army officers, and by Rodríguez. Che refused to answer most questions, but 'staunchly defended his belief in revolution and socialism'. When asked if he was Cuban or Argentine, he replied 'I'm Cuban, Argentine, Peruvian, Ecuadorian, etc ... You understand?' Later, when asked what he was thinking about, he reportedly said 'the immortality of the revolution'. Meanwhile, those guarding Che began dividing among themselves the personal effects and money taken from him after his capture. Rodríguez took Che's watch, which he frequently displayed to journalists over the years.[64]

Che's fate was decided in La Paz; as Bolivia had no death penalty, the government decided against a trial. Instead, they concluded he should be killed – but in a way that would make it appear he'd died from wounds received in combat. Early on the morning of Monday, 9 October, the commanders in La Higuera received the order to kill Che. They decided an NCO should do the deed, with instructions – apparently on Rodríguez's advice – to ensure no bullet entered his head or heart. That same day, a memo was sent to the US, stating that Che had been captured by the Bolivian unit they'd 'been training for some time'.'[65]

Last words

Rodríguez – who described Che as 'a mess … hair matted, clothes ragged and torn' – claimed to have tried to get the order to kill Che countermanded, as his orders were to take him to Panama. Although the US and the CIA had long seen Che as a thorn in their sides, it seems they would have preferred he was transferred to one of their 'black' sites, for interrogation. A Memorandum sent by National Security Council official Walt Rostow to US president Johnson on 11 October, described the decision to murder Che as 'stupid' – fearing he'd be 'even more dangerous in death than in life … a martyr for his cause'. Nonetheless, the US saw 'the passing of another of the aggressive, romantic revolutionaries' as likely to have 'a strong impact in discouraging would-be guerrillas' within Latin America.[66]

Shortly before Che was murdered, Willy and Aniceto were shot in the other schoolroom – thus confirming he was about to suffer the same fate. According to Rodríguez, once he'd told him he was about to be shot, Che's last words were: 'It is better this way. I should have never been captured alive. Tell my wife to remarry and try to be happy.' Rodríguez then left the schoolroom – later writing that Che 'was conducting himself like a man. He was facing his death with courage and grace.' As none of the NCOs volunteered, lots were drawn – the one selected was Sergeant Marío Terán. Just before noon, and extremely nervous, he entered the schoolroom to carry out his orders. According to him, Che seemed to grow before his eyes: he was 'big, very big, enormous … his eyes shone intensely'. But nerves got the better of him when Che apparently said: 'Calm yourself, man, and aim well. You're only going to kill a man.' Che then quietly asked for him to wait while he tried to stand up. Completely unnerved, Téran ran out without shooting. Ordered back in at around 1.10 pm, he fired blindly, hitting Che in the chest and one side of his body, but apparently not killing him. Several other soldiers then burst in, as they too wanted to be able to say they'd shot the famous Che Guevara. So more bullets were fired into him: in all, there were nine bullet wounds – two of which were fatal.[67]

A death is announced

When Che's death was announced by Bolivian government, many didn't believe it at first. Among the many reactions, Mandel 'spoke of "a severe shock, all the more as I regarded him as a personal friend"', and mourned 'a great friend, an exemplary comrade, a heroic militant'. A year after his murder, Che's long-term friend Tita commented that she'd read the news of his death with 'trembling hands and bated breath', as she viewed his 'valiant body on a miserable canvas, his beautiful head with the beard and long hair of a guerrilla', noting 'the gaze of his large eyes that transcends death'.[68]

Che's youngest brother heard of his death from a newspaper on 10 October: 'Bolivia announces that Che has died', with a photograph showing his body. Up until that time, neither he – nor any other family member – had known he was in Bolivia. He immediately called on his father, and the family then met up at their sister Celia's house. No one wanted to believe it was true – Celia kept saying 'What do you think? It must be a trick photo.' Che's father agreed, saying 'I tell you that the photo is a fake, it's not Ernesto.' In part, this was because 'Ernesto looked too thin.' Che's father and sister were too distraught to verify the reports, so the family decided to send Roberto, who was a lawyer. When he arrived at Vallegrande, he was told Che's body had been buried in a secret location. An exhumation request was refused; then it was said the body had been cremated. Frustrated, he was forced to return to Argentina. Later, according to Che's youngest brother, Castro invited Roberto to Cuba, where he confirmed Che's death: 'A Bolivian soldier had sent Che's diary and hands to Cuba.' On 15 October, Castro publicly announced Che's death, and declared three days of national mourning. The family soon learned that Che had been killed after having been captured alive – though it would be some time before photos of him standing in front of the La Higuera school appeared.[69]

Unsurprisingly, the person most shocked was March. Before leaving for Bolivia, Che had suggested she enrol at the university to study History, which she'd done in November 1966. She was carrying out important historical research in the Escambray Mountains when Castro broke the 'terrible news' of Che's death to her. Celia Sánchez then travelled to Santa Clara and took her to the airport. When she arrived in Havana, Castro met her; she spent a week, alone, at his house, before moving to another house with the children. Castro visited every day, and March detected that 'he, too, was deeply mourning the irreparable loss that Che's passing represented'. On 18 October, a solemn vigil for Che took place in Revolution Plaza – at which Castro declared that 8 October, the date of Che's last battle, would now be known as the 'Day of the Heroic Guerrilla'.

Although Castro asked her to attend, she declined, telling him she 'didn't have the strength to behave with the composure demanded ... in such a ceremony.'[70]

Instead, she stayed with the children (who as yet weren't fully aware of what had happened to their father), watching the event on television. In November, they returned to their family home. Although mostly occupied with their children's needs, there were 'inevitable moments' when she would hear the verses of the last poem he'd written for her. She was 33 years old, and their children were aged 7, 5, 4 and 2 – they, and her studies, kept her busy. During her grief, she felt 'the absence of the man who had been my first love'. But she also felt she wasn't alone, as at times she 'heard his voice ringing in my head: "Help me now Aleida, be strong"'. Gadea, his first wife, wrote a short piece about him for a magazine, which was published in January 1968. In it, she wrote: 'You are no longer here in body, Ernesto Che Guevara, but your example is, so is your work, and the principles for which you fell ... You will always be present in our struggles.' Her words would soon prove to be more prophetic than she imagined at the time of writing. Although those responsible for Che's murder had killed a man, they'd also helped give birth to the romantic revolutionary legend that Che became.[71]

Conclusion

Guevarism – Che's Legacy

'Our every action is a battle cry against imperialism, and a call for the unity of the peoples against the great enemy of the human race: the United States of America.'[1]

This quotation – from his *Message to the Tricontinental* (16 April 1967) – captures one of Che's main political legacies: internationalism. In the first decade following his murder, Che became a heroic symbol of struggle – for a future and better world – for many rebellious and revolutionary young people around the world. Although his ideas and writings were based almost entirely on his experiences in Cuba and Latin America, they nonetheless achieved worldwide influence. Not just in dominated Third World countries, but also in the developed West.

Particularly appealing were his commitment to international solidarity; his call for the creation of a new revolutionary type of moral human; his advocacy of what in effect was 'permanent revolution' in the construction of a socialism that was 'more radical, more egalitarian, more fraternal, and more consistent with the communist ethic'; and his uncompromising rejection of dogmatism, bureaucracy, and accommodation with imperialism and capitalist exploitation: 'Socialism, for Che, represented the historical project of a new society based on values of equality, solidarity, collectivism, revolutionary altruism, free discussion, and mass participation.'[2]

Yet trying to assess Che's overall political legacy is complicated by two facts. Firstly, his books, articles and speeches – many of which have yet to be translated into English – amount to a massive collection. One of the most complete editions of his writings is a 1977 nine-volume collection – in Spanish. Secondly, Che never had time to gather his many ideas on different aspects of revolution and socialism into a coherent whole.

Revolutionary or Romantic?

Che's short history has been described, positively, as a 'subversive and romantic epic'. Many of his critics, however, have dismissed the enduring appeal of his ideas and his example – especially for young people – as simply 'a case of "adolescent revolutionary romanticism" and radical chic'. A typically negative view sees Che as 'a utopian-romantic anarchist' whose ideals for a future world were unrealistic. Christopher Hitchens argued that Che's popularity was merely an example of 'classic romantic idolatry'; and that he 'belongs more to the romantic tradition than the revolutionary one', as 'to endure as a romantic icon, one must not just die young, but die hopelessly'. While Farber sees Che as having a 'romantic and quixotic notion of honor and self-sacrifice in pursuit of righting wrongs'. Even some sections of the revolutionary left have seen Che's actions as 'romantic and suicidal madness, perhaps well intentioned but irrelevant to reality'. Che is partly responsible for this perception, revealing that he joined Castro's rebels from 'a tie of romantic adventurous sympathy, and … the conviction that it would be worth dying on a foreign beach for such a pure ideal'.[3]

Thus Che has often been compared to the great romantic revolutionaries of the nineteenth century – in particular, to Simon Bolívar who, like Che, struggled to liberate Latin America from imperialism. However, as Löwy makes clear, it would be wrong to see Che as 'a man from the past, a survival from another epoch, an anachronism in the computer age'. Instead, Che should be seen as 'the avenging prophet of future revolutions, the revolutions of the "wretched of the earth", the starved, oppressed, exploited, and humiliated peoples of the three continents dominated by imperialism'.[4]

Over-riding any romantic streak was Che's love of humanity and what he saw as his revolutionary internationalist duty to free the downtrodden of the world from hunger, poverty and exploitation. Rather than a mere romantic fad, Che's popularity has much more to do with his political and ideological legacy. This is perhaps why, nearly sixty years after his death, he still remains a 'powerful symbol of one of the most outstanding examples in modern history of resistance to injustice, inequality, exploitation, and political domination'.[5]

There is also evidence that – in private, at least – some Soviet leaders were not completely hostile to Che's 'revolutionary adventurism'. According to Feder Burlatsky: 'There was still some sympathy for him … There was a romantic aura around him; he reminded people of the Russian Revolution … Some compared him to Trotsky.' While Nikolai Metutsov – despite stating that Che was 'contaminated by Maoism … And … can be considered a Trotskyite because he went to Latin America to stimulate the revolutionary movement' – concluded that, 'deep down, what was most profound in him was his aspiration to help man on the basis of Marxism-Leninism'.[6]

Guevarism

During the 1960s, Che's political thought was seen as demonstrating a 'perfect, albeit unusual – even among revolutionaries – agreement between thought and action'. This unity – a distinct political tendency often described as 'Guevarism' – was 'a real inspiration for an international workers' movement locked within the confines of the Cold War'. Even before his murder, his example and his ideas had begun to inspire many of those wanting another, fairer, world. Since then, 'Guevarism' has continued to influence individuals and groups right up to the early twenty-first century – whether the Zapatistas in Mexico, or Hugo Chávez in Venezuela.[7]

'Guevarism' is often applied almost exclusively to his *foco* theory of guerrilla warfare and its relevance for the most of the countries in Latin and Central America. However, 'Guevarism' is a much wider concept, encompassing a comprehensive body of political thought. That political thought marks Che out as an original and undogmatic – though somewhat eclectic – interpreter of, and contributor to, a more libertarian Marxism. Though, as pointed out by Llorente, 'his main ideological affinities seem to defy any simple classification', thus making it difficult to decide where precisely Che can be situated within Marxism.[8]

Those in the West protesting about the USA's war in Vietnam saw Che as a martyr who'd been killed 'in an effort to come to the aid of the Vietnamese people' – and thus a 'shining symbol of internationalism' and a 'revolutionary who knew no frontiers'. Also attractive was his vision of socialism and communism being about much more than increased production and consumption. For many young people on the revolutionary left in the late 1960s and early 1970s, his ideas gained even greater relevance when combined with Trotsky's views on 'permanent revolution' and bureaucracy: 'The fusion of these ingredients proved to be extremely explosive.' For many, Che's death in 1967 did not extinguish the 'light' of his thought – Löwy, writing in the early 1970s, concluded that 'Nothing will ever succeed in extinguishing that light.' However, Guevarism is 'not a … polished system of thought with an answer to everything'. His murder in Bolivia in 1967 interrupted 'a process of independent political maturation and intellectual development'. Consequently, 'On many questions … his thinking remains incomplete.'[9]

The varied nature of Guevarism has led to confusion of where, exactly, to place Che within Marxism: was he was a Stalinist, a Maoist or a Trotskyist? Some have pointed to Che's early admiration of Stalin as showing he was neither a libertarian Marxist nor a Trotskyist. Certainly, in the early 1950s, Che first came to a socialist position via some of Stalin's writings. And, during a speech in December 1964, he himself stated that he'd got involved in communism through Stalin. His biggest critics, such as Farber, see Che as growing up 'with the political legacy of a Stalinized Marxism', thus making his revolutionary political thought and practice 'irremediably undemocratic, based on a conception of socialism from above rather than below'.[10]

Even those sympathetic to Che accept that he had 'an extremely inadequate grasp of Stalinism as a political phenomenon', and that his writings 'contain virtually no real analysis of Stalinism'. However, on the few occasions Che did refer to Stalinism, he tended to identify it with 'repression in defense of the revolution', because 'Every revolution, like it or not, inevitably has its share of Stalinism, simply because every revolution faces capitalist encirclement.' A partial explanation of this inadequate grasp of Stalinism can be explained by the fact that his many activities and responsibilities left him little time 'for intellectual pursuits', while the real threats from US aggression faced by the revolution in Cuba 'no doubt reinforced his acceptance of his own understanding of Stalinism'.[11]

As regards Trotskyism, while always denying he was a Trotskyist, Che displayed an undogmatic willingness to consider Trotsky's writings – at a time when Trotskyism was considered a dreadful heresy by most 'orthodox' communists, especially those within the Soviet bloc. The first sign of this came as early as 1960, when he told a Peruvian revolutionary that he hadn't read any Trotskyist literature and so asked him for a book by Trotsky. He was given *The Permanent Revolution*, which he read and discussed – proof of Che's 'rejection of dogmatism'. Che also wanted Trotsky's works to be part of Cuba's Marxism education programme – and, in 1961, condemned the destruction of the plates of Trotsky's *The Permanent Revolution*, which Cuba's Trotskyists had wanted published; and it was Che who, in 1964, invited one of the leaders of the Trotskyist Fourth International to Cuba, to help him in the debates taking place about economic policies. As Llorente comments: 'This freedom from dogmatism is, in any case, surely one source of Guevara's appeal to many Marxists.'[12]

Che's desire to 'internationalise the revolution', and his arguments against the Soviet 'stages' view of History – instead arguing for combined and simultaneous struggle for national liberation and socialism – is also close to Trotsky's view of permanent revolution. This has led some to argue that 'Che had more in common with Latin American Trotskyism than with the established Communist parties'. Che was unique as a ruling communist leader in being so sympathetic to Trotskyism. And we now know that Che had Trotsky's *History of the Russian Revolution* with him when he went to fight his last mission in Bolivia – along with his notes on it: 'Trotsky, writes Guevara, "sheds light on a whole series of events of the great revolution that had remained hidden by myth. At the same time, he makes isolated statements whose validity still remains absolute today."[13]

As a minister – despite the great Sino-Soviet split – Che was similarly tolerant towards Maoism and those wanting to read material from Communist China. He had been interested in Mao and the Chinese Revolution before he went to Cuba – and had even proudly seen his first daughter, Hildita, as a little Mao. Che's views about guerrilla warfare were also an important departure from classical Bolshevism and Marxism – and closer to Maoism. However, as Llorente says, it's wrong to see Che as 'a Trotskyist or Maoist (or Stalinist). Guevara borrowed from many different currents within the Marxist tradition … His fundamentally antidogmatic, nonsectarian orientation enabled him to use ideas from different currents within Marxism … to forge a distinctive political project.' Regardless of Che's overall political stance, there are three main aspects of Guevarism that many revolutionaries have found attractive: the *foco* theory of guerrilla warfare, the transition to socialism, and revolutionary internationalism.[14]

Guerrilla warfare

Despite what some of Che's critics have written, he didn't see guerrilla warfare as an exciting adventure, or as an end in itself. For him, it was 'merely a means to an end: the conquest of political power'. Nonetheless, given the failure of his Congolese and Bolivian missions, many argue that his *foco* theory was nothing more than a romantic, unrealistic dream. Even those like Ali, who rejects what he sees as Che's 'total' reliance on guerrilla warfare as the way forward, doesn't see his choice of Bolivia as wrong – pointing out that: 'Only a few years later Che, isolated in his last tragic months, had become an icon for the Bolivian peasants.' Thus his defeat in Bolivia doesn't necessarily prove that the *foco* theory was mistaken. Based on Cuban experience, the idea was that initially, *focos* should be 'located in regions of highly dispersed and relatively sparse population'. Once the initial group numbered 120–150, other 'germ-carrying cells' would split from 'the mother cell' and establish themselves in new areas. However, as seen in Chapter 10, Che's Bolivian group never got the chance to grow that big.[15]

Che's failure to liberate Latin America from the grip of the 'Yankee Octopus' has been unfavourably compared with Bolívar's success. Bolívar, however, was fighting against a decrepit empire, while Che was fighting against an empire which was the most powerful in the world, and one with a record of military interventions second to none. More generally, others have claimed his murder in 1967 'marked the beginning of the end for revolutionary movements around the world. This is disputed by others, who have pointed out that 'Since the 1960s, a spectre haunts the sleep of the powerful and inspires the dreams and struggles of the oppressed in Latin America: "Guevarism".' Additionally, as argued by

Debray: 'For a revolutionary, failure is a springboard. As a source of theory it is richer than victory: it accumulates experience and knowledge.'[16]

Even those who are generally sympathetic towards Che, sometimes misread his views on guerrilla warfare. For instance, Harris has mistakenly argued that Che advocated a 'kind of military vanguardism' that reduced the 'popular revolution to a special form of guerrilla warfare'. Elsewhere, he comments that 'Che's failed mission in Bolivia proved, among other things, that a well-trained and committed revolutionary guerrilla force is not sufficient to detonate a successful revolution.' However, Che himself never argued that a guerrilla band, on its own, *was* sufficient to bring about a successful revolution. Nor did he believe guerrilla warfare could replace mass working-class action, arguing instead that: 'It is essential to stress again that the people's guerrilla war is a mass struggle. We cannot accept the contraposition that is sometimes made between mass struggle and guerrilla warfare.' What he did argue was that, in the right conditions, it *could* be a catalyst.[17]

Yet even Löwy says Che had a 'rigid and uncompromising adherence to the method of armed struggle'. However, as Llorente points out, there are plenty of other occasions on which Che had modified that view from the beginning. Though in his farewell letter to his parents, he stated 'I believe in armed struggle as the only solution for those peoples who fight to free themselves, and I am consistent with my beliefs', elsewhere he concedes it's not always necessary. In his essay *Guerrilla Warfare: A Method*, he said: 'a peaceful struggle can be carried out through mass movements that compel – in special situations of crisis – governments to yield.' Even in his uncompromising *Message to the Tricontinental*, although he says 'the real liberation of the peoples ... will be the result of armed struggle', he qualifies it by adding 'in the majority of cases'.[18]

Neither was it unreasonable to conclude, in the 1960s, that armed struggle – specifically guerrilla warfare in countryside – was likely to be necessary in the majority of cases. Che argued that it was US imperialism which kept the Latin American dictators in power, thus making 'nonviolent national liberation virtually impossible'. Che was also clear that 'when "faced with the dilemma of choosing between the people or imperialism"', Latin America's ruling classes would always side with US interests.[19]

Although Che had said that 'It is not necessary to wait until all the conditions for making revolution exist; the insurrection [*foco*] can create them,' he also made it clear – even in his first book, *Guerrilla Warfare* – that certain conditions were necessary. Yet even some of his supporters have either misunderstood or distorted this – including Régis Debray in his *Revolution in the Revolution?* According to Pombo, Che's bodyguard, Che was critical of the way Debray had explained the *foco* theory. What Che argued was that a *foco* could *hasten* 'the crystallization of both the "subjective" and "objective" conditions required for successfully taking power'.[20]

Che also saw guerrilla warfare as necessary because US imperialism would attempt to topple any radical government, even if it won in free elections. As well as what Che had witnessed in Guatemala in 1954, this is precisely what happened later in Chile in 1973. Thus Che argued that the only way to overcome that was by defeating the oppressor army – and that could only be done by 'a people's army, which cannot be created overnight'. The establishment of a guerrilla *foco* would provide the initial experience for that people's army. Che also believed that an armed insurrection in the countryside could succeed, as in Cuba, because in most Latin American countries peasants lacked land. He maintained those beliefs to the very end – his final communiqué, which he wasn't able to send, 'contains a highly compressed restatement of his vision of a guerrilla force as the agent and catalyst of national liberation.'[21]

In fact, so many guerrilla groups emerged in Latin and Central America following his death that the 1970s became known as 'The Years of Combat'. Claiming to follow 'in Che's footsteps', these groups took up armed struggle against the direct and indirect dominance over the continent exerted by US imperialism. However, these groups were mainly urban-based, not rural, which had been central to Che's ideas of guerrilla warfare. Though these were defeated, from the late 1970s – as poverty and inequality increased because of the neoliberal globalisation pushed by the US – various new revolutionary movements began to appear in the region. This was especially true in Central America, where such groups – inspired by Che – recognised the need to combine guerrilla warfare with urban actions and mass political mobilisations. Such movements had some success in countries such as El Salvador and Guatemala; and especially so in Nicaragua, where the Sandinistas overthrew the US-backed dictatorship of Samoza in 1979.[22]

Transition to socialism

During the Great Debate, Che had set out many of his ideas about the transition to socialism. However, the openness of comradely debate he'd enjoyed in Cuba during the Great Debate wasn't really possible internationally – mainly as a result of the Cold War and the Sino-Soviet split, but also because of the revival of Trotskyism in the West. Consequently, his criticisms of Soviet economic and foreign policies – which he saw as arising from their neglect of Marx – had led to accusations of Maoism and even Trotskyism. In fact, Che accepted that 'In many respects I have expressed opinions that could be closer to the Chinese side.' Nonetheless, several have argued that Che's most important legacy lies in his ideas on the transition to socialism: not just his economic ideas, but also those relating to political and philosophical matters. Perhaps the two most important elements were his attempts to create a new human consciousness, and his revolutionary humanism.[23]

Che saw transforming human consciousness, from the very beginning of the transition to socialism, as crucial. As Tablada points out, Che 'thought the creation of the new social consciousness required as much effort as that devoted to developing socialism's material base'. On 21 December 1963, at one of his regular departmental meetings, Che said: 'communism is a phenomenon of consciousness and not solely a phenomenon of production ... what Marx defined as communism ... cannot be attained if man ... does not have a new consciousness toward society'. In this respect, Che was echoing what Marx and Engels had written in *The German Ideology*: 'Both for the production on a mass scale of this communist consciousness, and for the success of the cause itself, the alteration of men on a mass scale is necessary ... [to remove] all the muck of ages.'[24]

Despite his critics, Che's arguments for the creation of a new human consciousness was not '"revolutionary romanticism", [or] a dream of a utopian paradise ... It is a Marxist-Leninist understanding of how social being determines social consciousness, and how both elements can only be transformed jointly, through social practice.' It was Che's view that, while there were objective limitations on what was possible at any one time, it was also 'man's *own actions* that transform his conditions and *create a new objective situation* that opens up *new options and possibilities*'.[25]

More generally, his writings and speeches also reveal certain basic moral considerations that were fundamental to his aim of creating new human beings with a moral outlook and a set of moral values and commitments. As we have seen, he saw moral values as crucial to the transition from capitalism to socialism, and from socialism to communism. As early as May 1959, in a speech given to students at Havana University, he emphasised the importance of a moral outlook, asking them 'to consider whether "if it is not better to have a bit less money, but to know that a great mass of peasants is benefiting [from this]".' While, in 1963, he said to a senior Polish administrator in his Ministry of Industries, who was disillusioned by the Polish government's greater interest in 'doing business' rather than providing mutual solidarity and aid: 'They're screwed. A country in which moral principles do not prevail ... cannot be called a socialist country.'[26]

In these respects, Che was ahead of most of the Marxists of his time, and his thinking stands as 'an important departure from the mainstream of the Marxist tradition'. His foregrounding of moral concerns was an example of what Llorente has described as a 'kind of *moral vanguardism*', with Che seeing the political vanguard as, 'in the last analysis, a moral vanguard' whose example would help others change their consciousness. Che thus anticipated 'to a certain extent the "ethical turn" in later twentieth-century Marxist theory'. Che's personal austerity was part of the mix – in his 'Farewell' to Castro, he proudly noted that he'd left no material possessions to his wife and children. As Sinclair noted, 'How many other Latin American politicians could say the same on leaving politics?'[27]

Regarding Che's revolutionary humanism, Besancenot and Löwy argue that Che developed this as a result of his travels and his own thinking, *before* moving towards Marxism. This then led him to adopt a Marxist humanism 'in which humanity and the individual were everything, the root and the goal of the egalitarian project'. For this, Che studied Marx's early writings, which saw revolution as coming from 'the intervention of humanity in its own destiny, a conscious intervention, both individual and collective'. This approach led Che to develop a revolutionary humanism that was at odds with both social democracy and 'orthodox' communism – although, on this, Besancenot and Löwy state: 'Che's thought has limits. It is, in part, incomplete and tentative.'[28]

Nonetheless, Che – determined to end all forms of human alienation – became an important contributor to Marxist humanism. It's clear he was familiar with several of Marx's early work which 'identifies communism with humanism'. Whether or not he'd read this particular work, Che built his life on Marx's idea that '*for man the supreme being is man*, and thus ... the *categorical imperative* [is] *to overthrow all conditions* in which man is a debased, enslaved, neglected and contemptible being'. Set against the 'orthodox' communism of the 1960s, Che's writings on this can be seen as constituting a 'recovery of the humanist tradition of Marxism'. Unfortunately, there is no *one* work in which his humanism is fully developed and systematically expressed. Nonetheless, as Löwy concludes, Che's commitment to 'socialist humanism is surely part of what makes him one of the revolutionary figures from the Third World who has best stood the test of time'.[29]

However, it can be argued that Che's greatest legacy as regards the transition to socialism lies not in his pre-1965 writings and speeches, but in his *Critical Notes on Political Economy*. These were completed between his guerrilla missions to the Congo and Bolivia, and strongly criticised the Soviet Union's economic 'bible', the *Manual of Political Economy*. Although Che left government – and Cuba – shortly after the end of the Great Debate, he didn't stop researching and theorising about the best ways to bring about the transition to socialism. Although he'd made limited criticisms of this *Manual* before, these extensive notes show how his earlier views had deepened. They were taken to Cuba by March, after her secret visit to him in Prague – and were then handed over to his deputy, Borrego. But they weren't published until 2006, well after the collapse of the Soviet Union and the 'socialist' countries of Eastern Europe.

Che made several points in the 'Introduction' – which mainly emphasised the importance of Marx's *Capital*, and many of Lenin's writings. In Che's opinion, the Soviet Union had increasingly ignored these. For him, 'the intransigent dogmatism of Stalin's epoch had been succeeded by inconsistent pragmatism' which was leading Marxist economics to 'dangerous defeats'. Aware that many would criticise him for airing his views, he reminded them Marx had pointed out the failure of 'bourgeois science to criticise itself', which resulted in it 'falling back on apologetics instead' – an attitude which could 'be applied today, disgracefully, in the science of Marxist economics'.[30]

In particular, Che continued his strong criticisms of Soviet methods: 'We think ... Marxist research in the field of economics is walking along dangerous paths ... in all aspects of the life of the socialist countries.' He criticised Stalin for having 'underestimated communist education and instituted an unrestricted culture of authority' – and for having embedded 'capitalist levers'. Yet he saw Stalin's successors as having compounded his errors. As a result, because of the Soviet Union's use of 'capitalist elements', he thought it 'debatable' for the Manual to claim there was 'no danger of capitalism returning to the USSR'.[31]

Che saw these notes as preparatory work for what would be an economic manual to aid Cuba's transition to socialism. He also hoped his constructive criticisms would enable the Soviet bloc countries to avoid the dangers he saw in their moves towards 'market socialism'. He'd sketched out a comprehensive plan for this work – one of his closest colleagues later commented how Che 'based himself on Marxist theory' and was 'capable of getting to the root of the issue because he was so studious.' He'd completed the first part – a biography of Marx and Engels – but the remainder of the project remained just notes, along with suggestions for his own further study. According to Yaffe, there was a 'remarkable consistency' between these *Critical Notes* and his arguments during the Great Debate. Although Ali sees the work as 'essentially voluntarist' – which he believes applies to most of Che's other writings – he argues that in the twenty-first century, these ideas are still important enough for Cuba's future to warrant further consideration, noting that 'it includes prescient warnings of why the Soviet Union might collapse into capitalism'.[32]

Che's *Critical Notes* also develop his ideas about socialist democracy – a crucial element in the transition to socialism. Löwy, for instance, argues that Che 'came close to the idea of socialist democracy, a democratic planning process in which the people themselves, the workers, "the masses", to use his terminology, will make the major economic decisions'. In those *Critical Notes*, Che wrote that instead of the plan being 'an economic decision by the masses', the Soviet model was 'a mechanistic, non-Marxist technique'. Instead, Che argued that: 'The masses must be able to direct their fate, to decide which share of production will be assigned respectively to accumulation and consumption.' Sadly, Che's ongoing '"heroic creation" of a new revolutionary socialism and a new democratic communism' was brutally cut short by his murder in Bolivia in 1967.[33]

Besancenot and Löwy thus later qualify their earlier criticisms of Che's legacy on socialist democracy by pointing out that his *Critical Notes* show that towards the end of his life, he was giving more thought to 'the principle of a socialist democracy in which the people themselves make the important economic decisions'. In particular, he wrote that the masses 'should have the possibility to direct their own destinies, to decide how much is going to accumulation and how much to consumption'. They also point out that Che returns to this issue several times, for instance commenting that the people 'will settle the important problems of the country (rates of growth, accumulation/consumption)'. Thus, these *Critical Notes* are 'undeniably an important stage in Guevara's path towards a communist and democratic alternative to the Stalinist model of the Soviet Union'. In them, Che 'is getting considerably closer to the ideal of democratic socialist planning, such as Ernest Mandel formulated it'. As they point out, although Che doesn't 'draw all the political conclusions – democratization of power, political pluralism, freedom of organization ... the importance of this new vision of economic democracy cannot be denied'. Had he not been killed at the age of 39, it seems fair to assume that this theme would have been expanded upon.[34]

Internationalism

Che's 'battle cry' – for worldwide military resistance to 'Yankee imperialism' – was made public in his *Message to the Tricontinental*, just six months before he was captured and murdered by a counter-insurgency force trained by the CIA. That 'battle cry' succinctly encapsulates and reflects his commitment to internationalism and the fight against imperialism – and it proved to be a call which reached many 'receptive ears'. It was certainly been taken up in Latin America, the continent he was most keen to see liberated. Although his optimism that the success of the Cuban Revolution could be repeated in other Latin American states ultimately proved unfounded, there were many prepared to heed his call. Various urban and rural guerrilla groups struggled, unsuccessfully, in countries such as Peru, Colombia, Uruguay, Argentina and Bolivia itself. In the mid- and late-1970s, even Mandel seemed to support the idea of a 'strategy of armed struggle' in Latin America as the only way forward, given the lack of democracy and US domination in the region.

However, Che's call for international solidarity spread well beyond Latin America after 1967, with his ideas proving particularly popular with many young revolutionaries in Western Europe. In France, the Revolutionary Communist Youth, formed in France in 1965, had 'one of its main political and moral reference points in the thought and action of Che'. One of its founders saw Che as 'the revolutionary without frontiers' who was 'sensitive to the fate of all the exploited'.[35]

It has been argued that Che's legacy of internationalism can also be seen in Cuba's active involvement in both Latin America and the rest of the world. In 1975, less than ten years after Che's death, Cuba gave military aid to newly independent Angola – as well as weapons, this aid included volunteer soldiers, despite Soviet opposition. Even when the US offered to end its embargo on Cuba if Castro would stop aiding the Angolans, he refused. For more than a decade, 50,000 Cubans helped beat off incursions from apartheid South Africa. These defeats of South African forces also helped Namibia gain its independence, and ultimately contributed to the collapse of apartheid itself. This was recognised by Nelson Mandela, whose first visit abroad following his release in 1991 was to Cuba, 'to pay homage to Cuban internationalism'. This was precisely the principle that Che had fought for over so many years, and for which he gave his life.[36]

As a doctor, Che would also have been proud that Cuba has provided much international medical aid – even after the collapse of the Soviet Union in 1991 ended Soviet assistance. The Latin American School of Medicine, set up in 1999, caters for students from over eighty countries. In addition, thousands of Cuban doctors have been sent to Latin American and African countries – the two continents where Che had tried to aid or ignite revolution. Cuba has also responded with medical aid when countries are devastated by natural disasters. When Pakistan suffered a major earthquake at end of 2005, Cuba sent field hospitals, medicines, and over 1,000 doctors – more than the rest of the world put together.

Ultimately, Che – who didn't believe in borders – was the living embodiment of revolutionary solidarity. Though some dismissed his internationalism as a romantic delusion, he never hesitated in dedicating his life to a better future for the many, and to struggle against every form of exploitation, humiliation and oppression, wherever it existed – something he saw, like Marx, as being the ethical duty of all humans to do. Another who had worked with Che in MININD said:

> his vocation was to combat what he had seen in Latin America, the situation of the miners and the indigenous populations, and of the African people,

> not to stay here [Cuba] in comfort. Che was an internationalist. He was not a revolutionary because he wanted to be a minister, but to fight for the poor.[37]

Be like Che!

Che's legacy within Cuba is – like other aspects of 'Guevarism' – disputed. Some, like Farber – who sees Che as 'a failed quixotic figure' – have argued that his politics have their greatest appeal outside of Cuba; this is challenged by others, such as Yaffe. Nonetheless, since his murder, Che has been held up as an example to which the citizens of Cuba should aspire. It was Castro who first exhorted future generations to 'Be like Che!' This has become 'one of the most emblematic slogans of the Cuban Revolution', and is based on the fact that he 'set a personal example in everything'. While few are able to match his gruelling work ethic, or his rejection of an easy life, as Llorente says: 'there are plainly some ways in which we can and should strive to "be like Che"'. In present-day Cuba, Che remains a political model of revolutionary idealism and sacrifice, and the call to 'Be like Che!' remains a popular one.[38]

As regards the legacy of Che's economic ideas, there has been what Yaffe has described as 'the *Guevarista* pendulum', following his departure from Cuba in 1965. Although many of his colleagues continued his novel approach, his ideas never met with consensus, and their influence has ebbed and flowed. Despite this having 'limited his legacy', many of his policies have nonetheless become 'embedded in Cuban society'.[39]

In 1987, Castro noted that 'Che would have been horrified' at some of the problems which emerged after Cuba had become more dependent on Soviet aid, and the consequent increased influence of Soviet advisors. By the early 1980s, those problems had strengthened the *Guevarista* tendency within Cuba. As a result, from 1986, Cuba began moving away from the Soviet model and back to Che's ideas. These changes included once again measuring production 'in terms of output, not values [profit]; bureaucracy was slashed, private markets were closed, and non-material incentives were revived' – as was voluntary labour. In 1987, on the twentieth anniversary of Che's death, Castro declared: 'We are rectifying all kinds of shoddiness and mediocrities that were precisely a negation of the ideas of Che, of the revolutionary thought of Che.'[40]

Although the collapse of the Soviet Union in 1991 – and an even harsher US blockade – led to another swing away from Che's economic ideas, this was openly 'conceded as a move away from the Guevarista model'. From 2000, however, there was a swing back to Che's economic ideas – accompanied by a political campaign known as the 'Battle of Ideas'. As Yaffe notes this 'invoked a return to Guevara's concept that education and culture are essential to create commitment to political ideas'. In 2004, an advisor to the Cuban Minister of the Economy commented:

> the way in which [Che] thought about problems is still relevant today and the way he identified the underlying problem was more profound then than any other person in our context ... I am trying to go back to Che's ideas, because I am now able to appreciate what he was trying to do.'

In 2005, the financial autonomy of enterprises was removed, while the central bank became responsible for allocating and approving all financial transactions, leading to 'a degree of financial centralisation not seen' since Che.[41]

Yaffe sees Che's main legacy in Cuba to be his political desire to create a new society, with new social-relations and new values. As she says, Che 'accepted that short-term growth could be secondary to the goal of creating a democratic, socialist society'. Thus merely focusing on production figures fails 'to capture the essence of [Che's] contribution to the economics of revolution'. In particular, Che's legacy was to address the problem of how to 'increase consciousness and productivity simultaneously' – this explains 'the continued recourse to Guevarista analysis whenever and wherever history throws up similar challenges'.[42]

Latin America's 'Pink Tide'

In his eulogy for Che, delivered on 18 October 1967, Castro stated: 'They are mistaken when they think that his death is the end of his ideas.' As it turned out, Che's cold-blooded murder was by no means the end of 'Guevarism'. On the contrary, Che became 'a universal model of revolutionary courage and commitment'. Arguably, Che's 'most explosive idea was that the revolution is permanent', giving his revolutionary legacy 'an enduring global significance'. However, as Sinclair argues, the impact of his ideas have proved longer-lasting in Latin America: 'For there has been no man with so great an ideal of unity for that divided and unlucky continent since Bolívar.' One of those inspired by Che's legend to struggle for a better life for others was Salvador Allende. He had a meeting with Che in early 1959, describing it to Régis Debray in 1971: 'Che ... was lying in the hammock, stripped to the waist and ... having a violent attack of asthma.' Allende was 'impressed by his immense intelligence ... and by his candour'.[43]

Che's influence has perhaps been greatest in mass social movements, as opposed to groups following the route of armed struggle. According to one assessment:

> Che does not symbolize a method of rural guerrilla warfare, but a certain spirit, both ethical and political, formed from revolt against the domination of imperialism, rage against capitalist social injustice, intransigent struggle against the established order, and the intense desire for a socialist and revolutionary transformation of society.

By the end of the twentieth century, several radical social movements were challenging the economic and political domination of the US empire and neoliberal capitalism – known as the 'Washington Consensus'. In 1998, a dramatic shift leftwards in Latin American politics began with the election of Hugo Chávez as president of Venezuela. Chávez frequently referred to Che's legacy in his speeches, often wore a Che shirt when addressing his audiences, and posters were displayed showing Chávez flanked by Che and Simon Bolívar. In 2006, Chávez called for the anti-imperialism and anti-capitalism advocated by Che, stating: 'I have discovered Che the critical thinker, Che the transformer of the economic system, Che of the stage of industrialisation of Cuba, Che and his reflections in Africa, Che and his criticisms of the soviet model and the Soviet manual'. In addition, Chávez ordered the mass distribution of Che's 'Man and Socialism in Cuba', and called for a 'Bolivarian Revolution' against the 'Washington Consensus', seeing it as following Che's revolutionary legacy by creating 'a democratic, humanist socialism'. All this was very close to Che's long-held ideals of 'Pan-American unity, anti-imperialism, and humanist socialism', and has been described as 'the first radical, socialist-oriented revolution in Latin America' since the 1980s.[44]

In 2004, Che's daughter, Aleida, travelled to Venezuela to interview Chávez – the result was a book and a documentary, called *Chávez: Venezuela and the New Latin America*. Oliver Stone also made a documentary about this: *South of the Border: Hugo Chavez and the New Latin America*. Aleida was part of the international 'Hands off Venezuela' campaign opposing US interference in Venezuela; while his son, Camilo, said: '[Che] is a devil for the U.S. government and American multinationals ... many North-Americans admire and respect El Che ... they fight injustice in American society under his banner.' Che's image was later adopted by activists in the Mexican community within the US, in their campaigns for equal educational and civil rights, and for a change in US immigration policy.[45]

Chávez's election victory heralded a radical democratic socialist electoral 'Pink Tide' that then swept through the region – described by W.I. Robinson as potentially a 'new model of revolutionary struggle and popular transformation from below for the 21st century ... based on mass popular struggles'. In 2005, Evo Morales – leader of the Movement toward Socialism (MAS) – was elected president of Bolivia. After his victory, photos of Che were placed in the parliament building and in the presidential offices; while, in his inauguration speech, he paid tribute to 'Che Guevara, who fought for a new world in equality'. His party included two who had fought with Che in his Bolivian campaign: Osvaldo 'Chato' Peredo and Loyola Guzmán – the latter was part of Morale's first government. Morales – a strong admirer of Che's politics – stated that: 'I admire Che because he fought for equality, for justice [and] he did not just care for ordinary people; he made their struggle his own.' In January 2006, Morales gave a speech, stating: 'The struggle that Che Guevara left uncompleted, we shall complete.' On 14 June 2006 – Che's 78th. birthday – Morales became the first Bolivian president to visit the village of La Higuera, where Che had been killed. That year, Rafael Correa won the presidential elections in Ecuador. Correa also referred to Che's influence – both Chavez and Morales were special guests at his inauguration, during which he said: 'A sovereign, dignified, just and socialist Latin America is beginning to rise.' As Harris notes: 'Exactly the kind of language Che used.'[46]

By then, Cuba and Venezuela had formed the Bolivarian Alternative for the Americas (ALBA). This was a project designed to achieve 'just and sustainable development' for Latin American and Caribbean countries – in opposition to the 'free trade' social and economic policies of global neoliberalism. By 2009, Bolivia, Ecuador, Nicaragua, Dominica and Honduras, with several other collaborating countries, had also joined ALBA, forming a 'radical anti-neoliberal regional bloc'. Many of the key players in the ALBA project 'have laid claim to Guevara's legacy in this process', with Yaffe arguing that 'As long as revolutionary states set out to build new societies with economic and social justice, Guevara's theory and practice will remain relevant and influential. In the economics of revolution, his legacy will grow in significance – particularly in Latin America.'[47]

Although that 'Pink Tide' later subsided, a second one spread in the late 2010s and early 2020s – affecting countries such as Mexico, Argentina, Bolivia, Peru, Honduras, Colombia, Brazil and Chile. Thus seeming to support Harris's view that 'Che's revolutionary life and death continue to inspire those who struggle against ... injustices, particularly in Latin America.'[48]

¡Ya Basta!

The earliest signs of Latin America's 'Pink Tide' appeared in Chiapas, southern Mexico, with the emergence of the Zapatista revolutionary movement. On 1 January 1994, the Zapatista Army of National Liberation (EZLN) publicly declared war on neoliberalism and the Mexican government, with its main leaders citing 'Guevara's political ideas and practice' as their inspiration to take up arms. Their cry of '¡Ya basta!' – 'Enough is enough!' – captures Che's stance on the exploitation and repression of peoples by international capitalism and global imperialism. 'Subcomandante Marcos', the leader of the movement, has made it clear how much Che's legacy has influenced him. As recently as 2006, 'Marcos' – now known as 'Galeano' – said: 'Che reminds us of what we have known since Spartacus … in the struggle against injustices, humanity finds a course that teaches it, makes it better, and more human.' He went on to deny that 'the end of history had occurred in the El Yuro ravine' in 1967. Instead of the 'time of rebellions' being over, he asserted that Che's dream of 'a better world' was still very much alive.[49]

According to Besancenot and Löwy, 'Guevarism is the essential ingredient' of the Zapatista uprising, which has become 'an example for the victims of neoliberalism, not only in Mexico, but throughout Latin America and the entire world'. Che's internationalism and his repeated calls for solidarity influenced the movements for global justice and for global resistance to capitalist neoliberalism that developed in the 1990s. Besancenot and Löwy have described this as the 'alterglobalist movement', consisting of: 'three distinct and complementary moments: the negativity of resistance, concrete proposals, and the utopia of another world'. For instance, in 2001, the World Social Forum adopted a Charter opposing the 'globalization led by the large multinational corporations', and calling instead for 'a globalization based on the values of solidarity that … will respect universal human rights … the environment … social justice, equality, and national sovereignty'.[50]

Although Che fought for many of those aims, his relevance in the twenty-first century is limited to some extent by the fact that he died before issues such as racism, patriarchy and feminism really came to the fore. Consequently, these issues do not figure importantly in his works. As Llorente observes: 'this is one reason that Guevara's writings may appear somewhat inadequate to those who take an interest in contemporary socialist theory'. However, as a mature revolutionary, he was 'staunchly antiracist' in a way 'that was missing among much of the Latin American left'. He was also full of praise for Franz Fanon's analysis of racism and colonialism, and it was he who pushed for *The Wretched of the Earth* to be published in Cuba. Regarding the position of women, Che argued for complete gender equality and had commented that, in Cuba, 'women still have to learn that they are just as good as a man in everything'.[51]

Additionally, given the multiple crises of the twenty-first century, there is arguably more need for Che's 'uncompromising internationalism' – and humanism – than ever before. Since the mid-1970s, the impacts of neoliberal 'globalisation' on many people, via 'forms of oppression, exploitation and marginalization', have been described as 'just as severe as they were in the 1960s'. Plus Che's belief that the biggest imperialist enemy was the US is seen by many as still valid today, given its various wars in Yugoslavia, Afghanistan and Iraq. While the worsening Climate and Ecological Crises – which the major economies seem unwilling to address in any serious way – cry out for international solutions. This has led to the rise of a global climate justice movement in the Global South, which is most impacted by these crises; and to the emergence of an international ecosocialist current.[52]

In the 1920s and 1930s, the multiple crises of poverty, fascism and war, were seen by many as the 'monsters' of the old world that was disintegrating, but from which a new and better world was struggling to emerge. Antonio Gramsci described it thus: 'The crisis consists precisely in the fact that the old is dying and the new cannot be born; in this interregnum a great variety of morbid symptoms appear.' Today, there are still 'monsters' – those Gramsci wrote about, and the new crises of climate change and pandemics. To many, it seems as though this 'old world is dying' too: 'We ... are revolutionary socialists. We believe that the old order is doomed and we must build a new one based on democracy, internationalism, ecosocialism, solidarity with the poor and the oppressed, and the total transformation of society to serve human need not private greed.' Che was certainly impatient to free humanity from the 'morbid symptoms' faced in the 1960s, and to create another, better, world. The need for such a world was underlined by the historian Eric Hobsbawm: 'If humanity is to have a recognizable future, it cannot be by prolonging the past or the present. If we try to build the third millennium on that basis, we shall fail. And the price of failure, that is to say, the alternative to a changed society, is darkness.'[53]

Many have seen Che as either typifying a generous 1960s' morality, or as someone too far ahead of his time. Either way, he has been dismissed as having no relevance today. Certainly, the world has changed a lot since his death. Nonetheless, writers such as Llorente argue that despite these big changes, 'it is not difficult to find many striking similarities between Guevara's time and our own'. The ideals he fought for – egalitarianism, and internationalist solidarity – are still on the agenda of many social and political movements today. As Ali said: 'the historical graph never rises consistently. It is a broken and contradictory line that can fall to zero and then rise again suddenly and without warning.'[54]

For Che, revolutionary internationalism was both a 'strategic imperative' and a 'moral requirement' – to be practiced 'through real and effective solidarity with people who are fighting against imperialism'. Che – and those in the 1960s who opposed imperialism – saw the USA's war against Vietnam was as important as the Spanish Civil War had been for those in the 1930s who opposed fascism. Che's *Message to the Tricontinental* was 'the first time, in a very long time, that a Communist leader of worldwide stature tried to outline an international revolutionary strategy that was not a function of a state's interests'. According to Besancenot and Löwy, Che was attempting to take communism back to the principles of the early Communist Third International, before Stalinism made it just part of USSR foreign policy.[55]

Che's actions and writings from the age of 26 increasingly showed a revolutionary determination to help humanity in Latin America – and elsewhere – 'to conquer conscious control over its social existence'. When Che was murdered in 1967, nuclear war was a serious threat. Today, given the mounting Climate and Ecological Crises, conquering that 'conscious control' has arguably 'become a matter of life and death' for all the inhabitants of the planet. Given his optimism, it is fair to assume that, if Che were alive today, he would still have confidence that humanity will ultimately 'succeed in realizing the noblest of all aspirations: the construction of a humane, classless, non-violent world socialism'. As such an 'unorthodox' communist and original thinker, it's likely – had he lived long enough – he would have been one of the first socialists to see how the Climate and Ecological Crises were impacting unfairly on the poor of both the Global South and the Global North. As Chávez – a strong admirer of Che – told the World Social Forum in 2006: 'There is nothing beyond the 21st century if we do not change. The choice is socialism or death, but death of the human species. Capitalism is destroying life on this planet.' Thus it's tempting to imagine Che giving a modern internationalist twist to his battle cry *'Death or Homeland'*, by adapting it to: *'Ecosocialism or Extinction!'*[56]

However, Che also exhibited the vital revolutionary attribute of daring to dream of another, and better, world – which is perhaps why despite his murder in 1967, he became 'the spark that does not die'. To dream and to hope are important for achieving a revolution – and are far from being utopian or unrealistic. In fact they are an accepted part of classical Marxism – a Marxism that Che increasingly came to see as having been abandoned by 'orthodox' communists and the 'actually existing socialism' they were implementing in Soviet bloc countries. Marx's intellectual activity was ultimately based on the desire for, and the necessity of, emancipation – and throughout his life, Marx believed revolutionaries had 'an elementary duty to fight' alongside all those suffering from exploitation, oppression and 'inhuman social conditions'. Che, too, believed this, and his dream of global emancipation – very much 'in the spirit of Marx' – was based firmly on the possibilities he saw in present-day realities and, despite what his critics said, was not divorced from existing material circumstances and conditions. On the contrary, his 'dreaming' was similar to what the Marxist philosopher Ernst Bloch termed 'Real Possible' hope that 'begins with the seed in which what is coming is inherent'. This helps explain why Che emphasised the role of subjective factors, against those 'orthodox' communists who, to him, seemed overly-wedded to purely objective factors and the 'here and now'.[57]

Che shared Marx's view that it was a 'categorical imperative' for revolutionaries to stand with the exploited and oppressed – wherever they were. Furthermore, Che's dream of abolishing exploitation, oppression, inequality, unfreedom and alienation – via the creation of a classless society – was one shared by many revolutionaries in past centuries. Then, however, material and cultural conditions had been insufficiently developed to allow such a dream to become reality. Thus, in that sense, such latter-day revolutionaries were indeed 'utopians', because their hopes were not based on the realities of their worlds – even though their rebellions were justified by being part of the global struggle by humans against inhuman conditions. Furthermore, those early utopians paved the way forward by developing dreams and ideals, and ways of thinking and acting, that Che saw as finally making it possible to realise those dreams and hopes. For Che, revolutionary hope was necessary for revolutionary politics and practice. Although he was attacked by 'orthodox' communists for holding such views, one Marxist who also stressed the importance of dreaming a concrete vision of a socialist future was none other than Lenin. According to Lenin, revolutionaries 'should dream!' – even if those dreams 'may run ahead of the natural march of events'. For him, 'If there is some connection between dreams and life then all is well.' Thus, as Mandel argued, 'hopes and dreams are … categories of revolutionary Realpolitk'.[58]

In many ways, there seems to be more need than ever for Che's revolutionary internationalism, commitment and humanism – and his determination to dream of a better future for humanity. His determination to stand with the world's exploited and oppressed was what led to him risking – and losing – his life in Bolivia. So perhaps Che's greatest legacy to the twenty-first century is his optimism to continue struggling for a better world, despite temporary setbacks and defeats. It is appropriate that the last words should be those of Che himself:

> The outcome of today's struggles is not important. As far as the final result is concerned it does not matter whether one movement or another is temporarily defeated.
>
> What is decisive is the determination to struggle which is maturing daily, the awareness of the need for revolutionary change and the certainty of its possibility.[59]

Endnotes

Introduction

1. Guevara, J.M., with Vincent, A., 2017, *Che, My Brother*, Cambridge, Polity Press, p.201.
2. Guevara, C.,1965, 'Notes on Man and Socialism in Cuba', in Hansen, J., (ed.), 1967, *Che Guevara Speaks: Selected Speeches and Writings*, New York, Pathfinder Press, p.136. Usually known as simply 'Man and Socialism in Cuba', it was written by Che in 1965, as he was on his way to help revolutionary fighters in the Congo.
3. Besancenot, O. & Löwy, M., 2009, *Che Guevara: His Revolutionary Legacy*, p.111; Harris, R.L., 2007, *Death of a Revolutionary: Che Guevara's Last Mission*, New York, Norton & Company, p.20
4. Part of the interview can be seen on: www.youtube.com/watch?v=xELHGR_ur0Q [Accessed 08/05/22]
5. The full text of Che's *Message* can be seen at: www.marxists.org/archive/guevara/1967/04/16.htm [Accessed 08/05/22]
6. Yaffe, H., 2009, 'Che Guevara: The Economics of Revolution', Basingstoke, Palgrave Macmillan, p.viii; Stutje, J.W., 2009, *Ernest Mandel: A Rebel's Dream Deferred*, London, Verso, p.163; Farber, S., 2016, *The Politics of Che Guevara: Theory and Practice*, Chicago, Haymarket Books, pp.xvi-xvii
7. Alexandre, M., (ed.), 1968, *Viva Che!* London, Lorrimer Publishing, p.99
8. Yaffe, H., 2009, 'Che Guevara: The Economics of Revolution', pp.1–2. A trailer for that film can be viewed on: www.youtube.com/watch?v=0_LAiSdIXos [Accessed 08/05/22]
9. Zanelli, M., ed., 2017, *Che Guevara: tu y TODOS*, Milan, Skira, back cover
10. Neruda, P., 1978, *Memoirs*, Harmondsworth, London, pp.299, 322–3, 330
11. Mandel, E., 1978, 'Why I am a Marxist,' in Achcar, G., ed., 1999, *The Legacy of Ernest Mandel*, London, Verso, pp.245–7
12. Mandel, E., 'Why I am a Marxist,' in Achcar, G., ed., *The Legacy of Ernest Mandel*, pp.248–9
13. Mandel, E., 'Why I am a Marxist,' in Achcar, G., ed., *The Legacy of Ernest Mandel*, p.251; Löwy, M., 2007, *The Marxism of Che Guevara: Philosophy, Economics, Revolutionary Warfare*, Lanham, Rowman & Littlefield, p.17
14. Mandel, E., 'Why I am a Marxist,' in Achcar, G., ed., The Legacy of Ernest Mandel, p.255; Löwy, M., *The Marxism of Che Guevara: Philosophy, Economics, Revolutionary Warfare*, pp.24–5
15. Mandel, E., 'Why I am a Marxist,' in Achcar, G., ed., *The Legacy of Ernest Mandel*, London, Verso, Mandel, pp.252–3
16. The term, *mucama*, originated from the time of slavery in nineteenth-century Brazil, and referred to a black – usually young and attractive – female house slave.
17. Anderson, J.L., 2010, *Che Guevara: A Revolutionary Life*, London, Bantam Books, pp.70, 412

Chapter 1

1. Anderson, J.L., 2010, *Che Guevara: A Revolutionary Life*, London, Bantam Books, p.29. *'Serna'* was an abbreviation of his mother's surname.
2. Lynch, E.G., 2007, *The Young Che: Memories of Che Guevara*, London, Vintage Books, p.58
3. Ibid. p.59
4. Anderson, J.L., *Che Guevara: A Revolutionary Life*, p.4
5. Lynch, E.G., *The Young Che: Memories of Che Guevara*, p.74; Luther, E. with Henken, T., 2001, *The Life and Work of Che Guevara*, Indianapolis, Alpha Books, p.6
6. Lynch, E.G., *The Young Che: Memories of Che Guevara*, pp.62, 77
7. Luther, E. with Henken, T., *The Life and Work of Che Guevara*, p.7
8. Lynch, E.G., *The Young Che: Memories of Che Guevara*, pp.96–97
9. Ibid. p.97–98; Luther, E. with Henken, T., *The Life and Work of Che Guevara*, p.7
10. Lynch, E.G., *The Young Che: Memories of Che Guevara*, p.87
11. Ibid. p.97–99
12. Ibid. p.99–100
13. Luther, E. with Henken, T., *The Life and Work of Che Guevara*, p.9
14. Anderson, J.L., *Che Guevara: A Revolutionary Life*, p.18
15. Lynch, E.G., *The Young Che: Memories of Che Guevara*, pp.110–111; Anderson, J.L., *Che Guevara: A Revolutionary Life*, p.18
16. Luther, E. with Henken, T., *The Life and Work of Che Guevara*, p.8
17. Anderson, J.L., *Che Guevara: A Revolutionary Life*, p.15
18. Lynch, E.G., *The Young Che: Memories of Che Guevara*, pp.108–109
19. Anderson, J.L., *Che Guevara: A Revolutionary Life*, p.16
20. Ibid. p.22; Lynch, E.G., *The Young Che: Memories of Che Guevara*, pp.153–154.
21. Luther, E. with Henken, T., *The Life and Work of Che Guevara*, pp.9–10
22. Lynch, E.G., *The Young Che: Memories of Che Guevara*, p.125
23. Luther, E. with Henken, T., *The Life and Work of Che Guevara*, p.10
24. Lynch, E.G., *The Young Che: Memories of Che Guevara*, pp.115–16
25. Luther, E. with Henken, T., *The Life and Work of Che Guevara*, p.12
26. Ibid. p.11
27. Harris, R.L., 2011, *Che Guevara: a Biography*, Santa Barbara, Greenwood, p.4
28. Guevara, J.M., 2017, *Che, My Brother*, Cambridge, Polity Press, p.58;
29. Harris, R.L., *Che Guevara: a Biography*, p.3
30. Luther, E. with Henken, T., *The Life and Work of Che Guevara*, p.13
31. Lynch, E.G., *The Young Che: Memories of Che Guevara*, p.111; Luther, E. with Henken, T., *The Life and Work of Che Guevara*, p.12
32. Harris, R.L., *Che Guevara: a Biography*, p.6; Lynch, E. G, *The Young Che: Memories of Che Guevara*, p.119
33. Lynch, E.G., *The Young Che: Memories of Che Guevara*, pp. 120,122–123
34. Ibid. p.128, 135

Chapter 2

1. Guevara, E.C., 2021, *The Motorcycle Diaries*, Dublin, Penguin Classics, p.149
2. Harris, R.L., 2011, *Che Guevara: a Biography*, Santa Barbara, Greenwood, p.8; Luther, E. with Henken, T., 2001, *The Life and Work of Che Guevara*, Indianapolis, Alpha Books, p.16
3. Lynch, E.G., 2007, *The Young Che: Memories of Che Guevara*, London, Vintage Books, pp.136–7
4. Lynch, E.G., *The Young Che: Memories of Che Guevara*, pp.138–9

5. Luther, E. with Henken, T., *The Life and Work of Che Guevara*, p.17; Guevara, J.M. with Vincent, A., 2017, *Che, My Brother*, Cambridge, Polity Press, p.55
6. Lynch, E.G., *The Young Che: Memories of Che Guevara*, p.140
7. Harris, R.L., *Che Guevara: a Biography*, Santa Barbara, Greenwood, p.6
8. Luther, E. with Henken, T., *The Life and Work of Che Guevara*, p.15; Lynch, E.G., *The Young Che: Memories of Che Guevara*, pp.124–5
9. Anderson, J.L., *Che Guevara: A Revolutionary Life*, London, Bantam Books, p.22
10. Ibid. p.33
11. Ibid. p.33
12. Ibid. p.34
13. Gadea, H., 2008, *My Life with Che*, New York, Palgrave Macmillan, p.42
14. Luther, E. with Henken, T., *The Life and Work of Che Guevara*, p.17
15. Anderson, J.L., *Che Guevara: A Revolutionary Life*, p.38
16. Harris, R.L., *Che Guevara: a Biography*, p.8; Guevara, E.C., *The Motorcycle Diaries*, p.149
17. Anderson, J.L., *Che Guevara: A Revolutionary Life*, pp. 35–6
18. Ibid. p. 36
19. Ibid. p. 36; Guevara, J.M. with Vincent, A., *Che, My Brother*, p.60
20. Luther, E. with Henken, T., *The Life and Work of Che Guevara*, p.15; Anderson, J.L., *Che Guevara: A Revolutionary Life*, p.27
21. Guevara, J.M. with Vincent, A., *Che, My Brother*, p.59; Lynch, E.G., *The Young Che: Memories of Che Guevara*, p.139
22. Luther, E. with Henken, T., *The Life and Work of Che Guevara*, p.23
23. Anderson, J.L., *Che Guevara: A Revolutionary Life*, p. 54; Guevara, J.M. with Vincent, A., *Che, My Brother*, pp.81–2.
24. Lynch, E.G., *The Young Che: Memories of Che Guevara*, p.146; Anderson, J.L., *Che Guevara: A Revolutionary Life*, pp. 40–1
25. Guevara, J.M. with Vincent, A., *Che, My Brother*, p.37
26. Lynch, E.G., *The Young Che: Memories of Che Guevara*, p.152
27. Anderson, J.L., *Che Guevara: A Revolutionary Life*, p.46
28. Lynch, E.G., *The Young Che: Memories of Che Guevara*, p.312
29. Guevara, J.M. with Vincent, A., *Che, My Brother*, p.37
30. Anderson, J.L., *Che Guevara: A Revolutionary Life*, p. 47
31. Lynch, E.G., *The Young Che: Memories of Che Guevara*, p.142; Luther, E. with Henken, T., *The Life and Work of Che Guevara*, p.21
32. Lynch, E.G., *The Young Che: Memories of Che Guevara*, p.139
33. Guevara, J.M. with Vincent, A., *Che, My Brother*, p.55; Lynch, E.G., *The Young Che: Memories of Che Guevara*, p.138
34. Anderson, J.L., *Che Guevara: A Revolutionary Life*, p. 49; Luther, E. with Henken, T., *The Life and Work of Che Guevara*, p.22
35. Luther, E. with Henken, T., *The Life and Work of Che Guevara*, p.22; Guevara, J.M. with Vincent, A., *Che, My Brother*, p.76
36. Anderson, J.L., *Che Guevara: A Revolutionary Life*, p.50
37. Guevara, J.M. with Vincent, A., *Che, My Brother*, p.53
38. Anderson, J.L., *Che Guevara: A Revolutionary Life*, p. 52
39. Guevara, E.C., *The Motorcycle Diaries*, p.149
40. Harris, R.L., *Che Guevara: a Biography*, p.19; Lynch, E.G., *The Young Che: Memories of Che Guevara*, p.144
41. Guevara, J.M. with Vincent, A., *Che, My Brother*, pp.78–9; Luther, E. with Henken, T., *The Life and Work of Che Guevara*, p.24

42. Anderson, J.L., *Che Guevara: A Revolutionary Life*, p.59; Luther, E. with Henken, T., *The Life and Work of Che Guevara*, p.26
43. Luther, E. with Henken, T., *The Life and Work of Che Guevara*, p.25; Lynch, E.G., *The Young Che: Memories of Che Guevara*, pp.155–7
44. Lynch, E.G., *The Young Che: Memories of Che Guevara*, pp.159–61
45. Ibid. p.161; Luther, E. with Henken, T., *The Life and Work of Che Guevara*, pp.24–5
46. Anderson, J.L., *Che Guevara: A Revolutionary Life*, p.61
47. Lynch, E.G., *The Young Che: Memories of Che Guevara*, pp.167–6; Guevara, J.M. with Vincent, A., *Che, My Brother*, p.80
48. Lynch, E.G., *The Young Che: Memories of Che Guevara*, p. 171
49. Ibid. .159
50. Ibid. p.173, 175
51. Ibid. .176; Guevara, J.M. with Vincent, A., *Che, My Brother*, p.79; Luther, E. with Henken, T., *The Life and Work of Che Guevara*, p.26
52. Guevara, J.M. with Vincent, A., *Che, My Brother*, p.61; Luther, E. with Henken, T., *The Life and Work of Che Guevara*, p.27
53. Guevara, J.M. with Vincent, A., *Che, My Brother*, p.62
54. Lynch, E.G., *The Young Che: Memories of Che Guevara*, p.141
55. Anderson, J.L., *Che Guevara: A Revolutionary Life*, p.66; Guevara, J.M. with Vincent, A., *Che, My Brother*, p.63

Chapter 3

1. Guevara, E.C., 2021, *The Motorcycle Diaries*, London, Penguin Books, p.3,
2. Harris, R.L., 2011, *Che Guevara: a Biography*, Santa Barbara, Greenwood, p.23
3. Anderson, J.L., *Che Guevara: A Revolutionary Life*, London, Bantam Books, p.68
4. Guevara, J.M. with Vincent, A., 2017, *Che, My Brother*, Cambridge, Polity Press, p.82
5. Ibid. pp.83–5
6. Ibid. p.82
7. Guevara, E.C., *The Motorcycle Diaries*, London, Penguin Books, p.9; Symmes, P., 2000, *Chasing Che: A Motorcycle Journey in Search of the Guevara Legend*, New York, Vintage Books, p.49
8. Guevara, E.C., *The Motorcycle Diaries*, p.3
9. Ibid. pp.13–14
10. Ibid. pp.16, 19
11. Ibid. p.29–31; Luther, E. with Henken, T., 2001, *The Life and Work of Che Guevara*, Indianapolis, Alpha Books, p.33
12. Guevara, E.C., *The Motorcycle Diaries*, pp.35, 37–8
13. Ibid. pp.40–41; Anderson, J.L., *Che Guevara: A Revolutionary Life*, p.73
14. Guevara, E.C., *The Motorcycle Diaries*, pp.42–4; Luther, E. with Henken, T., *The Life and Work of Che Guevara*, p.36
15. Guevara, E.C., *The Motorcycle Diaries*, pp.46–8
16. Ibid. p.53
17. Ibid. pp.55–6; Luther, E. with Henken, T, *The Life and Work of Che Guevara*, p.39
18. Luther, E. with Henken, T., *The Life and Work of Che Guevara*, pp.39–40; Guevara, E.C., *The Motorcycle Diaries*, pp.58, 65–8 In 1973 – six years after Che's murder – the US helped engineer a military coup to topple Allende, who'd been elected president in 1970.
19. Anderson, J.L., *Che Guevara: A Revolutionary Life*, p.78

20. Guevara, E.C., *The Motorcycle Diaries*, pp.90, 96; Luther, E. with Henken, T., *The Life and Work of Che Guevara*, pp.40–1; Anderson, J.L., *Che Guevara: A Revolutionary Life*, p.80
21. Guevara, E.C., *The Motorcycle Diaries*, p.100
22. Ibid. p.102
23. Ibid. p.103
24. Löwy, M., 2007, *The Marxism of Che Guevara: Philosophy, Economics, Revolutionary Warfare*, Lanham, Rowman & Littlefield Publishing, p.119; Anderson, J.L., *Che Guevara: A Revolutionary Life*, p.82
25. Luther, E. with Henken, T., *The Life and Work of Che Guevara*, p.41; Anderson, J.L., *Che Guevara: A Revolutionary Life*, p.83
26. Guevara, E.C., *The Motorcycle Diaries*, p.121–2
27. Ibid. p.130; Harris, R.L., 2011, *Che Guevara: a Biography*, Santa Barbara, Greenwood, p.33
28. Guevara, J.M. with Vincent, A., Che, My Brother, p.84; Symmes, PChasing Che: A Motorcycle Journey in Search of the Guevara Legend, p.180
29. Guevara, E.C., *The Motorcycle Diaries*, pp.133, 138
30. Ibid. pp.138–9; Anderson, J.L., *Che Guevara: A Revolutionary Life*, p.88
31. Guevara, E. C, *The Motorcycle Diaries*, pp.142–3
32. Guevara, E.C., *The Motorcycle Diaries*, pp.143–4
33. Lynch, E.G., *The Young Che: Memories of Che Guevara*, p.179
34. Guevara, J.M. with Vincent, A., *Che, My Brother*, p.85; Luther, E. with Henken, T., *The Life and Work of Che Guevara*, p.43; Harris, R.L., *Che Guevara: a Biography*, pp.35–6
35. Guevara, J.M. with Vincent, A., *Che, My Brother*, pp.85–6; Lynch, E.G., *The Young Che: Memories of Che Guevara*, p.180; Luther, E. with Henken, T., *The Life and Work of Che Guevara*, p.44
36. Guevara, J.M. with Vincent, A., *Che, My Brother*, p.86; Lynch, E.G., *The Young Che: Memories of Che Guevara*, p.181
37. Harris, R.L., *Che Guevara: a Biography*, p.37

Chapter 4

1. Guevara, C., 1969, *Reminiscences of the Cuban Revolutionary War*, Harmondsworth, Penguin Books, p.38
2. Guevara, C., 2002, *Back on the Road: a Journey to Central America*, London, Vintage, p.viii; Sinclair, A., 1998, *Che Guevara*, Thrupp/Stroud, Sutton Publishing, p.1
3. Guevara, C., *Back on the Road: a Journey to Central America*, p.xv; Guevara, J.M. with Vincent, A., 2017, *Che, My Brother*, Cambridge, Polity Press, pp.88–9
4. Guevara, J.M. with Vincent, A., *Che, My Brother*, p.87
5. Lynch, E.G., 2007, *The Young Che: Memories of Che Guevara*, London, Vintage Books, p.182; Luther, E. with Henken, T., 2001, *The Life and Work of Che Guevara*, Indianapolis, Alpha Books, p.49
6. Guevara, C., *Back on the Road: a Journey to Central America*, pp.4–5
7. Luther, E. with Henken, T., *The Life and Work of Che Guevara*, pp.50–1; Guevara, C., *Back on the Road: a Journey to Central America*, pp.xvi, 17–18
8. Luther, E. with Henken, T., *The Life and Work of Che Guevara*, p.50; Lynch, E.G., *The Young Che: Memories of Che Guevara*, p.191; Harris, R.L., 2011, *Che Guevara: a Biography*, Santa Barbara, Greenwood, p.40
9. Guevara, C., *Back on the Road: a Journey to Central America*, pp.9–11, 13
10. Ibid. pp.15, 18
11. Harris, R.L., *Che Guevara: a Biography*, p.41; Lynch, E.G., *The Young Che: Memories of Che Guevara*, p.197; Guevara, J.M. with Vincent, A., *Che, My Brother*, p.89

12. Anderson, J.L., 2010, *Che Guevara: A Revolutionary Life*, London, Bantam Books, p.107; Luther, E. with Henken, T., *The Life and Work of Che Guevara*, p.53
13. Guevara, C., *Back on the Road: a Journey to Central America*, pp.22–4; Luther, E. with Henken, T., *The Life and Work of Che Guevara*, p.54
14. Guevara, C., *Back on the Road: a Journey to Central America*, pp.26, 132
15. Luther, E. with Henken, T., *The Life and Work of Che Guevara*, p.54
16. Guevara, C., *Back on the Road: a Journey to Central America*, pp.26, 29, 32; Luther, E. with Henken, T., *The Life and Work of Che Guevara*, p.55
17. Guevara, C., *Back on the Road: a Journey to Central America*, pp.30–5
18. Lynch, E.G., *The Young Che: Memories of Che Guevara*, pp.200–1
19. Guevara, C., *Back on the Road: a Journey to Central America*, p.36
20. Anderson, J.L., *Che Guevara: A Revolutionary Life*, p.117
21. Gadea, H., 2008, *My Life with Che*, London, Frontline Books, pp.24–5
22. Ibid. p.27
23. Ibid. p. 27; Guevara, C., *Back on the Road: a Journey to Central America,* pp.38–9; Löwy, M., 2003, 'Neither imitation nor copy', internationalviewpoint.org/spip.php?article270 [Accessed 31/07/22]
24. Gadea, H., *My Life with Che*, p.30; Guevara, C., *Back on the Road: a Journey to Central America*, p.45
25. Gadea, H., *My Life with Che*, p.54
26. Guevara, C., *Back on the Road: a Journey to Central America*, p.39; Luther, E. with Henken, T., *The Life and Work of Che Guevara*, p.59; Anderson, J.L., *Che Guevara: A Revolutionary Life*, p.126
27. Luther, E. with Henken, T., *The Life and Work of Che Guevara*, p.57; Lynch, E.G., *The Young Che: Memories of Che Guevara*, p.206
28. Gadea, H., *My Life with Che*, pp.62–3; Lynch, E.G., *The Young Che: Memories of Che Guevara*, p.218
29. Gadea, H., *My Life with Che*, pp.65–6; Anderson, J.L., *Che Guevara: A Revolutionary Life*, p.133
30. Guevara, C., *Back on the Road: a Journey to Central America*, pp.59–60; Lynch, E.G., *The Young Che: Memories of Che Guevara*, pp.226–7
31. Guevara, C., *Back on the Road: a Journey to Central America*, p.57
32. Ibid. p.59
33. Ibid. p.61
34. Ibid. p.64; Guevara, J.M. with Vincent, A., *Che, My Brother*, p.94
35. Guevara, C., *Back on the Road: a Journey to Central America*, pp.64–5, 67–8; Lynch, E.G., *The Young Che: Memories of Che Guevara*, p.234; Sinclair, A., Che Guevara, p.14
36. Guevara, J.M. with Vincent, A., *Che, My Brother*, p.95
37. Gadea, H., *My Life with Che*, p.84
38. Guevara, C., *Back on the Road: a Journey to Central America,* pp.74, 77, 79; *The Militant*, 23 September 1963, Vol. 27 – No.33, New York, The Militant Publishing Association, p.4; Wall, D., 2018, *Hugo Blanco: A revolutionary for life*, London, Merlin Press, p.1; Symmes, P., 2000, *Chasing Che: A Motorcycle Journey in Search of the Guevara Legend*, New York, Vintage Books, p.244
39. Anderson, J.L., *Che Guevara: A Revolutionary Life*, pp.147–8
40. Guevara, C, *Back on the Road: a Journey to Central America*, p.83; Gadea, H., *My Life with Che*, pp.95, 97
41. Gadea, H., *My Life with Che*, pp.94; Luther, E. with Henken, T., *The Life and Work of Che Guevara*, p.62; Anderson, J.L., *Che Guevara: A Revolutionary Life*, p.150.
42. Lynch, E.G., *The Young Che: Memories of Che Guevara*, p.240

Chapter 5

1. Guevara, E.C., 2021, *Reminiscences of the Cuban Revolutionary War*, London, Penguin Classics, pp.9–10
2. Lynch, E.G., 2007, *The Young Che: Memories of Che Guevara*, London, Vintage Books, p.243; Guevara, J.M. with Vincent, A., 2017, *Che, My Brother*, Cambridge, Polity Press, p.92; Sinclair, A., 1998, *Che Guevara*, Thrupp/Stroud, Sutton Publishing, p.16
3. Guevara, C., 2002, *Back on the Road: a Journey to Central America,* London, Vintage, pp.84–5
4. Gadea, H., 2008, *My Life with Che*, London, Frontline Books, p.125; Guevara, C., *Back on the Road: a Journey to Central America,* p.85
5. Guevara, J.M. with Vincent, A., *Che, My Brother*, p.97; Guevara, C., *Back on the Road: a Journey to Central America,* p.88
6. Lynch, E.G., *The Young Che: Memories of Che Guevara*, pp.248–9; Guevara, J.M. with Vincent, A., *Che, My Brother*, p.98;
7. Guevara, C., *Back on the Road: a Journey to Central America,* pp.91–2; Lynch, E.G., *The Young Che: Memories of Che Guevara*, pp.256–9; Luther, E. with Henken, T., 2001 *The Life and Work of Che Guevara*, Indianapolis, Alpha Books, p.63
8. Anderson, J.L., 2010, *Che Guevara: A Revolutionary Life*, London, Bantam Books, p.157; Gadea, H., 2008, *My Life with Che*, p.133; Guevara, C., *Back on the Road: a Journey to Central America,* pp.95, 97
9. Gadea, H., *My Life with Che*, p.134; Anderson, J.L., *Che Guevara: A Revolutionary Life*, p.159; Lynch, E.G., *The Young Che: Memories of Che Guevara*, p.265
10. Lynch, E.G., *The Young Che: Memories of Che Guevara*, pp.265, 269–70
11. Guevara, J.M. with Vincent, A., *Che, My Brother*, p.98; Gadea, H., *My Life with Che*, p.143
12. Lynch, E.G., *The Young Che: Memories of Che Guevara*, pp. 262–3
13. Guevara, J.M. with Vincent, A., *Che, My Brother*, p.99; Harris, R.L., *Che Guevara: a Biography*, p.60
14. Guevara, C., *Back on the Road: a Journey to Central America*, p.99; Gadea, H., *My Life with Che*, p.144
15. Gadea, H., *My Life with Che*, p.147; Sinclair, A., *Che Guevara*, p.18; Guevara, J.M. with Vincent, A., *Che, My Brother*, p.101
16. Gadea, H., *My Life with Che*, p.149; Anderson, J.L., *Che Guevara: A Revolutionary Life*, p.172
17. Ibid. pp.153–4
18. Guevara, C., *Back on the Road: a Journey to Central America*, p.94; Anderson, J.L., *Che Guevara: A Revolutionary Life*, p.175
19. Gadea, H., *My Life with Che*, pp.163, 166; Guevara, C., *Back on the Road: a Journey to Central America*, pp.101–06
20. Gadea, H., *My Life with Che*, pp.167–8
21. Ibid. p.202
22. Lynch, E.G., *The Young Che: Memories of Che Guevara*, p. 297
23. Gadea, H., *My Life with Che*, p.172
24. Luther, E. with Henken, T,. *The Life and Work of Che Guevara*, p.75; Lynch, E.G., *The Young Che: Memories of Che Guevara*, p. 282; Gadea, H., *My Life with Che*, p.173
25. Luther, E. with Henken, T., *The Life and Work of Che Guevara*, pp.75–6; Lynch, E.G., *The Young Che: Memories of Che Guevara*, pp. 285–6, 298–9; Guevara, C., *Back on the Road: a Journey to Central America*, p.117
26. Anderson, J.L., *Che Guevara: A Revolutionary Life*, p.184
27. Ibid. p.187; Gadea, H., *My Life with Che*, p.202
28. Gadea, H., *My Life with Che*, p.202

29. Ibid. p.186
30. Anderson, J.L., *Che Guevara: A Revolutionary Life*, p.190
31. Gadea, H., *My Life with Che*, p.193
32. Lynch, E.G., *The Young Che: Memories of Che Guevara*, pp. 288–90; Guevara, C., *Back on the Road: a Journey to Central America*, pp.110–11
33. Guevara, C., *Back on the Road: a Journey to Central America,* p.109–11; Guevara, J.M. with Vincent, A., *Che, My Brother*, p.102
34. Guevara, J.M. with Vincent, A., *Che, My Brother*, p.103; Gadea, H., *My Life with Che*, p.195; Harris, R.L., 2011, *Che Guevara: a Biography*, Santa Barbara, Greenwood, p.67
35. Gadea, H., *My Life with Che*, p.203
36. Ibid. p.205; Lynch, E.G., *The Young Che: Memories of Che Guevara*, pp. 305–07
37. Lynch, E.G., *The Young Che: Memories of Che Guevara*, p. 307
38. Guevara, C., *Back on the Road: a Journey to Central America*, pp.111–12
39. Ibid. pp.116; Lynch, E.G., *The Young Che: Memories of Che Guevara*, p. 302

Chapter 6

1. Guevara, C., 1969, Guerrilla Warfare, Hardmondsworth, Penguin Books, p.68
2. Sinclair, A., 1998, *Che Guevara*, Thrupp/Stroud, Sutton Publishing, p.36; Lynch, E.G., 2007, *The Young Che: Memories of Che Guevara*, London, Vintage Books, pp. 126–7
3. March, A., 2012, *Remembering Che: My Life with Che Guevara*, Melbourne, Ocean Press, p.7
4. Guevara, E.C., 2021, *Reminiscences of the Cuban Revolutionary War*, London, Penguin Classics, p.17; Guevara, J.M. with Vincent, A., 2017, *Che, My Brother*, pp.108–09; Gadea, H., 2008, *My Life with Che*, p.216
5. Guevara, J.M. with Vincent, A., *Che, My Brother*, p.109
6. Guevara, J.M. with Vincent, A., *Che, My Brother*, p.110; Anderson, J.L., 2010, *Che Guevara: A Revolutionary Life*, London, Bantam Books, p.213
7. Gadea, H., *My Life with Che*, pp.209, 215–16
8. Anderson, J.L., *Che Guevara: A Revolutionary Life*, p.215
9. Guevara, E.C., *Reminiscences of the Cuban Revolutionary War*, p.33
10. Besancenot, O. & Löwy, M., 2009, *Che Guevara: His Revolutionary Legacy*, New York, Monthly Review Press, p.43; Guevara, C., Guerrilla Warfare, Hardmondsworth, Penguin Books, p. 29; Guevara, E.C., *Reminiscences of the Cuban Revolutionary War*, pp.26, 30
11. Anderson, J.L., *Che Guevara: A Revolutionary Life*, p.229
12. Guevara, E.C., *Reminiscences of the Cuban Revolutionary War*, p.54
13. Guevara, E.C., *Reminiscences of the Cuban Revolutionary War*, p.76
14. Guevara, E.C., *Reminiscences of the Cuban Revolutionary War*, pp.82, 84; Harris, R.L., 2011, *Che Guevara: a Biography*, Santa Barbara, Greenwood, p.75
15. Anderson, J.L., *Che Guevara: A Revolutionary Life*, p.227; Luther, E. with Henken, T., *The Life and Work of Che Guevara*, p.100; Reid-Henry, S., 2009, *Fidel & Che: A Revolutionary Friendship*, p.170,
16. Anderson, J.L., *Che Guevara: A Revolutionary Life*, p.231
17. Reid-Henry, S., *Fidel & Che: A Revolutionary Friendship*, pp.170, 328
18. Ibid. p.170; Anderson, J.L., *Che Guevara: A Revolutionary Life*, p.281
19. Harris, R.L., *Che Guevara: a Biography*, p.76; Guevara, E.C., *Reminiscences of the Cuban Revolutionary War*, p.104
20. Guevara, E.C., *Reminiscences of the Cuban Revolutionary War*, p.106; Harris, R.L., *Che Guevara: a Biography*, p.75

21. Guevara, E.C., *Reminiscences of the Cuban Revolutionary War*, pp.110–11; Reid-Henry, S., *Fidel & Che: A Revolutionary Friendship*, p.165
22. Guevara, E.C., *Reminiscences of the Cuban Revolutionary War*, p.116
23. Anderson, J.L., *Che Guevara: A Revolutionary Life*, p.266; Guevara, E.C., *Reminiscences of the Cuban Revolutionary War*, p.123
24. Guevara, E.C., *Reminiscences of the Cuban Revolutionary War*, pp.150, 152
25. Guevara, J.M. with Vincent, A., *Che, My Brother*, pp.115–16
26. Anderson, J.L., *Che Guevara: A Revolutionary Life*, p.290; Gadea, H., *My Life with Che*, p.218
27. Guevara, J.M. with Vincent, A., *Che, My Brother*, pp.112–13; Anderson, J.L., *Che Guevara: A Revolutionary Life*, pp.293–4
28. Guevara, E.C., *Reminiscences of the Cuban Revolutionary War*, p.206
29. Reid-Henry, S., *Fidel & Che: A Revolutionary Friendship*, pp.174–5
29. Anderson, J.L., *Che Guevara: A Revolutionary Life*, pp.310–11
30. Guevara, E.C., *Reminiscences of the Cuban Revolutionary War*, p.212
31. Luther, E. with Henken, T., *The Life and Work of Che Guevara*, p.108
32. Guevara, E.C., *Reminiscences of the Cuban Revolutionary War*, pp.201, 205; Anderson, J.L., *Che Guevara: A Revolutionary Life*, p.315
33. Anderson, J.L., *Che Guevara: A Revolutionary Life*, p.318
34. Guevara, E.C., *Reminiscences of the Cuban Revolutionary War*, p.214
35. Guevara, E.C., *Reminiscences of the Cuban Revolutionary War*, p.217
36. Anderson, J.L., *Che Guevara: A Revolutionary Life*, pp.323–25
37. Ibid. p.338
38. Gadea, H., *My Life with Che*, p.218; Anderson, J.L., *Che Guevara: A Revolutionary Life*, pp.297, 319
39. March, A., *Remembering Che: My Life with Che Guevara*, pp.34–5
40. Ibid. pp.7, 36
41. Ibid. pp 38–9
42. Ibid. p.40
43. Ibid. pp.41–2, 45
44. Ibid. pp.47, 49–50
45. March, A., *Remembering Che: My Life with Che Guevara*, p.52
46. Guevara, E.C., *Reminiscences of the Cuban Revolutionary War*, p.219
47. Guevara, E.C., *Reminiscences of the Cuban Revolutionary War*, p.220
48. Guevara, E.C., *Reminiscences of the Cuban Revolutionary War*, p.221
49. Luther, E. with Henken, T., *The Life and Work of Che Guevara*, p.116
50. March, A., *Remembering Che: My Life with Che Guevara*, pp.58–9
51. Luther, E. with Henken, T., *The Life and Work of Che Guevara*, p.115

Chapter 7

1. Guevara, C., 1967, *Che Guevara Speaks: Selected Speeches and Writings*, New York, Pathfinder Press, pp.20–21
2. Reid-Henry, S., 2009, *Fidel & Che: A Revolutionary Friendship*, p.202; Luther, E. with Henken, T.,2001, *The Life and Work of Che Guevara*, Indianapolis, Alpha Books, p.153
3. Guevara, E.C., 2021, *Reminiscences of the Cuban Revolutionary War*, p.221; Yaffe, H., 2009, 'Che Guevara: The Economics of Revolution', Basingstoke, Palgrave Macmillan, p.43
4. March, A., 2012, *Remembering Che: My Life with Che Guevara*, p.67; Luther, E. with Henken, T., *The Life and Work of Che Guevara*, p.119

5. Gadea, H., 2008, *My Life with Che*, London, Frontline Books, p.219
6. March, A., *Remembering Che: My Life with Che Guevara*, pp.66–7
7. Luther, E. with Henken, T., *The Life and Work of Che Guevara*, p.117
8. March, A., *Remembering Che: My Life with Che Guevara*, pp.61, 65
9. Ibid. p.65
10. Harris, R.L., 2011, *Che Guevara: a Biography*, Santa Barbara, Greenwood, p.93
11. Gadea, H., *My Life with Che*, p.221
12. Luther, E. with Henken, T., *The Life and Work of Che Guevara*, p.122
13. Ibid. p.122; March, A., *Remembering Che: My Life with Che Guevara*, p.69
14. Luther, E. with Henken, T., *The Life and Work of Che Guevara*, pp.123–4
15. March, A., *Remembering Che: My Life with Che Guevara*, pp.73, 76–7
16. Ibid. pp.77–8
17. Ibid. pp.91–2
18. Ibid. p.85
19. Luther, E. with Henken, T., *The Life and Work of Che Guevara*, pp.130–1
20. www.irishtimes.com/culture/art-and-design/visual-art/the-irish-artist-who-captured-the-image-of-che-guevara-1.576934 [Accessed 07/10/22] In September 2011, there was a festival in Kilkee to commemorate the 50th. anniversary of Che's visit. Since then, there's been an annual festival there: www.youtube.com/watch?v=w0U59qWW8bs [Accessed 07/10/22]
21. Yaffe, H., 2009, 'Che Guevara: The Economics of Revolution', Basingstoke, Palgrave Macmillan, pp.10, 13
22. March, A., *Remembering Che: My Life with Che Guevara*, pp.79–80
23. Ibid. pp.79–81
24. Ibid. p.107
25. Luther, E. with Henken, T., *The Life and Work of Che Guevara*, p.131
26. Ibid. pp.133–4
27. Ibid. p.136
28. March, A., *Remembering Che: My Life with Che Guevara*, p.95
29. Luther, E. with Henken, T., *The Life and Work of Che Guevara*, pp.151–2
30. March, A., *Remembering Che: My Life with Che Guevara*, p.99
31. Luther, E. with Henken, T., *The Life and Work of Che Guevara*, p.162
32. Guevara, E.C., 1961, 'The Sin of the Revolution', in Gerassi, J., ed.,1969, *Venceremos!: The speeches and writings of Ernesto Che Guevara*, London, Panther Books, p.191; March, A., *Remembering Che: My Life with Che Guevara*, p.100
33. Luther, E. with Henken, T., *The Life and Work of Che Guevara*, p.157
34. Since then, the economic blockade has been intensified. In 2020, the US blocked a shipment to Cuba of vital Covid supplies, leading Oxfam in 2021 to condemn the blockade which, among other things, *'restricts access to suppliers of medicines, technology, food and other essential products.'* Despite the UN's General Assembly regularly voting for the blockade to be lifted (in 2021, 184 nations supported Cuba's call for the blockade to end – only the US, Israel and Ukraine voted against), it was still in force in 2023.
35. Guevara, J.M. with Vincent, A., *Che, My Brother*, p.126
36. Guevara, J.M. with Vincent, A., *Che, My Brother*, p.126; March, A., *Remembering Che: My Life with Che Guevara*, pp.65–7
37. March, A., *Remembering Che: My Life with Che Guevara*, pp.93, 99,103
38. Ibid. pp.103–06

39. The French shipping firm that owned *La Coubre* placed all documents relating to its investigation into the causes of the explosion under a 150–year embargo, while the US has steadfastly refused to make public its own documents relating to the explosion.
40. Luther, E. with Henken, T., *The Life and Work of Che Guevara*, p.153
41. Ibid. p.156. At the time, the CIA denied any involvement in the attempted invasion; but, in 1998, they released documents that confirmed their role.
42. Luther, E. with Henken, T., *The Life and Work of Che Guevara*, pp.158–9; Guevara, J.M. with Vincent, A., *Che, My Brother*, p.123
43. Guevara, J.M. with Vincent, A., *Che, My Brother*, pp.128, 130
44. Luther, E. with Henken, T., *The Life and Work of Che Guevara*, p.148
45. Ibid. p.163
46. Anderson, J.L., 2010, *Che Guevara: A Revolutionary Life*, London, Bantam Books, p.502
47. The US called it a 'quarantine', as a blockade in peacetime is against international law.
48. Luther, E. with Henken, T., *The Life and Work of Che Guevara*, p.171
49. Ibid. p.177; March, A., *Remembering Che: My Life with Che Guevara*, pp.107–08
50. content.time.com/time/subscriber/article/0,33009,869742-2,00.html [Accessed 20/11/22]
51. Harris, R.L., *Che Guevara: a Biography*, p.100
52. Guevara, E.C., 'letter to his Family', ed., Gerassi, J., *Venceremos! The speeches and writings of Ernesto Che Guevara*, p.568; Harris, R.L., *Che Guevara: a Biography*, p.104
53. Guevara, J.M. with Vincent, A., *Che, My Brother*, p.124; Luther, E. with Henken, T., *The Life and Work of Che Guevara*, p.176; March, A., *Remembering Che: My Life with Che Guevara*, p.107

Chapter 8

1. Guevara, E.C., 1965, 'Man and Socialism in Cuba', in Silverman, B., 1971, *Man and Socialism in Cuba*, New York, Atheneum, p.343
2. Farber, S., 2016, *The Politics of Che Guevara: Theory and Practice*, Chicago, Haymarket Books, p.96
3. Yaffe, H., 2009, 'Che Guevara: The Economics of Revolution', Basingstoke, Palgrave Macmillan, pp.1–2; Stutje, J.W., 2009, *Ernest Mandel: A Rebel's Dream Deferred*, London, Verso, p.152. See also Yaffe's Ph. D. thesis: Yaffe, H., 2007, *Ernesto 'Che' Guevara: socialist political economy and economic management in Cuba, 1959–1965*, Ann Arbor, ProQuest LLC: etheses.lse.ac.uk/2311/ [Accessed 19/12/22]
4. Stutje, J.W., *Ernest Mandel: A Rebel's Dream Deferred*, p.148; Castro, F., 1967, 'In Tribute to Che', in Guevara, C., 1969, *Reminiscences of the Cuban Revolutionary War*, Harmondsworth, Penguin Books, pp.21–2 (my emphasis)
5. Löwy, M., 2007, *The Marxism of Che Guevara: Philosophy, Economics, Revolutionary Warfare*, Lanham, Rowman & Littlefield, p.27
6. Löwy, M., *The Marxism of Che Guevara: Philosophy, Economics, Revolutionary Warfare*, p.60
7. Stutje, J.W., *Ernest Mandel: A Rebel's Dream Deferred*, p.150
8. Stutje, J.W., *Ernest Mandel: A Rebel's Dream Deferred*, p.149. Mandel's time in Cuba can be found on: walterlippmann.com/ernest-mandel-and-cuba/ [Accessed 19/12/22]
9. Samary, C., 'Mandel's Views on the Transition to Socialism', in Achar, G., ed., 1999, *The Legacy of Ernest Mandel*, London, Verso, p.152; Mandel, E., 'What is the Bureaucracy?', in Ali, T., (ed.), 2013, *The Stalinist Legacy: Its Impact on Twentieth-Century World Politics*, Chicago, Haymarket Books, p.78
10. Samary, C., 'Mandel's Views on the Transition to Socialism', in Achar, G., ed., *The Legacy of Ernest Mandel*, p.155

11. Ibid. pp.155–6; Stutje, J.W., *Ernest Mandel: A Rebel's Dream Deferred*, p.149
12. Ibid. p.187; Toussaint, E., 'Ernest Mandel, Revolutionary Cuba and Che Guevara', in CounterPunch, [Accessed 12/01/24]
13. Löwy, M., *The Marxism of Che Guevara: Philosophy, Economics, Revolutionary Warfare*, p.xxxiii.
14. Harris, R.L., 2011, *Che Guevara: a Biography*, Santa Barbara, Greenwood, p.12; Yaffe, H., 'Che Guevara: The Economics of Revolution', p.45
15. Yaffe, H., 'Che Guevara: The Economics of Revolution', pp.2, 45,
16. Ibid. p.51
17. Ibid. p.49
18. Yaffe, H., 2007, *Ernesto 'Che' Guevara: socialist political economy and economic management in Cuba, 1959–1965*, Ph. D. thesis, Ann Arbor, ProQuest LLC, p.3, etheses.lse.ac.uk/2311/ [Accessed 19/12/22]
19. Silverman, B., 1971, *Man and Socialism in Cuba*, New York, Atheneum, p.11; Yaffe, H., 'Che Guevara: The Economics of Revolution', pp.52, 66
20. Yaffe, H., 'Che Guevara: The Economics of Revolution', p.53
21. Guevara, E.C., 1964, 'On the Budgetary System of Financing', in Silverman, B., *Man and Socialism in Cuba*, p.143; Yaffe, H., 'Che Guevara: The Economics of Revolution', p.54
22. Yaffe, H., 'Che Guevara: The Economics of Revolution', pp.56, 59, 63
23. Marx, K., 'Critique of the Gotha Programme', in Fernbach, D., ed., 1974, *The First International after Marx*, Harmondsworth, Penguin Books, p.345; Löwy, M., *The Marxism of Che Guevara: Philosophy, Economics, Revolutionary Warfare*, p.38
24. Löwy, M., *The Marxism of Che Guevara: Philosophy, Economics, Revolutionary Warfare*, p.39; Guevara, E.C., 1963, 'On the Concept of Value', in Silverman, B., *Man and Socialism in Cuba*, p.231
25. Guevara, E.C., 'On the Concept of Value', in Silverman, B., Man and Socialism in Cuba, p.231; Löwy, M., *The Marxism of Che Guevara: Philosophy, Economics, Revolutionary Warfare*, p.40
26. Löwy, M., *The Marxism of Che Guevara: Philosophy, Economics, Revolutionary Warfare*, pp.41–2
27. Guevara, E.C., 1964, 'On the Budgetary System of Financing', in Gerassi, J., ed., Guevara, C., *Venceremos!: The speeches and writings of Ernesto Che Guevara*, p.422
28. Guevara, E.C., 'On the Budgetary System of Financing', in Silverman, B., *Man and Socialism in Cuba*, p.143; Yaffe, H., 'Che Guevara: The Economics of Revolution', pp.2, 20,46.
29. Farber, S., *The Politics of Che Guevara: Theory and Practice*, p.xvi; Yaffe, H., 'Che Guevara: The Economics of Revolution', p.20; Tablada, C., 1990, Che Guevara: Economics and Politics in the Transition to Socialism, New York, Pathfinder Press, pp. 111–2
30. Löwy, M., *The Marxism of Che Guevara: Philosophy, Economics, Revolutionary Warfare*, p.49
31. Guevara, C., 1965, 'Socialist Planning', Gerassi, J., ed., *Venceremos!: The speeches and writings of Ernesto Che Guevara*, p. 562
32. Löwy, M., *The Marxism of Che Guevara: Philosophy, Economics, Revolutionary Warfare*, p.34; Guevara, C., 1965, 'Socialist Planning', Gerassi, J., ed., Guevara, C., Venceremos!: The speeches and writings of Ernesto Che Guevara, p.554
33. Löwy, M., *The Marxism of Che Guevara: Philosophy, Economics, Revolutionary Warfare*, pp.50–51
34. Ibid. pp.41–2
35. Farber, S., *The Politics of Che Guevara: Theory and Practice*, pp.21–2

36. Marx, K., 'Theses on Feuerbach', in Colletti, L., ed., 1975, *Early Writings*, Harmondsworth, Penguin Books, p.422
37. Löwy, M., *The Marxism of Che Guevara: Philosophy, Economics, Revolutionary Warfare*, p.54, 61; Guevara, E.C., 1964, 'Man and Socialism in Cuba', in Silverman, B., *Man and Socialism in Cuba*, pp.341, 343
38. Löwy, M., *The Marxism of Che Guevara: Philosophy, Economics, Revolutionary Warfare*, p.56
39. Ibid. p.56; Guevara, C., 1964, 'On The Budgetary System of Financing', Gerassi, J., ed., Guevara, C., Venceremos!: The speeches and writings of Ernesto Che Guevara, p.410; Guevara, E.C., 'Man and Socialism in Cuba', in Silverman, B., Man and Socialism in Cuba, p.123
40. Marx, K., 'Economic and Philosophical Manuscripts', in Colletti, L., (ed.), *Early Writings*, p.348; Tablada, C., *Che Guevara: Economics and Politics in the Transition to Socialism*, p.77; Silverman, B., *Man and Socialism in Cuba*, pp.123–4, 342–3;.
41. Yaffe, H., 'Che Guevara: The Economics of Revolution', p.64
42. Ibid. p.66; Farber, S., *The Politics of Che Guevara: Theory and Practice*, pp.11, 18; Llorente, R., 2018, www.hamptonthink.org/read/a-travesty-of-scholarship-a-review-of-samuel-farbers-the-politics-of-che-guevara [Accessed 08/01/23]
43. Löwy, M., *The Marxism of Che Guevara: Philosophy, Economics, Revolutionary Warfare*, pp.59–60
44. Guevara, C., 1962, 'On Being A Communist Youth', Gerassi, J., ed., Guevara, C., *Venceremos!: The speeches and writings of Ernesto Che Guevara*, pp.303–04
45. Yaffe, H., 'Che Guevara: The Economics of Revolution', p. 214
46. Löwy, M., *The Marxism of Che Guevara: Philosophy, Economics, Revolutionary Warfare*, pp.64–5
47. Yaffe, H., 'Che Guevara: The Economics of Revolution', pp.201–2
48. Ibid. pp.202–3
49. Löwy, M., *The Marxism of Che Guevara: Philosophy, Economics, Revolutionary Warfare*, p.5
50. Ibid. pp.5, 10
51. Ibid. p.6
52. Yaffe, H., 'Che Guevara: The Economics of Revolution', p.133
53. Ibid. pp.134, 138
54. Ibid. p.144; Farber, S., *The Politics of Che Guevara: Theory and Practice*, pp.68–9; Toussaint, E., 'Ernest Mandel, Revolutionary Cuba and Che Guevara', in CounterPunch, [Accessed 12/01/24]
55. Yaffe, H., 'Che Guevara: The Economics of Revolution', pp.131–2
56. Farber, S., *The Politics of Che Guevara: Theory and Practice*, pp.67–8
57. Ibid., pp.17, 65; Principe, M., 2017, sdonline.org/issue/75/debunking-myth-or-distorting-record-samuel-farber-che-guevara [Accessed 08/01/23]; Anderson, J.L., 2010, *Che Guevara: A Revolutionary Life*, London, Bantam Books, p.574
58. Guevara, C., 1963, 'On Party Militancy', Gerassi, J., ed., Guevara, C., Venceremos!: The speeches and writings of Ernesto Che Guevara, pp.347–8; Löwy, M., *The Marxism of Che Guevara: Philosophy, Economics, Revolutionary Warfare*, pp.12–13
59. Farber, S., *The Politics of Che Guevara: Theory and Practice*, pp.19, 118; Löwy, M., *The Marxism of Che Guevara: Philosophy, Economics, Revolutionary Warfare*, pp.12–13; Marx, K., 'The Eighteenth Brumaire of Louis Bonaparte' in Fernbach, D., ed., 1973, *Surveys from Exile*, Harmondsworth, Penguin Books, p.146
60. Guevara, C., 1969, *Guerrilla Warfare*, Harmondsworth, Penguin Books, pp.13–14; Yaffe, H., 'Che Guevara: The Economics of Revolution', p.223

61. Yaffe, H., 'Che Guevara: The Economics of Revolution', p.200; Marx, K., 'Critique of the Gotha Programme', in Ferbach, D., ed., 1974, *The First International and After*, Harmondsworth, Penguin Books, p.346
62. Guevara, C., 1962, 'Our Industrial Tasks', Gerassi, J., ed., Guevara, C., *Venceremos!: The speeches and writings of Ernesto Che Guevara*, p.286; Guevara, E.C., 1965, 'Man and Socialism in Cuba', Silverman, B., *Man and Socialism in Cuba*, p.346
63. Löwy, M., *The Marxism of Che Guevara: Philosophy, Economics, Revolutionary Warfare*, p.17; Guevara, E.C., 1965, 'Man and Socialism in Cuba',Silverman, B., Man and Socialism in Cuba, p.341
64. Guevara, C., 1962, 'On Being a Communist Youth', and Guevara, C., 1965, 'Man and Socialism in Cuba', Gerassi, J., ed., Guevara, C., *Venceremos!: The speeches and writings of Ernesto Che Guevara*, pp. 308, 540–1, 544; Löwy, M., *The Marxism of Che Guevara: Philosophy, Economics, Revolutionary Warfare*, p.18
65. Farber, S., *The Politics of Che Guevara: Theory and Practice*, p.76
66. Lorente, R., www.hamptonthink.org/read/a-travesty-of-scholarship-a-review-of-samuel-farbers-the-politics-of-che-guevara [Accessed 08/01/23]; Farber, S., *The Politics of Che Guevara: Theory and Practice*, Chicago, Haymarket Books, p.78
67. Guevara, C., 1963, 'On Party Militancy', Gerassi, J., ed., Guevara, C., Venceremos!: The speeches and writings of Ernesto Che Guevara, p.347; Löwy, M., *The Marxism of Che Guevara: Philosophy, Economics, Revolutionary Warfare*, pp.19–20
68. Löwy, M., *The Marxism of Che Guevara: Philosophy, Economics, Revolutionary Warfare*, p.6; Yaffe, H., 'Che Guevara: The Economics of Revolution', p.232
69. Löwy, M., *The Marxism of Che Guevara: Philosophy, Economics, Revolutionary Warfare*, pp.14–15; Marx, K., 'Economic and Philosophical Manuscripts', in Colletti, L., ed., *Early Writings*, Harmondsworth, Penguin Books, p.348; Guevara, C., 1964, 'On the Budgetary System of Finance', Gerassi, J., ed., Guevara, C., *Venceremos!: The speeches and writings of Ernesto Che Guevara*, pp.410–11
70. Guevara, C., 1964, 'On the Budgetary System of Finance', Gerassi, J., ed., Guevara, C., *Venceremos!: The speeches and writings of Ernesto Che Guevara*, p.410
71. Löwy, M., *The Marxism of Che Guevara: Philosophy, Economics, Revolutionary Warfare*, p.8
72. Ibid. p.22. That chapter was republished in the very first issue of the journal 'Tricontinental'
73. Löwy, M., *The Marxism of Che Guevara: Philosophy, Economics, Revolutionary Warfare*, p.23; Farber, S., *The Politics of Che Guevara: Theory and Practice*, p.82
74. Guevara, C., 1966–7, *Message to the Tricontinental*: 'Create two, three…many Vietnams', Gerassi, J., ed., Guevara, C., *Venceremos!: The speeches and writings of Ernesto Che Guevara*, p.581; Farber, S., *The Politics of Che Guevara: Theory and Practice*, p.82; Principe, M., sdonline.org/issue/75/debunking-myth-or-distorting-record-samuel-farber-che-guevara [Accessed 08/01/23]
75. Löwy, M., *The Marxism of Che Guevara: Philosophy, Economics, Revolutionary Warfare*, p.65; Stutje, J.W., *Ernest Mandel: A Rebel's Dream Deferred*, p.152; Toussaint, E., 'Ernest Mandel, Revolutionary Cuba and Che Guevara', in CounterPunch, [Accessed 12/01/24]

Chapter 9

1. Guevara, E.C., ed. Deutschmann, D., 1987, *Che Guevara and the Cuban Revolution: Writings and Speeches of Ernesto Che Guevara*, Leichhardt (Sydney), Pathfinder/Pacific & Asia, p.375. Castro can be heard reading this out in public on 3 October 1965: www.youtube.com/watch?v=dwshXWL1jSY [Accessed 08/02/23]

2. Llorente, R., 2018, *The Political Theory of Che Guevara*, Lanham, Rowman & Littlefield International, p.46; Sinclair, A., 1998, *Che Guevara*, Thrupp/Stroud, Sutton Publishing, pp.84, 87
3. Löwy, M., 2007, *The Marxism of Che Guevara: Philosophy, Economics, Revolutionary Warfare*, Lanham, Rowman & Littlefield Publishing, p.100; Guevara, E.C., ed. Deutschmann, D., *Che Guevara and the Cuban Revolution: Writings and Speeches of Ernesto Che Guevara*, p.356
4. Llorente, R., *The Political Theory of Che Guevara*, p.55; Guevara, E.C., 2001, *The African Dream: The Diaries of the Revolutionary War in The Congo*, London, Harvill Press, p.7
5. March, A, 2012, *Remembering Che: My Life with Che Guevara*, pp.108, 113. Che's eulogy to 'El Patojo' was published in *Verde Olivo* in August 1962 – and can been seen in the 2021 edition of *Reminiscences of the Cuban Revolutionary War*, pp.227–30
6. Anderson, J.L., 2010, *Che Guevara: A Revolutionary Life*, London, Bantam Books, pp.510, 530–32, 550.
7. Harris, R.L., 2011, *Che Guevara: a Biography*, Santa Barbara, Greenwood, p.100; Sinclair, A., *Che Guevara*, p.84; Luther, E. with Henken, T., 2001, *The Life and Work of Che Guevara*, Indianapolis, Alpha Books, p.192;
8. Luther, E. with Henken, T, *The Life and Work of Che Guevara*, p.183. An interview (in French) Che gave to Radio Television Suisse after that Conference, can be seen at: www.youtube.com/watch?v=y5X0L_SPgoE [Accessed 14/02/23]
9. Anderson, J.L., *Che Guevara: A Revolutionary Life*, pp.561, 574–5; Luther, E. with Henken, T, *The Life and Work of Che Guevara*, p.182
10. Anderson, J.L., *Che Guevara: A Revolutionary Life*, p.580
11. Ibid. pp.581–2; Luther, E. with Henken, T, *The Life and Work of Che Guevara*, p.185
12. Reid-Henry, S., 2009, *Fidel & Che: A Revolutionary Friendship*, London, Sceptre, p.316; Luther, E. with Henken, T, *The Life and Work of Che Guevara*, pp.186–7; Harris, R.L., *Che Guevara: a Biography*, pp.99–100; Gerassi, J., ed., 1969, Guevara, C., *Venceremos!: The speeches and writings of Ernesto Che Guevara*, London, Panther Books, p.508 Che at UN, 11 Dec 1964: www.youtube.com/watch?v=bufHojkoGtw www.youtube.com/watch?v=bufHojkoGtw&t=93s [Accessed 23/03/23] Full text of speech on: www.marxists.org/archive/guevara/1964/12/11.htm www.emersonkent.com/speeches/homeland_or_death.htm [Accessed 23/03/23]
13. Reid-Henry, S., 2009, *Fidel & Che: A Revolutionary Friendship*, London, Sceptre, p.317; Anderson, J.L., *Che Guevara: A Revolutionary Life*, p.583. Che – US-Cuba relations, on 'Face the Nation', 13 December 1964: www.youtube.com/watch?v=xELHGR_ur0Q [Accessed 23/03/23] On 18 December, Che's return journey from New York was delayed in Dublin because of fog. While there, he was interviewed (the interpreter was Aer Lingus air steward, Felima Archer): www.youtube.com/watch?v=vBYUOOEHbJw [Accessed 23/03/23]
14. Luther, E. with Henken, T, *The Life and Work of Che Guevara*, p.182; Harris, R.L., *Che Guevara: a Biography*, p.101–02.
15. Anderson, J.L., *Che Guevara: A Revolutionary Life*, p.551
16. Ibid. pp.539, 541
17. Luther, E. with Henken, T, *The Life and Work of Che Guevara*, p.184
18. Luther, E. with Henken, T, *The Life and Work of Che Guevara*, p.187
19. Deutschmann, D., *Che Guevara and the Cuban Revolution: Writings and Speeches of Ernesto Che Guevara*, pp.338–9, 344. For the speech, see: www.marxists.org/archive/guevara/1965/02/24.htm [Accessed 23/03/23]

20 Reid-Henry, S., *Fidel & Che: A Revolutionary Friendship*, p.319; Anderson, J.L., *Che Guevara: A Revolutionary Life*, pp.589–90; Harris, R.L., *Che Guevara: a Biography*, p.123

21. Anderson, J.L., *Che Guevara: A Revolutionary Life*, p.584; Guevara, E.C., *The African Dream: The Diaries of the Revolutionary War in The Congo*, p.7
22. Anderson, J.L., *Che Guevara: A Revolutionary Life*, pp.587–8
23. Reid-Henry, S., *Fidel & Che: A Revolutionary Friendship*, p.324
24. Anderson, J.L., *Che Guevara: A Revolutionary Life*, pp.569
25. Reid-Henry, S., *Fidel & Che: A Revolutionary Friendship*, p.325
26. Harris, R.L., *Che Guevara: a Biography*, , p.125
27. Luther, E. with Henken, T., *The Life and Work of Che Guevara*, p.189; Gadea, H., 2008, *My Life with Che*, p.232. Russell Brand can be seen reading out Che's last letter to his children on: www.youtube.com/watch?v=Bb6S9hraP3g [Accessed 08/04/23]
28. Luther, E. with Henken, T., *The Life and Work of Che Guevara*, p.191; Gadea, H., *My Life with Che*, pp.226, 230–1
29. Harris, R.L., *Che Guevara: a Biography*, pp.103–04
30. Guevara, E.C., ed. Deutschmann, D., *Che Guevara and the Cuban Revolution: Writings and Speeches of Ernesto Che Guevara*, p.375; Luther, E. with Henken, T., *The Life and Work of Che Guevara*, p.189
31. Luther, E. with Henken, T., *The Life and Work of Che Guevara*, p.191; March, A, *Remembering Che: My Life with Che Guevara*, pp.111–12
32. March, A., *Remembering Che: My Life with Che Guevara*, pp.109, 112; Harris, R.L., *Che Guevara: a Biography*, p.126
33. March, A., *Remembering Che: My Life with Che Guevara*, pp.117–20,
34. Ibid. pp. 115–16
35. Luther, E. with Henken, T., *The Life and Work of Che Guevara*, p.184; March, A., *Remembering Che: My Life with Che Guevara*, p.114
36. Guevara, E.C., *The African Dream: The Diaries of the Revolutionary War in The Congo*, pp.xiv, xlv; Harris, R.L., *Che Guevara: a Biography*, p.132; March, A., *Remembering Che: My Life with Che Guevara*, p.114
37. Luther, E. with Henken, T., *The Life and Work of Che Guevara*, p.194; Guevara, J.M. with Vincent, A., 2017, *Che, My Brother*, Cambridge, Polity Press, p.136
38. March, A., *Remembering Che: My Life with Che Guevara*, p.115
39. Luther, E. with Henken, T., *The Life and Work of Che Guevara*, p.192
40. Guevara, E.C., *The African Dream: The Diaries of the Revolutionary War in The Congo*, p.14
41. Ibid. pp.1, 72
42. Ibid. p.15
43. Ibid. p.20
44. March, A., *Remembering Che: My Life with Che Guevara*, p.121; Luther, E. with Henken, T, *The Life and Work of Che Guevara*, p.195
45. Guevara, E.C., *The African Dream: The Diaries of the Revolutionary War in The Congo*, p.24; Luther, E. with Henken, T., *The Life and Work of Che Guevara*, pp.196–7; March, A., *Remembering Che: My Life with Che Guevara*, p.119; Anderson, J.L., *Che Guevara: A Revolutionary Life*, pp.613
46. Guevara, E.C., *The African Dream: The Diaries of the Revolutionary War in The Congo*, pp.23, 26
47. Ibid. pp.29, 49; Luther, E. with Henken, T., *The Life and Work of Che Guevara*, p.198
48. Luther, E. with Henken, T., *The Life and Work of Che Guevara*, p.198; Guevara, E.C., *The African Dream: The Diaries of the Revolutionary War in The Congo*, p.49
49. Guevara, E.C., *The African Dream: The Diaries of the Revolutionary War in The Congo*, p.57
50. Ibid. p.68

51. Ibid. pp.125,129
52. Anderson, J.L., *Che Guevara: A Revolutionary Life*, p.623
53. Guevara, E.C., *The African Dream: The Diaries of the Revolutionary War in The Congo*, pp.131–2, 234
54. Ibid. pp.148, 151
55. Ibid. pp.181–2
56. Ibid. pp.186, 209
57. Ibid. pp.1, 216–18; Luther, E. with Henken, T., *The Life and Work of Che Guevara*, p.202
58. Reid-Henry, S., *Fidel & Che: A Revolutionary Friendship*, p.345; Anderson, J.L., *Che Guevara: A Revolutionary Life*, p.638
59. Luther, E. with Henken, T., *The Life and Work of Che Guevara*, p.202
60. March, A., *Remembering Che: My Life with Che Guevara*, pp.122–4
61. Anderson, J.L., *Che Guevara: A Revolutionary Life*, p.642; Guevara, J.M. with Vincent, A., *Che, My Brother*, p.143
62. Guevara, E.C., *The African Dream: The Diaries of the Revolutionary War in The Congo*, pp.10, 235
63. Ibid. pp.233–4
64. Harris, R.L., *Che Guevara: a Biography*, p.141. A video on the legacy of Che's Congo campaign, made 50 years on, can be seen on: www.youtube.com/watch?v=c5puG74hS3M [Accessed 28/04/23]
65. March, A., *Remembering Che: My Life with Che Guevara*, pp.127–30
66. Ibid. pp.130, 132
67. Guevara, E.C., *The African Dream: The Diaries of the Revolutionary War in The Congo*, p. 235

Chapter 10

1. Deutschmann, D., 1987, *Che Guevara and the Cuban Revolution: Writings and Speeches of Ernesto Che Guevara*, Leichhardt, (Sydney), Pathfinder/Pacific & Asia, p.360
2. March, A., 2012, *Remembering Che: My Life with Che Guevara*, pp.135–7, 143
3. March, A, *Remembering Che: My Life with Che Guevara*, pp.134–7; Harris, R.L., 2007, Death of a Revolutionary: Che Guevara's Last Mission, New York, Norton & Company, p.87; Reid-Henry, S., 2009, *Fidel & Che: A Revolutionary Friendship*, London, Sceptre, p.351; Guevara, J.M. with Vincent, A., 2017, Che, My Brother, Cambridge, Polity Press, p.137
4. Luther, E. with Henken, T., 2001, *The Life and Work of Che Guevara*, Indianapolis, Alpha Books, p.207;
5. Harris, R.L., *Death of a Revolutionary: Che Guevara's Last Mission*, pp.88–9; Guevara, J.M. with Vincent, A., *Che, My Brother*, p.151; Ali, T., 2008, *Pirates of the Caribbean: Axis of Hope*, London, Verso, pp.97–8
6. March, A., *Remembering Che: My Life with Che Guevara*, p.139
7. Ibid. pp.137–8
8. Ibid. pp.140–41
9. Ibid. p.142; Luther, E. with Henken, T., *The Life and Work of Che Guevara*, p.210
10. Anderson, J.L., *Che Guevara: A Revolutionary Life*, p.666; March, A, 2012, *Remembering Che: My Life with Che Guevara*, pp.143; Luther, E. with Henken, T., 2001, *The Life and Work of Che Guevara*, p.210
11. Anderson, J.L., 2010, *Che Guevara: A Revolutionary Life*, London, Bantam Books, pp.667; March, A., *Remembering Che: My Life with Che Guevara*, pp.142–3,145

12. Luther, E. with Henken, T., *The Life and Work of Che Guevara*, pp.208, 211
13. Harris, R.L., *Che Guevara: a Biography*, p.148
14. Deutschmann, D., *Che Guevara and the Cuban Revolution: Writings and Speeches of Ernesto Che Guevara*, p.357; Luther, E. with Henken, T.,*The Life and Work of Che Guevara*, . p.212
15. Anderson, J.L., *Che Guevara: A Revolutionary Life*, pp.660–1
16. Ibid. p.524
17. Deutschmann, D., *Che Guevara and the Cuban Revolution: Writings and Speeches of Ernesto Che Guevara*, pp.356, 358–9
18. Deutschmann, D., *Che Guevara and the Cuban Revolution: Writings and Speeches of Ernesto Che Guevara*, p.355
19. Guevara, E.C., 2021, *The Bolivian Diary*, London, Penguin Books, pp.30, 34. Guevara, J.M. with Vincent, A., *Che, My Brother*, p.153. Extracts, in English, of Inti's book can be found via: s3–eu-west-1.amazonaws.com/s3–euw1–ap-pe-ws4–cws-documents.ri-prod/9781138824287/ch10/5._Inti_Peredo,_My_Campaign_with_Che,_1970.pdf [Accessed 08/05/23] On 9 September 1969, Inti was assassinated in La Paz, by Bolivian security forces.
20. March, A., *Remembering Che: My Life with Che Guevara*, p.144
21. Guevara, C., 1969, *Guerrilla Warfare*, Hardmondsworth, Penguin Books, p.53
22. Guevara, C., *Guerrilla Warfare*, pp.39, 116; Harris, R.L., *Che Guevara: a Biography*, p.157
23. Guevara, E.C., *The Bolivian Diary*, pp.49, 52, 60
24. Ibid. pp.52, 62–3
25. Ibid. pp.64–5, 67
26. Ibid. pp.69, 71
27. Ibid. pp.72–3
28. Ibid. pp.75–7
29. Ibid. pp.79–80, 83–4
30. Debray, R., 1968, Revolution in the Revolution? Armed Struggle and Political Struggle in Latin America, Harmondsworth, Penguin Books, p.9
31. Guevara, E.C., *The Bolivian Diary*, p.87
32. Harris, R.L., Death of a Revolutionary: Che Guevara's Last Mission, p.116; Luther, E. with Henken, T., *The Life and Work of Che Guevara*, p.217
33. Stutje, J.W., 2009, *Ernest Mandel: A Rebel's Dream Deferred*, London, Verso, p.161
34. Guevara, E.C., *The Bolivian Diary*, pp.92, 218
35. Ibid. pp.94, 96
36. Ibid. pp.98, 100, 103
37. Harris, R.L., *Che Guevara: a Biography*, p.160
38. Guevara, E.C., *The Bolivian Diary*, pp.105–06, 220
39. Luther, E. with Henken, T., *The Life and Work of Che Guevara*, pp.218–19
40. Guevara, E.C., *The Bolivian Diary*, p.118
41. Ibid. pp.112–5, 117–18
42. Ibid. pp.119, 121–2, 126
43. Reid-Henry, S., 2009, *Fidel & Che: A Revolutionary Friendship*, London, Sceptre, p.367; Guevara, E.C., *The Bolivian Diary*, pp.131–2
44. Guevara, E.C., *The Bolivian Diary*, p.221; nsarchive.gwu.edu/document/24582–document-3–cia-intelligence-information-cable-presence-ernesto-che-guevara-bolivian [Accessed 08/05/23]
45. Guevara, E.C., *The Bolivian Diary*, pp.136, pp.139–40

46. Ibid. pp.144, 146, 148
47. Ibid. pp.148–50
48. Ibid. pp.223–4, 226–7
49. Ibid. pp.153, 155; Harris, R.L., *Death of a Revolutionary: Che Guevara's Last Mission*, p.139; Sinclair, A., 1998, *Che Guevara*, Thrupp/Stroud, Sutton Publishing, p.105
50. Guevara, E.C., *The Bolivian Diary*, p.157
51. Ibid. pp.166–7
52. Ibid. pp.168, 170–1
53. Stutje, J.W., *Ernest Mandel: A Rebel's Dream Deferred*, pp.162–3; Reid-Henry, S., *Fidel & Che: A Revolutionary Friendship*, pp.368–70
54. Guevara, E.C., *The Bolivian Diary*, pp.173–4, 178
55. Ibid. pp.178, 180–2
56. Harris, R.L., Death of a Revolutionary: Che Guevara's Last Mission, p.147
57. Guevara, E.C., *The Bolivian Diary*, pp.197–8, 201
58. Anderson, J.L., *Che Guevara: A Revolutionary Life*, p.699; Guevara, E.C., *The Bolivian Diary*, pp.201, 203
59. Anderson, J.L., *Che Guevara: A Revolutionary Life*, p.699
60. Guevara, E.C., *The Bolivian Diary*, p.205
61. Ibid. pp.207–8
62. Sinclair, A., *Che Guevara*, p.106
63. Neruda, P., 1978, *Memoirs*, Harmondsworth, Penguin Books, p.323
64. Luther, E. with Henken, T., *The Life and Work of Che Guevara*, p.221; Reid-Henry, S., *Fidel & Che: A Revolutionary Friendship*, p.373; Harris, R.L., *Che Guevara: a Biography*, pp.166
65. nsarchive2.gwu.edu/NSAEBB/NSAEBB5/docs/doc09.pdf [Accessed 08/05/23]
66. Anderson, J.L., *Che Guevara: A Revolutionary Life*, pp.705; Luther, E. with Henken, T., *The Life and Work of Che Guevara*, pp.221–2; Harris, R.L., *Che Guevara: a Biography*, p.175; nsarchive2.gwu.edu/NSAEBB/NSAEBB5/docs/doc07.pdf [Accessed 08/05/23]
67. Reid-Henry, S., *Fidel & Che: A Revolutionary Friendship*, p.373; nsarchive2.gwu.edu/NSAEBB/NSAEBB5/docs/doc15.pdf
    newsable.asianetnews.com/life/cia-files-finally-reveal-che-gueveras-final-words-moments-before-he-was-killed-in-bolivia [Accessed 08/05/23]
    There are in fact several versions of Che's 'last words.' After his dead body had been photographed – with his captors and murderers standing around it – his hands were cut off for later fingerprinting, and he was buried in a mass secret grave, along with other guerrillas.
68. Stutje, J.W., *Ernest Mandel: A Rebel's Dream Deferred*, p.163; Lynch, E. G, 2007, *The Young Che: Memories of Che Guevara*, London, Vintage Books, p.311
69. Guevara, J.M. with Vincent, A., 2017, *Che, My Brother*, pp.134, 143–4, 147–8. In 1997, thirty years after Che's murder, a Cuban-Argentine forensics team finally discovered his remains, which were then flown back to Cuba.
70. March, A., *Remembering Che: My Life with Che Guevara*, pp.146–7
71. Ibid. pp.147, 149; Gadea, H, 2008, *My Life with Che*, London, Frontline Books, p.233. Several years after Che's murder, March eventually remarried. A 1994 film (in French, without subtitles) about Che's life and his *Bolivian Diary*, can be seen on YouTube: www.youtube.com/watch?v=tL5Ntt9qyM0 [Accessed 17/05/23]

Conclusion

1. Deutschmann, D., 1987, *Che Guevara and the Cuban Revolution: Writings and Speeches of Ernesto Che Guevara*, p.359
2. Löwy, M., 2007, *The Marxism of Che Guevara: Philosophy, Economics, Revolutionary Warfare*, Lanham, Rowman & Littlefield, pp.120–21
3. Besancenot, O. & Löwy, M., 2009, *Che Guevara: His Revolutionary Legacy*, New York, Monthly Review Press, pp.29, 113; www.nybooks.com/articles/1997/07/17/goodbye-to-all-that/ [Accessed 17/05/23]; Farber, S., 2016, *The Politics of Che Guevara: Theory and Practice*, Chicago, Haymarket Books, p.7; Harris, R.L., 2007, *Death of a Revolutionary: Che Guevara's Last Mission*, New York, Norton & Company, p.294; Guevara, C., 1969, *Reminiscences of the Cuban Revolutionary War*, Harmondsworth, Penguin Books, p.39
4. Löwy, M., *The Marxism of Che Guevara: Philosophy, Economics, Revolutionary Warfare*, p.107
5. Harris, R.L., Death of a Revolutionary: Che Guevara's Last Mission, p.295
6. Harris, R.L., 2011, *Che Guevara: a Biography*, Santa Barbara, Greenwood, p.124; Anderson, J.L., 2010, *Che Guevara: A Revolutionary Life*, London, Bantam Books, pp.549, 552
7. Besancenot, O. & Löwy, M., *Che Guevara: His Revolutionary Legacy*, pp.29, 113
8. Llorente, R., 2018, *The Political Theory of Che Guevara*, Lanham, Rowman & Littlefield International, p.105
9. Löwy, M., *The Marxism of Che Guevara: Philosophy, Economics, Revolutionary Warfare*, pp.109, 111, 120
10. Farber, S., *The Politics of Che Guevara: Theory and Practice*, p.xviii
11. Llorente, R., *The Political Theory of Che Guevara*, pp.108–09
12. Ibid. p.106
13. Llorente, R., 2018, *The Political Theory of Che Guevara*, p.107; Principe, M., 2017, sdonline.org/issue/75/debunking-myth-or-distorting-record-samuel-farber-che-guevara [Accessed 17/05/23]
14. Llorente, R., *The Political Theory of Che Guevara*, p.109
15. Debray, R., 1968, *Revolution in the Revolution?*, Harmondsworth, Penguin Books, pp.50, 79; Ali, T., 2008, *Pirates of the Caribbean: Axis of Hope*, London, Verso, p.93n
16. Harris, R.L., *Death of a Revolutionary: Che Guevara's Last Mission*, p.264; Besancenot, O. & Löwy, M., *Che Guevara: His Revolutionary Legacy*, pp.79, 84, 86; Debray, R., *Revolution in the Revolution?* pp.24, newmilitant.com/to-the-people-of-latin-america-1974/ [Accessed 17/05/23]
17. Harris, R.L., Death of a Revolutionary: Che Guevara's Last Mission, pp.267, 279; Guevara, E.C., 2001, *The African Dream: The Diaries of the Revolutionary War in The Congo*, London, Harvill Press, p.241
18. Löwy, M., *The Marxism of Che Guevara: Philosophy, Economics, Revolutionary Warfare*, p.67; Llorente, R., *The Political Theory of Che Guevara*, p.53; Deutschmann, D., *Che Guevara and the Cuban Revolution: Writings and Speeches of Ernesto Che Guevara*, pp.356, 372;
19. Llorente, R., *The Political Theory of Che Guevara*, p.54
20. Guevara, C., *Guerrilla Warfare*, 1969, Harmondsworth, Penguin Books, pp.13, 146; Llorente, R., *The Political Theory of Che Guevara*, pp.55, 146 (n.77)
21. Llorente, R., *The Political Theory of Che Guevara*, p.56
22. Besancenot, O. & Löwy, M., *Che Guevara: His Revolutionary Legacy*, p.84
23. Yaffe, H., 2009, 'Che Guevara: The Economics of Revolution', Basingstoke, Palgrave Macmillan, p.235
24. Tablada, C., 1990, *Che Guevara: Economics and Politics in the Transition to Socialism*, New York, Pathfinder Press, pp.215–17; Arthur, C. J., ed., 1974, *The German Ideology*, London, Lawrence & Wishart, pp.94–5

25. Tablada, C., 1990, *Che Guevara: Economics and Politics in the Transition to Socialism*, New York, Pathfinder Press, pp.86–7 [my emphasis]
26. Llorente, R., *The Political Theory of Che Guevara*, p.112
27. Ibid. p.113; Sinclair, A.,1998, *Che Guevara*, Thrupp/Stroud, Sutton Publishing, p.63
28. Besancenot, O. & Löwy, M., *Che Guevara: His Revolutionary Legacy*, pp.31, 35, 45
29. Llorente, R., *The Political Theory of Che Guevara*, pp.109, 111; Marx, K, 'Introduction, A Contribution to the Critique of Hegel's Philosophy of Right', in Colletti, L., ed., 1975, *Early Writings*, Harmondsworth, Penguin Books, p.251
30. Yaffe, H., 'Che Guevara: The Economics of Revolution', , pp.240–41
31. Ali, T., *Pirates of the Caribbean: Axis of Hope*, p.144; Yaffe, H., 'Che Guevara: The Economics of Revolution', pp. 249–50. Trotsky had warned of the possibility of capitalism returning, some 20–30 years before Che.
32. Yaffe, H., 'Che Guevara: The Economics of Revolution', pp.233, 239; Ali, T., Pirates of the Caribbean: Axis of Hope, p.145
33. Löwy, M., *The Marxism of Che Guevara: Philosophy, Economics, Revolutionary Warfare*, pp.127–8
34. Besancenot, O. & Löwy, M., *Che Guevara: His Revolutionary Legacy*, pp.76–7, 107
35. Ibid. p.88
36. Ali, T., Pirates of the Caribbean: Axis of Hope, p.138
37. Yaffe, H., 'Che Guevara: The Economics of Revolution', p.257
38. Farber, S., *The Politics of Che Guevara: Theory and Practice*, p.xv; Llorente, R., *The Political Theory of Che Guevara*, p.123
39. Yaffe, H., 'Che Guevara: The Economics of Revolution', pp.260, 262
40. Ibid. pp.264–5
41. Ibid. pp.265–8
42. Ibid. pp.260–1
43. Kenner, M. & Petras, J., (eds.), 1972, *Fidel Castro Speaks*, Harmondsworth, Penguin Books, p.249; Harris, R.L., *Death of a Revolutionary: Che Guevara's Last Mission*, pp.279–80; Sinclair, A., *Che Guevara*, pp. 109–10, 113; Ali, T., *Pirates of the Caribbean: Axis of Hope*, pp.118–19. newmilitant.com/to-the-people-of-latin-america-1974/ [Accessed 17/05/23]
44. Besancenot, O. & Löwy, M., *Che Guevara: His Revolutionary Legacy*, p.82; Harris, R.L., *Death of a Revolutionary: Che Guevara's Last Mission*, pp.281, 290; Robinson, W. I., 'Transformative Possibilities in Latin America', in *Global Flashpoints: Reactions to Imperialism and Neoliberalism*, 2007, ed. L. Panitch & C. Leys, The Merlin Press, London, p.148
45. walterlippmann.com/an-interview-with-camilo-guevara-son-of-el-che/ [Accessed 18/05/23] Stone's film is available on YouTube: www.youtube.com/watch?v=Yg4ZdDiq0YM [Accessed 18/05/23]
46. Robinson, W. I., 'Transformative Possibilities in Latin America', in *Global Flashpoints: Reactions to Imperialism and Neoliberalism*, 2007, ed. L. Panitch & C. Leys, p.141; robinson.faculty.soc.ucsb.edu/Assets/pdf/trans_poss_in_latinamerica.pdf.pdf p.1, [Accessed 18/05/23]; Harris, R.L., *Death of a Revolutionary: Che Guevara's Last Mission*, pp.283, 292, 295
47. Yaffe, H., 'Che Guevara: The Economics of Revolution', p.275
48. Harris, R.L., Death of a Revolutionary: Che Guevara's Last Mission, p.280
49. Farber, S., *The Politics of Che Guevara: Theory and Practice*, p.xvi; Besancenot, O. & Löwy, M., Che Guevara: His Revolutionary Legacy, p.120

50. Besancenot, O. & Löwy, M., *Che Guevara: His Revolutionary Legacy*, pp.80, 100; fsmm2018.org/principles-of-the-world-social-forum/?lang=en [Accessed 18/05/23]
51. Llorente, R., *The Political Theory of Che Guevara*, pp.121–2
52. Ibid. p.56
53. Gramsci, A, 1971, *Selections from the Prison Notebooks,* London, Lawrence & Wishart, p.276; Faulkner, N., et al, 2021, *System Crash: An activist guide to making revolution*, London, Resistance Books, p.120; Hobsbawm, E, 1994, *Age of Extremes: The Short Twentieth Century 1914–1991*, London, Michael Joseph, p.585
54. Llorente, R., *The Political Theory of Che Guevara*, p.120; Ali, T., 2008, Pirates of the Caribbean: Axis of Hope, p.27
55. Besancenot, O. & Löwy, M., *Che Guevara: His Revolutionary Legacy*, pp.93, 96
56. Mandel, E, 'Why I am a Marxist', in Achcar, G., ed., 1999, *The Legacy of Ernest Mandel*, London, Verso, p.255; Harris, R.L., *Death of a Revolutionary: Che Guevara's Last Mission*, p.285
57. Mandel, E., 1983, 'Emancipation, science and politics in Karl Marx', in de Jong, A., ed., 2022, *Ernest Mandel: Hope and Marxism*, London, Resistance Books, p.186; Bloch, E., 1995, *The Principle of Hope, Vol. 1*, Cambridge (Mass.), The MIT Press, p. 238
58. Lenin, V. I., 1902, *'What is to be done?'*, in *Lenin: Selected Works, Vol. 1,* 1975, Moscow, Progress Publishers, pp.225–6; Mandel, E., 1978, 'We Must Dream', in de Jong, A., ed., 2022, *Ernest Mandel: Hope and Marxism*, p.124
59. Debray, R., 1967, *Revolution in the Revolution? Armed Struggle and Political Struggle in Latin America*, p.24. The full text of *Guerrilla Warfare: A Method* can be seen on: www.marxists.org/archive/guevara/1963/09/guerrilla-warfare.htm [Accessed 17/05/23]

Bibliography/Further Reading

Guevara's writings/speeches

Guevara, C., 1969, *Guerrilla Warfare*, Harmondsworth, Penguin Books

Guevara, E.C., 2021, *Reminiscences of the Cuban Revolutionary War*, London, Penguin Classics

Guevara, C., 1969, *Reminiscences of the Cuban Revolutionary War*, Harmondsworth, Penguin Books

Guevara, E.C., 2021, *The Motorcycle Diaries*, London, Penguin Books

Guevara, E.C., 2002, *Back on the Road: a Journey to Central America*, London, Vintage Books

Guevara, E.C., 2001, *The African Dream: The Diaries of the Revolutionary War in The Congo*, London, Harvill Press

Guevara, E.C., 2021, *The Bolivian Diary*, London, Penguin Books

Guevara, C., 1967, *Che Guevara Speaks: Selected Speeches and Writings*, New York, Pathfinder

Guevara, E.C., ed. Deutschmann, D., 1987, *Che Guevara and the Cuban Revolution: Writings and Speeches of Ernesto Che Guevara*, Leichhardt (Sydney), Pathfinder/Pacific & Asia

Guevara, E.C., ed. Gerassi, J., 1969, *Venceremos! The speeches and writings of Ernesto Che Guevara*, London, Panther Books

Biographies on Guevara

Alexandre, M., ed., 1968, *Via Che!* London, Lorrimer Publishing

Anderson, J.L., 2010, *Che Guevara: A Revolutionary Life*, London, Bantam Books

Gadea, H., 2008, *My Life with Che: The Making of a Revolutionary*, London, Frontline Books

Guevara, J.M. with Vincent, A, 2017, *Che, My Brother*, Cambridge, Polity Press

Harris, R.L., 2007, *Death of a Revolutionary: Che Guevara's Last Mission*, New York, Norton & Company

Harris, R.L., 2011, *Che Guevara: a Biography*, Santa Barbara, Greenwood

Luther, E. with Henken, T., 2001, *The Life and Work of Che Guevara*, Indianapolis, Alpha Books

Lynch, E.G., 2007, *The Young Che: Memories of Che Guevara*, London, Vintage Books

March, A., 2012, *Remembering Che: My Life with Che Guevara*, Melbourne, Ocean Press

Sandison, D., 2001, *Che Guevara*, London, Chancellor Press

Reid-Henry, S., 2009, *Fidel & Che: A Revolutionary Friendship*, London, Scepter

Sinclair, A., 1998, *Che Guevara*, Thrupp, Stroud, Sutton Publishing

Sinclair, A., 2006 *Viva Che! The Strange Death and Life of Che Guevara*, Stroud, Sutton Publishing

Symmes, P., 2000, *Chasing Che: A Motorcycle Journey in Search of the Guevara Legend*, New York, Vintage Books

Zambelli, D., et al., 2017, *Che Quevara: tú y TODOS*, Milan, Skira

Guevarism

Ali, T., 2008, *Pirates of the Caribbean: Axis of Hope*, Verso, London

Besancenot, O. & Löwy, M., 2009, *Che Guevara: His Revolutionary Legacy*, New York, Monthly Review Press
Debray, R., 1968, *Revolution in the Revolution? Armed Struggle and Political Struggle in Latin America*, Harmondsworth, Penguin Books
Farber, S., 2016, *The Politics of Che Guevara: Theory and Practice*, Chicago, Haymarket Books
Llorente, R., 2018, *The Political Theory of Che Guevara*, Lanham, Rowman & Littlefield International
Löwy, M., 2007, *The Marxism of Che Guevara: Philosophy, Economics, Revolutionary Warfare*, Lanham, Rowman & Littlefield Publishing
Silverman, B., ed., 1971, *Man and Socialism in Cuba: The Great Debate*, New York, Atheneum
Tablada, C., 1990, *Che Guevara: Economics and Politics in the Transition to Socialism*, New York, Pathfinder Press
Yaffe, H., 2009, 'Che Guevara: The Economics of Revolution', Basingstoke, Palgrave Macmillan
Yaffe, H., 2014, 'Ernesto "Che" Guevara: socialist political economy and economic management in Cuba, 1959–1965', (2007 Ph. D. thesis), Ann Arbor, ProQuest

Websites

companeroche.com/
www.marxists.org/archive/guevara/index.htm
nsarchive.gwu.edu/briefing-book/cuba-intelligence/2020–10–09/che-guevara-cia-mountains-bolivia
nsarchive.gwu.edu/document/24582–document-3–cia-intelligence-information-cable-presence-ernesto-che-guevara-bolivian
nsarchive.gwu.edu/document/24585–document-6–cia-memorandum-cuban-inspired-guerrilla-activity-bolivia-june-14–1967
www.counterpunch.org/2024/01/12/ernest-mandel-revolutionary-cuba-and-che-guevara/

Index